Comrades No More

The BCSIA Studies in International Security book series is edited at the Belfer Center for Science and International Affairs at Harvard University's John F. Kennedy School of Government and published by The MIT Press. The series publishes books on contemporary issues in international security policy, as well as their conceptual and historical foundations. Topics of particular interest to the series include the spread of weapons of mass destruction, internal conflict, the international effects of democracy and democratization, and U.S. defense policy.

A complete list of BCSIA Studies appears at the back of this volume.

Comrades No More

The Seeds of Political Change in Eastern Europe

Renée de Nevers

BCSIA Studies in International Security

The MIT Press
Cambridge, Massachusetts
London, England

This book was typeset in Palatino by Wellington Graphics and was printed and bound in the United States of America.

Library of Congress Cataloging-in-Publication Data

De Nevers, Renée
Comrades no more : the seeds of political change in Eastern Europe / Renée de Nevers.
p.   cm.   (BCSIA studies in international security)
Includes bibliographical references and index.
ISBN 0-262-04193-6 (hardbound : alk. paper)—ISBN 0-262-54129-7 (pbk, : alk. paper)
1. Europe, Eastern—Politics and government—1989– 2. Europe, Eastern—Politics and government—1945–1989. 3. Soviet Union—Politics and government—1985–1991. I. Title. II. Series.

JN96.A58 D4 2002
320.947′09′049—dc21   2002032168

On the cover: Cartoon of Polish leader Wojciech Jaruzelski by Jeff Danziger.
© Jeff Danziger. Used with permission.

Printed in the United States of America

10 9 8 7 6 5 4 3 2 1

Contents

Tables and Figures

Acknowledgments

Over the years working on this project, I benefited enormously from the friendly advice, criticism, and wisdom of my teachers and colleagues. Jack Snyder, Charles Gati, Robert Legvold, and Warner R. Schilling were my teachers and advisers. Their criticisms, suggestions, and support were invaluable along the way. Many colleagues offered their comments on different parts of the manuscript. Michael E. Brown read early drafts and pushed me to "be smarter, write better." I am indebted to him for his faith in me over the years, and for his friendship. Lynn Eden provided insightful comments and advice, as well as humor and support. I thank Elizabeth Kier and Jeffrey Legro for their comments on parts of the manuscript, and two anonymous reviewers for the MIT Press for their useful comments and suggestions.

Initial research for this study was done at the International Institute for Strategic Studies, where I was a Research Fellow from 1988–90. I am grateful to François Heisbourg, Hans Binnendyjk, and John Cross for their insights and support while I endeavored to keep abreast of rapidly changing events in Eastern Europe. My colleagues on the fifth floor, particularly Ian Gambles and Tim Zimmermann, helped enliven the research process. I completed the first draft that led to this book while a Predoctoral Fellow at the Center for International Security and Arms Control (now the Center for International Security and Cooperation) at Stanford University. David Holloway, Gail Lapidus, Condoleezza Rice, and Phillippe Schmitter read and commented on various drafts of this work; I greatly appreciate the time and effort they spent to help me improve the manuscript. Many thanks to David Holloway and Michael May for creating a lively scholarly community there, and to Coit D. Blacker, Lynn Eden, Robert Hamerton-Kelly, John Harvey, Elizabeth Cousens, Jeffrey Knopf, and Michael Elleman, among others. A large part of the book was written at the Belfer Center for Science and International Affairs at the John F. Kennedy School of Government. I would like to thank

Graham Allison, Steven Miller, Michael Brown, and Sean Lynn-Jones in particular for their support for this project and the research I conducted while at BCSIA. Additionally, the intellectual interaction and sense of community among the research fellows there helped push me to refine my arguments and broadened my understanding of international relations theory. I thank my colleagues Miriam Fendius Elman, Elizabeth Rogers, Rachel Bronson, John Matthews, Owen Coté, Fiona Hill, Dan Lindley, Pascal Vennesson, Marie Chevrier, Chantal de Jonge Oudraat, Taylor Seybolt, Christopher Layne, Robert Newman, Bradley Thayer, and Milada Vachudova for creating a critical sense of community there. Thanks also to Pauline Jones Luong, Mark Kramer, Celeste Wallander, Carol Saivetz, Lis Tarlow, and Tim Snyder at Harvard. Rose McDermott, Elizabeth Kier, Jon Mercer, Ted Hopf, Mlada Buchovansky, Sarah Mendelson, Dawn Opstad, Sharon Weiner, and Clif Hubby helped me weather different parts of the process, and Karen Motley and Miriam Avins provided useful guidance through the editorial process. Thanks also to Kennette Benedict at the MacArthur Foundation for her support during the final stages of the project. Columbia University's Harriman Institute and the Institute for the Study of World Politics provided additional financial support.

I thank my family for their love, forbearance, and encouragement throughout. Finally, my thanks to Brian Taylor, for his patience, humor, criticism, love, and unwavering support.

Eastern Europe

Introduction

The Warsaw Pact crumbled in 1989. The disintegration of Soviet control in Eastern Europe signified the end of the Cold War, the most momentous change in the international system since 1945; moreover, this collapse was almost entirely peaceful.[1] Why did this happen? An explanation of this bloodless upheaval is important for comprehending both the sources of regime change, and the prospects for peaceful transitions in the future.

This book examines how international forces influenced domestic change and shaped the transformation of Eastern Europe in 1989. It has two goals. First, I aim to develop an explanation for why a peaceful collapse of communism occurred throughout the Warsaw Pact. Second, by examining the interaction of internal and external variables during the transformation of the East European political system at the end of the 1980s, I hope to improve our understanding of how factors at different levels of analysis affect processes of political change.[2]

---

1. The only obvious rival is the collapse of the Soviet Union itself. While some may disagree that the collapse of the Warsaw Pact ended the Cold War, it had "system-wide implications" for the bipolarity that governed international politics after World War II. On this point see Rey Koslowski and Friedrich V. Kratochwil, "Understanding Change in International Politics: The Soviet Empire's Demise and the International System," *International Organization*, Vol. 48, No. 2, (Spring 1994) pp. 215–247.

2. I use "transformation" here to refer to the collapse of the existing regimes in the East European states of the Warsaw Pact. My intent is not to examine the transition to democracy in its entirety; that is a larger task, and one that addresses a different set of questions than those that I consider. For some recent discussions of the transition process in Eastern Europe since 1990, See Adam Przeworski, *Democracy and the Market: Political and Economic Reforms in Eastern Europe and Latin America* (Cambridge: Cambridge

An abundance of books have appeared in recent years that have scrutinized different aspects of the collapse of communist regimes in Eastern Europe.[3] Yet several critical questions remain unanswered. Why did this sweeping upheaval happen in 1989? It was not inevitable that this disintegration should happen when it did, or that it should encompass the whole bloc—much less that this transformation should remain almost entirely peaceful. Moreover, the disintegration of communism in Eastern Europe was not uniform in process. In some states, the process of reform was initiated from above, by the regime in power; in others, it was impelled from below, by expanding popular protests against communist rule. Reforms were also initiated at different times and rates in the disparate East European states. Why was there such variation in this process, while the end results—a commitment to democratization—proved to be so similar?[4]

University Press, 1991); Luiz Carlos Bresser, Jose Maria Marvall, and Adam Przeworski, eds., *Economic Reforms in New Democracies: A Social-Democratic Approach* (Cambridge and New York: Cambridge University Press, 1993); and Juan J. Linz and Alfred Stepan, *Problems of Democratic Transition and Consolidation: Southern Europe, South America, and Post-Communist Europe* (Baltimore, Md.: Johns Hopkins University Press, 1996).

3.   Among them are Michael Waller, *The End of the Communist Power Monopoly* (Manchester and New York: Manchester University Press, 1993); Peter Cipkowski, *Revolution in Eastern Europe: Understanding the Collapse of Communism in Poland, Hungary, East Germany, Czechoslovakia, Romania, and the Soviet Union* (New York: Wiley, 1991); Ivo Banac, ed., *Eastern Europe in Revolution* (Ithaca and London: Cornell University Press, 1992); Roger East, *Revolutions in Eastern Europe* (London and New York: Pinter Publishers, 1992); Charles Gati, *The Bloc that Failed: Soviet-East European Relations in Transition* (Bloomington and Indianapolis, Indiana University Press, 1990); J.F. Brown, *Surge to Freedom: The End of Communist Rule in Eastern Europe* (Durham and London: Duke University Press, 1991); Timothy Garton Ash, *We the People: The Revolution of 1989 Witnessed in Warsaw, Budapest, Berlin and Prague* (Cambridge: Granta Books, 1990); Philip Zelikow and Condoleezza Rice, *Germany Unified and Europe Transformed: A Study in Statecraft* (Cambridge and London: Harvard University Press, 1995); Michael J. Sodaro, *Moscow, Germany and the West from Khrushchev to Gorbachev* (Ithaca and London: Cornell University Press, 1990); Elizabeth Pond, *Beyond the Wall: Germany's Road to Unification* (Washington, D.C.: Brookings Institution, 1993); Andrei Codrescu, *The Hole in the Flag: A Romanian Exile's Story of Return and Revolution* (New York: William Morrow, 1991); Jacques Lévesque, *The Enigma of 1989: The USSR and the Liberation of Eastern Europe* (Berkeley, Calif.: University of California Press, 1997); and Gale Stokes, *The Walls Came Tumbling Down: The Collapse of Communism in Eastern Europe* (New York: Oxford University Press, 1996).

4.   The success of these countries in democratizing has varied since 1990. Yet at the end of 1989 each had specified that its goal was to hold free elections in a more open political arena. Poland was the only exception to this, since partially free elections had already been held in Poland in June 1989, which resulted in the formation of a Solidarity-led government in the fall of 1989.

Many recent books have brought to light elements of the story that were not evident at the time, enriching our understanding of these events. Yet few have attempted to examine the process in an analytical way, by comparing the impact of particular variables across the different cases. By doing so, this book will contribute to our understanding of the differential rates and processes of change in regime transitions.

The Argument

I address two main questions in this book. First, what accounts for the variation in the way the transition progressed in different states in Eastern Europe? Why did some of these transformations involve a cooperative interaction between the existing regime and nascent opposition movements, while others did not? And what made individuals in some states decide to object to the continuation of policies they had tolerated for decades, with such dramatic consequences? Second, how does the interaction of international, domestic, and cognitive factors explain why these transitions occurred when they did, and why they assumed the particular shape that they did?

The changes that occurred in Eastern Europe in 1989 can only be fully understood by examining the interaction of international influences and domestic factors. This study offers three central propositions to explain the process of reform that unfolded in Eastern Europe. First, international factors at two levels were critical to the process of reform. Change in the Soviet Union was necessary to activate the transition process, yet it was not sufficient to induce the bloc-wide change that occurred. Internal change within Eastern Europe itself was an additional necessary catalyst that provoked change encompassing the entire Warsaw Pact. Second, the relationship between regime and society helps explain whether a regime was likely to risk its dominant position by introducing political reforms; this to a large extent determined the nature of the transitions that emerged in different states in the region. Third, changes in individual states created a demonstration effect, which changed domestic calculations over time as it resonated throughout the Warsaw Pact.

External change was clearly necessary if reforms were to emerge in Eastern Europe. So long as the Soviet Union was prepared to demand bloc-wide cohesion, there would be little reason to expect political change in the non-Soviet states of the Warsaw Pact. This is not to suggest that bloc cohesion could have been maintained indefinitely, but for the short to medium term new challenges to communist control were unlikely to emerge from within the existing system.

Yet external factors did not have a uniform impact throughout the bloc. Two propositions can be advanced about the role that international influences played in bringing about a transition. First, change in the Soviet Union was a *necessary*, but not sufficient condition for the succession of upheavals that destroyed the Warsaw Pact.[5] Second, the spread of reforms throughout the bloc was neither a given nor inevitable until *comprehension* of the change in Moscow's attitude spread widely throughout Eastern Europe. This required awareness that Moscow's attitude toward autonomy within the region had truly and dramatically changed. Recognition of this change did not prevail in the bloc, however, until it was proven, when the process of reform was well under way in the first states to take the Soviet Union at its word about noninterference and its tolerance for political change, Poland and Hungary.

An examination of two critical moments during 1988–89 illustrates both the importance of regime-society relations in shaping the nature of reforms, and how the interaction of domestic and international factors affected domestic decisions in this period. I distinguish between early and late reformers within the Warsaw Pact to delineate these two points. The first critical period occurred when East European regimes made the decision either to initiate or to reject political reforms after the Soviet Union introduced perestroika, and began to encourage reform in the Warsaw Pact. The only external factor operating at this point was the change under way in the Soviet Union. The second critical period occurred later, and involved those states that rejected their first opportunity to introduce reforms. At this point, change within the Warsaw Pact itself as well as change in the Soviet Union affected internal choices.

I argue that a regime's initial decision to introduce or reject reforms was shaped by two key factors: whether the regime or government believed it could survive in a more open political climate, and whether it recognized the need to introduce reforms.[6] How the regime answered

---

5. The Warsaw Pact officially survived as a political alliance until July 1, 1991. But for military purposes, it was defunct by January 1990. See Raymond L. Garthoff, *The Great Transition: American-Soviet Relations and the End of the Cold War* (Washington, D.C.: Brookings Institution, 1994), p. 616.

6. It is important to keep in mind that in almost all cases of transition, the East European states included, disagreements within the ruling regime or group were widespread. The argument being made here refers to the position of the dominant group in the leadership; the differences of view and their impact on the reform processes will be examined in the case studies. On the issue of leadership disagreements, see Phillippe Schmitter and Guillermo O'Donnell, "Opening Authoritarian Regimes," in *Transitions from Authoritarian Rule*, vol. 4 (Baltimore, Md.: Johns Hopkins University Press, 1986),

these questions helps explain whether it was likely to be willing to initiate reforms when the opportunity to do so presented itself.

Comprehension of the urgency of reform developed in those states where the regime was cognizant both of its own economic shortcomings, and of the crucial linkages between economic and political reform in the search for solutions to the country's problems. The regime's perception of its ability to remain in power was colored primarily by its appreciation of its own legitimacy, or the lack of it. If the regime was both aware of the need for reform, and felt that it had sufficient domestic support to risk competition in a more liberal environment, then it would be willing to initiate reforms; if not, early reforms emerged only in response to popular protest.[7]

Second, in those states that rejected the option of early reform another factor was critical to the process: a cognitive change in *comprehension* within them, by either the elites or the populations, about what was possible. But this change only unfolded after reforms had progressed quite far in the early reforming Warsaw Pact states in 1989, and these external changes critically shaped the internal shift in attitude. Cognitive blinders prevented some leaders from grasping the full extent of the changes going on around them, while at the same time the realization began to spread at the popular level throughout the bloc that substantial change was feasible for the first time, and indeed, might be unavoidable. A "demonstration effect" thus developed, provoked by the diffusion of ideas from state to state. This demonstration effect played a critical role in impelling reform, because both elite and popular perceptions changed in response to changes resonating from outside the state. The demonstration effect provoked a surge in popular willingness to risk protest against unpopular regimes, while it simultaneously convinced some East European leaders that their only hope of continued survival was to jump on the wave of reform before they were destroyed by it. Yet a regime's perception of its own legitimacy, and thus its prospects, continued to constrain the choices open to it. These changes in perspective by elites and population altered both the way reforms were initiated in Eastern Europe, and their scope.

The states that chose to introduce reforms early were Poland and Hungary. The Polish regime, though aware of its unpopularity, recog-

---

p. 18; and Samuel P. Huntington, *The Third Wave: Democratization in the Late Twentieth Century* (Norman and London: University of Oklahoma Press, 1991), chap. 3.

7. In most states in the Warsaw Pact, popular dissent did not exist on a large enough scale to impel change in early 1989.

nized the urgency of reform to address the country's economic problems, and faced popular agitation for change. The Hungarian regime endorsed the prospect of reform and felt secure in initiating political change.

The late reforming states were the German Democratic Republic (GDR), Czechoslovakia, Bulgaria, and Romania. In both the GDR and Czechoslovakia, reforms emerged after widespread popular protests left politically bankrupt regimes with no choice but to concede the need for substantial political reform. The Bulgarian regime sustained a relatively high degree of legitimacy; in the face of a slowly emerging opposition and the popular upheavals elsewhere, members of the regime initiated reforms. The Romanian regime led by Nicolae Ceaușescu was overthrown after popular protests provoked violence; several communist officials then installed a new government and proclaimed their intention to introduce reforms from above, with support from the street protests below.

The argument of this book both explains a critical event, the collapse of the Warsaw Pact, and has more general implications for the development of theory. First, by improving our understanding of when domestic and international factors promote regime change, it may help us develop measures for predicting similar changes in other states. Second, the end of the Cold War ended the bipolar competition between the United States and the Soviet Union. The conclusion of their ideologically motivated competition meant that sustaining client states around the globe became less important to both superpowers.[8] Moreover, international financial institutions and donor states have reconsidered their lending practices in response to changed attitudes about the utility of free market mechanisms and foreign aid.[9] As a result, a variety of states worldwide have encountered a significant reduction in external support. In states that have lost external backing either of a patron state or international institutions, these external changes are likely to affect domestic conditions in ways that parallel the internal changes in Eastern Europe. Yet it is not clear that they will opt for democratization, as did the Warsaw Pact states in 1989.[10]

---

8. In the Soviet case this was obviously strongly motivated by economic as well as political factors.

9. For one study that has looked at this question, see Stephen John Stedman, "Conflict and Conciliation in Sub-Saharan Africa," in Michael E. Brown, ed., *The International Dimensions of Internal Conflict* (Cambridge, Mass.: MIT Press, 1996), pp. 235–265.

10. Clearly, the Warsaw Pact states have succeeded to different degrees in their efforts to move toward more democratic, market-oriented systems, and by some estima-

This study can help clarify the conditions that made democratization the dominant choice in this region; these may apply in other cases as well. Third, and more broadly, understanding the ways that international events influence domestic policy choices in these critical cases will help improve our comprehension not only of sources of regime change, but also of the gray area where domestic and international politics interact.

Testing the Argument

I develop my argument in the first chapter, examine the Soviet Union's role in Eastern Europe in the next chapter, and then test my argument in five case studies.

In Chapter 1, I first examine competing hypotheses on the collapse of the Warsaw Pact to determine their strengths and weaknesses in explaining these cases. I then develop my argument on how internal and external variables interacted to induce change in Eastern Europe. In doing so, I utilize international relations theories that look at the relationship between domestic and international politics, as well as some concepts from the literature on transitions to democracy, and psychology and sociology. My main goal is to develop propositions that explain the nature of change in the various countries of the Warsaw Pact and the role that external factors played in shaping this evolution.

How did internal factors shape the reform process, and how important were they? If the regime's perception of its relationship with society was truly significant, one would expect to see reform only in those states where the regime had a predisposition toward significant change of its domestic system, or where opposition to the regime was sufficiently strong to demand change. Conservative regimes that doubted their ability to survive would have little inducement to initiate change at all, particularly at a time when Moscow's demands for conformity were lessening.[11] That the transformation eventually incorporated all the members of

---

tions, few are succeeding completely. Nonetheless, this was the stated aim at the end of the period under examination here. For one assessment of the prospects for both East European and former Soviet republics to solidify democratic control, see Charles Gati, "The Mirage of Democracy," *Transition*, Vol. 2, No. 6 (March 22, 1996).

11. One must keep in mind that, prior to 1989, a great deal of skepticism existed about the seriousness of Moscow's intentions regarding the implementation of democratization and market reforms in the Soviet Union. Therefore, there was little reason to assume that Moscow was likely to *require* that its allies adopt radical reforms in the near future.

the Warsaw Pact suggests that domestic factors alone cannot explain the emergence of reforms in these states.

If the external influences from within Eastern Europe proved to be decisive in changing peoples' attitudes toward their current governments, as proposed here, then one would expect to find coincidences in the progression of events from country to country, as the political climate changed in response to the diffusion of ideas from countries that initiated reforms early in the process. Similarly, if such a demonstration effect occurred, one would expect that there would be a correlation between the access to information about external events in a particular country, and the speed and intensity with which emulation emerged.

I argue that there were four distinct patterns by which regime change in Eastern Europe occurred. Reform occurred relatively early or late; and was either introduced from above, by the regime in power, or induced from below, by mounting popular pressure for change. Chapters 3 through 6 examine each of these patterns in greater detail.

The cases of Poland, Hungary, and Bulgaria are considered individually in Chapters 3, 4, and 6, since they fell into three distinct categories within my argument. In Poland early reforms were stimulated by domestic opposition to the regime; Hungary presents an example of early reform from above. In Bulgaria, reforms were introduced comparatively late in the process, by the ruling regime. I examine the GDR and Czechoslovakia together in Chapter 5, because these are both cases of late reform induced by popular pressure. Finally, in Chapter 7 I examine the Romanian case. Because it is the only state in the Warsaw Pact in which a violent upheaval occurred, and in which the impetus for reform was initially unclear, the Romanian case provides an opportunity to reexplore the balance between external and internal catalysts in promoting change.

In the concluding chapter, I examine how this analysis enriches our understanding of how domestic and international factors interact as catalysts for change. I briefly examine the impact that the nature of change in Eastern Europe has had on subsequent developments in the different states in the region. Finally, I consider the implications of this analysis for future research.

Having outlined my argument and the chapters ahead, let me add a note on what this book is not. The book does not aim to provide a definitive history of the transformation of Eastern Europe in 1989; as noted earlier, many books have appeared in recent years documenting the transitions in one or more states in Eastern Europe. Instead, this book analyzes some of the causes for the transformations in Eastern Europe and compares variables across cases to develop a theoretically informed explanation with relevance for all. Because my goal is social science rather than history, I have relied on a mix of primary and secondary sources.[12]

---

12. As Theda Skocpol has pointed out, "Redoing primary research for every investigation would be disastrous; it would rule out most comparative-historical research." Skocpol, "Emerging Agendas and Recurrent Strategies," in Theda Skocpol, ed. *Vision and Method in Historical Sociology* (Cambridge: Cambridge University Press, 1984), p. 382, as quoted in Ian S. Lustick, "History, Historiography, and Political Science: Multiple Historical Records and the Problem of Selection Bias," *American Political Science Review*, Vol. 90, No. 3 (September 1996), pp. 605–618.

Chapter 1

Legitimacy, the Demonstration Effect, and the Collapse of the Warsaw Pact

The East-West divide in Europe that persisted from the end of World War II until 1989 was both a cause and consequence of the Cold War. Having liberated most of Eastern Europe from the Nazis, the Soviet Red Army stayed, and with it Soviet control.[1] The Western allies had agreed that new governments in the East European states should be "democratic and friendly" to the Soviet Union, but by 1950 it was clear that these governments would be ruled by communist and socialist parties backed by, and beholden to, Moscow. The consolidation of the Soviet bloc was further confirmed by the creation of the Warsaw Pact, a political-military alliance, in 1955; ostensibly this was a response to NATO's (the North Atlantic Treaty Organization) inclusion of West Germany, but it further hardened the dividing line in Europe.[2]

---

1. Through much of the Cold War, the term "Eastern Europe" was used to describe the states of the Warsaw Pact, and sometimes Yugoslavia and Albania as well. With the collapse of the East-West divide in Europe, many states in this region rejected the term, and distinctions between Central Europe and South Eastern Europe have become common. Moreover, the collapse of the Soviet Union at the end of 1991 led to the depiction of former Soviet republics such as Ukraine, Belarus, and the Baltic States as "Eastern Europe." For the sake of brevity and simplicity, and because it was the accepted term during the period I study, I use Eastern Europe to refer to those states that were part of the Warsaw Pact: Bulgaria, Czechoslovakia, East Germany (the German Democratic Republic), Hungary, Poland, and Romania.

2. The Council of Economic Mutual Assistance, established in 1949, became a mechanism for coordinating planning and trade among the socialist countries. For more on the establishment of these alliances, see Zbigniew K. Brzezinski, *The Soviet Bloc: Unity and Conflict,* rev. and enl. ed. (Cambridge, Mass.: Harvard University Press, 1967), pp. 456–463.

Though there was some initial popular support for socialism in Eastern Europe, bolstered by promises of land reform and greater equality, this dissipated as communist control in the region emulated the Stalinist model, with its premium on repression and violence. Though communist rule became more relaxed after Stalin's death, throughout the Cold War Moscow faced the challenge of balancing its desire for bloc cohesion against the need for viable regimes in Eastern Europe. Cohesion favored the adoption of uniform policies, while viability meant giving the regimes more latitude as they strove to achieve a modicum of popular acceptance, if not approval. This tension was evident in the periodic crises in the bloc, most prominently the Hungarian revolution of 1956, the Prague Spring and Soviet invasion of Czechoslovakia in 1968, and the rise of the Solidarity movement in Poland in 1980, which led to the declaration of martial law by the Polish regime in December 1981. All of these crises were rooted in the conflict between popular aspirations for greater freedom and Moscow's desire for control. By the 1980s, the conventional wisdom was that Moscow would tolerate limited political and economic flexibility deemed necessary to keep the population quiescent, while the East European states' membership in the Eastern bloc was not open to question.

Moscow's insistence on continued loyalty to the Soviet Union was made most explicit in the Brezhnev Doctrine, enunciated in November 1968 after the Soviet invasion of Czechoslovakia. The Soviet Union claimed for itself the right to interfere if socialism was threatened anywhere in Eastern Europe.[3] The presence of Soviet troops in East Germany, Czechoslovakia, Hungary, and Poland underscored Moscow's intent to preserve Soviet control in the region, and ensured its ability to do so. The paralysis of the East-West divide created by Soviet and NATO troops facing each other in Europe sustained the conviction that this division was both resilient and critical to Europe's continued stability during the Cold War.

When Mikhail S. Gorbachev assumed power as General Secretary of the Communist Party of the Soviet Union (CPSU) in March 1985, neither East nor West anticipated any change in this arrangement—certainly not without war. Yet Gorbachev dramatically changed the relationship between Eastern Europe and the Soviet Union over the next five years, as the Cold War decayed. Gorbachev initiated a sweeping series of reforms

---

3. Leonid Brezhnev, "Speech to the Fifth Congress of the Polish United Workers' Party (November 12, 1968)," as reprinted in Gale Stokes, ed., *From Stalinism to Pluralism: A Documentary History of Eastern Europe since 1945*, 2nd ed. (Oxford: Oxford University Press, 1996), pp. 132–134.

in the Soviet Union in the second half of the 1980s, and invited his East European allies to follow suit. Few substantial changes had appeared in Eastern Europe by mid-1988. Poland had just begun to explore negotiations with limited aims between the regime and opposition groups, and the governing socialist party in Hungary had begun to revamp its leadership, elevating more reform-minded leaders.[4] But by the end of 1989, less than five years after Gorbachev came to power in the Soviet Union, the communist-led regimes in all the East European member states of the Warsaw Pact had either crumbled or conceded the need for free elections, to be held over the next few months.

What happened? Why had only two states in the Eastern bloc moved to introduce even limited reforms at the beginning of 1989? And what led to the collapse of the communist regimes throughout the bloc by the end of that year?

I argue that a combination of international and domestic factors explain the changes in Eastern Europe in the late 1980s. Once the Soviet Union invited reform, those regimes that recognized the urgency of reform, or that calculated that they could hold on to power during a reform process, cautiously moved toward political liberalization in order to have the chance to mend their economies. The introduction of reforms in these states, Poland and Hungary, changed political calculations in the rest of the bloc. Populations became more ready to demand change, and some within the other East European regimes became convinced that the previous system was no longer viable as they watched the reform processes in these two states—and the Soviet Union's acceptance of their changes.

This explanation highlights the role of individuals' perception, which mattered in several ways. It was not enough that the Soviet Union declare a policy of noninterference and "freedom of choice"; leaders and populations had to believe this. It was not enough for people to want greater freedoms; they must throw off their apathy and demand them.

Finally, leaders' perceptions of their own standing influenced their attitudes toward risk-taking and the prospect of change. Few political science theories examine the mechanisms by which large political changes

---

4. I use the term "reform" throughout this book as a shorthand for the initiation of a very complex process that included the introduction of a democratic form of government and the transition from a centrally planned economy to a capitalist, market-based economy. While this is not an entirely satisfactory term, I know of no precise words to depict the initiation of reform. It could be argued that the closest such word is revolution, but this has other meanings and connotations that do not coincide with the issue here. In this book, "reform" is used both to refer to early efforts to introduce economic or political reforms, and to the larger process of political change that occurred in 1989. The distinction should be clear from the context.

outside a country affect the behavior of individuals within it. This chapter constructs an explanation of the events of 1989 that does so. This is not a "theory" per se. Rather, the events of 1989, a critical episode in twentieth-century history, merit an effort to comprehend in greater depth the processes that shaped the collapse of the Warsaw Pact. I first look at the prevailing explanations for the collapse of the Warsaw Pact, each of which describes a necessary but insufficient cause for the collapse of the communist regimes in Eastern Europe. I then focus on the factors that led to early reform or its rejection, and the factors that finally led those states holding out against reform to concede the need for reforms, or to crumble.

Domestic and International Explanations

Three basic arguments have been proposed to explain the Warsaw Pact's collapse. Some observers maintain that Western influence was critical to the collapse of Eastern Europe's communist regimes since the West presented an alternative to the socialist system imposed on the Eastern bloc, and constrained the Soviet Union to change its foreign policies; these influences grew stronger starting in the 1970s as a result of the Helsinki process. Many observers contend that the process of change in the Soviet Union in the late 1980s impelled the collapse of the communist-run regimes in Eastern Europe. This theory is an extension of the argument that the socialist system created by the Soviet Union and exported to its allies was doomed to collapse, and also reflects the conviction that without Soviet dominance the Eastern Europeans would spontaneously reject communism and embrace democracy. Finally, some see the collapse of the authoritarian regimes in the Warsaw Pact as a classic transition to democracy, and essentially the same as democratic transitions in Southern Europe and Latin America.

Each of these explanations clarifies some facets of the process, but none can explain adequately why the collapse of the Warsaw Pact took place as it did, and when it did. Indeed, intermingled internal and external factors catalyzed the process of change in Eastern Europe. As Peter Gourevitch argues, "international relations and domestic politics are therefore so interrelated that they should be analyzed simultaneously, as wholes."[5] The international system alone is indeterminate; a state's environment may exert strong pulls on it, but the state always has some

---

5. Peter Gourevitch, "The Second Image Reversed: The International Sources of Domestic Politics," *International Organization,* Vol. 32, No. 4 (Autumn 1978), pp. 881–912.

choice in responding to external events. To understand the choice we must look both within and outside the state. The collapse of the Warsaw Pact presents a unique opportunity to examine the interrelationship of domestic and international variables, because it is one in which a significant external change affected all of these states, yet internal responses to this change varied widely within the Warsaw Pact.

THE IMPACT OF THE WEST

Some argue that the West can take credit for inducing the transformation of Eastern Europe, and of the Soviet Union. Western influence was clearly important as a model, an ideal, and in some cases a succor to dissent in Eastern Europe during the Cold War. Yet the West played a largely passive role in the changes in Eastern Europe in 1989; it did not cause them.

Arguments about the role of the West can be separated into three main strands. First, East-West competition during the Cold War compelled change in the Soviet Union, a necessary precursor to changes in Eastern Europe. The Western military build-up led the Soviet Union to conclude that it could not sustain the military confrontation with the West. Therefore, Gorbachev instituted reforms in the Soviet Union, which led to the collapse of its control in Eastern Europe and eventually the destruction of the Soviet Union itself.[6]

A second interpretation is that the apparent success of the Western economic and political system presented a critical challenge to the socialist system. It provided a constant refutation of Marxist-Leninist claims that the capitalist system was fatally flawed, and doomed to collapse under the weight of its "internal contradictions." The health of the West magnified the poverty of the socialist system in the East, and also height-

---

6. The logic of this argument is similar to claims that change in the Soviet Union was sufficient to induce the changes that occurred in Eastern Europe. See Pipes, *Survival is Not Enough: Soviet Realities and America's Future* (New York: Simon and Schuster, 1984); see also John Lewis Gaddis, "Hanging Tough Paid Off," *Bulletin of the Atomic Scientists,* Vol. 45 (January–February 1989), pp. 11–14; Richard Perle, "Military Power and the Passing Cold War," in Charles W. Kegley, Jr., and Kenneth L. Schwab, eds., *After the Cold War: Questioning the Morality of Nuclear Deterrence* (Boulder, Colo.: Westview Press, 1991); Caspar Weinberger, *Fighting for Peace* (New York: Warner Books, 1990); and Peter Schweizer, *Victory: The Reagan Administration's Secret Strategy that Hastened the Collapse of the Soviet Union* (New York: Atlantic Monthly Press, 1994). For more theoretical analyses of external influences on the Soviet Union, see Jack Snyder, "International Leverage on Soviet Domestic Change," *World Politics,* Vol. 42, No. 1 (October 1989), pp. 1–30; and Daniel Deudney and G. John Ikenberry, "The International Sources of Soviet Change," *International Security,* Vol. 16, No. 3 (Winter 1991/92), pp. 74–118.

ened resentment among Eastern Europe's inhabitants, many of whom felt that they belonged with the West by virtue of their history and culture.[7]

Third, some believe that the expansion in East-West ties that developed out of the "Helsinki process" catalyzed the process of democratization in the East. The Helsinki process grew out of efforts to improve East-West relations in the early 1970s, when a relaxation between the United States and the Soviet Union made progress in arms control and détente possible. The Conference on Security and Cooperation in Europe (CSCE) culminated in the signing of the "Final Act" in Helsinki in August 1975, which provided for increased East-West ties and agreed definitions of human rights that each side would respect. Though originally this conference was promoted by the Soviet Union, the Helsinki process enabled the West to insist that Moscow live up to its human rights commitments, and to advocate greater freedom of movement and East-West exchanges.[8] Thus, it helped catalyze change by expanding cross-border contacts and exchanges of ideas across the Cold War divide. The Western peace movement also argues that its efforts to sustain ties with dissidents in Eastern Europe during the 1980s, efforts given sanction by the Helsinki process, induced the process of change in Eastern Europe.[9]

---

7. For some discussions of East European attitudes toward the West prior to the collapse of the Warsaw Pact, see J.F. Brown, "Eastern Europe's Western Connection," in Lincoln Gordon, ed., *Eroding Empire: Western Relations with Eastern Europe* (Washington, D.C.: Brookings Institution, 1987); Joseph Rothschild, *Return to Diversity: A Political History of East Central Europe Since World War II* (New York: Oxford University Press, 1989); and Stephen R. Graubard, ed., *Eastern Europe . . . Central Europe . . . Europe* (Boulder, Colo.: Westview Press, 1991).

8. See Vojtech Mastny, *Helsinki, Human Rights, and European Security* (Durham, N.C.: Duke University Press, 1986); see also J.F. Brown, *Surge to Freedom: The End of Communist Rule in Eastern Europe* (Durham, N.C.: Duke University Press, 1991), chap. 1; and John J. Maresca, *To Helsinki: The Conference on Security and Cooperation in Europe, 1973–75* (Durham, N.C.: Duke University Press, 1985).

9. For an example of the kind of exchange that grew out of the Helsinki process, and some discussions of the influence of Western concepts in the Soviet Union and Eastern Europe, see Mary Kaldor, ed., *Europe from Below: An East-West Dialogue* (London: Verso, 1991); an earlier example is Timothy Garton Ash, *The Uses of Adversity: Essays on the Fate of Central Europe* (New York: Vintage, 1990). See also Thomas Risse-Kappen, "Did `Peace Through Strength' End the Cold War? Lessons from INF," *International Security*, Vol. 16, No. 1 (Summer 1991), pp. 162–188; Thomas Risse-Kappen, "Ideas Do Not Float Freely: Transnational Coalitions, Domestic Structures, and the End of the Cold War," *International Organization*, Vol. 48, No. 2 (Spring 1994), pp. 185–214; Mary Kaldor, "Cold War Europe: Taking the Democratic Way," *The Nation*, April 22, 1991, pp. 514–519; and Mary Kaldor, "Who Killed the Cold War?" *Bulletin of the Atomic Scientists* (July/August 1995), pp. 57–60.

While Western influences were clearly significant, they did not induce the changes that occurred in 1989. The impact of the West did not change significantly during the period immediately prior to the collapse of the Warsaw Pact. The East-West confrontation had been static since the 1950s, and the Carter-Reagan arms build-up was notable in its size, but Soviet experts discount this as a factor in the introduction of perestroika.[10] The Western model challenged the Soviet Union and Eastern Europe, but this challenge was more or less constant. Similarly, influences stemming from the CSCE process and the peace movement were present since the mid-1970s. That the Western alternative was an important aspiration in Eastern Europe can be seen in the adoption of "western" values and institutions since 1989, but it is unlikely that the attraction of the West alone could have impelled the collapse of the Warsaw Pact.

THE SOVIET UNION AS A CATALYST FOR CHANGE

Another compelling argument is that once the Soviet Union began to introduce substantial political and economic reforms, change in Eastern Europe was inevitable.[11] At its most stark, this mirrors the argument that the socialist system created by the CPSU was doomed to collapse.[12] Some an-

---

10. Most assessments of the causes for Gorbachev's new thinking point to a reassessment of Soviet aims with regard to the West, but not to a reevaluation in light of its inability to "keep up," as is sometimes claimed in the West. Gorbachev's change in policy had more to do with Soviet domestic difficulties, and the realization that Soviet foreign policy had worked against its own interests. See Chapter 2.

11. As Jack F. Matlock, Jr., points out, this was the "glib" response of many who viewed the Soviet Union through conservative lenses and considered the collapse of the Soviet Union itself as inevitable. See Matlock, *Autopsy on an Empire* (New York: Random House, 1995), p. 7, and chaps. 8 and 11; for this viewpoint see also Michael Waller, *The End of the Communist Power Monopoly* (Manchester: Manchester University Press, 1993).

12. The most famous such assertion was made by U.S. President Ronald Reagan, who prematurely relegated communism to "the ash-heap of history." Among scholars making this argument, one of the most vehement was Richard Pipes, who also argued that the United States could hasten the Soviet Union's collapse. More reasoned analyses of the socialist system's problems have been offered by scholars such as Seweryn Bialer, who pointed out the inherent weaknesses of the Soviet economic and political structure, while at the same time cautioning that the system had sufficient resources to muddle along for decades. See Z, "To the Stalin Mausoleum," in Graubard, ed., *Eastern Europe . . . Central Europe . . . Europe* (Boulder, Colo.: Westview, 1991), pp. 283–339; Pipes, *Survival is Not Enough;* and Bialer, *The Soviet Paradox: External Expansion, Internal Decline* (New York: Knopf, 1986). For analyses of U.S.-Soviet relations during the 1980s, see Walter LaFeber, *America, Russia and the Cold War, 1945–1990*, 6th ed. (New York: McGraw-Hill, 1991), pp. 310–316; Matthew Evangelista, "Sources of Moderation

alysts considered the Soviet socialist system to be unreformable, and doomed to crumble under its own weight. The East European states shared the defects of the Soviet-imposed socialist economic system, with the added liability that communism was imposed in these states, in the face of varying degrees of resistance.[13] Once Soviet control was removed, therefore, change in Eastern Europe was inevitable.

While the alterations in the Soviet Union's foreign and domestic policy in the second half of the 1980s resulted in a revision of Moscow's policies toward Eastern Europe, and these changes were necessary to the collapse of the communist regimes in Eastern Europe, Soviet actions and policy alone cannot account for the timing of events, or the way reforms resonated throughout the bloc. Nor can they explain the variations in the reform processes in Eastern Europe. Furthermore, the argument that change in the Soviet Union was sufficient to cause the collapse of the Warsaw Pact does not correspond with what people in Eastern Europe, the Soviet Union, or the West believed at the time.

Soviet "encouragement" of reform did not result in a uniform response in the Warsaw Pact, as would be expected if change in the Soviet Union were sufficient to induce change. Moreover, while he favored reform in Eastern Europe as well as in the Soviet Union, Gorbachev does not appear to have anticipated change of the sort that transpired in Eastern Europe. It is reasonable to conclude that neither the East European population nor its leaders could be confident of the range of options open to them in 1989, and this ambiguity fundamentally influenced the nature and pace of change in Eastern Europe. Chapter 2 examines how Soviet policy toward Eastern Europe changed, and analyzes in more detail Moscow's impact on developments within the Warsaw Pact.

---

in Soviet Security Policy," in Philip E. Tetlock, Jo L. Husbands, Robert Jervis, Paul C. Stern, and Charles Tilly, eds. *Behavior, Society, and Nuclear War,* vol. 2 (New York: Oxford University Press, 1991), pp. 254–354; George W. Breslauer and Philip E. Tetlock, eds., *Learning in U.S. and Soviet Foreign Policy* (Boulder, Colo.: Westview Press, 1991); and Alexander L. George, Philip J. Farley, and Alexander Dallin, eds., *U.S.-Soviet Security Cooperation: Achievements, Failures, Lessons* (New York: Oxford University Press, 1988).

13. I use the term "communist" here as short-hand to refer to the socialist and communist parties that claimed to represent the "leading role in society" in the states of Eastern Europe. These parties had a variety of names, and implemented a variety of policies that were intended to move their states toward the goal of Soviet-style communism. On the Soviet Union's imposition and manifestations of control in Eastern Europe, see Brzezinski, *The Soviet Bloc;* William E. Griffith, ed., *Communism in Europe: Continuity, Change, and the Sino-Soviet Dispute* (Cambridge, Mass.: MIT Press, 1965); and Rothschild, *Return to Diversity,* chap. 3.

TRANSITIONS TO DEMOCRACY AND REFORM IN EASTERN EUROPE

Finally, a substantial literature exists on transitions to democracy. Prior to 1989, the transitions literature focused on cases in Southern Europe and Latin America; in recent years East European cases have been incorporated into new studies, to refine our current understanding of transition processes.[14] This literature offers important clues that can help explain the process of transition in Eastern Europe. Scholarship on authoritarian decline also indicates that there were clear parallels between the crumbling political structures in Eastern Europe and in certain similarly crumbling authoritarian regimes elsewhere.[15]

At the same time, there are important differences between Eastern Europe and other cases of democratic transition.[16] Many authoritarian regimes, for example, do not rely on a particular ideology, as did the East

---

14. Some recent works in this vein include Adam Przeworski, *Democracy and the Market: Political and Economic Reforms in Eastern Europe and Latin America* (Cambridge: Cambridge University Press, 1991); Samuel P. Huntington, *The Third Wave: Democratization in the Late Twentieth Century* (Norman, Okla.: University of Oklahoma Press, 1991); George W. Breslauer, ed., *Dilemmas of Transition in the Soviet Union and Eastern Europe* (Berkeley, Calif.: University of California at Berkeley, 1991); Doh Chull Shin, "On the Third Wave of Democratization," *World Politics*, Vol. 46 (October 1994), pp. 135–170; Luiz Carlos Bresser, Jose Maria Marvall, and Adam Przeworski, eds., *Economic Reforms in New Democracies: A Social-Democratic Approach* (Cambridge: Cambridge University Press, 1993); Philippe C. Schmitter, *Some Propositions about Civil Society and the Consolidation of Democracy* (Vienna: Institut fur Hohere Studien, 1993); *The Transition to Democracy: Proceedings of a Workshop* (Washington, D.C.: National Academy Press, 1991); Juan J. Linz, *Problems of Democratic Transition and Consolidation: Southern Europe, South America, and Post-Communist Europe* (Baltimore, Md.: Johns Hopkins University Press, 1996).

15. However, there has been disagreement about how the causes of authoritarian decline affect the transition process. Dankwart Rustow has argued that while factors influencing the decline of a regime are important preconditions of the transition process, this does not tell us anything useful about the transition itself, and the way it will progress. Other scholars, such as Samuel Huntington, have countered this claim by arguing that some factors that may be important as preconditions can also shape the nature of the transition, and therefore are important to the process of transition. Dankwart Rustow, "Transitions to Democracy," *Comparative Politics*, Vol. 2, No. 3 (April 1970), pp. 337–363; and Samuel P. Huntington, "Will More Countries Become Democratic?" *Political Science Quarterly*, Vol. 99, No. 2 (Summer 1984), pp. 23–41.

16. The question of comparability between Eastern Europe and other cases of democratic transition has been the subject of vigorous debate. For representative examples, see Philippe C. Schmitter and Terry Lynn Karl, "The Conceptual Travels of Transitologists and Consolidologists: How Far to the East Should They Attempt to Go?" *Slavic Review*, Vol. 53, No. 1 (Spring 1994), pp. 173–185; and Valerie Bunce, "Should Transitologists Be Grounded?" *Slavic Review*, Vol. 54, No. 1 (Spring 1995), pp. 111–127.

European regimes.[17] Even upon first seizing power, other authoritarian regimes have often declared their intent to rule as "caretaker" governments until democracy can be established or reestablished, as the case may be. In other cases, democratic values may be promoted as a means to secure support, at least temporarily, for a given leadership. Liberalization can hold out the promise of partial democratization or pluralism in the future. None of these options are open to an avowedly communist regime. Democratization would require, at a minimum, acceptance of the need for greater pluralism. Yet only by maintaining the leading role of the party and guiding society toward the future could the goals of socialism, the aim of the ruling parties in Eastern Europe, be reached.[18]

The transitions literature can provide useful insights into the process by which states with authoritarian regimes shift to more democratic systems, but it cannot explain the collapse of the Warsaw Pact, for two reasons. First, the transitions literature focuses on the details of how transitions progress, rather than explaining why they begin in the first place. It cannot explain the timing of transitions, why they took the initial form that they took. Second, and more important, the transitions literature is primarily process-oriented, and concentrates on domestic processes. Few scholars in this area consider the impact that external actors or events may have had in shaping either the climate leading to a transition,

---

17. There is general agreement in the democratization literature on what constitutes an authoritarian government. Simply put, political systems in which "significant procedural proscriptions on political contestation or inclusiveness" exist can be defined as authoritarian. In other words, a regime would be considered authoritarian if the choice of the state's government is not determined by a competitive process, either because there are no means for elections or these are substantially restricted in their scope. Donald Share, "Transitions to Democracy and Transition through Transaction," *Comparative Political Studies*, Vol. 19, No. 4 (January 1987), p. 527. A more exhaustive description catalogs the following sorts of regimes as authoritarian: "political systems with limited, not responsible, political pluralism, without elaborate and guiding ideology, but with distinctive mentalities, without extensive nor intensive political mobilization, except at some points in their development, and in which a leader or occasionally a small group exercises power within formally ill-defined limits but actually quite predictable ones." Juan J. Linz, "Totalitarian and Authoritarian Regimes," in Fred I. Greenstein and Nelson W. Polsby, eds., *Handbook of Political Science*, vol. 3 (Reading, Mass.: Addison-Wesley, 1975), p. 264. See also Robert A. Dahl, *Polyarchy: Participation and Opposition* (New Haven, Conn.: Yale University Press, 1971), esp. chap. 1.

18. On communist succession problems in the past, see Chalmers Johnson, ed., *Change in Communist Systems* (Stanford, Calif.: Stanford University Press, 1970); and Myron Rush, *How Communist States Change their Rulers* (Ithaca, N.Y.: Cornell University Press, 1974).

or the nature of the transition itself.[19] Just as we cannot argue that change in the Soviet Union *caused* the collapse of these regimes, we also cannot claim that only domestic factors determined the upheavals that occurred.

This chapter examines the interaction of international and domestic variables by looking at how actions at the level of the individual were affected by international developments. It includes elements of a two-level game, taking into account the fact that individuals and regimes respond not only to external influences but also, and critically in these cases, to domestic-level factors in making calculations about what policies to follow. State leaders cannot take action internationally without considering the domestic implications of their decisions. Robert Putnam has discussed how international pressures can "reverberate" and change domestic calculations about international negotiating positions; in the East European states in 1989, international reverberations changed domestic calculations about acceptable domestic policies as well.[20] I examine this interaction below.

Early Reform: Domestic Factors and Regime Perceptions

Why did the introduction of reform vary from country to country in Eastern Europe? Overall, the process took two forms. First, in some states (Poland and Hungary) reforms emerged early and cautiously, in response to the Soviet Union's changed policies, while in East European states whose regimes rejected the option of change, reform was provoked late in 1989. These were East Germany, Czechoslovakia, Bulgaria, and Romania. Second, in some countries (Poland, Hungary, and Bulgaria), reform was introduced from above, by the regime in power at the time; in others (East Germany, Czechoslovakia, and to some degree Romania), reform was compelled from below, by mounting popular pressure. In this section I examine the two factors that appear to have influenced a regime's choice of whether or not to introduce reforms early: these are the regime's comprehension of the need for substantial changes in governance, and its judgment of its ability to survive in a more open political environment.

---

19. A notable exception, and one likely significantly to influence future research, is Huntington, *The Third Wave*, pp. 85–99.

20. Robert D. Putnam, "Diplomacy and Domestic Politics: The Logic of Two-Level Games,"*International Organization*, Vol. 42, No. 3 (Summer 1988), pp. 427–461.

THE URGENCY OF REFORM

I seek to explain the East European regimes' decisions to introduce significant *political* reforms. Yet this choice cannot be understood without acknowledging the relationship between political and economic reforms within the socialist camp, because centralized control in the Soviet Union, Eastern Europe, and some other communist-ruled countries encompassed both political governance and the state's control of the economy.

The socialist system that developed in the Soviet Union and was exported to Eastern Europe was based on the goal of cultivating the state's productive forces in order to create the abundance that would be necessary if a true communist system, based on Marxist principles, was to be realized.[21] To ensure that industrialization received sufficient priority, the Soviet Union developed a centralized planning system that coordinated all aspects of the economy, from supplies to outputs. This meant that the regime had extremely broad control over the functioning of the state; it also required the development of a massive bureaucratic infrastructure to plan all the economic activities of the state's industries to the lowest levels. Since planners determined both the types and quantities of goods produced, as well as their prices, this centralization virtually precluded the functioning of market mechanisms in the economy. This centralization has important implications for change in the system, because the degree of transformation of the economy that would need to accompany any change in the governance of the state is extremely large. Rather than simply exchanging one set of officials for another set, a new government in a post-totalitarian state must decide whether it wishes to revamp the entire centralized structure of the state and how to go about doing so, in the face of unknown obstacles and the certainty of societal upheavals. Moreover, central control discourages entrepreneurship or innovation by industrial managers, making the introduction of capitalism more problematic.[22]

In spite of satisfactory economic growth in the Soviet Union and Eastern Europe until well into the 1960s, regimes within the socialist camp made a variety of attempts to tinker with elements of the socialist economic system during the postwar period. These efforts generally involved modifications meant to improve the performance of the socialist

---

21. The most important such principle was "from each according to his ability, to each according to his needs." For a good overview of the Soviet economic system, see Alec Nove, *The Soviet Economic System*, 2nd ed. (London: George Allen & Unwin, 1980).

22. Juan J. Linz, "Transitions to Democracy," *Washington Quarterly*, Vol. 13, No. 3 (Summer 1990), p. 156.

system, such as changing the price structure, or allowing enterprises somewhat greater autonomy, rather than efforts to replace it, which was not an option.[23] Yet these "refinements" were evidence that even when working comparatively well, the centralized economic system was not performing to the satisfaction of its proponents.[24]

In spite of their rhetorical support for the socialist model, some East European leaders recognized that the socialist economic system needed repair. In 1968, however, it became clear that states could pursue only limited economic reform without venturing into political quicksand. The reforms associated with the "Prague Spring" in Czechoslovakia in 1968 were a bid to improve both the state's economic and political mechanisms, but when the Czechoslovakian regime, led by Alexander Dubček, began to allow the expansion of political modifications intended to improve relations with society and, by extension, to help improve economic conditions, political reforms spiraled out of control. The consequence, the Soviet invasion of Czechoslovakia and the subsequent repression, was to make political reforms taboo in Eastern Europe for nearly twenty years.[25]

Until the mid-1970s, the East European regimes were able to run their economies without substantial reforms, partly because they received fuel at well below world market prices from the Soviet Union.[26] The start of the Helsinki process in the early 1970s also made a partial opening to the

23. See Jan Adam, *Why Did the Socialist System Collapse in Central and Eastern European Countries? The Case of Poland, the Former Czechoslovakia and Hungary* (Houndmills, Basingstoke, Hampshire: Macmillan Press, 1996), chap. 7; Charles Gati, *Hungary and the Soviet Bloc* (Durham, N.C.: Duke University Press, 1986), pp. 156–159. On the socialist economic system, see also Iván T. Berend, *Central and Eastern Europe, 1944–1993: Detour from the Periphery to the Periphery* (Cambridge: Cambridge University Press, 1996), chaps. 5 and 6; János Kornai, *Overcentralization in Economic Administration* (Oxford: Oxford University Press, 1959); and Kornai, *Economics of Shortage* (Amsterdam: North-Holland Press, 1980).

24. George W. Breslauer, "Is the Soviet System Transformable? The Perennial Question," in Breslauer, ed., *Dilemmas of Transition in the Soviet Union and Eastern Europe* (Berkeley, Calif.: University of California at Berkeley, 1991), pp. 1–14; and J.F. Brown, *Eastern Europe and Communist Rule* (Durham, N.C.: Duke University Press, 1988), especially chap. 4.

25. For detailed accounts of the Prague Spring, see Gordon H. Skilling, *Czechoslovakia's Interrupted Revolution* (Princeton: Princeton University Press, 1976); Jiri Valenta, *Soviet Intervention in Czechoslovakia, 1968: Anatomy of a Decision* (Baltimore, Md.: Johns Hopkins University Press, 1979); and Zdeněk Mlynar, *Nightfrost in Prague: The End of Humane Socialism* (New York: Karz, 1980).

26. On Soviet fuel pricing and its implicit subsidies to Eastern Europe, see Paul Marer, "The Political Economy of Soviet Relations with Eastern Europe," and John P. Hardt, "Soviet Energy Policy in Eastern Europe," both in Sarah Meiklejohn Terry, ed., *Soviet Policy in Eastern Europe* (New Haven, Conn.: Yale University Press, 1984).

West possible, which gave these regimes access to cheap Western credits.[27] Finally, many of these regimes did not hit the limits of their growth potential under the existing system until the mid-1970s. So long as they had sufficient manpower to continue expanding even in very inefficient, labor-intensive modes of production, economic growth was still possible.[28]

By the early 1980s, however, the need for substantial economic changes was clearly recognized in some East European states, such as Hungary and Poland. The East European economies stagnated by the end of the 1970s for a variety of reasons: all lost their access to cheap fuel; most had high levels of accumulated debt in most of the Warsaw Pact states, due to bad management of the credits they had received from the West; and all had reached or were reaching the natural limits of labor-intensive growth.[29] This led to adverse terms of trade both within the Soviet-dominated Council for Mutual Economic Assistance (CMEA) and with Western trading partners. In combination with the rise of Solidarity in 1980, a clear indication of popular discontent, there was a growing comprehension in some of these states that tinkering would not work; only substantial modifications of the economic system would solve the system's problems.

Thus, when Mikhail Gorbachev came to power in the Soviet Union in 1985, some leaders were aware of the need for substantial economic reform—but more regimes should have comprehended the problems they faced. Many regimes in the Eastern bloc faced economic conditions that should have led their leaders to consider at a minimum significant economic reforms, if not political changes as well; by 1985, previous economic reforms without political modifications had clearly failed. Moreover, while economic conditions in some states were far worse than in

---

27.   The CSCE made possible expanded economic ties, which in the long run weakened the East European states because of the debt they compiled. See Mastny, *Helsinki, Human Rights, and European Security;* and Brown, *Surge to Freedom,* chap. 1.

28.   Adam, *Why Did the Socialist System Collapse in Central and Eastern European Countries?* pp. 138–142.

29.   The Soviet Union introduced a system of price averaging in the mid-1970s in response to the rapid rise in prices and the inability of its allies to pay world prices. When the international oil market collapsed at the end of the decade, this left the East European states paying prices substantially more than the new world market prices. See Adam, *Why Did the Socialist System Collapse in Central and Eastern Europe?* chap. 8; on energy inefficiency in the Eastern bloc see also Jacek Rostowski, "Economic Structure and Material and Energy Intensity in Eastern Europe," in Reiner Weichhardt, ed., *The Economies of Eastern Europe under Gorbachev's Influence* (Brussels: NATO, 1988), pp. 53–79.

others, none of the East European economies were actually healthy. But the early 1980s economic problems were not always enough to make a regime recognize the need for economic reforms, let alone political changes.

This is partly explained by the fact that introducing significant economic reforms would clearly impinge on political issues.[30] To introduce elements of a market economic system was to reject the Marxist-Leninist ideology that was the basis for rule in the Soviet Union and Eastern Europe.[31] Yet by the mid-1980s some East European leaders appeared to have understood that even major economic changes, in the absence of political changes, would not resolve their problems.[32] The acceptance of major economic reforms therefore implied a changed attitude toward political orthodoxy as well.

What factors would lead a regime to recognize the need for political reforms?[33] First, clearly, a regime must see the need for significant *eco-*

---

30. Hungary's cautious efforts to reform in the 1960s and 1970s are a case in point; having begun economic liberalizations in the mid-1960s, the Hungarian government faced pressure and suspicion from the Soviet leadership about the aims of these reforms, and after the Warsaw Pact invaded Czechoslovakia in 1968, the second half of the planned reforms was postponed and eventually dropped. Some aspects of the original reform program survived, however, and generated a rise in prosperity in Hungary. See Berend, *Central and Eastern Europe, 1944–1993*, pp. 146–152. See also Chapter 3.

31. Indeed, his own devotion to socialism notwithstanding, Gorbachev faced substantial opposition within the Soviet Union because of the consequences of his reforms for the state's core ideological beliefs. For a particularly famous criticism, see Nina Andreyeva, "I Cannot Forgo My Principles," in Alexander Dallin and Gail W. Lapidus, eds., *The Soviet System: From Crisis to Collapse*, rev. ed. (Boulder, Colo.: Westview Press, 1995), pp. 288–296. See also E.K. Ligachev, *Zagadka Gorbacheva* [The mystery of Gorbachev] (Novosibirsk: Interbook, 1992).

32. This was especially apparent in Poland, where the already struggling economy had been thrown into chaos by the strikes Solidarity organized in 1980–1981. See Timothy Garton Ash, *The Polish Revolution: Solidarity* (New York: Scribner's, 1983).

33. By "regime" I mean what some in Eastern Europe referred to during the transition as "the powers that be." In the Soviet Union and the Warsaw Pact (as well as in most other putatively socialist states), a distinction was made between the "government" and the "party." In theory, government officials were responsible for directing state business, but in practice the party, "the leading force in society," dictated and largely oversaw policymaking. The ruling parties in Eastern Europe also had a variety of names ranging from the "Hungarian Socialist Worker's Party" to the "Communist Party of Czechoslovakia." To avoid confusion, I will refer to the "regime" or the "Communist Party" throughout, unless I am discussing individual leaders. For an overview of differences in governance and party practices during the Cold War, see Richard F. Staar, *Communist Regimes in Eastern Europe*, 5th ed. (Stanford, Calif.: Hoover Institution Press, 1988).

nomic reforms, beyond earlier endeavors to tinker with the system. This awareness could be caused by an economic crisis or economic stagnation. In the absence of such recognition, an East European regime would not be likely to accept the need for political reforms. Or a regime might understand the linkages between economic and political reforms—that economic reforms alone would not succeed in solving the state's problems. Such regimes would be in agreement with the ideas being promoted by Gorbachev from 1985 on. Finally, a regime would likely recognize the need for political changes if it were aware that it faced serious problems in its relations with society, and that these were only likely to be solved by introducing political as well as economic reforms.

I measure regime awareness of the urgency of reform with four indicators. First, I examine the nature of reform efforts prior to 1985 for evidence of the regime's attitude toward economic reform. If earlier reforms were limited to changes at the margins of the system, the regime was unlikely to see the need for political reform. If it had begun to introduce market elements, the regime would be more likely to perceive that political reforms were crucial as well.

The second indicator is the degree of "orthodoxy" of a state's economic and political structure. By orthodoxy, I mean the degree to which the state adhered to the Soviet model and Marxism-Leninism. If a regime's commitment to socialist ideals had begun to erode by the 1980s, for whatever reason, then it would be more likely to acknowledge problems with the existing system. Unshaken faith in the correctness of Marxist-Leninist values, if only as a justification for the regime's continuance in power, should make a regime more hostile to political changes.

Another way to measure a regime's orthodoxy is through its ties with Moscow. Links with the Soviet leadership played a critical role in the survival of East European leaders from the late 1940s on. Under Stalin, absolute conformity to Soviet positions came to be required—particularly after the dispute between the Yugoslavian leader Josip Broz Tito and Stalin in the late 1940s.[34] During Khrushchev's and Brezhnev's tenure, patronage by the right members of the Soviet leadership could determine the political survival or success of an East European leader, depending on which factions held sway in Moscow. Similarly, changes in a leader's orientation—toward more reformist or conservative views—could influence

---

34. On the split between Stalin and Tito, see Brzezinski, *The Soviet Bloc*, pp. 185–209; Milovan Djilas, *Conversations with Stalin* (New York: Harcourt, Brace & World, 1962); and Adam B. Ulam, *Titoism and the Cominform* (Cambridge, Mass.: Harvard University Press, 1952).

Moscow's decision to support particular factions within an East European regime, especially during periods of instability.[35]

After Mikhail Gorbachev came to power in the Soviet Union in 1985, reform-minded elements in the Communist Party of the Soviet Union gained authority in the Soviet leadership.[36] The make-up and inclination of many of the East European regimes, however, did not mirror this shift. If an East European regime sided with more reformist elements in the Soviet leadership, then one would expect the regime would be open to political reforms, even if its ultimate goal was not democratization. Conversely, an East European regime that maintained strong ties to the hard-line elements in the Soviet leadership would be less likely to initiate reforms. The degree of commitment by the regime to socialist ideals would probably coincide with its alignment with reformers or hard-liners in Moscow.

A third indicator that a regime saw the need for political as well as economic reforms is the magnitude of the problems facing its state. If the state faced a serious economic crisis, it should be less likely to sustain its faith in its ability to rule without reforms. The party leadership should be aware that the socialist economic model was not working; indeed, a protracted economic crisis could erode a regime's commitment to Marxism-Leninism. A regime might see that it must modify its political strategies and look for new solutions if it hoped to preserve its position.[37]

---

35. On the relationship between the Soviet leadership and the regimes in Eastern Europe, particularly during crises, see, among others, Gati, *Hungary and the Soviet Bloc;* and Valenta, *Soviet Intervention in Czechoslovakia, 1968.*

36. However, they were neither the majority nor totally in control. For some discussions of differences within the Politburo during the late 1980s, see Archie Brown, *The Gorbachev Factor* (Oxford: Oxford University Press, 1996); Matlock, *Autopsy on an Empire;* Seweryn Bialer, *Politics, Society, and Nationality Inside Gorbachev's Russia* (Boulder, Colo.:Westview Press, 1989), chaps. 3–7; Michael Tatu, "The 19th Party Conference," *Problems of Communism,* Vol. 37, Nos. 3–4 (May–August 1988), pp. 1–15; and John B. Dunlop and Henry S. Rowen, "Gorbachev versus Ligachev, The Kremlin Divided," *The National Interest* (Spring 1988), pp. 18–29. See also Chapter 2.

37. Pressure for change has also arisen from economic growth, which can create strains within rigid societies. Rapid industrialization, with its requirement for skilled or semi-skilled workers, may help labor organizations gain members and bargaining power. Expanding job opportunities and rising living standards can also change popular impressions of individual rights and willingness to accept rigid limits to these freedoms. As a result, economic growth could lead to increased pressures on a regime for liberalizations, or for democratization. For example, economic growth created new pressures on the government in Spain in the late 1960s and early 1970s. In much of Eastern Europe, rapid industrialization from the 1950s on led to the creation of an urban, industrialized workforce, but the centralized planning system made it impossible

Moreover, the economy would also affect popular attitudes toward the regime. If the economy was in relatively good condition and capable of meeting popular expectations, then the population should be more pliable; while if the economy was in poor condition, then the population should be more restive, or even open in its disapproval of the regime.

Of course, determining the magnitude of the economic problems facing a state can be difficult. A regime that was unwilling drastically to change its economic system for ideological reasons might overstate its economic successes as proof that reforms were unnecessary, as in Romania. Or if the state's economy was not in crisis, or if the regime successfully contended that it was not, as in East Germany, then the regime would be less likely to acknowledge that reforms might be potentially beneficial. Some of the East European economies were in far worse condition in 1989 than was believed at the time. Since I seek to measure a regime's cognizance of the need for reform, I use the interpretations generally accepted by the regime and outside observers during the late 1980s, not newer evidence, which sometimes tells a less sanguine story.[38]

The fourth indicator is a regime's willingness to use the opportunity presented by Gorbachev to expand its reform efforts. A regime's response can be measured by examining any attempts it made to change the system between 1985 and 1988, during the initial period of reform in the Soviet Union. The statements of party leaders during this period should also demonstrate their attitude toward reform. East European leaders who supported the changes in Moscow with enthusiasm should favor political reforms; those who made neutral or negative comments about

---

to continue the pace of growth that the workers were led to expect. This was a major cause of many of the crises in Poland, in particular, and led to the formation in 1980 of Solidarity, the first independent trade union in the Eastern bloc—a direct threat to the Communist-controlled system. On the situation in Spain, see Kenneth Maxwell, "The Emergence of Democracy in Spain and Portugal," *Orbis*, Vol. 27, No. 1 (Spring 1983), pp. 151–184. For some discussions of the role of modernization on transitions, see Adam Przeworski and Fernando Limongi, "Modernization: Theories and Facts," *World Politics*, Vol. 49 (January 1997), pp. 155–183; Huntington, *The Third Wave*, pp. 59–71; and Seymour Martin Lipset, *Political Man: The Social Bases of Politics* (Baltimore, Md.: Johns Hopkins University Press, 1981).

38. Sometimes outside observers and the ruling regime had very different interpretations of the economy's condition. This is particularly evident in the case of Romania. However, since Ceaușescu's continued belief in the rightness of his policies, regardless of the suffering they caused the Romanian population, was central to his attitude toward reform in Eastern Europe, it is easy to conclude that Ceaușescu was not cognizant of the need for reform. See Chapter 7.

Soviet and other East European reforms probably dismissed the need for political reforms.[39]

POLITICAL SURVIVAL AND LEGITIMACY

A regime's outlook on reform was not the only factor influencing whether it introduced reforms between 1985 and 1988. A regime's calculation of its ability to survive in a more open political climate also played a critical role. A regime might be able to control the reform process, and perhaps its pace, if it began a process of liberalization or took steps toward more democratic governance, particularly if there was little or no popular pressure for such changes.[40] Yet a regime would only be likely to take this risk if it presumed that it had a reasonable chance to continue exercising power in a freer political environment. If the regime felt that this was unlikely, then in the absence of other stresses it would not be expected to risk its control by expanding political competition. How would a regime make this calculation?

First, the regime's perception of its own *legitimacy* was critical to whether it would be willing to risk introducing political reforms. Discussing legitimacy as it pertains to Eastern Europe is difficult, at best. How one defines legitimacy, however, is important. Seymour Martin Lipset points to the ability of the regime to sustain the belief among the population that "the existing political institutions are the most appropriate ones for the society."[41] In terms of compatibility of institutions and values, clearly the East European regimes failed to gain legitimacy during much of the Cold War. Alternatively, what is critical about legitimacy as a factor in political life may be that it reflects the degree to which those who seek to rule are accepted by those they rule; thus, legitimacy is an impor-

---

39. There were three types of response to Gorbachev's relaxation of control in the Warsaw Pact and his calls for reform in 1987–88: enthusiastic but cautious efforts to introduce reforms; pro-forma attempts to keep pace with change in the Soviet Union; and outright rejection of the need to follow Moscow's lead. Poland and Hungary fall in the first category; Czechoslovakia and Bulgaria in the second; and East Germany and Romania in the third.

40. Initiating a process of liberalization has enabled other authoritarian regimes to maintain at least partial authority during and after a transition toward democracy. See, for example, Adam Przeworski, "Some Problems in the Study of Transition to Democracy," in Guillermo O'Donnell, Philippe C. Schmitter, and Laurence Whitehead, eds., *Transitions from Authoritarian Rule* (Baltimore, Md.: Johns Hopkins University Press, 1986) part III, pp. 51–53; and O'Donnell and Schmitter, "Tentative Conclusions about Uncertain Democracies," in *Transitions from Authoritarian Rule*, Part IV, p. 7.

41. Lipset, *Political Man*, p. 64.

tant measure of the relationship between rulers and ruled.[42] Governments are confronted with the need to answer the question "who are you that I should obey you?"[43] Legitimacy is thus an ongoing process. As Robert Jackman has pointed out, legitimacy is not something that either exists or does not; it is more appropriate to think of it as a spectrum. Sustaining legitimacy requires constant attention.[44] Recognizing that legitimacy is something that they must constantly work on, regimes can resort to different tactics to try to enhance their legitimacy.[45]

Moreover, the lack of legitimacy, or the loss of it, need not mean regime collapse. Loss of legitimacy can ensue when the state "fails consistently to cope with existing tasks, or proves unable to cope with new tasks suddenly thrust upon it by crisis circumstances." Nonetheless, the state may be able to preserve its stability, particularly if it retains effective means of coercion.[46] Similarly, illegitimate regimes are perfectly capable of perpetuating their rule indefinitely—if no alternative to their rule is available.[47]

Legitimacy in Eastern Europe thus must be examined in the context of Soviet control. This had negative consequences for regime legitimacy in two ways. First, the imposition of communist-led governments by the Soviet Union hurt the latent appeal that communist principles might have held for the local population. Second, continued Soviet control diminished a regime's ability to augment its legitimacy in the eyes of the people it ruled. Dependence on Soviet patronage meant that any at-

---

42. Robert W. Jackman, *Power Without Force: The Political Capacity of Nation-States* (Ann Arbor: University of Michigan Press, 1993), p. 95.

43. Clifford Geertz, "The Judging of Nations: Some Comments on the Assessment of Regimes in the New States," *European Journal of Sociology*, Vol. 18, No. 2, pp. 245–261, as cited in Jackman, *Power Without Force*, p. 98.

44. Jackman, *Power without Force*, p. 95.

45. The loss of legitimacy may reduce the regime's effectiveness in governing, which in the long run could lead to increased pressures on the regime for change. For a discussion of the relationship between legitimacy and effectiveness, see Seymour Martin Lipset, "Some Social Requisites of Democracy: Economic Developments and Political Legitimacy," *American Political Science Review*, Vol. 53, No. 1 (March 1959), pp. 69–105; see also Lipset, *Political Man*, pp. 64–70; and Jackman, *Power Without Force*, pp. 98–99.

46. Theda Skocpol, *States and Social Revolutions: A Comparative Analysis of France, Russia, and China* (Cambridge: Cambridge University Press, 1979), p. 32.

47. Adam Przeworski cites Weber on this point: "People may submit from individual weakness and helplessness *because there is no acceptable alternative.*" Max Weber, *Economy and Society*, vol. 1 (New York: Bedminster, 1968), p. 213; in Przeworski, "Some Problems in the Study of Transition to Democracy," p. 51.

tempts by the East European regimes to modify the means by which they ruled, both politically and economically, were subject to veto from Moscow. This hindered efforts to reshape policies so as to gain greater support from the population.[48]

Yet Soviet backing also meant that the East European communist regimes could not be toppled by domestic threats so long as Moscow supported their continuation in power. This applied to the ruling regimes, but not necessarily to individual leaders, who could lose their positions if they disagreed with Moscow.[49]

East European leaders were clearly constrained in the range of policy options open to them, and this had important implications for legitimacy within the Warsaw Pact. First, the events of 1956, 1968, and 1980–81 meant that the inhabitants of Eastern Europe knew that both they and the regimes that ruled them had limited freedom to act. Therefore populations were likely to acquiesce in an East European regime's continued rule. People tend to tolerate unpopular rulers, particularly if they perceive that the alternative is likely to be worse.[50] Second, an East European regime could not hope to achieve widespread popular support, due to popular hostility toward Soviet influence. Nonetheless, by improving the standard of living, being perceived to be responsive to the needs of the population, and appearing to defend the country's interests as far as was possible within the bounds of Soviet control, an East European regime could gain some degree of approbation from the population. There was

---

48.   Charles Gati has pointed out that the Soviet Union, in considering what policies it would allow its East European allies to adopt, faced the dilemma of choosing between demanding conformity with Moscow's own practices or allowing variation that might enhance the domestic viability of these regimes. See Gati, *Hungary and the Soviet Bloc*, chap. 9. See also Zvi Gitelman, "Power and Authority in Eastern Europe," in Chalmers Johnson, ed., *Change in Communist Systems* (Stanford, Calif.: Stanford University Press, 1970), p. 243; and Sarah Meiklejohn Terry, "Theories of Socialist Development in Soviet-East European Relations," in Terry, ed., *Soviet Policy in Eastern Europe* (New Haven, Conn.: Yale University Press, 1984), pp. 221–254.

49.   The most obvious example of this is the demise of Walter Ulbricht, who was replaced as party leader in the German Democratic Republic because of his opposition to Moscow's new relationship with the Federal Republic of Germany. See David Childs, *The GDR: Moscow's German Ally* (London: George Allen and Unwin, 1983), pp. 80–87; and Robert Hutchings, *Soviet-East European Relations: Consolidation and Conflict, 1968–1980* (Madison: University of Wisconsin Press, 1983), pp. 94–95.

50.   Similarly, the lack of an alternative will keep the population quiescent, as Przeworski has pointed out. Giuseppe di Palma, "Legitimation From the Top to Civil Society: Politico-Cultural Change in Eastern Europe," *World Politics*, Vol. 44, No. 1 (October 1991), pp. 49–80.

certainly variation in the level of legitimacy within Eastern Europe, both over time, and from country to country.[51] Given this diversity, the *relative* legitimacy of an East European regime is a valid factor to consider.

I argue that if a regime perceived that its rule was considered relatively legitimate in the eyes of the state's population, then it should feel that it could survive in a more open political climate. For the East European states, this assumes that membership in the Warsaw Pact, friendship with the Soviet Union, and a government that could be considered at least nominally "socialist" in nature, if not still controlled by the Moscow-backed communist party, continued.[52] That is, a regime's assessment of its legitimacy assumed that the basic parameters of the system would remain. The removal of these parameters was critical to the eventual spread of reform, but these parameters seemed stable when the process began. Similarly, a regime that did not feel that its rule was perceived to be legitimate would not take the risk of introducing domestic political reforms, in the absence of other stimuli.

How can we measure a regime's perception of its legitimacy? Economic factors are not practical measures of this variable, because most governments strive to improve economic performance and to satisfy popular expectations. Efforts by an East European regime to shield the country from complete adherence to the Soviet model might indicate earlier endeavors to improve its standing with the population. But this could also reflect particular aspects of the state's internal structure, or the impulses of a particular leader.[53]

---

51. In Poland, for example, Wladislaw Gomulka enjoyed widespread support after he stood up to the Soviets in 1956; but within ten years he was widely unpopular, since he had failed to address the country's economic problems and satisfy popular needs. Conversely, Hungary's János Kádár went from revilement for his presumed complicity in the Soviet invasion of Hungary in 1956, to having higher approval than most leaders in Eastern Europe due to his efforts to strengthen Hungary's economy and the overall moderation of his rule. See J.F. Brown, *Eastern Europe and Communist Rule;* Andrzej Korbonski, "Poland," in Teresa Rakowska-Harmstone, *Communism in Eastern Europe,* 2nd ed. (Bloomington, Ind.: Indiana University Press, 1984), pp. 50–85; Jane L. Curry and Luba Fajfer, eds., *Poland's Permanent Revolution: People versus Elites, 1956 to the Present* (Washington, D.C.: American University Press, 1996); and Gati, *Hungary and the Soviet Bloc.*

52. A third parameter was that the Soviet Union did not want to see "communists" being hung from lamp-posts, as they had been during the Hungarian revolution in 1956. Based on author's interviews in Eastern Europe, 1988–89.

53. For example, agriculture in Poland was never collectivized, despite Stalin's desire to see the East European satellite regimes imitate the Soviet economic model. But this step was not taken because it would clearly lead to more civil unrest at a time when

One way to measure legitimacy may be to examine the extent of repression of society. A low level or lack of repression could mean that the regime perceived that its rule would not be imperiled by the presence of opposing views, albeit on a minimal scale. The outer limits of dissent in Eastern Europe were set by Moscow, at least prior to 1985, and a low level of repression would mean allowing a broader range of publications, greater access to information about the outside world, and travel to the West.

A high level of repression—a lack of tolerance for divergent views, and a refusal to trust the population with access to information or travel—could indicate that the regime doubted its own legitimacy. But it could also imply that the regime believed in its own legitimacy, and thus its right to use coercive means to sustain its rule.[54] Therefore the use of repression alone is indeterminate as an indicator of the regime's faith in its own legitimacy. However, when the motives behind a regime's use of repressive means are apparent from private comments by the leadership to Soviet or other East European elites, it should be possible to distinguish what the use of repression implies about a regime's perception of its legitimacy.

Finally, the failure of repression to curb dissent reveals a regime's low legitimacy. If a regime could not prevent dissent, it might eventually condone relatively open opposition out of concern that regime-society relations would only be worse if it tried to quell such dissent. Moreover, toleration in a climate of low legitimacy could indicate that the regime wanted to improve its popular status.

---

the communist regime's hold over the country was extremely fragile. Other examples are somewhat less troubling. In Hungary, for example, Party Secretary János Kádár managed to gain grudging popular support over time by tolerating passive opposition to the regime and not demanding active support for the system; improving the quality of life through minor economic revisions; and importantly, by making clear his lack of enthusiasm for the Soviet invasion of Czechoslovakia in 1968. This gave the impression that he was allowing as much variation as the parameters of the socialist system would tolerate at the time, and even pushing the limits. As a result, by the early 1980s the population in Hungary seemed to accept that given the alternatives within the Soviet-dominated parameters, Kádár's rule was relatively benign. Romania's leader Nicolae Ceauşescu openly defied the Soviet Union and condemned the invasion of Czechoslovakia, a move that made him widely popular in Romania at the time. Nonetheless, his utter myopia about popular needs and his megalomania destroyed all vestiges of popular support for his rule by the late 1980s—though not his perception of his legitimacy.

54. Reinhard Bendix, *Kings or People: Power and the Mandate to Rule* (Berkeley, Calif.: University of California Press, 1978), pp. 16–17.

INTRA-REGIME CONFLICT

The introduction of political reforms can also be affected by conflict within a regime, which might induce different factions within it to initiate political changes. Conflicts within regimes about policy choices are common, particularly during transitions.[55] If a regime did not face significant external pressures for change, then we should find elements within the regime compelling the initiation of reforms, if they occurred. A common cause of internal conflict within a regime is the succession problem that authoritarian regimes confront. Succession problems are especially likely when the way a regime came to power, or the personalized nature of rule by a single figure, means that no regularized means of transferring authority from one individual or group to another exists.

Power struggles within the ruling group may focus on the issue of succession, or factions may use very different issues as a pretext for conflict. For example, the leadership in an authoritarian state may disagree among itself about what policies it ought to follow; this would hinder its ability to govern effectively. Such power struggles could leave the regime paralyzed, or some group within the leadership might choose to look outside the current ruling structure for allies, and attempt to coopt previously excluded groups within society into supporting its views; this could lead to the initiation of reforms of the type seen in some Eastern European states.[56] Regime-initiated reform of this sort could involve a negotiated settlement with opposition groups or the closest equivalents, and an agreement on a political settlement that would allow the previous rulers to continue to participate in some way in governing the state.[57]

---

55. Some scholars have argued that divisions within regimes are present in all cases of authoritarian decline, which suggests that regime conflict is a necessary condition for decline. This coincides with a general assumption about the nature of transitions to democracy; O'Donnell and Schmitter cite the examples of recent transitions in Latin America and Southern Europe to make this point. See O'Donnell and Schmitter, "Tentative Conclusions about Uncertain Democracies," p. 18.

56. Przeworski, "Some Problems in the Study of Transition to Democracy," p. 56.

57. Samuel Huntington argues that almost all transitions involve some negotiations between government and opposition groups. He lays out a typology of three broad types of transition processes: transformations, in which elites in power take the lead in bringing about democratization; replacements, in which authoritarian regimes collapse or are overthrown and opposition groups take the lead in promoting democratization; and transplacements, in which government and opposition groups work together to establish democracy. Negotiations are particularly important in this last category. See Huntington, *The Third Wave*, pp. 109–163; see also Schmitter and O'Donnell, "Negotiating Pacts," in Guillermo O'Donnell, Phillippe C. Schmitter, and

In Eastern Europe, a group within a regime's leadership might also find political allies outside the state. Communist party officials could generate political resources abroad as well as at home—in the other countries in the Eastern bloc, and most notably in the Soviet Union.[58] By the late 1980s there were clearly differences of opinion within most of the ruling communist parties in Eastern Europe, despite the surface unity most of them retained for public consumption.[59] Different groups involved in intraparty conflicts could try to coopt *external* support for their positions in the internal conflicts underway from like-minded groups in other states, especially the Soviet Union. The degree to which this was happening could have been critical to the shape that the process of change took from country to country, depending on the strength of various contingents in gaining external as well as internal support.[60]

Laurence Whitehead, eds., *Transitions from Authoritarian Rule* (Baltimore, Md.: Johns Hopkins University Press, 1986), part IV.

58. Ellen Commisso uses this term to describe this relationship in "Introduction: State Structures, Political Processes, and Collective Choice in CMEA States," *International Organization*, Vol. 40, No. 2 (Spring 1986), pp. 195–238. She discusses the question of recruiting cross-border support primarily with regard to economic issues in the CMEA, but the same logic applies in political decision-making in other areas of state policy. This awareness of cross-border ties is certainly not new; Condoleezza Rice extensively analyzed the nature of cross-border party-military ties in *Uncertain Allegiance: The Soviet Union and the Czechoslovak Army, 1948–1983* (Princeton: Princeton University Press, 1984), as did Christopher D. Jones in *Soviet Influence in Eastern Europe: Political Autonomy and the Warsaw Pact* (New York: Praeger, 1981).

59. However, the factionalism that existed in Eastern Europe was not new in the 1980s; intraparty strife has played a role in the majority of leadership changes throughout the region. Due to the nature of the hegemonic system in Eastern Europe, and its roots in Soviet communism, open factionalism was proscribed in these states, which meant that differences over policy could not be played out publicly, as they are in Western political systems. Instead, "if coalitions form, they tend to be within the party rather than between party groups and social forces or institutions outside it." See Commisso, "Introduction: State Structures, Political Processes, and Collective Choice in CMEA States," pp. 211–213.

60. Steven R. David's refinement of alliance formation theory in third world cases, "omnibalancing," also helps explain why some regimes in Eastern Europe allied with the conservatives in the Soviet Union against domestic pressures for change, while others risked the introduction of reforms. David argues that to understand alliance formation in the third world, we must look not only at the external threats that confront a regime, but also at its domestic opposition; regimes are likely to bandwagon with an external threat if they perceive a *greater* threat to their continued rule from an internal opponent. Similarly, I argue that a regime was unlikely to initiate reforms if it believed that its domestic political survival was at stake. See David, "Explaining Third World Alignment," *World Politics*, Vol. 43 (January 1991), pp. 233–256.

SUMMARY

Given the two variables—a regime's awareness of the need for reforms, and its perception of its own ability to survive, as well as the possibility of intra-regime conflicts—how would we expect different regimes to respond to the prospect presented to them by Gorbachev's reforms? Four variations are possible. First, if the regime rated its ability to survive as good, and recognized the need for reforms, then the regime would be likely to respond to the changes in the Soviet Union by introducing reforms. This is represented by Box A in Table 1. In this case, reforms should emerge from above, initiated by the regime in the absence of substantial domestic opposition to its rule. Hungary fits this model.

Second, a state whose regime was confident of its ability to survive but did not acknowledge the need for reforms would not be expected to change its policies in response to Soviet reforms. Rather, it might applaud Soviet policies, but it would be unlikely substantially to revise its own economic or political policies in a similar fashion. This is represented by Box B. Bulgaria fits in this category, as does Romania.[61]

What of a state whose regime did not feel that it was likely to survive in a more open political environment but recognized the need for reforms? In this third case, Box C, one would expect the regime to experiment with some economic reforms in the hope of improving its circumstances. Substantial political reform, however, would be unlikely in the absence of popular domestic pressure on the regime. If such domestic pressure existed the regime might feel compelled to respond by trying to introduce at least some political changes intended to broaden its base of support, once the Soviet Union made clear that it would tolerate wider attempts to revise the socialist system. This model best describes the reform process in Poland.

Finally, in a state where the regime was not confident of its ability to survive in a more open political climate, and which did not believe that its system needed reform, little response to Gorbachev's reforms would be expected. This is Box D of Table 1. In this case, the regime might ignore the reforms underway in the Soviet Union, or reject them as irrelevant to its circumstances, by arguing that its own system was functioning satisfactorily. East Germany and Czechoslovakia both fit this model.

Thus, reforms beginning prior to 1989, as a response to change in the Soviet Union alone, would be expected in the cases of A and C. In B and

---

61. Keep in mind that this table shows only the distinction between states that chose to reform *early* and those that did not; once early reforms had begun, the demonstration effect began to operate in the *late* reforming states (which indicate no reforms in this table), dramatically changing political developments there.

Table 1. The Regime's Relationship to Society and the Introduction of Reform in the Late 1980s.

		Regime's Initial Awareness of Need for Political Reform	
		YES	NO
Regime's Perceived Ability to Survive in a More Open Political Climate	YES	A: Reforms likely	B: No Reforms
	NO	C: Reforms unlikely without domestic pressure	D: No Reforms

D, no significant reforms would be anticipated. They might pay lip service to reforms, given the Warsaw Pact's legacy of imitating Soviet policies at home. Yet we would not expect substantial changes to the system to emerge in these states absent other pressures.

Late Reform: Cognitive Processes and the Demonstration Effect

In the states where reform was *not* the choice of the regime when Gorbachev inaugurated perestroika, what caused reforms to ensue? In three states reform was initiated from below, but in one state it was initiated from above. These variations raise several questions. What made some populations protest, when they had been quiescent before? What changed a regime's perceptions about its circumstances, and how did this affect the outcome of events? And what role did external influences play in catalyzing or shaping this process?

We need to look at two elements to understand the nature of change in these states: the cognitive processes by which people interpret the world and events; and the diffusion of ideas from *outside* particular states, which changed the environment within which both regime and population were operating.

Both the regimes and populations in the later reforming states were affected by changes in the political climate. The introduction of reforms in the Soviet Union, and then the beginning of cautious reforms in Poland and Hungary, which "tested the waters" of Soviet tolerance, demonstrated that Soviet tolerance had radically changed. As a result, the modifications introduced within some states, and then by each successive East European state adopting reforms, expanded the limits of the possible.[62] Equally critical to the process was the *cognition* of this change, by both leaders and private citizens, which helps explain what people believed was possible. This section examines how cognitive process and the diffusion of ideas affected Eastern Europe in 1989.

COGNITIVE PROCESSES AND EASTERN EUROPE

People interpret information with a variety of cognitive tools. Humans' cognitive capacities are limited, and given the vast amounts of information they confront every day, it would be impossible for people to process all this information as totally new data, without reference to some context by which to recognize objects or events. Therefore, humans use a variety of simplifying "knowledge structures" to help interpret the information they receive.[63]

Among the most common cognitive tools are schema, the "building blocks of cognition."[64] Deborah Welch Larson characterizes a schema as "a generic concept stored in memory, referring to objects, situations, events, or people."[65] It is not a specific picture of an object or situation, but rather a collection of ideas or attributes that are stored as a generic image of an object or situation. When a person thinks of a dog, for example, the image of a Weimaraner probably does not come to mind (unless the person is a fan of William Wegman), but rather a more common dog

---

62. Such a demonstration effect is not unique to the East European cases, but has occurred among other states with similar characteristics. See Barrington Moore, Jr., *Social Origins of Dictatorship and Democracy: Lord and Peasant in the Making of the Modern World* (Boston: Beacon Press, 1966), p. 414; Linz, "Totalitarian and Authoritarian Regimes," p. 348; and Huntington, *The Third Wave*, pp. 100–105.

63. The use of psychological theories to examine political decision-making has been promoted most prominently by Robert Jervis. For some notable examples of work in this vein, see Robert Jervis, *Perception and Misperception in International Politics* (Princeton: Princeton University Press, 1976); Deborah Welch Larson, *Origins of Containment: A Psychological Explanation* (Princeton: Princeton University Press, 1985); Yuen Foong Khong, *Analogies at War: Korea, Munich, Dien Bien Phu, and the Vietnam Decisions of 1965* (Princeton: Princeton University Press, 1992); and Jonathan Mercer, *Reputation and International Politics* (Ithaca, N.Y.: Cornell University Press, 1996). See also Ernest May, *"Lessons" of the Past: The Use and Misuse of History in American Foreign Policy* (New York: Oxford University Press, 1973); and Richard Neustadt and Ernest May, *Thinking in Time: The Uses of History for Decision-Makers* (New York: Free Press, 1976).

64. David Rumelhart, "Schemata: The Building Blocks of Cognition," in Rand Spiro, Bertram Bruce, and William Brewer, eds., *Theoretical Issues in Reading Comprehension* (Hillsdale, N.J.: Lawrence Erlbaum Associates, 1980), pp. 33–34, as cited in Khong, *Analogies at War*, p. 27, fn.23.

65. Larson, *Origins of Containment*, p. 51.

without the distinctive features associated with a particular breed.[66] Analogies may be the most obvious example of schemas in our daily lives, and as elements of political decision-making. The appeasement of Hitler at Munich in 1938 is perhaps the best known political analogy, and has been used by a variety of leaders to justify standing firm (rather than negotiating) to avoid the danger of greater conflicts later.

Five facets of the way people use analogies and apply them to their experiences are pertinent.[67] First, analogies play a role because they come to represent the "lessons" people learn from their personal experiences and key events in their lives, and then use in making future judgements. People tend to call on analogies to interpret new situations they face, and by reference to the analogy, they draw lessons about what behavior is appropriate in the new situation. Second, the analogies that people draw on the most tend to be instilled by dramatic events in their lives. Moreover, people learn the most from first-hand experiences, and from incidents that happen early in their adult lives, when their beliefs are being molded. Thus, dramatic events, particularly those with which an individual had personal experience at a young age, tend to shape their later views of their environment.[68] Munich's "failure" to prevent World War II shaped the thinking of a generation of political leaders, for example. Third, people tend to choose analogies on the basis of superficial similarities. This is known as the "availability heuristic"; rather than looking for the best fit between new information and the range of available schema in one's repertoire, people tend to assume that the analogies that come to mind first are the most appropriate, though surface similarities can be misleading.[69] Yet regardless of the fit, people tend to "fill in" information that they have not actually received but which concurs with their expectations of what should be happening, given the analogy with which they are working. For example, U.S. leaders assumed that Ho Chi Minh and his Chinese allies had ambitions reaching beyond Vietnam, because they used the analogy of Hitler's territorial demands after Munich. Fourth,

---

66. See Richard Nisbett and Lee Ross, *Human Inference: Strategies and Shortcomings of Social Judgment* (Englewood Cliffs, N.J.: Prentice-Hall, 1980), pp. 32–33.

67. I provide only an abbreviated description of the processes by which individuals process information. For a broader discussion, see Nisbett and Ross, *Human Inference*, pp. 17–42, and for a discussion of the implications for political decision-makers, see Jervis, *Perception and Misperception in International Politics*, esp. pp. 217–282.

68. Jervis, *Perception and Misperception in International Politics*, pp. 227–252.

69. Nisbett and Ross, *Human Inference*, pp. 18–19; and Khong, *Analogies at War*, pp. 35–36.

people are more sensitive to information that confirms their beliefs or schemas; this is called "top-down processing." And fifth, peoples' beliefs persevere. Once an analogy or script has been chosen, it becomes difficult to dislodge. Just as they notice new data that confirms their beliefs, people will also tend to ignore or discount information that does not fit the schema that has been chosen.[70]

Can we use a knowledge of how analogies and other schema operate to explain leadership decisions and the rise of mass protests in Eastern Europe in 1989? Not conclusively. We cannot be certain what East European leaders were thinking during this period, nor can we completely trust their recollections, or those of their aides. As with most former rulers, those in the Warsaw Pact want to justify their behavior, and to shape, to the degree possible, the way they will be remembered for posterity. The communist rulers in Eastern Europe were deposed, and most were thoroughly discredited. Some, as a result, are embittered and unwilling to explain past events from their perspective. Other former leaders may see their memoirs as their only chance to rewrite the record and try to portray their roles in a more favorable light. This gives them incentive to distort the truth. For similar reasons, those further down the chain of command have an incentive to paint their superiors as worse than they were, to absolve themselves of guilt for the evils of the system. In the absence of satisfactory memoirs or diaries, and because similar problems reduce the value of interviews, we are forced to rely on the documentary record at the time. This does not allow substantial insights into the private thoughts of these leaders.

Can a cognitive evaluation be useful, given these difficulties? I believe it can, so long as it is estimated within its constraints. We know that humans share similar patterns in their cognitive responses, so it is not rash to assume that cognitive processes would have effects on the Warsaw Pact leaders that are comparable to their effects on Western leaders, for whom a better record of their thoughts or experiences at a particular time may be available. Moreover, while it would not be practical to try to analyze the formative experiences of the central figures in the East European leadership, the historical record provides us ample evidence of the major events they experienced, particularly the shared events of the Cold War period. Additionally, having already drawn distinctions between the East European leaders by evaluating which favored and which rejected reform, it is reasonable to speculate about the likely reactions

---

70. Jervis, *Perception and Misperception in International Politics*, p. 274. See also Bernard Berelson and Gary A. Steiner, *Human Behavior: An Inventory of Scientific Findings* (New York: Harcourt, Brace & World, 1964), p. 529.

these leaders who did not favor reform would have had to the events unfolding around them in 1989. Finally, this cognitive deliberation is intended to supplement the larger argument I make here, rather than to be its sole support; it adds nuance to the larger analysis of events.

How might analogies have affected leaders' perceptions in Eastern Europe? In the previous section, I hypothesized that the leadership in these states should have had more conservative ideologies and strong ties with the conservative members of the leadership in Moscow. These leaders were likely to be older than the reform-minded leaders. Indeed, with the exception of Polish leader Wojciech Jaruzelski, no Communist Party leader in the Warsaw Pact had been in power for *less* than fifteen years in 1985.[71]

It seems reasonable to assume that the series of dramatic crises and interventions that accented Soviet–East European relations during the Cold War would be the basis for some widely shared schemas within the Warsaw Pact. The Soviet Union invaded Hungary in October 1956 to quell an incipient revolution and Hungary's withdrawal from the Warsaw Pact; it intervened in Czechoslovakia in August 1968 at the "request" of local party officials to ensure the continuation of socialism and communist party rule in Czechoslovakia; and in December 1981, it pressured the Polish government to declare martial law to prevent Solidarity, the independent trade union, from gaining greater strength and threatening the cohesion of the bloc. These events had in common popular involvement or protest in an effort to reform the existing system, and leaderships that either initiated changes or made concessions to popular demands along the way. Moscow tolerated these modifications up to a point, though its concern about the direction of change was evident in the pressure it placed on each of the regimes to address Soviet concerns about the aims of these liberalizing processes. Finally, in each case, the Soviet Union acted to prevent an attempt at liberalization, reform, or protest from threatening communist party control.

It is reasonable to argue that some lessons would be widely shared within the Warsaw Pact as a result of these experiences.[72] I suggest that

---

71. Significantly, political reforms in Hungary did not begin until the Hungarian Socialist Workers Party had replaced János Kádár, who had been in power since 1956, with Károly Grósz in the summer of 1988. Yet there was internal conflict in virtually all the East European regimes.

72. Western analysts drew analogies from events such as the Prague Spring and the subsequent enunciation of the Brezhnev Doctrine, to conclude that the Soviet Union was unwilling to allow its control over Eastern Europe to come into question, and this judgment did not change easily in the late 1980s. This shaped Western policy toward Eastern Europe during the Cold War period, even as late as 1989. Indeed, Michael R.

three broad lessons were shared by leaders and populations in Eastern Europe. First, liberalization was dangerous and difficult to control. From the regimes' perspective, liberalization would not solve the problems it was meant to address, but might make the situation worse.[73] Second, Soviet toleration for reform was clearly limited. Third, in the final analysis, the Soviet leadership would be unwilling to countenance the introduction of a more pluralist system, moves too far away from "socialism," or withdrawal from the Warsaw Pact. In other words, Moscow would draw the line at any fundamental challenge to its authority within the Pact.

To the degree that one can speculate about the attitudes of the East European leadership, how does our understanding of cognitive processes lead us to expect them to respond to the changes around them in 1989? The analogies of Soviet interventions and their consequences would be particularly strong.[74] This could color a regime or leader's interpretation of Gorbachev's introduction of reforms in important ways. This history would be expected to induce a skeptical attitude toward Moscow's sincerity in encouraging substantial reform. The arguments within the Soviet leadership about the nature and pace of reforms in Russia should reinforce doubts among East European leaders about the durability of this round of reforms. Most critical for our purposes, the history of Soviet intervention would probably influence the degree to which an East European leader believed that Moscow would support him. Well into 1989—indeed, until it was proven otherwise—there was a widespread belief throughout much of Eastern Europe that the Soviet Union would not accept the overthrow of one of its allies in the Warsaw Pact. This may help explain why the East European leaders who opposed reform seemed un-

---

Beschloss and Strobe Talbott maintain that in January 1989 Henry Kissinger, acting as President Bush's emissary, proposed a deal to Gorbachev, whereby the Soviet Union would promise not to use force, while the United States would promise not to exploit developments in Eastern Europe to hurt "legitimate" Soviet security interests. Though this came to naught, it was an indication that Western leaders still perceived the Soviet Union and the Warsaw Pact in the same mold that had existed during the Cold War. See Beschloss and Talbott, *At the Highest Levels: The Inside Story of the End of the Cold War* (Boston: Little, Brown, 1993), pp. 13–21.

73. Both the Prague Spring and the rise of Solidarity in 1980 had their roots in efforts to improve the country's economic conditions; yet neither solved any problems, and instead left the country worse off than it had been before.

74. Given the age of particular leaders, the experience of the Soviet imposition of control over Eastern Europe after World War II probably had a strong impact, particularly for a leader who had been active in the nascent communist party at the time. This could have created an even more rigid impression that the Soviet Union would not let go of Eastern Europe. See Brzezinski, *The Soviet Bloc*, chaps. 1–7; and Adam B. Ulam, *Expansion and Coexistence* (New York: Praeger, 1968), chaps. 8 and 10.

able to recognize growing evidence suggesting that Soviet tolerance was changing. Indeed, this may also explain why no one predicted the events of 1989; these changes were difficult to comprehend in the West as well.[75]

In retrospect, the evidence of greater Soviet toleration for variation in Eastern Europe seems obvious; its acceptance of Polish Round Table negotiations, the dropping of the socialist party's "leading role" in Hungary, the defeat of Poland's ruling party, as well as Gorbachev's enunciation that no state should intervene in another's affairs, are clearly very different from the pattern of previous periods of reform and unrest within the Warsaw Pact. But an East European regime could easily focus on the limits that remained in place—such as the Soviet troops remaining in Eastern Europe—which suggested that Moscow could easily act to quell reforms if it chose to do so. Moreover, Poland and Hungary remained very cautious about the reforms that they were implementing well into 1989; neither directly threatened continued rule by the socialist party in power until August 1989, and even then the Polish regime and Solidarity negotiated a coalition government.[76] Moreover, the Polish Communist Party made it plain that it had cleared its consent to this move with Moscow. Clearly, there was a great deal of confusion throughout Eastern Europe about what the Soviet reaction would be—it remained possible to presume that some Soviet-imposed constraints remained. It should not be surprising, therefore, that virtually none of the nonreforming East European leaders took advantage of the model presented by Poland and Hungary and attempted to introduce power-sharing agreements in their own countries.[77] Nor is it surprising that popular pressure for reform remained low well into 1989, since the populace had learned the same lessons that leaders had from earlier Soviet efforts to sustain its control in Eastern Europe.

EXTERNAL INFLUENCES, DIFFUSION, AND THE DEMONSTRATION EFFECT

Cognitive factors help explain the political paralysis in East Germany, Czechoslovakia, Bulgaria, and Romania in early 1989; what then led to the changes that eventually occurred? I argue that the interaction of external influences and the diffusion of ideas created a demonstration

---

75. U.S. President George Bush's caution about Gorbachev's sincerity through much of 1989 is one such reminder. See Beschloss and Talbott, *At the Highest Levels.*

76. Indeed, the Romanian leader Nicolae Ceauşescu advocated an invasion of Poland to prevent this event. He clearly did not recognize that Moscow would not stop this process. See Chapter 3.

77. The Bulgarian regime did introduce reforms from above, but only after ousting its top leader, Todor Zhivkov. See Chapter 6.

effect, primarily at the popular level in Eastern Europe, which played a decisive role in inducing change. What led thousands of citizens in East Germany, Czechoslovakia, and later Romania to break their earlier lethargy and demonstrate against the ruling regime?[78]

Timur Kuran, in examining how tiny opposition movements can mushroom so quickly into substantial protest, discusses how preference falsification can affect an individual's willingness to take the risks involved in protest. An individual who is considering protest must weigh the balance between the rewards of being true to one's convictions and the risks of possible punishment for making one's objections known, against the psychological cost of not protesting. Kuran calls this preference falsification: "the suppression of one's wants entails a loss of personal autonomy, a sacrifice of personal integrity. It thus generates lasting discomfort, the more so the greater the lie."[79] Each individual has a threshold at which he or she can no longer accept the internal costs of pretense and tacit acceptance of an illegitimate regime's continued rule. For most citizens of states that repress dissent, this threshold is relatively high.

Kuran argues that changes in a superpower's actions will not necessarily lead to widespread changes elsewhere (in this case meaning Eastern Europe) because individuals will not necessarily be moved to react to the superpower's actions, which seem distant from their lives. The key, he argues, is when a few individuals, or a few more than previously, become willing to risk punishment to display their dissatisfaction with the regime: "A single person's reaction to an event of global importance may make all the difference between a massive uprising and a *latent bandwagon* that never takes off."[80] As individuals react even in quite small

---

78. Some recent works have discussed the importance of changing popular attitudes to the transformation that occurred in Eastern Europe, including Albert O. Hirschman, "Exit, Voice, and the Fate of the German Democratic Republic: An Essay in Conceptual History," *World Politics*, Vol. 45, No. 2 (October 1992), pp. 173–202; Timur Kuran, "Now out of Never: The Element of Surprise in the East European Revolution of 1989," *World Politics*, Vol. 44, No.1 (October 1991), pp. 7–48; Susanne Lohmann, "The Dynamics of Informational Cascades: The Monday Demonstrations in Leipzig, East Germany, 1989–91," *World Politics*, Vol. 47 (October 1994), pp. 42–101; Norman M. Naimark, "'Ich will hier raus': Emigration and the Collapse of the German Democratic Republic," and Tony R. Judt, "Metamorphosis: The Democratic Revolution in Czechoslovakia," both in Ivo Banac, ed., *Eastern Europe in Revolution* (Ithaca, N.Y.: Cornell University Press, 1992), pp. 72–116; and Peter Cipkowski, *Revolution in Eastern Europe: Understanding the Collapse of Communism in Poland, Hungary, East Germany, Czechoslovakia, Romania, and the Soviet Union* (New York: John Wiley, 1991).

79. Timur Kuran, "Now out of Never," p. 18.

80. Ibid., p. 22. Emphasis in the original.

numbers, the threshold of toleration for increasing numbers of individuals can rapidly be lowered, and thus widespread protests can result.[81]

In Kuran's view, the key lies in an individual's need to be true to him or herself. But what is the catalyst? What makes the first few people change their views about what they can tolerate? How is this initial threshold changed?

The demonstration effect, or suggestive effect, is a concept that has been developed in sociological studies that examine why an individual switches from one choice of action to another.[82] These studies have

---

81. Susanne Lohmann expands on Kuran's threshold concept by arguing that both the surprise and inevitability of the revolution in East Germany in 1989 can be explained by the dispersed nature of information about East Germany's situation. She contends that East Germans were discontented, but there was no outlet for this, and insufficient knowledge that this discontent was shared. Lohmann sees the demonstrations that began in Leipzig in September 1989 as an "informational cascade" that played a critical role in expanding the information available to the population about the country's situation. This is helpful, but it does not explain what beyond knowledge impels change, leaving questions about how much information is necessary to be credible and to change peoples' preferences. It is also not entirely accurate to argue that the East Germans or other East Europeans did not know that their discontent was shared; this was, I believe, widely known, but the limits of what was believed to be politically tenable were not clear. See Lohmann, "The Dynamics of Informational Cascades," pp. 42–101.

82. Sociologists have also studied the role that diffusion and contagion play in shaping events or policies. The diffusion/contagion literature clearly supports the argument that external ideas can both shape and trigger behavior across borders. Yet it leaves unanswered the question of why an individual would change his or her beliefs and actions. These hypotheses have been used in studies of domestic politics, such as the diffusion of ideas or innovations among the American states. In the study of international relations, diffusion and contagion hypotheses have been used to examine coups, the spread of war, and the influence of international economic forces. Diffusion is "the spread of a particular type of behavior through time and space as the result of the cumulative impact of a set of statistically independent events." Diffusion occurs when events or ideas build on each other to produce a response. Contagion occurs when a response is sparked without the cumulation of cues; the spread of ideas is considered contagious when a single example of some behavior either encourages similar behavior, or reduces an observer's inhibitions about taking similar actions. See Manus Midlarsky, "Analyzing Diffusion and Contagion Effects: The Urban Disorders of the 1960's," *American Political Science Review,* Vol. 72, No. 3 (September 1978), p. 1006; on statistical tests, see also Richard P.Y. Li and William R. Thompson, "The `Coup Contagion' Hypothesis," *Journal of Conflict Resolution,* Vol. 19, No. 1 (March 1975), pp. 63–88; and Benjamin Most and Harvey Starr, "Theoretical and Logical Issues in the Study of International Diffusion," *Journal of Theoretical Politics,* Vol. 2, No. 4 (1990), pp. 391–412. For applications, see Jack L. Walker, "The Diffusion of Innovations Among the American States," *American Political Science Review,* Vol. 63, No. 3 (September 1969), pp. 880–899; Virginia Gray, "Innovation in the States: A Diffusion Study," *American Political Science Review,* Vol. 67, No. 4 (December 1973), pp. 1174–1193. On the diffusion of

shown that imitation and suggestion may help shift an individual's choice to a different alternative. For example, individuals tend to adopt decision-theoretical approaches when choosing among alternatives if this is the strategy followed by people that they consider to be role models, such as teachers or parents. But individuals also tend to rely on more impulsive, nontheoretical decision-making if such strategies are displayed by the media; media images can be an important link in the process of change. For example, publicized suicides (such as that of Marilyn Monroe) lead to a significant statistical rise in the number of single vehicle fatalities that can be deemed suicides. Similarly, there is a jump in the homicide rate following televised and highly publicized prize fights within the region to which the fights were broadcast, but not elsewhere in the country.[83] Further, when the effects of television reports of violence are compared with laboratory experiments testing the effect that behaviors presented on the media may have, it seems clear that the violent behavior patterns seen on television serve as "mediating mechanisms" that can affect peoples' behavior and induce them to switch from one choice of action to another.[84]

The demonstration effect induced change in Eastern Europe in four ways. First, the demonstration effect changed the "shadow of the past" in Eastern Europe. One of the crucial obstacles to change in Eastern Europe was the strong perception that basic, fundamental change in the system was simply not an option. This was the obvious conclusion drawn from Eastern Europe's painful experience with efforts to reform the socialist system, which resulted in dramatic crises in 1956, 1968, and 1980–81. This lesson was one of the obstacles that Gorbachev confronted when he tried to encourage reform in Eastern Europe; indeed, it is no accident that con-

---

innovations, see Everett M. Rogers, *Diffusion of Innovations*, 4th ed. (New York: Free Press, 1983).

83. The regional effect also applies in the suicide examples; local but highly publicized suicides lead to rises in the fatality rate within the region that received news reports about these events. The methodology in both cases indicates delays of a few days after each of these events, but with consistent rises in the rates of fatalities and homicides. See David P. Phillips, "Suicide, Motor Vehicle Fatalities, and the Mass Media: Evidence Toward a Theory of Suggestion," *American Journal of Sociology*, Vol. 84, No. 5 (1979), pp. 1150–1171; Phillips, "The Impact of Mass Media Violence on U.S. Homicides," *American Sociological Review*, Vol. 48 (August 1983), pp. 560–568; and Kenneth A. Bollen and David P. Phillips, "Imitative Suicides: A National Study of the Effects of Television News Stories," *American Sociological Review*, Vol. 47 (December 1982), pp. 802–809.

84. Laboratory studies examined changes in the level of violent behavior by children after watching such behavior acted out on television. Phillips, "Suicide, Motor Vehicle Fatalities, and the Mass Media," p. 1169.

cern over whether the "Brezhnev Doctrine" still applied persisted in Eastern Europe well into 1989, or that Gorbachev was queried on this issue until he finally disavowed it that year.[85]

How people use analogies helps to explain how the demonstration effect changed peoples' attitudes and behavior in Eastern Europe in 1989. That so little had changed in Eastern Europe prior to 1989 is an indication of the power of long-held cognitive beliefs; the drama of Soviet interventions in earlier years was not easily overridden by the creeping changes of détente and perestroika as they affected Eastern Europe before 1989.[86] By late 1988 and early 1989, however, people in Eastern Europe were restive, unsettled by the spread of change in the Soviet Union and in its relations with the West. But most were not prepared to change their own behavior in ways that would indicate their willingness to reject continued socialist rule in the region.[87] External changes to this point had not triggered a change in individual attitudes.[88] What remained necessary was some indication or *proof* that change was possible, and a suggestion—or model—to follow to introduce change.

This is where the demonstration effect operated to shift attitudes sufficiently to induce change. By the fall of 1989, the Eastern Europeans had new prototypes of behavior to counter the old—the Soviet acceptance of a Solidarity activist as prime minister in Poland and the Hungarian government's decision to allow thousands of East Germans to flee to the West.

---

85. Notably, in spite of Gorbachev's evident acceptance and even encouragement of massive change in the Eastern bloc early in 1989, it was not until December 1989 that the Soviet leadership flatly repudiated the Brezhnev Doctrine and the invasion of Czechoslovakia. See "Statement on 1968 Invasion of Czechoslovakia," TASS, December 4, 1989, in *BBC Summary of World Broadcasts: Soviet Union*, December 6, 1989. See Chapter 2.

86. This is not to suggest that perestroika was moving slowly before 1989. But its impact on Eastern Europe was limited, while Gorbachev and his reform-minded allies focused on other issues, and many East European leaders fence-sat, waiting to see if this policy would survive.

87. The exception is Poland. However, popular protest was far more common a response in Poland than in many other states in the Eastern bloc throughout the Cold War, so mass protests in Poland do not represent a switch in behavior that indicates the impact of a demonstration effect.

88. The thirtieth anniversary of the Soviet intervention in Czechoslovakia in August 1988 illustrated this point. More people than in previous years (and especially more young people) were willing to risk open protest by marking this anniversary. But the regime was fully prepared to crush indications of protest, which left little hope that change was possible there as long as force remained an option. The contrast with November 1989 is all the more striking as a result.

The demonstration effect primarily affected populations in the late reforming states. In some states, the level of open resistance to the regime leapt practically overnight, and continued to grow as the communist regimes' impotence without Soviet backing became clear. In East Germany and Czechoslovakia, the population realized that an alternative to the existing system was feasible, and began to protest against the continuation of the status quo, provoking the collapse of the communist regimes.

Second, the progression of changes from country to country provided a model for the successive states both of ways to mediate change, and of ways to reject the existing regime. The progressive opening of "Round Table" negotiations in successive East European states is the most visible example of this modeling.[89]

Third, and coincident with the appearance of a model, the demonstration effect showed the rulers in these states that the old methods were no longer viable. Some regimes—or groups within them—were convinced by the dramatic changes in neighboring states that continued rule by the previous methods was not a good survival strategy. This led some regimes to adopt what might be called a "finger to the wind" strategy; regimes that previously had been resistant to reform opted to risk initiating some changes, to avoid being swept away by popular reaction and discontent. In Bulgaria, for example, members of the leadership read the signs of change elsewhere and the nascent stirrings of protest at home, and chose to change their attitudes toward reform, remove the party's preeminent leader, and introduce at least moderate reforms.

The alternative reaction by the regime was paralysis. Regimes with some legitimacy could choose to risk introducing reforms; regimes with

---

89. That diffusion of this sort would create such a model is not unique to Eastern Europe. Elbaki Hermassi has pointed out that throughout world history, revolutions have introduced new political ideals and principles of legitimacy that can exert strong effects beyond the boundaries of the country in which they originate, with the potential for triggering waves of revolution and counterrevolution. In this respect, one should note that time matters; the ideas available to an actor or state are determined by the events that have happened earlier. Gershenkron noted this in his analysis of the differences in opportunity open to states attempting economic modernization at different times. "Late" modernizers can skip some of the trial-and-error stages that the "early" modernizers went through, and can progress directly toward later, better technology. Theda Skocpol looked more specifically at the effects of social revolutions; previous revolutions may shape the choices made by later revolutionaries, who have more models available to them than did the revolutionaries who preceded them. See Elbaki Hermassi, "Toward a Comparative Study of Revolutions," *Comparative Studies in Society and History*, Vol. 18, No. 2 (April 1976), esp. p. 214; Gershenkron, *Economic Backwardness in Historical Perspective* (Cambridge, Mass.: Harvard University Press, 1962); and Theda Skocpol, *States and Social Revolutions*.

no hope of gaining popular support did not have this option. Their only choices would be to resort to force, or to stall. The use of force, however, would imply that the regime perceived such action to be justified, regardless of whether its rule was considered to be legitimate by the population. Yet by the end of 1989, it no longer appeared to be true that a regime with little or no legitimacy could sustain its rule so long as it was willing to resort to force.[90] What is particularly noteworthy about this is that *external* developments seem to have tipped this calculation. It would appear that so long as they believed that the Soviet Union would not let them fall, the hard-line regimes in Eastern Europe were willing to contemplate and even order the use of force, notwithstanding their lack of domestic legitimacy.[91] In addition to the effect that ideology had as a legitimating factor in Eastern Europe, even if it was no longer believed, it allowed rulers to deceive even themselves about their right to continue in power—but only for so long.[92] This is why cognitive processes matter. Because they continued to believe that they had Soviet backing, these regimes rejected change. But once they comprehended that this support was truly gone, they had no alternative means of gaining support, because they could not contemplate alternative strategies. Thus, they remained paralyzed while popular protests against their rule multiplied.

Fourth, the demonstration effect caused the process of reform to accelerate in ensuing cases. One of the remarkable features of the East European cases is the rapidity with which the impact of early efforts at reform began to resonate through the bloc. As the process continued, peoples' thresholds of toleration changed more rapidly, signaling a faster reaction to external events. Moreover, due to the demonstration effect, the new political model of choice was endorsed throughout much of Eastern Europe with little argument or stalling. Thus, the struggle to overthrow communist rule that took ten years in Poland took perhaps two months in East Germany, weeks in Czechoslovakia, and a matter of days in Romania.

---

90. This accords with Reinhard Bendix's observation that the pursuit of power is one of the elements that helps legitimacy develop: "wherever a mandate to rule is to sway the minds and hearts of men, it requires the exercise of force or the *awareness* that those who rule are able, and will not hesitate, to use force if that is needed to assert their will." Bendix, *Kings or People*, pp. 16–17. See also Skocpol, *States and Social Revolutions*, pp. 32–33; and Przeworski, "Some Problems in the Study of Transition to Democracy," p. 51.

91. In some cases, Soviet support seems to have made these regimes perceive themselves as legitimate; being legitimate in the eyes of their patrons was sufficient.

92. Timothy Garton Ash, *We the People: The Revolution of '89* (Cambridge: Granta Books, 1990), p. 137.

Thus, while it was necessary that Gorbachev declared the "freedom of choice" of his allies in December 1988, it was also necessary that some state prove that significant changes were possible, and that Moscow would accept them. Just as publicized violence sparks a rash of mimicry, the cumulative effect of tentative steps to change the political systems in the early reforming states in Eastern Europe sparked a rash of imitation across the bloc. Changes in Eastern Europe had an especially powerful effect within the bloc because this region had strong shared experiences under communist control; reforms in the Soviet Union itself did not resonate in the same way because the points of reference between the Soviet Union and the East European states were much weaker.[93]

The demonstration effect that arose in Eastern Europe affected the Soviet Union as well, as was seen in efforts by the Baltic communist parties to declare their independence from Moscow's central control in late 1989, and in the rise of nationalism and independence movements in regions as diverse as Georgia and Estonia.[94] In addition, Nicaragua's socialist government mimicked this example and called for elections in the aftermath of Eastern Europe's shift—and lost dramatically, as did most East European communist parties. Nonetheless, the fact that Nicaragua's leadership was persuaded to call elections in a way that mirrored the process in Eastern Europe points to the power of example as a catalyst for change in the international arena.[95]

Though the diffusion of external influences is difficult to measure, certain behaviors should offer proof that external change affected the political climate in different countries. If citizens in a state could receive foreign sources of information, particularly television but also radio broadcasts or newspapers, this indicates that information about outside events was available. Similarly, if coverage of events in neighboring countries by the state's official press was available, its tone and objectivity—or lack thereof—should give clues about the regime's view of processes underway elsewhere. Information about contacts between opposition groups in neighboring countries also points to the influence of external forces.

But the most convincing proof of the demonstration effect is mimicry. If opposition leaders adopted demands or appeals similar to those in

93. Li and Thompson, "The `Coup Contagion' Hypothesis," p. 66; and Midlarsky, "Analyzing Diffusion and Contagion Effects."

94. See Mark Kramer, "The Collapse of East European Communism and the Repercussion within the Soviet Union," forthcoming in *Journal of Cold War Studies*, Vol. 5, No. 3 (Summer 2003).

95. The Sandinistas' gamble on elections suggests that their calculation of legitimacy versus risk differed from that of the late reformers in Eastern Europe.

other reforming states, or if the population made appeals to foreign governments or other external groups to aid their reform efforts, this suggests both that these domestic groups were aware of what was going on elsewhere, and that their own goals were changing as a result of this knowledge. Similarly, if a regime moved to adopt the types of policies underway elsewhere, such as constitutional revisions or Round Table negotiations, this demonstrates that external factors were shaping the internal political domain. Figure 1 lays out the alternative paths to reform in Eastern Europe.

THE CASE STUDIES

I offer three central propositions to explain the process of reform that unfolded in Eastern Europe. First, change of the nature that was seen throughout the region could not have occurred in the absence of the changes in the Soviet Union; external change in the Soviet Union was necessary but not sufficient to the transition that ensued. Second, the relationship between regime and society can help explain whether a regime was likely to risk its ruling position, and thus the way that reforms emerged in different states in the region. The regime's choice was shaped by its evaluation of the need for significant political changes and its judgment of its ability to survive in a more open political climate. Third, change within Eastern Europe itself was a necessary catalyst to change, and created a demonstration effect that resonated through the Warsaw Pact. Both the cognitive process by which people interpret events, and the diffusion of ideas from state to state in Eastern Europe, help explain why a demonstration effect occurred.

Chapter 2 examines Soviet policy toward Eastern Europe. I use Chapters 3 through 7 to determine how well the three hypotheses explain the collapse of the Warsaw Pact by measuring the variables laid out here: the regime's recognition of the need to reform; its perception of its legitimacy, or lack thereof; cognitive attitudes of the main actors in each state; and the demonstration effect. Table 2 classifies the six East European cases with regard to the propositions presented here.

If the regime's perception of its relationship with society was truly significant, then one would expect to see reform introduced early only in those states where the regime had a predisposition toward significant change of its domestic system, or where opposition to the regime was sufficiently strong to induce change. Even in cases of early reform, there should be weak indications of a demonstration effect. Both regimes and populations were aware of the changes underway in the Soviet Union, where perestroika began; and they would have paid attention to changes in other early reforming states. Similarly, one would expect early reforms

Figure 1. Alternative Paths to Reform.

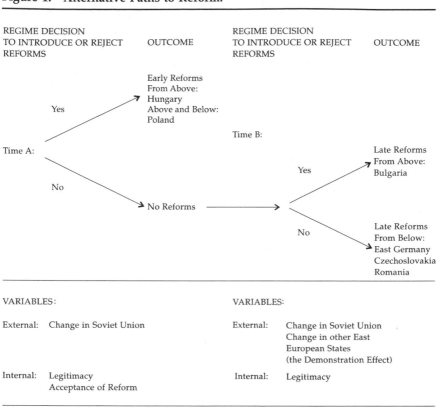

REGIME DECISION
TO INTRODUCE OR REJECT   OUTCOME
REFORMS

REGIME DECISION
TO INTRODUCE OR REJECT   OUTCOME
REFORMS

Yes → Early Reforms
From Above:
Hungary
Above and Below:
Poland

Time A:

Time B:

No → No Reforms →

Yes → Late Reforms
From Above:
Bulgaria

No → Late Reforms
From Below:
East Germany
Czechoslovakia
Romania

VARIABLES:

External: Change in Soviet Union

Internal: Legitimacy
Acceptance of Reform

VARIABLES:

External: Change in Soviet Union
Change in other East
European States
(the Demonstration Effect)

Internal: Legitimacy

to be introduced cautiously, with due attention to the response of the Soviet Union, given previous experiences with political reforms in the Warsaw Pact.

Conservative regimes that doubted their ability to survive would have little inducement to initiate change at all. Moreover, they would be expected to perceive reforms elsewhere in the bloc not only as a violation of socialist principles, but also as a threat to their own positions, and to the Warsaw Pact's integrity.

If the external influences from within Eastern Europe played a decisive role in changing peoples' attitudes toward their current governments in the late reforming states, then evidence of a demonstration effect should be strong in the later reforming states. One would expect to find coincidences in the progression of events from country to country, as the

Table 2. Classifications of the Six East European Cases.

		Regime's Initial Awareness of Need for Political Reform	
		YES	NO
Regime's Perceived Ability to Survive in a More Open Political Climate	YES	A: Early reforms from above	B: Late reforms from above
		Hungary	**Bulgaria**
	NO	C: Early reforms from below	D: Late reforms from below
			East Germany **Czechoslovakia**
		Poland	**Romania**

political climate changed in response to the diffusion of ideas from countries that initiated reforms early in the process. Similarly, if a demonstration effect occurred, there should be a correlation between the level of information about external events that was available in a particular country, and the speed and intensity of emulation.

Chapter 2

Gorbachev and Eastern Europe

Mikhail Gorbachev's primary interest when he came to power as General Secretary of the Communist Party of the Soviet Union (CPSU) in March 1985 was to revitalize the Soviet economy. His awareness of the need for economic and societal reform in the Soviet Union was long-standing; from the time he was the CPSU party boss in Stavropol in the 1970s he had been interested in making the system work better.[1] By the late 1970s and early 1980s, Gorbachev recognized the need for significant change if the Party and government were to address the country's problems, which ranged from a stagnant and militarized economy and bureaucratic inertia to alcoholism and pervasive social malaise.[2]

Gorbachev also was aware that domestic changes could not succeed without substantial changes in Soviet foreign policy.[3] When Gorbachev came to power at least some members of the Soviet elite believed that

---

1. Archie Brown, *The Gorbachev Factor* (Oxford: Oxford University Press, 1996), pp. 41–42.

2. Gorbachev was not alone in this belief; even conservative members of the Politburo recognized that the system needed significant reforms. See Yegor Kuz'mich Ligachev, *Inside Gorbachev's Kremlin* (New York: Pantheon Books, 1993).

3. This point has been made by both Soviet and Western scholars. See S.F. Akhromeyev and G.M. Kornienko, *Glazami Marshala i Diplomata: Kriticheskiy vzglyad na vneshnyuyu politiki SSSR do i posle 1985 goda* [Through the eyes of a marshall and a diplomat: A critical view of the foreign policy of the USSR before and after 1985] (Moscow: Mezhdunarodnye Otnosheniya, 1992), p. 68; and Raymond Garthoff, *The Great Transition: American-Soviet Relations and the End of the Cold War* (Washington, D.C.: The Brookings Institution, 1994), p. 193.

Moscow's foreign policy was exacerbating the country's woes. Gorbachev's understanding of the general principles of balancing behavior in world politics led him to conclude that the Soviet military build-up and Moscow's aggressive foreign policy positions were perceived as threatening by other states, and were thus counterproductive to the Soviet Union's own interests.[4] In the belief that in the long run, Soviet domestic interests could only be met by developing better ties with the West to reduce military competition and to gain greater access to Western technology and economic credits, Gorbachev accepted the need to change Moscow's foreign policy behavior in order to change the Soviet Union's international image. This required both revitalizing and expanding détente with the United States and Europe, to convince the West that the Soviet Union was a reliable member of the international community. It also required fundamental changes in Moscow's policy toward Eastern Europe, which was an obstacle to Soviet efforts to gain the confidence of the West.

This chapter provides a brief overview of the reforms Gorbachev introduced in the Soviet Union, and of Moscow's policy toward Eastern Europe during his tenure. This helps explain how Soviet policy toward Eastern Europe fit with Gorbachev's broader goals for the Soviet Union, and also provides useful background information for the chapters that follow. The chapter first surveys the main threads of Gorbachev's reforms. It then focuses on Soviet policy toward Eastern Europe, looking at Moscow's long-term goals with regard to Eastern Europe, Gorbachev's goals when he came to power, the policies he implemented, and their implications for Soviet policy and for Eastern Europe.

The Introduction of Reforms

Three main threads of Gorbachev's policies deserve attention here because developments in these areas affected Soviet policy toward Eastern Europe: perestroika, or restructuring of Soviet politics and economics; arms control and improved relations with the United States; and

---

4. On Soviet motivations, see William Wohlforth, "Realism and the End of the Cold War," *International Security*, Vol. 13, No. 3 (Winter 1994/95), pp. 91–129; Wohlforth, *The Elusive Balance: Power and Perceptions during the Cold War* (Ithaca, N.Y.: Cornell University Press, 1993); Coit D. Blacker, *Hostage to Revolution: Gorbachev and Soviet Security Policy, 1985–91* (New York: Council on Foreign Relations Press, 1993); R. Craig Nation, *Black Earth, Red Star: A History of Soviet Security Policy, 1917–1991* (Ithaca, N.Y.: Cornell University Press, 1992); and Garthoff, *The Great Transition.*

East-West relations in Europe. Policies in each of these areas developed over time; no precise strategies existed when Gorbachev came to power in March 1985.[5]

PERESTROIKA

On coming to power, Gorbachev first had to prepare the ground for the changes he wanted to introduce.[6] His first year in office was spent primarily on this task, making preparations for the 27th CPSU Party Congress to be held in February 1986, as well as making some important personnel changes in the Politburo to consolidate his power.[7] Gorbachev did try to encourage greater efficiency in economic production, and curtailed alcohol sales as a way to promote greater productivity at work.

At the 27th Party Congress Gorbachev presented the first detailed outline of the themes of perestroika (restructuring) and glasnost (openness—Gorbachev's catchword for the push toward greater transparency in the Soviet system) that dominated Soviet domestic policy for the next five years.[8] Perestroika came to be used as short-hand for, in essence, the overhauling of the Soviet Union's economic, political, and social system

---

5. For some comprehensive studies of the Gorbachev period, see Richard Sakwa, *Gorbachev and His Reforms, 1985–1990* (New York: Prentice-Hall, 1991); Brown, *The Gorbachev Factor*; Alexander Dallin and Gail W. Lapidus, eds., *The Soviet System: From Crisis to Collapse/Soviet System in Crisis* (Boulder, Colo.: Westview Press, 1995); Jerry F. Hough, *Democratization and Revolution in the USSR, 1985–1991* (Washington, D.C.: Brookings Institution, 1997).

6. Scholars evaluate Gorbachev's policies in a variety of ways. Archie Brown proposes that Gorbachev's policies went through six stages: preparing the ground for reform (1985–1986); radical political reform (1987–1988); transformation at home and abroad (early 1989-autumn 1990); Gorbachev's "turn to the right" (winter 1990–1991); the Novo-Ogarevo Process, an "attempt to achieve voluntary agreement on the new union treaty" (April-August 1991); and from coup to collapse (August–December 1991). *The Gorbachev Factor*, pp. 160–211, and chap. 8.

7. Thane Gustafson and Dawn Mann, "Gorbachev's First Year: Building Power and Authority," *Problems of Communism*, Vol. 25, No. 3 (May–June 1986), pp. 1–19; and Garthoff, *The Great Transition*, pp. 205–206.

8. The concepts of glasnost and perestroika dominated politics in the late 1980s, but by 1990–1991 they were eclipsed by new issues in the political and economic debate, among them nationalism and separatism, the need for market reforms, and attacks on the rule of the Communist Party. Indeed, by 1988, it was clear that perestroika and glasnost were creating a number of problems in the Soviet Union. The economic reforms themselves were not generating an economic turnaround, and nationalist unrest was on the rise in various parts of the country, including Armenia, Azerbaijan, and the Baltic republics.

through the introduction of reforms.[9] Linkages between perestroika and the "new political thinking" in foreign policy that Gorbachev advocated were also publicly acknowledged.[10] These were the first open statements of the direction Soviet policy would take; it took another year for these policies to be translated into practice.

Domestic political reforms began in earnest in 1987, as Gorbachev and his allies began to move to limit the Party's oversight in economics and politics. Simultaneously, divisions within the Party leadership over the reform policies began to appear.[11] In January 1987 Gorbachev criticized the CPSU for stagnation, particularly during the Brezhnev era, and called for multicandidate elections for some posts. The June 1987 CPSU Plenum accepted some diminution of the Party's centralized economic control, and endorsed Gorbachev's proposal for an all CPSU conference, the first to be held since 1941.[12] Gorbachev and his allies thus began to push for significant changes in policy, which inspired significant criticism against the direction of reforms from more conservative forces. This was to be a recurring pattern: as Gorbachev pushed harder to implement reforms that threatened basic Communist Party tenets, opposition to his proposals rose.[13] In spite of growing objections within the Party leader-

---

9. Gorbachev's advocacy of perestroika grew out of his sense that the Soviet system had become "rotten," and needed substantial reform. His first use of this term was in 1984, prior to his appointment as General Secretary. See Brown, *The Gorbachev Factor,* pp. 79–82.

10. Mikhail Gorbachev, "Political Report of the CPSU Central Committee to the 27th Party Congress," February 25, 1986 (Moscow: Novosti Press Agency, 1986).

11. Akhromeyev and Kornienko, *Glazami Marshala i Diplomata,* p. 153; Ligachev, *Inside Gorbachev's Kremlin,* pp. 90–134; and V. A. Medvedev, *V Komande Gorbacheva: Vzglyad Iznutri* [On Gorbachev's team: a view from inside] (Moscow: Bylina, 1992) pp. 113–56. Divisions within the party are also discussed by Gorbachev in his memoirs, *Zhizn' i Reformi* [Life and reforms] (Moscow: Novosti, 1995), and by Nikolai Ryzhkov in *Perestroika: Istoriya Predatel'stv* [Perestroika: History of betrayal] (Moscow: Novosti, 1992).

12. Gorbachev proposed the holding of a CPSU conference as a way to expedite his efforts to democratize the Party and the Soviet Union's political system. Party Congresses were by tradition held every five years, and Gorbachev did not want to wait until 1991, the date of the next CPSU congress, to push through more reform measures. The most signficant reform at the Party Conference held in 1988 was the establishment of the Congress of Peoples' Deputies to replace the Supreme Soviet, and agreement on the election of its representatives.

13. Of course, dissatisfaction with Communist Party rule also rose, which made the Communist Party's position more fragile, and complicated efforts to find policy solutions. For some analyses of the rise of opposition movements in the Soviet Union and Russia, see M. Steven Fish, *Democracy from Scratch: Opposition and Regime in the New*

ship, Gorbachev denounced Stalin in his speech on the seventieth anniversary of the Bolshevik Revolution in November 1987, beginning a reexamination of the history of the Soviet period.[14]

In 1988, Gorbachev pushed for further separation of Party and state by limiting the Party's oversight of economics and beginning the process of restructuring the government to give greater authority to state, rather than Party, institutions.[15] In May 1989, after multicandidate elections for two-thirds of its delegates, the new Congress of Peoples' Deputies opened, taking the place of the Supreme Soviet.[16] By this point perestroika had led to dramatic political changes in the Soviet Union: open criticism of the Communist Party; increasing demands for greater democratic accountability of the leadership; and by the end of 1989, attacks on the Communist Party's leading role.

While political reforms had a dramatic impact on the Soviet Union by 1989, economic reforms had failed to revive the Soviet economy. [17] If anything, economic trends were getting worse, for three reasons. First, as was

---

Russian Revolution (Princeton: Princeton University Press, 1995), esp. pp. 32–51; Brown, *The Gorbachev Factor,* pp. 160–211; and Michael McFaul and Sergei Markov, *The Troubled Birth of Russian Democracy: Parties, Personalities, and Programs* (Stanford, Calif.: Hoover Institution Press, 1993), pp. 1–21.

14.   Up to this point, only the Brezhnev period of "stagnation" had been open to criticism; now the Party's rule since Lenin's death was questioned as well. On opposition within the Soviet leadership and concern about Gorbachev's attack on Stalin, see Seweryn Bialer, "The Changing Soviet Political System: The Nineteenth Party Conference and After," in Bialer, ed., *Politics, Society, and Nationality Inside Gorbachev's Russia* (Boulder. Colo.: Westview Press, 1989), pp. 199–208.

15.   See Gordon Hahn, *Russia's Revolution From Above, 1985–2000: Reform, Transition and Revolution in the Fall of the Soviet Communist Regime* (New Brunswick, Conn.: Transaction Publishers, 2002).

16.   Notably, dissident physicist Andrei Sakharov and then Communist Party rebel Boris Yeltsin were elected to the new Congress of People's Deputies. The May 1989 elections were interpreted as a resounding victory for glasnost and perestroika, first, because they were held, and second, because the vote tallys for Central Committee members running unopposed were published; even votes against Gorbachev were publicized. The elections were followed by astoundingly open debates during the first session of the new Congress in May and June 1989. On the voting rules, see Brown, *The Gorbachev Factor,* pp. 188–190.

17.   For some analyses of Soviet economic reforms under Gorbachev, see David Dyker, *Restructuring the Soviet Economy* (London: Routledge, 1992); Stephen Whitefield, *Industrial Power and the Soviet State* (Oxford: Clarendon Press, 1993); Peter Rutland, *The Politics of Economic Stagnation in the Soviet Union: The Role of Local Party Organs in Economic Management* (Cambridge: Cambridge University Press, 1993); and Ed A. Hewett, *Reforming the Soviet Economy: Equality versus Efficiency* (Washington, D.C.: Brookings Institution, 1988).

also true in the political realm, when Gorbachev came to power he had no clear idea of what he wanted or needed to change economically. He knew that the economic system was not functioning well, but it was not obvious how it should be changed, especially since Gorbachev was *not* considering moving to a market-based economy when he initiated reforms. He moved in this direction in the next five years out of necessity, but continued until the end to strive to create a "socialist" market economy.

Second, Gorbachev could not consolidate control over economics as he could—at least for a while—over the domestic political arena and foreign affairs, partly because far more ministries were involved in the implementation of economic policy. These ministries remained entrenched in their habits, and their leaders were profoundly threatened by the changes Gorbachev was proposing.[18] Equally, the Party itself was threatened by the economic changes under consideration. Relinquishing Communist Party control over the economy presented a fundamental threat to Marxism-Leninism, and the Party's basis for rule. The CPSU agreed to lessen centralized control over the economy in 1987, but it did not do so willingly; moreover, most of its leaders continued to believe that competition was bad, and the sale of land was simply out of the question.

Third, Gorbachev's support for the curtailment of alcohol production and sales in 1985 seriously damaged the state's tax base beginning in his first year in power. This compounded the difficulty of instituting the reforms that were introduced later.[19] In itself, this would not seem significant, but it highlights the lack of comprehension by the Soviet leadership of how state revenues functioned, and the full scope of changes necessary in the economic sphere—to say nothing of the importance of alcohol in quelling social discontent in the Soviet Union.

ARMS CONTROL AND RELATIONS WITH THE UNITED STATES
Gorbachev recognized the need to limit military competition to create a climate for "normal" relations with the United States and Europe. He also recognized that military reductions would allow the Soviet Union to focus its attention inward, and to free resources for domestic revitalization. Soviet efforts in arms control under Gorbachev took two forms: unilateral measures by Moscow to disarm, and bilateral arms control talks with the United States.

---

18. Whitefield, *Industrial Power and the Soviet State*, p. 180, as cited by Brown, *The Gorbachev Factor*, p. 132.

19. For an analysis of the anti-alcohol campaign, see Stephen White, *Russia Goes Dry: Alcohol, State and Society* (Cambridge: Cambridge University Press, 1996).

Moscow's unilateral arms control moves had two central aims: to prove Soviet sincerity in its efforts to reduce military tensions, and to put the United States on the defensive, giving the Soviet Union the moral and political high ground in the arms control arena.[20]

The Soviet Union's early concessions were greeted with skepticism in the West, since the Soviet Union was famous for unilateral moves that contained little substance. Moscow's initial moves appeared to continue this trend; they proposed real adjustments, but did not create significant changes in the overall military balance. For example, the Soviet Union's moratorium on nuclear testing, announced in August 1985, and its call for a chemical-weapons-free zone in Central Europe were seen as little more than propaganda efforts.[21] Moscow's silence about the nuclear reactor accident at Chernobyl in 1986 also hurt its credibility, though later its candor about the extent of the problems at Chernobyl was an indication that the Soviet Union was responding in a new way to external concerns.[22] This was followed by acknowledgement that the radar at Krasnoyarsk violated the Anti-Ballistic Missile (ABM) Treaty, and the Soviet Union halted construction of this facility.[23] Though these latter moves were early indications that the Soviet leadership was behaving differently toward the outside world, their significance was not immediately obvious.

More impressive unilateral steps came in 1988. In February 1988 Gorbachev proposed that the Soviet Union withdraw its troops from Afghanistan by March 1989. In December 1988, Gorbachev announced a unilateral reduction of the Red Army by 500,000 troops, including 50,000 from Eastern Europe, along with their equipment.[24] These two moves

---

20. Jacques Lévesque refers to Gorbachev's policy in arms control as a "controlled avalanche" of proposals designed for this effect. Lévesque, *The Enigma of 1989: The USSR and the Liberation of Eastern Europe* (Berkeley, Calif.: University of California Press, 1997), p. 25.

21. In January 1986, Gorbachev called for the complete abolition of nuclear weapons by the end of the century, and for the first time accepted on-site verification measures as a possibility in the intermediate-range nuclear forces negotiations with the United States. "Text of Statement by M.S. Gorbachev, General Secretary of the CPSU Central Committee," from *Izvestiya*, January 16, 1986, in *BBC Summary of World Broadcasts: Soviet Union* [hereafter *SWB:SU*], January 17, 1986.

22. Garthoff, *The Great Transition*, pp. 276–278.

23. Ibid., pp. 317–318; Harald Müller, "The Internalization of Principles, Norms, and Rules by Governments: The Case of Security Regimes," in Volker Rittberger, ed., *Regime Theory and International Relations* (Oxford: Clarendon Press, 1993), pp. 368–375.

24. Gorbachev, "Speech to the United Nations General Assembly," *Pravda*, December 8, 1988. On the Soviet leadership's decision-making regarding Afghanistan, see Sarah

provided tangible evidence that the Soviet Union's attitude toward the use of force was changing, and that it wanted to reduce the military threat its forces presented to Europe.[25]

Gorbachev also revived bilateral progress in arms control. U.S.-Soviet arms control had been stalled since the end of 1983, when the Soviet Union walked out of both the Intermediate-range Nuclear Force (INF) negotiations and the Strategic Arms Reduction (START) negotiations in protest against the U.S. deployment of intermediate-range missiles in Europe.[26] The United States and the Soviet Union also were in conflict over the U.S. Strategic Defense Initiative (SDI) and the Krasnoyarsk radar installation, and the implications of these for the ABM Treaty. Some proposals for a renewal of talks had been made during former General Secretary Konstantin Chernenko's tenure, but negotiations did not resume until after the first summit meeting of Gorbachev and U.S. President Ronald Reagan, in Geneva in October 1985.

E. Mendelson, *Changing Course: Ideas, Politics, and the Soviet Withdrawal from Afghanistan* (Princeton: Princeton University Press, 1998).

25. As one indication of how slowly perceptions change, Western scholars and policymakers continued to question the "durability" both of Gorbachev's tenure and of the "new thinking" Gorbachev was introducing in Soviet policy, while U.S. government officials rejected the possibility that substantial changes had appeared in Soviet political and military strategy even after Gorbachev's announcement of unilateral troop withdrawals from Europe at the end of 1988. Indeed, in early 1989, Secretary of Defense Frank Carlucci stated that "there is no evidence that Gorbachev and his allies will abandon communism or their drive to expand Soviet influence." Frank Carlucci, *Annual Report to the Congress, Fiscal Year 1990*, January 17, 1989, p. 3., as cited by Garthoff, *The Great Transition*, p. 533. Garthoff, among others, elaborates on U.S. skepticism about Soviet intentions during this period. See also Michael R. Beschloss and Strobe Talbott, *At the Highest Levels: The Inside Story of the End of the Cold War* (Boston: Little, Brown, 1993).

26. NATO decided to deploy intermediate range forces in Europe as a response to Soviet deployments of SS-22 missiles in eastern parts of the Soviet Union in the late 1970s. Interestingly, friction had arisen between the Soviet Union, Hungary, and East Germany during Moscow's campaign against NATO's INF deployments in late 1983. Hungary and East Germany had claimed that small states could play a positive role in the international arena, while the Soviet leadership had insisted that the bloc unite behind Soviet policies. This argument had continued in the Soviet press in 1984 and 1985, even after Gorbachev's appointment. On the INF debate and U.S.-Soviet arms control during the 1970s and 1980s, see Raymond L. Garthoff, *Detente and Confrontation: American-Soviet Relations from Nixon to Reagan* (Washington, D.C.: The Brookings Institution, 1994); and Strobe Talbott, *Deadly Gambits: The Reagan Administration and the Stalemate in Nuclear Arms Control* (New York: Vintage Books, 1984). On the Soviet–East European dispute over INF, see Ronald Asmus, *Eastern Europe and Moscow: Documentation of a Dispute*, Radio Free Europe Occasional Papers, No. 1 (Munich: Radio Free Europe, 1985).

In 1986, Gorbachev proposed that negotiations on the INF be separated from those on the longer-range missiles that were the subject of the START talks; he also agreed to exclude British and French INF forces from discussions on U.S.-Soviet missiles in Europe, an option that his predecessors had rejected.[27] Concrete results in U.S.-Soviet discussions began to emerge in 1987.[28] The United States and the Soviet Union reached a tentative agreement on the "zero option" for INF in Europe in September 1987; this treaty was signed in December 1987 and ratified in June 1988. U.S.-Soviet talks on banning underground nuclear tests opened in November 1987, and START negotiations began to show progress after agreement was reached on the INF accord. The START I treaty, which was signed in 1991, included the first real reductions in the number of strategic nuclear warheads for both states.[29]

EAST-WEST RELATIONS IN EUROPE

Soviet policy toward Europe changed dramatically under Gorbachev. Gorbachev and his advisers recognized that there were clear advantages in distinguishing between the United States and Europe in the areas of arms control and foreign trade. Europe probably would be increasingly important to the Soviet Union as a trade partner—more so than the United States—in its effort to renovate its economy. Gorbachev also argued that the Soviet Union should stop viewing Europe through the lens of the U.S.-Soviet competition. One consequence was the establishment in the Soviet Union of a research institute devoted to Europe (The Institute of Europe) in 1988.

Much of the "new thinking" in foreign policy, introduced in 1986, affected Soviet policy toward Europe, and its military policy in particular. The new political thinking suggested the existence of universal values and interests. Rather than being one concept, it was a series of new ideas that provided the groundwork for the changes in Soviet foreign policy under Gorbachev. Among its central elements were a belief in "humani-

---

27. Garthoff, *Détente and Confrontation*, p. 279.

28. Gorbachev and Reagan's summit meeting in Reykjavik, Iceland, in October 1986, proved fruitless in terms of immediate results, but it did break many of the logjams in U.S.-Soviet negotiations. It is best remembered for the near agreement between the two leaders to do away with all nuclear weapons, something U.S. negotiators neither anticipated nor desired. For an in-depth discussion of the Reykjavik summit, see Garthoff, *The Great Transition*, chap. 6; and Brown, *The Gorbachev Factor*, pp. 231–233.

29. The underground test ban made the Comprehensive Test Ban Treaty possible, though this was only realized in 1996. On the history of U.S.-Soviet negotiations, see *The Future of U.S. Nuclear Weapons Policy* (Washington, D.C.: National Academy of Sciences, 1997), pp. 12–23.

tarian universalism," an emphasis on interdependence rather than class interests, and "freedom of choice," which was to play an important role in Eastern Europe.[30]

Universal principles were in enshrined in concepts such as "reasonable sufficiency" of both nuclear and conventional weapons.[31] This implied the importance of expanding efforts in nuclear arms control. In the conventional realm, it mandated revisions in the Soviet Union's military doctrine, and led to a shift toward "defensive defense."[32] Physical proof of the changes in Soviet military policy on the ground appeared both in changes in Soviet and Warsaw Pact exercises, and later in the Soviet Union's unilateral reduction of forces in Europe, announced in 1988 and begun in 1989.[33] The Soviet Union also agreed to conclude the ongoing Mutual and Balanced Force Reduction Talks (MBFR) on conventional forces in Europe, which had dragged on since the mid-1970s, and to begin new conventional force talks in 1989. These resulted in agreement on substantial cuts in forces by both alliances in Europe, restrictions on the number of troops based outside their home state, and limits to each country's forces from the Atlantic to the Urals.[34] The impact of both the unilateral cuts and the conventional forces agreement was to reduce significantly the physical threat to Western Europe.

Europe also was critical to the evolution of Gorbachev's foreign policy because his strong bilateral ties with particular European leaders helped shape his views about Europe, and his confidence in the Europeans as potential allies. This helped him to reduce East-West tensions, and

---

30. Gorbachev, *Zhizn' I Reformii*, vol. 2, pp. 81–101; and Brown, *The Gorbachev Factor*, pp. 220–225.

31. "Reasonable sufficiency" first emerged as a goal in Gorbachev's speech at the 27th CPSU Congress in February 1986. M.S. Gorbachev, "Political Report to the CPSU Central Committee to the 27th Party Congress of the CPSU," *Pravda*, February 26, 1986, pp. 2–10.

32. On the Soviet Union's efforts to change its military doctrine in the late 1980s, see Akhromeyev and Kornienko, *Glazami Marshala i Diplomata*, pp. 68–74, 121–127; Jack Snyder, "International Leverage on Soviet Domestic Change," *World Politics*, Vol. 42, No. 1 (October 1989), pp. 1–31; Steven M. Meyer, "The Sources and Prospects of Gorbachev's New Political Thinking on Security," *International Security*, Vol. 13, No. 2 (Fall 1988); Nation, *Black Earth, Red Star*, pp. 287–304; and Blacker, *Hostage to Revolution*.

33. Nation, *Black Earth, Red Star*, pp. 292–293; and Garthoff, *The Great Transition*, pp. 306–307.

34. It should be noted that the CFE Treaty entailed few changes in NATO's forces in Europe. On the CFE Treaty, see Richard A. Falkenrath, *Shaping Europe's Military Order: The Origins and Consequences of the CFE Treaty* (Cambridge, Mass.: MIT Press, 1995).

allowed him either to take or accept additional risks as they arose in Eastern Europe. Among the leaders who made a significant impact on Gorbachev were British Prime Minister Margaret Thatcher, Spanish Prime Minister Felipe Gonzalez, French President François Mitterand, and German Chancellor Helmut Kohl. Thatcher played a particularly important role in the early development of Gorbachev's thinking. In her first meetings with him in December 1984, even before he was appointed General Secretary, Thatcher was blunt in explaining how the Soviet Union came across on the international stage.[35]

Soviet Policy Toward Eastern Europe

During the Cold War, Eastern Europe mattered to the Soviet Union in several ways. First, the "fraternal socialist community" provided proof of the ideological claims made by Marxism-Leninism; socialism's spread to Eastern Europe was evidence of its ascendancy, and signaled its first steps toward the inevitable victory over capitalism. Second, Soviet dominance in Eastern Europe was a concrete reminder of the Soviet Union's strength. Its gains in the victory over fascism in World War II were embodied in Eastern Europe, and especially in socialist East Germany.[36] Similarly, the Warsaw Pact created a buffer zone between the Soviet Union and the West. Given the magnitude of Soviet casualties and devastation in World War II, this barrier between the Soviet Union and its presumed opponents had become critical to the Red Army's military doctrine and planning for a war in Europe.[37] Third, particularly by the 1980s, the East European states provided potential models of "socialist experimentation" that the Soviet Union could study.[38]

---

35. Gorbachev, *Zhizn' i Reformii*, vol. 2, pp. 81–101; and Brown, *The Gorbachev Factor*, pp. 115–117.

36. J.F. Brown, *Eastern Europe and Communist Rule* (Durham, N.C.: Duke University Press, 1988), pp. 30–33. On East Germany's importance see also Michael J. Sodaro, *Moscow, Germany, and the West from Khrushchev to Gorbachev* (Ithaca, N.Y.: Cornell University Press, 1990).

37. On Soviet military doctrine during the Cold War, see Raymond L. Garthoff, *Soviet Military Doctrine* (Glencoe, Ill.: Free Press, 1953); and Harriet Fast Scott and William F. Scott, *Soviet Military Doctrine: Continuity, Formulation, and Dissemination* (Boulder, Colo.: Westview Press, 1988). For a recent analysis, see also Andrei A. Kokoshin, *Soviet Strategic Thought, 1917–91* (Cambridge, Mass.: MIT Press, 1998).

38. The other obvious model available to the Soviet Union was China, and it too received attention. On Soviet interest in reform concepts in Eastern Europe, see Karen Dawisha, *Eastern Europe, Gorbachev, and Reform: The Great Challenge* (Cambridge: Cambridge University Press, 1988), pp. 20–21; and Brown, *The Gorbachev Factor*, p. 135; on

While Eastern Europe was not an immediate Soviet priority after Gorbachev came to power, and Gorbachev did not have a clear plan with regard to Eastern Europe when he became General Secretary, he wanted Soviet relations with Eastern Europe to change in several ways. He wanted to see more independent, reformed states in Eastern Europe. But he wanted them to change along lines similar to those he thought necessary in the Soviet Union. Eastern Europe would still be socialist, just as he expected the Soviet Union to remain socialist, but there was a lot of latitude in what reformed socialism might look like. Part of Gorbachev's interest in an independent, reformed Eastern Europe grew from his desire that these states be better trading partners for the Soviet Union. Finally, Gorbachev expected the East European states to remain friendly to the Soviet Union; indeed, he wanted them to remain allies. Gorbachev envisioned a gradual reduction of the importance of the two military blocs in Europe, concurrent with a waning of the distinctions between the two halves of Europe. He even appears to have accepted the possibility that German unification might be necessary to achieve his goals, but he expected this process to evolve over a very long period.[39]

While Eastern Europe was integral to the changes that Gorbachev wanted to make, particularly in foreign policy, Soviet policy goals evolved over time. The changes that were made in Soviet policy toward Eastern Europe had different results than initially desired. These policy changes can be broken into four categories: noninterference; economic policy; foreign policy; and domestic political reform.

NONINTERFERENCE

The adoption of a policy of noninterference toward Eastern Europe had two aims. First, Gorbachev clearly wanted to change the principle on which relations between the Soviet Union and Eastern Europe had been based during the Cold War period. Given his criticism of the system as a whole, and the new policies he introduced in Soviet domestic politics and foreign policy, Gorbachev apparently found the previous system, whereby the East European leaders understood that they should follow the Soviet Union's example, both wrong and inefficient.

The adoption of noninterference also indicated that Gorbachev wanted to shed the responsibility of resolving Eastern Europe's problems, by making the leadership of these countries responsible for their

comparisons with China, see Wlodzimierz Brus, "Marketisation and Democratization: The Sino-Soviet Divergence," *Cambridge Journal of Economics*, Vol. 14, No. 4 (December 1993), pp. 423–440.

39. Lévesque, *The Enigma of Reform*, pp. 43, 69–74.

own affairs. Thus, the Soviet Union would no longer order the East Europeans to follow its lead, nor would it take care of these states; therefore, they would be less of a burden to the Soviet Union.[40]

The shift to a policy of noninterference took place very early on in Gorbachev's tenure, though its implications were not immediately recognized—or believed—by most East European leaders. According to Gorbachev, in his informal meetings with the leaders of the Warsaw Pact states following the funeral of Chernenko, his predecessor as General Secretary, he stressed the importance of respecting the sovereignty of all states, and stressed the responsibility of each party for its country's conditions. Less than a month later, when the Warsaw Pact was renewed for thirty years at a meeting of the heads of governments in Sofia, Bulgaria, Gorbachev reiterated these points, and also explained the need for changes in the Soviet Union's domestic politics.[41]

Noninterference remained central to Soviet policy toward Eastern Europe as it evolved during 1986–1988. A fundamental assumption of Gorbachev's policy during this period was that the Eastern European states were all independent, and the Soviet Union was not pushing them to adopt a particular path. This was reflected in Gorbachev's comments during the 27th Party Congress, which stressed the importance of "unconditional respect in international practice for the right of every people to choose the paths and forms of its development."[42] Those in the Soviet Union concerned with policy toward Eastern Europe emphasized that these states should not be treated as "younger brothers," and Gorbachev

---

40. Craig Nation has argued that when the Soviet Union began seriously to reassess its security policies and relationship with the West, it began to see the Warsaw Pact as a liability. So long as the Soviet Union insisted on command of this region, it was not likely to be taken seriously in its bid to improve East-West relations. Eastern Europe was also a barrier to domestic reform, because the Soviet Union was burdened with sustaining these dependent satellite regimes while trying to resolve its own domestic problems, which ranged from the transformation of its economy to the creation of a more democratic political system. See Nation, *Red Earth, Black Star*, pp. 307–308. See also Valerie Bunce, "The Empire Strikes Back: The Evolution of the Eastern Bloc from a Soviet Asset to a Soviet Liability," *International Organization*, Vol. 39, No. 1 (Winter 1985), pp. 1–46. For an examination of implicit Soviet subsidies to Eastern Europe in the 1970s and early 1980s, see Michael Marrese and Jan Vanous, *Soviet Subsidization of Trade with Eastern Europe: A Soviet Perspective* (Berkeley, Calif.: Institute of International Studies, 1983); for an evaluation of the costs of empire to the Soviet Union, see Peter Liberman, *Does Conquest Pay? The Exploitation of Occupied Industrial Societies* (Princeton: Princeton University Press, 1996), pp. 120–145.

41. Gorbachev, *Zhizn' i Reformi*, vol. 2, pp. 311–312.

42. *Pravda*, February 26, 1986, as cited in Dawisha, *Eastern Europe, Gorbachev, and Reform*, p. 164.

stressed that the Soviet Union should "show modesty" in making suggestions to its allies, given its past record.[43] By 1987, Gorbachev's foreign policy spokesmen were stressing the need for "equal dialogue" with the Soviet Union's allies, while the stress on noninterference continued.[44] And as Soviet domestic policy became more radicalized in 1988, Gorbachev's pronouncements on noninterference strengthened as well. In his December 1988 speech to the United Nations, Gorbachev emphasized both noninterference and "freedom of choice" for all states, an indication to his Warsaw Pact allies that their maneuvering room was virtually limitless.[45]

ECONOMIC POLICY

The Soviet Union was anxious to improve economic ties with the East European states. Gorbachev and his allies retained an ongoing interest in Eastern Europe's experiences with reform, and Soviet leaders had watched carefully during the previous decades to see what had worked in Eastern Europe. At the same time, Moscow wanted better trade ties with its East European allies.[46] Gorbachev wanted to reshape the pricing structure for Soviet raw materials within the Council for Mutual Economic Assistance (CMEA), for example, and to receive high-quality goods in intrabloc trade; the East European practice when he came to power was to reserve its better products for hard currency trade with the West. Both of these steps would lessen Moscow's implicit economic subsidies to Eastern Europe. These desires were apparent at the 27th Party Congress, and Moscow's desire for better trade ties was increasingly evident in the development of a new policy within the Soviet Union beginning in 1986. Gorbachev wrote a memo to the Politburo in the summer of 1986 that analyzed the condition of socialist cooperation, and concluded

---

43. V.A. Medvedev, *Raspad: Kak On Nazreval v "Mirovoi Sisteme Sotsialisma"* [Collapse: How it developed in the world socialist system] (Moscow: Mezhdunarodnie Otnoshenia, 1994), p. 21; and Lévesque, *The Enigma of Reform*, p. 54.

44. Gorbachev, *Zhizn' i Reformi*, vol. 2, pp. 35, 318.

45. Gorbachev, "Speech to the United Nations General Assembly."

46. The price paid by East Europeans for Soviet oil and gas, for example, was determined by five-year averaging of world prices, rather than the current world market price. For a discussion of Soviet actions within the CMEA, see Michael Kraus, "Gorbachev's reforms and Eastern Europe," in Ronald D. Liebowitz, ed., *Gorbachev's New Thinking: Prospects for Joint Ventures* (Cambridge, Mass.: Ballinger, 1989); and Bunce, "The Empire Strikes Back." For an evaluation of the strengths and weaknesses of Soviet economic control in Eastern Europe, see Randall W. Stone, *Satellites and Commissars: Strategy and Conflict in the Politics of Soviet-Bloc Trade* (Princeton: Princeton University Press, 1996).

that relations needed to be rebuilt, including both the system of political relations with these states and the economic mechanisms between them. This led to a meeting of the CMEA in November 1986, at which new relations within the socialist community were discussed. This meeting was apparently one of the first serious indications to the leaders of Eastern Europe of the degree of change in interbloc relations that Gorbachev had in mind. According to one account, it was also one of the most frank meetings to date between the Soviet leader and his allies, and the tone of the discussion was sufficiently sharp that only muted reports of the meeting were given to the press.[47]

As his own policies developed, Gorbachev accepted and even encouraged greater trade between Eastern and Western Europe. There were several benefits to this. Increased trade with the West would enable the Eastern Europeans to acquire new technology and improve the quality of their manufactured goods. This would help improve their overall terms of trade, and it made higher-quality East European goods available to the Soviet Union through interbloc trade. Trade with the West would also encourage the Eastern Europeans to look beyond the Soviet Union to resolve their economic problems. Moreover, allowing increased East-West economic ties would be another indication that the Soviet Union was serious about allowing each country to choose its own course, and this would reinforce the sincerity of Moscow's commitment to noninterference.

FOREIGN POLICY

Eastern Europe had been an important factor in Soviet foreign policy during much of the Cold War. In addition to its ideological importance, Eastern Europe was integral to Soviet military doctrine because of its strategic location between the Soviet Union and the West. Gorbachev's foreign policy goals required substantial changes in Soviet military doctrine to emphasize defense, which meant that military planning regarding Eastern Europe had to change.[48]

Moreover, Soviet control over Eastern Europe implied that the Soviet "new thinking" did not represent a major change. Moscow needed to accept greater independence by the Eastern European states, both as partners within the Warsaw Pact and in their own political, social, and economic policies, to prove its sincerity in the political changes it was making in East-West relations. To this end, the Soviet Union moved to

---

47. Gorbachev himself notes that "taboos" were broken, which would have cost those people speaking out their jobs in earlier times. Gorbachev, *Zhizn' i Reformi*, vol. 2, pp. 315–316; and Medvedev, *Raspad*, pp. 27–29.

48. Akhromeyev and Kornienko, *Glazami Marshala i Diplomata*, p. 60.

"normalize" relations with its East European allies, moving away from communist ideology as a basis of relations.

The first indications of such change were seen in Gorbachev's endorsement of greater respect for the equality of all parties within the Warsaw Pact at its meeting in Bulgaria in April 1985.[49] This was followed by efforts in May 1987 to get Moscow's allies to state their views on policy, and to promote "equal dialogue" within the Warsaw Pact.[50] Significantly, in contrast with the standard statements following summit meetings, no mention of "unity and cohesion" in foreign policy was made in the communiqué; instead, it reported that "a thorough exchange of opinions on the development of cooperation among the allied socialist countries" was held at the meeting.[51]

Gorbachev's changed attitude toward Eastern Europe was apparent in Moscow's continued insistence on the independence of its allies, and the importance Gorbachev placed on their addressing their own unique challenges. While Gorbachev clearly encouraged the adoption of policies similar to perestroika, he did not demand them, and preferred to wait for changes from the East Europeans themselves.

Moscow did, however, take important steps to transform Soviet relations with Eastern Europe. Prior to 1985, Soviet policy toward Eastern Europe occupied an ambiguous position between foreign and domestic policy, with relations handled primarily by the Central Committee (CC) of the CPSU, and by the Department of Socialist Countries, rather than the Foreign Ministry. Important issues were handled through party-to-party ties. As part of his effort to "deideologize" foreign policy, Gorbachev wanted to shift away from this, and to give priority to state-to-state ties. This paralleled his desire to shift domestic responsibilities to state institutions and away from the CPSU. To this end, Gorbachev abolished the CC department responsible for relations with other communist parties in 1988, and transferred its responsibilities to the International Department of the CC. He also shifted more responsibility for the development of policy toward Eastern Europe to the Foreign Ministry, where his ally Eduard Shevardnadze held sway.[52]

---

49. Gorbachev, *Zhizn' i Reformi*, p. 313.

50. Medvedev, *Raspad*, p. 51; and Medvedev, *V Komande Gorbacheva*, p. 51.

51. "Warsaw Treaty Political Consultative Committee Communique," *Soviet News*, June 3, 1987.

52. Since 1985, the International Department had been led by Anatolii Dobrynin, former ambassador to the United States. Along with the reshuffling of responsibilities in 1988, the Department was overseen by a new Commission on International Policy, led by Aleksandr Yakovlev, and it gained a new head, Valentin Falin. It should be noted

POLITICAL REFORM

In the realm of political reform and the advocacy of domestic changes in Eastern Europe, Gorbachev was far less active, for three reasons. First, Gorbachev took the principle of noninterference quite seriously from very early in his tenure—indeed, one could argue that he took this policy too far. Gorbachev was unwilling to express his support for particular leaders in Czechoslovakia, for example, when endorsing a reformist candidate for party leadership in 1987 might have ensured the nomination of a reformer within the communist party leadership there.[53] The one major exception to this policy of noninterference was that Gorbachev was willing to criticize Romanian leader Nicolae Ceauşescu and to advocate perestroika-style policies in Romania.[54]

Second, there was no consensus within the Soviet leadership about political reforms in Eastern Europe, just as there was no agreement on the policies Gorbachev was introducing at home. While there was general agreement within the Party leadership in 1985 and 1986 that Soviet domestic policy needed changes, there was less accord in other areas. As a result, Gorbachev gave significant attention early in his term to consolidating his power within the Soviet leadership, so that he could carry out the policies he felt were necessary. Over time he also moved to wrest political control away from the CPSU, and to invest power in the state apparatus instead. This reflected his frustration with the obstruction he met within the Party to change, particularly as his policies became more radical.

The consequence was that as his efforts moved forward starting in 1987, Gorbachev met with increasing resistance and criticism at home. Chief of the General Staff, Marshall S.F. Akhromeyev, points out that the

---

that before it was abolished in 1988, reformers within the Department of Socialist Countries had been advocating that greater pressure should be put on the conservative regimes in Eastern Europe to adopt reforms. On these shifts in policy see Medvedev, *Raspad*, pp. 19–27; and Glenn R. Chafetz, *Gorbachev, Reform, and the Brezhnev Doctrine: Soviet Policy toward Eastern Europe, 1985–90* (Westport, Conn.: Praeger, 1993), pp. 69–71. On the restructuring of the International Department, see Mark Kramer, "The Role of the CPSU International Department," *Soviet Studies*, Vol. 42, No. 3 (July 1990), pp. 436–439.

53. Lévesque points out that on occasion his refusal to interfere in Eastern Europe led to missed opportunities by Gorbachev. *The Enigma of Reform*, pp. 59–65.

54. Gorbachev, *Zhizn' i Reformi*, vol. 2, p. 403; Medvedev, *Raspad*, pp. 194–223; and Georgii Shakhnazarov, *Tsena Svobodi: Reformatsiya Gorbacheva Glazami evo Pomoshchnika* [The value of freedom: Gorbachev's reforms through the eyes of his aide] (Moscow: Rossika * Zevs, 1993), pp. 101–102. See Chapter 7 for a discussion of Gorbachev's relations with Ceauşescu and Romania.

unity within the Politburo disappeared in 1987, due to the increasingly radical nature of the changes Gorbachev was introducing.[55] This resistance was most evident with regard to domestic policy. Only in 1988 did Gorbachev gain substantial control of the Politburo, which enabled him to push harder in domestic policy change.

Gorbachev finessed the problem of resistance to his foreign policy by concentrating power in the hands of an ever smaller group of people. By 1989, possibly two or three people appear to have been making decisions in the foreign policy realm. Moreover, there was virtually no discussion about major foreign policy developments within the Party leadership. One of Gorbachev's critics highlights the lack of debate by noting the contrast between the discussion of the "Andreyeva Letter," a letter to *Sovetskaya Rossia* published in March 1988, which had been seen as an attack on Gorbachev's leadership, and the crisis within East Germany in the fall of 1989.[56] This letter, which questioned perestroika's reappraisal of Stalinism as a way to attack Gorbachev and his reform policies, received two days of debate within the Politburo, while there was no discussion within the Politburo of the crisis that led to the collapse of the East German state, the Soviet Union's most important ally in the Eastern bloc.[57] There also were no discussions between political and military leaders about the impact that Gorbachev's foreign policy revisions might have on the military security of the Soviet Union.[58]

---

55. Akhromeyev and Kornienko, *Glazami Marshala i Diplomata*, p. 153; and A.S. Chernyaev, *Shest' Let s Gorbachevym: Po Dnevnikovym Zapisyam* [Six years with Gorbachev: From diary notes] (Moscow: "Progress"—"Kultura," 1993), p. 291.

56. The "Andreyeva Letter," which was published by an influential newspaper in March 1988, criticized the reappraisal of Stalin that Gorbachev had endorsed in the fall of 1987 because it threatened the foundation of the Soviet state. The letter was perceived to signal an attack on Gorbachev's leadership because it was published while he was out of the country, and other members of the Party leadership did nothing to repudiate it—indeed, Ligachev praised it. For an analysis of the Andreyeva affair and its impact on Gorbachev's position, see Brown, *The Gorbachev Factor*, pp. 172–174; and Michael Tatu, "The 19th Party Conference," *Problems of Communism*, Vol. 37, No. 3–4 (May–August 1988), pp. 1–15.

57. Instead, Gorbachev "informed" Politburo members of developments there. V.I. Boldin, *Krusheniye P'edestala* [Collapse of the pedestal] (Moscow: Izdatel'stvo "Respublika," 1995), pp. 184–187; and V.I. Vorotnikov, *A Bylo eto Tak . . . Iz Dnevnika Chlena Politburo TsK KPSS* [And that's the way it was: From the diary of a member of the Politburo of the Central Committee of the Communist Party of the Soviet Union] (Moscow: Sovyet Veteranov Knigoizdaniya, SI-Mar, 1995), pp. 308–311.

58. It is also notable that there were virtually no discussions within the Politburo or the CC about the spread of reform in Eastern Europe in 1989. This is probably due to the fact that Eastern Europe was increasingly being treated as a foreign policy issue,

Since there was no consensus within the Party leadership about Eastern Europe, noninterference also meant that continued conservatism within Eastern Europe was acceptable. Some of Gorbachev's reform-minded supporters advocated putting greater pressure on the more conservative East European regimes, but this did not happen, both because Gorbachev preferred to wait for changes from within Eastern Europe, and because of the resistance this would have met within the Soviet party leadership.[59] Gorbachev's preference for initiatives from the East Europeans themselves is evident in the support he gave to reformers within Eastern Europe. But he pointedly avoided offering suggestions to either reformers or conservatives.[60] This reserve followed from the policy of noninterference, and indicated Gorbachev's belief that these regimes would have greater success at enhancing their legitimacy if they initiated reforms on their own, in response to their own problems.

The third reason Gorbachev was less active in advocating policy reform in Eastern Europe is that he was too busy—distracted by the large number of issues demanding his attention in both domestic and foreign policy.[61] Especially by 1989, he was promoting massive changes in these areas, and facing ever-growing criticism from within the Party and from society.[62]

In late 1986, Yegor Ligachev, one of Gorbachev's potential rivals in the Politburo, began to indicate his opposition to the direction of reforms by reaffirming the importance of the Soviet Union's ideological heritage.[63] The dispute led by Ligachev was the first round of a cycle that recurred in Soviet domestic politics during the next six years, culminating

and the Party leadership was merely "informed" about developments in the Eastern bloc. On the absence of discussions between military and political leaders regarding foreign policy, see Akhromeyev and Kornienko, *Glazami Marshala i Diplomata*, pp. 70, 226–227.

59. Lévesque, *The Enigma of Reform*, p. 57.

60. See, for example, Gorbachev's insistence that the Polish communists could decide for themselves how to react to the reemergence of Solidarity in 1988. Medvedev, *Raspad*, p. 90.

61. Shakhnazarov, *Tsena Svobodi*, p. 100.

62. What is striking in the memoirs of many of Gorbachev's aides from this period is the absence of a discussion about developments in Eastern Europe; even for Gorbachev's foreign policy aides, the memoirs are heavily weighted toward internal political struggles over the direction of reform.

63. "Extracts of Report by Yegor Ligachev to 69th Anniversary Meeting," *SWB:SU*, November 7, 1986. See also John B. Dunlop and Henry S. Rowen, "Gorbachev Versus Ligachev: The Kremlin Divided," *The National Interest*, No. 11 (Spring 1988), pp. 18–29; and Ligachev, *Inside Gorbachev's Kremlin*, pp. 90–122.

in the attempted coup by hard-line forces in August 1991. Between 1986 and 1991, Gorbachev was confronted periodically with a resurgence of pressure from conservative elements in the Party and government. At times, he managed to fend off heated attacks on his leadership and at the same time to increase the pace of reforms, over hard-line objections.[64] At other times, he altered his policies so as to placate this constituency, and by late 1990 he had moved away from his reformist allies and closer to the conservatives in the party leadership.

Objections at the societal level rose as well. The policy of glasnost that accompanied perestroika opened the Party and Gorbachev himself to popular criticism. This criticism expanded as Gorbachev proved unable to meet the demands of society for real change, notwithstanding the fact that his hands were tied by bureaucratic inertia, Party resistance, and the sheer scope of the problems facing the country. Gorbachev's personal inability to embrace more democratic freedoms also hurt him in the long run, particularly after more democratic challengers emerged to push the issue, notably Boris Yeltsin.[65]

Added to the general societal discontent, criticism from the union republics within the Soviet Union began to emerge in 1987, with calls for greater autonomy and eventually independence. By 1989 this nationality issue had become a serious problem for the Soviet leadership, with demonstrations in Georgia, Armenia, Latvia, Lithuania, and Estonia.[66]

---

64. In late September 1988, Gorbachev was able to give one of his strongest supporters, Aleksandr Yakovlev, the important ideological portfolio that Ligachev had held, while Ligachev was shifted to agriculture, an important but extremely difficult job. Simultaneously, several other conservative Politburo members were "retired," including the potentially powerful KGB chief, Viktor Chebrikov, and Andrei Gromyko, the foreign minister for over three decades who had been retired from this position shortly after Gorbachev came to power and appointed chairman of the Presidium of the Supreme Soviet, while retaining a seat on the Politburo. This significantly strengthened Gorbachev's position, albeit temporarily. For some analyses of political currents within in the Soviet Union in the late 1980s, see Abel Aganbegyan and Timor Timofeyev, *The New Stage of Perestroika* (New York: Institute for East-West Security Studies, 1988); John B. Dunlop, *The Rise of Russia and the Fall of the Soviet Empire* (Princeton: Princeton University Press, 1993); and Brown, *The Gorbachev Factor*.

65. On the conflict between Yeltsin and Gorbachev, see Dunlop, *The Rise of Russia and the Fall of the Soviet Empire*. For an assessment of Gorbachev's beliefs, see Brown, *The Gorbachev Factor*.

66. On the role of nationalities in the Soviet Union, see Yuri Slezkine, "The USSR as a Communal Apartment, or How a Socialist State Promoted Ethnic Particularism," *Slavic Review*, Vol. 53, No. 2 (Summer 1994), pp. 414–453; Victor Zaslavsky, "Nationalism and Democratic Transition in Postcommunist Societies," *Daedalus*, Vol. 121, No. 2 (Spring 1992), pp. 97–122; Ronald Grigor Suny, *The Revenge of the Past: Nationalism, Revolution, and the Collapse of the Soviet Union* (Stanford, Calif.: Stanford University

The result of this overload of issues, resistance, and criticism was that little thought appears to have been given within the leadership to the consequences of its actions for Eastern Europe. Indeed, Shevardnadze noted that the enormity of the Soviet Union's domestic problems meant this in 1989—as pressures for reform there came to a head—"Eastern Europe was [put] on the back burner."[67] In particular, little attention was paid to the fact that perestroika could destroy the Soviet Union's political military bloc, the Warsaw Pact. There were some within the leadership who felt that Soviet policy changes would destroy the socialist community, but this view was not widely shared prior to 1989.[68] Gorbachev argued instead that the "renewal" of socialism would breathe new life into the socialist parties in Eastern Europe.[69] Gorbachev's faith in the ability of socialism to reform itself and the popularity of reformed socialism in Eastern Europe appears to be based on a misinterpretation of his own evident popularity in Eastern Europe. He wrongly believed that this implied support for reformed socialism, rather than for greater freedoms and democratization.

Conclusion

The policies that Gorbachev introduced in the Soviet Union had a significant impact on Eastern Europe. His own endorsement of glasnost and perestroika made expansion of the political debate within Eastern Europe possible, and his acceptance of the changes initiated in Eastern Europe was critical to the spread of reforms throughout the Warsaw Pact.

However, Gorbachev's policies toward Eastern Europe had far different effects than intended. In part, his policies were based on the view that externally mandated reforms could not respond to each country's specific

---

Press, 1993); and Roman Laba, "How Yeltsin's Exploitation of Ethnic Nationalism Brought Down an Empire," *Transition*, January 12, 1996, pp. 5–13.

67. Vladislav M. Zubok, "New Evidence on the "Soviet Factor" in the Peaceful Revolutions of 1989," *Cold War International History Project Bulletin*, Issue 12/13 (Fall/Winter 2001), p. 10.

68. Retrospective assessments of the "inevitability" of collapse, and tendencies to blame Gorbachev and his policies, must be taken with a grain of salt. One figure who convincingly argues that he believed the result of perestroika would be to destroy the socialist bloc is Marshall Akhromeyev, largely because his actions and his later explanations coincide. Akhromeyev resigned as head of the General Staff in December 1988, largely because, as he states in his memoirs, he did not want to preside over the "burial" of the Warsaw Pact. Akhromeyev and Kornienko, *Glazami Marshala i Diplomata*, p. 215.

69. Shakhnazarov, *Tsena Svobodii*, pp. 117, 123.

problems; these states must address their own circumstances. In addition, his inability or unwillingness to demand reform in Eastern Europe meant that the process of reform was shaped as much by internal factors in each of these states as by the example or influence of the Soviet Union.

Gorbachev believed that for reforms to be successful, the East European communist leaders must initiate them on their own, absent pressure from the Soviet Union. He also believed that by doing so, and in essence following his lead, these leaders would gain sufficient support to survive and remain viable political leaders. Gorbachev envisioned reformed socialist governments in Eastern Europe with far greater freedoms and links to the West, and friendship and gratitude for the Soviet Union; he failed to recognize that once he removed the constraints on what they could aspire to, the East Europeans would reject socialism altogether.

Chapter 3

Reform from Above and Below: Regime and Solidarity in Poland

Poland was the first East European state to take advantage of Soviet leader Mikhail Gorbachev's invitation to solve its problems through reform efforts. The results of Poland's political reform process that culminated in 1989 were far different from the hopes or expectations of any of the participants in the process. Neither regime nor opposition envisioned changes of such magnitude as the communists' loss of power, and the appointment of Tadeusz Mazowiecki, a Catholic intellectual and adviser to the previously illegal trade union Solidarity, as prime minister. The history of Poland's reform illustrates the lack of comprehension within Eastern Europe at the beginning of 1989 about the degree of change that Gorbachev would tolerate, as well as Gorbachev's failure to see how far reform in the bloc might go. Not surprisingly then, Soviet influence—and all parties' concern about Moscow's reaction to events—were critical to the nature and pace of change in Poland. The model of concrete Soviet political reforms, beginning in the summer of 1988, also played an important role in shaping the Polish regime's choices.

In this chapter, I first outline the process of reform in Poland, beginning in the early 1980s and concentrating on the years after Gorbachev came to power in the Soviet Union. I then examine the regime's recognition of the need for change, and its judgment of its ability to survive in a more open political climate. I then turn to external influences on the process in Poland, to determine the importance of Soviet and other sources of influence. Finally, I evaluate how well the argument presented in Chapter 1 explains the outcome in Poland.

Poland's Transition

PRECURSORS TO REFORM IN POLAND

The transformation in Poland began with the emergence of Solidarity. An increase in meat prices on July 1, 1980, stimulated a wave of protest strikes that by mid-August had spread across the nation, presenting the most severe threat to communist rule in the region since 1968.[1] The Polish government officially acknowledged Solidarity as an independent union on August 31, 1980, by signing the Gdansk agreement with Solidarity representatives led by Lech Wałęsa, an electrician at the Gdansk shipyard. The most important agreements legalized the workers' right to strike and to organize independent trade unions, and a significant portion of the population saw it as the basis for creating a new order in Poland.[2]

The crisis caused by Solidarity's rise was notable because far more people than before were willing to risk the regime's censure by showing their dissatisfaction with the failings of the existing economic and political structure.[3] An important impetus for this change in popular mood was the 1978 election of a Polish cardinal as Pope John Paul II. In a country where almost 90 percent of the population declared itself Roman Catholic even under communist rule, this was a source of immense national pride. Indeed, John Paul's visit to Poland in June 1979 fed the sense of "human dignity" that was to provide a crucial foundation for Solidarity's demands.[4] This was also the first time that workers and intellectuals

---

1. For analyses of Solidarity and its role in Poland, see Timothy Garton Ash, *The Polish Revolution: Solidarity* (New York: Scribner's, 1983); David Ost, *Solidarity and the Politics of Anti-Politics: Opposition and Reform in Poland since 1968* (Philadelphia: Temple University Press, 1990); Maciej Lopinski, Marcin Moskit, and Mariusz Wilk, *Konspira: Solidarity Underground,* trans. Jane Cave (Berkeley, Calif.: University of California Press, 1990); Roman Laba, *The Roots of Solidarity: A Political Sociology of Poland's Working Class Democratization* (Princeton: Princeton University Press, 1991); and W.J. Twierdochlebow, *Solidarnosc: A Biblio-Historiography of the Gdansk Strike and Birth of the Solidarity Movement* (Menlo Park, Calif.: Center for the Study of Opposition in Poland, 1985).

2. For details on the Gdansk agreement, see Joseph Rothschild, *Return to Diversity: A Political History of East Central Europe Since World War II* (New York: Oxford University Press, 1989), pp. 200–203; and Ash, *The Polish Revolution: Solidarity,* pp. 68–71.

3. However, Poland had a long history of protest against communist rule. See Zbigniew K. Brzezinski, *The Soviet Bloc: Unity and Conflict,* rev. and enl. ed. (Cambridge, Mass.: Harvard University Press, 1960 and 1967).

4. Ash, *The Polish Revolution: Solidarity,* pp. 28–30; and J.F. Brown, *Eastern Europe and Communist Rule* (Durham, N.C.: Duke University Press, 1988), pp. 183–184.

had joined forces in Poland against the regime.[5] This greatly strengthened the protest, since a substantial majority of the population was thus aligned against the regime.

Linkages between the state's economic problems in the 1970s and Solidarity's rise were evident when inflation and price increases for consumer goods (made necessary by the country's deteriorating balance of trade payments) sparked riots in 1976, and later the strikes in the summer of 1980. More fundamental to Solidarity's rise was the fact that the Party had never succeeded fully in securing control over society. The Polish United Worker's Party (PUWP, Poland's Communist Party), never enjoyed much popular approval because of its bonds with the Soviet Union, which even during the interwar period had undermined the party's image.[6] Additionally, Communist Party authority in Poland was always more limited than in the other East European states, because it had been forced to concede the role of the Catholic Church in Polish society.[7]

The PUWP leadership was divided in its efforts to find an appropriate reaction to the 1980 crisis, with some groups favoring serious reform of the political system.[8] Its fragmentation led to Wojciech Jaruzelski's ever-expanding role in running the state. A military officer and minister

---

5. Many intellectuals, both individuals and groups, supported the workers, and volunteered to advise the union in its negotiations with the regime. A Worker's Defense Committee (KOR) had been formed by a group of intellectuals committed to giving legal assistance and aid to workers who suffered during the government crackdown following workers' riots that erupted in June 1976, again in reaction to an announcement by the government of price increases. KOR was later to become one of the core elements of Solidarity. Andrzej Korbonski points out that KOR was also unique in that it made its existence and actions public, thereby encouraging other independent groups to form. See Andrzej Korbonski, "Soviet Policy toward Poland," in Sarah Mieklejohn Terry, ed., *Soviet Policy in Eastern Europe* (New Haven, Conn.: Yale University Press, 1984), pp. 56–57; and Rothschild, *Return to Diversity*, p. 199.

6. In the interwar period, the Polish Communist Party was closely tied to that in the Soviet Union, and advocated policies that would have continued the subordination of Poland to Russia; this did not endear the party to the Polish people. This party was dissolved by the comintern in 1938, and in 1941–1942 the United Polish Workers Party, the forerunner of the PUWP, was formed. See William P. Avery, "Political Legitimacy and Crisis in Poland," *Political Science Quarterly*, Vol. 103, No. 1 (1988), pp. 111–130. See also Brzezinski, *The Soviet Bloc*, pp. 10, 48.

7. Bartolomej Kaminski, *The Collapse of State Socialism: The Case of Poland* (Princeton: Princeton University Press, 1991), p. 13.

8. This paralleled developments in Czechoslovakia in 1968, and indicated that the party was in danger of disintegrating. The growing rifts within the Party, into hard-line and liberal factions, contributed to the stalemate in negotiations with the new union.

of defense at the beginning of the crisis, Jaruzelski was appointed prime minister in February 1981, replacing Jozef Pinkowski, whose tenure had lasted only six months. His appointment was welcomed by both the Roman Catholic church and Solidarity, partly because the military in general was held in esteem in Poland, and because Jaruzelski was regarded as a Polish patriot and a man of principle. This was due both to the long-standing pride in the Polish army as a patriotic institution and to the myth that Jaruzelski had refused in 1976 to order Polish troops to fire on Polish workers.[9] By mid-October 1981 he was First Secretary of the Party as well. Though he was considered to be a moderate, and had supported the opening of a dialogue with the union in 1980,[10] Jaruzelski appears to have begun planning a crackdown on Solidarity in July 1981, prior to his appointment as Party head.[11] In the event, Jaruzelski declared martial law on December 13, 1981, arguably to prevent a far worse fate from befalling Poland.[12]

The crisis caused by Solidarity had a profound impact not only on Poland, but also throughout the Eastern bloc and in the Soviet Union. It illustrated the depth of the Polish population's hostility to the existing system of government in Poland, and put on the country's agenda the issue of citizens' rights to a greater say in their governance. This crisis also illuminated the depth of the economic problems in Eastern Europe, and made clear that the socialist system transplanted in Eastern Europe had thus far failed to keep its promises to the citizenry.

---

9. Brown, *Eastern Europe and Communist Rule*, pp. 187–188.

10. Konrad Syrop, "Warsaw Unpacked," *Times Literary Supplement*, March 5, 1993, p. 10; this is a book review of, among others, Jaruzelski's memoir, *Stan Vojenny*, and of Rakowski, *Jak To Sie Stalo*.

11. One emigré report suggests that the idea of imposing martial law was broached as early as August 1980. See "Special Report: Poland in Crisis, 1980–81," Interview with Ryszard Kuklinski; and "Commentary," *Orbis*, Vol. 32, No. 1 (Winter 1988), pp. 3–31. See also "Unlikely Detonator of Change," interview with Wojciech Jaruzelski, *Time*, December 31, 1990, pp. 34–35; and Korbonski, "Soviet Policy toward Poland," pp. 86–87.

12. Uncertainty remains about Jaruzelski's role in ordering martial law. Jaruzelski himself claimed that he took this step to prevent the worse fate of a Soviet intervention. But recent documents suggest both that the Soviet leadership was not planning to invade Poland in December 1981, and that Jaruzelski himself *asked* the Soviet leadership for "fraternal assistance." On this point, see Mark Kramer, "Jaruzelski, The Soviet Union, and the Imposition of Martial Law in Poland: New Light on the Mystery of December 1981"; "The Anoshkin Notebook on the Polish Crisis, December 1981," trans. Mark Kramer; and "Commentary," Wojciech Jaruzelski, all in *Cold War International History Project Bulletin*, No. 11 (Winter 1988), pp. 5–39; and Kramer, "Poland, 1980–81: Soviet Policy during the Polish Crisis," *Cold War International History Project Bulletin*, No. 5 (Spring 1995), pp. 1, 116–126.

Though the government managed to imprison many of Solidarity's leaders when it introduced martial law, it failed to crush the union. Instead, Solidarity went underground. It managed to establish core organizations and to publish and distribute underground literature; in the mid-1980s, underground printing was widespread throughout Poland, with 1,000 to 1,700 independent publications in circulation.[13] Yet throughout the 1980s, there was considerable disagreement within Solidarity over the strategies it ought to adopt: should it try to work with the government to encourage incremental reforms, or should it continue more explicitly to oppose the regime in the hope of causing it to collapse?[14]

Most Poles reacted to the government's efforts to gain its acquiescence following the crackdown with sullen apathy and a thorough distrust of the regime's attempts to reform the economy.[15] But support for Solidarity waned as well. In 1984, only 39 percent of the population favored legalizing opposition groups.[16] Popular sympathy for government and union was evenly balanced at 25 percent in 1988, with the rest of the population declaring indifference.[17]

Having instituted martial law, the government faced the challenge of regaining popular trust. The initial crackdown in December 1981 was extremely effective, resulting in the arrest of hundreds of Solidarity activists

---

13. Poland was thought to have the most liberal press in Eastern Europe, and by the mid-1980s the regime had essentially accepted that it could not stop this press. See Anna Sabbat-Swidlicka, "Poland's Underground Press," in Vojtech Mastny, ed., *Soviet/East European Survey, 1983–4: Selected Research and Analysis from RFE/RL* (Durham, N.C.: Duke University Press, 1985), pp. 172–190. See also Abraham Brumberg, "Poland: The New Opposition," *New York Review of Books,* February 18, 1988; and Ost, *Solidarity and the Politics of Anti-Politics,* pp. 176–177.

14. Some Solidarity members even advocated armed struggle against the regime. See Stefan Malski, "Political Diversification of the Polish Underground," in Vojtech Mastny, ed., *Soviet/East European Survey, 1983–4: Selected Research and Analysis from RFE/RL* (Durham, N.C.: Duke University Press, 1985), pp. 190–195; and Gail Stokes, *The Walls Came Tumbling Down: The Collapse of Communism in Eastern Europe* (New York: Oxford University Press, 1993), pp. 105–106.

15. Christopher Barclay and Richard Ware, "Background Paper: Reforming Poland," House of Commons Library Research, No. 218, July 18, 1989, pp. 12–13.

16. Andrzej Rychard, "Poglady Politiyczne," in Adamski et al., *Polacy '84: Raport z Badania,* as cited in David S. Mason, Daniel N. Nelson, and Bohdan M. Szklarski, "Apathy and the Birth of Democracy: The Polish Struggle," *East European Politics and Society,* Vol. 5, No. 2 (Spring 1991), p. 219.

17. This figure is from an opinion poll by Stefan Nowak, cited in Abraham Brumberg, "Poland, the New Opposition," in *New York Review of Books,* February 18, 1988.

within a few hours. But the government did not adopt harsh repressive measures and lifted the repressive measures associated with martial law relatively quickly, formally rescinding martial law in July 1983. This was possible partly because the government had introduced legislation incorporating many of the provisions of the martial law period into the state's legal framework.[18] The goal was to give the appearance, at least, of normalization.

As part of its attempt to achieve a reconciliation with the population, the government found itself tolerating a far more open society in Poland than existed elsewhere in Eastern Europe. Both the official and unofficial presses were far more liberal than those in other Eastern bloc countries, and travel to the West in the mid-1980s was simpler than in most other states.[19] Yet the best the regime was able to do in the early 1980s was to neutralize opposition to the regime. The regime's inability to reach some compromise with society was a primary reason that, over the years, it tried increasingly unorthodox means to address the country's political stalemate. This laid the groundwork for the Party's later willingness to accept Gorbachev's invitation to experiment more broadly with substantial political reforms.

POLISH POLITICS AFTER GORBACHEV'S APPOINTMENT

Unlike the conservative leaders who preceded him, Gorbachev clearly endorsed Jaruzelski's policies shortly after his ascendance as party leader in the Soviet Union in 1985. Not only was Jaruzelski's rule sanctioned by Gorbachev during his July 1985 visit to Warsaw for the renewal of the Warsaw Pact, but Jaruzelski received individual commendation by Gorbachev at the 27th Party Congress in February 1986. Gorbachev's ringing endorsement of Jaruzelski at the 10th PUWP Congress in June 1986 confirmed the new Soviet leader's attitude.[20]

---

18. Kaminski, *The Collapse of State Socialism*, p. 218.

19. This was not the case throughout the 1980s. The imposition of travel restrictions in 1981 as part of martial law had the ironic consequence of helping Solidarity; in contrast to Hungary in 1956 and Czechoslovakia in 1968, dissidents did not have the option of escaping to the West, so they stayed and continued their struggle. The often forced emigration in Hungary and Czechoslovakia (as well as East Germany during the 1970s and 1980s) prevented strong and cohesive opposition to the regime from developing. When Poland did ease restrictions, many Solidarity activists left, but not enough to decimate the movement. See Grzegorz Ekiert, *The State Against Society: Political Crises and Their Aftermath in East Central Europe* (Princeton: Princeton University Press, 1996), pp. 289–290.

20. See Sarah Mieklejohn Terry, "The Future of Poland: *Perestroika* or Perpetual Crisis?" in William E. Griffith, ed., *Central and Eastern Europe: The Opening Curtain?* (Boulder, Colo.: Westview Press, 1989), pp. 201–202.

Jaruzelski welcomed Gorbachev's leadership as well, in the hope that the new Soviet leader might grant him the leeway needed to solve Poland's economic and political troubles. The reforms Gorbachev introduced during the next few years were greeted with enthusiasm by Jaruzelski, and Poland's political and economic reforms were analogous to many of the steps being introduced by Gorbachev.[21]

Not surprisingly, Poland supported the reforms Gorbachev announced at the 27th Party Congress more actively than any other country in the bloc. Indeed, the Party program that the Polish regime announced at the 10th PUWP Congress showed that it anticipated more latitude in trying to solve its domestic problems. The draft document played on traditional Polish patriotism to gain support for the regime, recognized the role of the Catholic Church as a legitimate actor in Poland's future, and acknowledged "class contradictions" in Polish society. In these respects, the Polish party went further than the Soviet Union had in reinterpreting socialism.[22]

Jaruzelski followed these changes with new efforts to address the PUWP's poor relations with the population. Crackdowns on dissent had continued and even intensified in 1985 and early 1986 with some notable successes on the regime's part; Zbigniew Bujak, Solidarity's underground leader since the imposition of martial law, was finally arrested early in 1986.[23] Yet Jaruzelski announced a complete amnesty for political prisoners that September. This helped the regime's standing with the population and the Church and removed one of the opposition's strongest rallying points, and also improved Poland's standing in the West.[24] Jaruzelski also formed a "Social Consultative Council" to advise the government in

---

21. As a result of this, and complementing it, a warm relationship developed between Gorbachev and Jaruzelski. Georgii Shakhnazarov, *Tsena Svobodi: Reformatsiya Gorbacheva Glazami evo Pomoshchnika* [The value of freedom: Gorbachev's reforms through the eyes of his aide] (Moskva: Rossika * Zevs, 1993), pp. 101, 117; Gorbachev, *Zhizn' i Reformi* [Life and reforms], vol. 2 (Moskva: Novosti, 1994) pp. 346–347; B.A. Medvedev, *Raspad: Kak On Nazreval v "Mirovoi Sisteme Sotsialisma"* [Collapse: How it developed in the "world socialist system"] (Moskva: Mezhdynarodnie Otnoshenia, 1994), p. 84.

22. "The Draft Program of the PZPR," *Trybuna Ludu* (Poland) (supplement), February 10, 1986, in *Foreign Broadcast Information Service: Eastern Europe* [hereafter *FBIS: EEU*], March 5, 1986.

23. Brown, *Eastern Europe and Communist Rule*, p. 198.

24. Shortly thereafter, the U.S. government lifted the economic sanctions it had imposed on Poland shortly after martial law was declared. Both the Church and Solidarity advocated lifting the sanctions at this point. See Brown, "Poland Since Martial Law," pp. 9–11; and Ekiert, *The State against Society*, pp. 302–303.

policy formation; its members included church activists and former Solidarity members as well as Party members. Few Solidarity figures accepted the invitation to participate, but some respected members of the intellectual community took part, with the stipulation that all proceedings be public. Only one meeting took place, with no clear agenda for discussion.[25] Jaruzelski's efforts to undercut Solidarity and give outside groups such as the Church at least a consultative voice in politics fit a pattern of efforts to liberalize the political spectrum seen in authoritarian states in other regions. He was the only East European leader at the time who appeared to be trying to coopt at least some segments of the population to support him—albeit with mixed results.

In contrast, the economic provisions of the plan announced at the 10th PUWP Congress did little to alter the state's centralized economic system. Instead, the plan essentially recommended a retreat from the few reforms that had been implemented during the previous five years. Interestingly, this proposal met with strong opposition from both the state's parliament, the Sejm, and the official trade unions, which were resistant to what they perceived as a retreat from the limited reform that had been already implemented after 1982: worker participation in management.[26] The economic situation in the country continued to deteriorate, which was probably one of the reasons the PUWP wanted to retreat from the earlier reforms; the regime was forced to implement austerity measures in December 1986.

In 1987, the regime presented new reform proposals that represented a serious attempt to introduce economic reforms. The proposals showed Jaruzelski's willingness to reconsider his economic policies, and also ech-

---

25. Jaruzelski stressed the importance of working for "the actual good of the nation. . . . Our goal will be the constant and irreversible quest for forms and institutions that will enhance democratization in the sense of genuine participation . . . and will at the same time, be appropriate to the conditions that obtain under a socialist system." "Jaruzelski: Speech to Consultative Council," *Trybuna Ludu*, December 8, 1986, in *FBIS:EEU*, December 15, 1986; Michael T. Kaufman, "Warsaw Learns a New Word: 'Democratization,'" *New York Times*, February 13, 1987; and Ost, *Solidarity and the Politics of Anti-Politics*, p. 173. For opposition concerns about the nature of the Council, see "Memorandum of a Conversation, 18 October 1986," in *Cold War International History Project Bulletin* [hereafter *CWIHP Bulletin*], Issue 12/13 (Fall/Winter 2001), pp. 96–98.

26. A new "official" trade union confederation was created in January 1983 to give the impression that trade unions were possible. But the best known of these, the OPZZ, was clearly progovernment rather than independent in orientation. J.F. Brown has pointed out that this was one of the few times prior to 1989 when these bodies actually functioned within the parameters of their intended role as channels for public opinion. See "Poland Since Martial Law," p. 15; and Kaminski, *The Collapse of State Socialism*, pp. 231–232.

oed the increasingly rapid pace of change being advocated in the Soviet Union.[27] The economic proposals presented in 1987 were similar to the second stage of the economic plan that Jaruzelski had launched in 1982: the government would be reorganized; all enterprises were to be induced to achieve greater efficiency and economy by greater decentralization of planning; and the country's price and income structures were to be remodeled.[28] The government also announced that a package of massive price increases would be introduced in early 1988, arguing that it would be less inflationary to raise prices all at once than to increase them gradually.[29] The government took the highly unusual step in November 1987 of holding a public referendum on the political and economic reforms it proposed. The referendum asked first whether the population would accept the necessary austerity measures to end shortages and to make more investment possible in the long run, and second if it would approve more democratization of the country through the granting of greater rights of participation to the public.

This was the regime's first attempt to open a political decision to nation-wide approbation—a first cautious step toward political liberalization. The regime did not present a truly open choice to the population, since the referendum asked for acceptance or rejection of one alternative presented by the government. Nonetheless, the regime saw some value in convincing the population to support the difficult measures, thereby implying that popular opinions mattered to the functioning of the state.

The referendum backfired. It failed to win the absolute majority that was required by the constitution because voter turnout was too low, even though it was accepted by almost two-thirds of those who voted, largely because many people did not understand the complicated balloting procedures and the phrasing of the propositions. Nonetheless, the relatively high "yes" vote was an acknowledgement of some support for the government's plans, both because a significant portion of those who voted

---

27. Gorbachev's visit to Poland in July 1987 demonstrated that he continued to back Jaruzelski and that his encouragement of greater experimentation by his allies was very real, since Gorbachev approved Jaruzelski's unorthodox methods of trying to solve the country's internal problems.

28. Barclay and Ware, "Background Paper: Reforming Poland," p. 8. See also Kaminski, *The Collapse of State Socialism*, pp. 228–229; *Eastern Europe and the USSR: Economic Structure and Analysis* (London: The Economist Intelligence Unit, 1988), p. 145; and Stokes, *The Walls Came Tumbling Down*, pp. 119–120.

29. Food was to increase by 110 percent, while gas, coal, and electricity would jump by 140 percent. This proved a forerunner of the "shock therapy" introduced after the change in government in 1989. See Barclay and Ware, "Background Paper: Reforming Poland," p. 9.

accepted the need for harsh austerity measures, and because so many people voted in an election for which Solidarity had advocated a national boycott.[30] However, the dire state of the economy meant that the government was compelled to go forward with a modified version of the measures. Energy price increases went ahead, though the government announced that increases in food prices would be phased in over four years rather than the originally planned two to three. The reform process slowed as a result.[31]

THE INITIATION OF REFORM

By the end of 1987, some leaders in both the regime and the opposition acknowledged the need for cooperation to solve the country's problems. Jaruzelski had begun making efforts to coopt segments of the population to discuss solutions to the country's problems in late 1986, with the formation of the Social Consultative Council. The editor of the Party's ideological journal, *Nowe Drogi*, asserted shortly thereafter that "this government is willing to share power, of course not on a 50–50 basis. The party will hold the deciding power."[32] The 1987 referendum was another effort to engage the population in support of the regime's economic reform efforts. In evaluating the planned economic reforms, some groups within the PUWP also examined the role the Party itself should play in society, concluding that "the party does not pretend to the right of owning a monopoly of rule," and "the subject of a socialist opposition" should be raised. Party spokesman Jerzy Urban suggested that plans existed to "limit the role of the Party in all areas of public life."[33] These statements and actions pointed to a willingness by the regime to consider solutions that were radical by the standards of the socialist bloc, though not so radical as to bring its control into question.

The opposition's attitude had changed as well. Solidarity had remained demoralized in the early Gorbachev period.[34] Recognizing that it must respond to the amnesty of political prisoners in the fall of 1986 if it

---

30. Brown, "Poland Since Martial Law," pp. 24–26.

31. *Eastern Europe and the USSR*, p. 148; and Barclay and Ware, "Background Paper: Reforming Poland," p. 9.

32. Ludwik Krasucki, cited in Kaufman, "Warsaw Learns a New Word: Democratization."

33. As quoted in Brumberg, "Poland: The New Opposition."

34. On declining identification with the union, see Mason, Nelson, and Szklarski, "Apathy and the Birth of Democracy," p. 208; see also Ekiert, *The State against Society*, p. 284; and Stokes, *The Walls Came Tumbling Down*, p. 111.

was to remain viable, Solidarity announced its willingness to talk with the regime, but only if Solidarity was first legalized.[35]

The 1987 referendum changed the union's attitude toward the regime. The outcome of the referendum presented a puzzle: why did the regime admit defeat, rather than doctor the results to claim victory? There appeared to be two possible explanations: the Party was split, and those favoring reform were unwilling to accept falsification of the results; or some in the Party simply wanted to ensure the honesty of the process.[36] Both alternatives suggested that a serious reform group existed within the regime, sparking a debate over whether the union should work with this group.[37] Bronislaw Geremek, one of the union's leading intellectuals, proposed an "anti-crisis pact" between opposition and society, suggesting that they work together to address the country's economic problems. Geremek's proposal was published in a new officially approved journal, rather than the underground press, an indication that some in the regime were open to the possibility of discussions.[38]

The reawakening of Solidarity as a political force during a short-lived round of strikes in May 1988 further recharged Poland's political climate.[39] Ironically, Solidarity's leadership was divided about supporting these strikes, because many Solidarity activists and intellectuals were more concerned with changing the country's economic and political sys-

---

35. Brumberg, "A New Deal in Poland?" *New York Review of Books*, January 15, 1987, p. 33; Wiktor Osiatynski, "The Roundtable Talks in Poland," in Jon Elster, ed., *The Roundtable Talks and the Breakdown of Communism* (Chicago: University of Chicago Press, 1996), p. 27; "Letter of Lech Wałęsa to the Council of State," in *CWIHP Bulletin*, Vol. 12/13 (Fall/Winter 2001), p. 94.

36. Aleksander Paszynski, "Questions After the Referendum," *Tygodnik Mazowsze*, (Poland), December 9, 1987, reprinted in *East European Reporter*, Vol. 3, No. 2 (March 1988), p. 34.

37. Jan Litynski, "The Referendum" in *Tygodnik Mazowsze*, December 2, 1987; Paszynski, "Questions after the Referendum" in *Tygodnik Mazowsze*, December 9, 1987; and "Warsaw's Regional Executive Statement of 13 December 1987," in *Tygodnik Mazowsze*, January 20, 1988, all reprinted in *East European Reporter*, Vol. 3, No. 2 (March 1988), pp. 33–35. See also Brumberg, "Poland: The New Opposition."

38. Osiatynski, The Roundtable Talks in Poland," p. 27. Historian Jerzy Holzer also wrote to both Jaruzelski and Wałęsa urging them to hold talks without preconditions. See "Historian Writes Jaruzelski, Weekly Responds," Warsaw PAP (Polish News Service), January 15, 1988, in *FBIS:EEU*, January 19, 1988; see also "Warsaw's Regional Executive Statement of 13 December 1987."

39. The strikes did not spread widely and came to a demoralizing close after a nine-day sit-in at the Gdansk shipyard, as workers yielded and returned to their jobs. *Time*, September 5, 1988, pp. 4–6.

tem than with fighting for higher pay.[40] The strikes also illustrated the growing divide between Solidarity activists and younger workers who were, by the late 1980s, alienated from the regime and distrustful of Solidarity's leadership.[41] This disaffection may have made the regime recognize that it could lose its opportunity to negotiate if did not talk with Solidarity while the union still commanded sufficient moral force in society to sway the population.[42]

The regime approached Lech Wałęsa about the possibility of negotiations between the regime and the union in July 1988.[43] In August, another round of strikes ensued, which by mid-month were spreading across the country, as in 1980. Workers were beginning to return to their jobs by the end of the month, giving the impression that the government's resistance had broken the workers' resolve.[44] On August 31, 1988, however, a regime representative met with Wałęsa, and the regime announced that it had offered to begin a dialogue between the government, opposition groups, and official organizations, as well as the Catholic Church. The regime proposed holding Round Table discussions on the country's future that would address, among other things, the question of the legality of independent trade unions, freedom of association, and the formation of a national council to deal with the country's problems—in effect, a discussion of limited power-sharing with opposition and societal groups.[45] Implicit in this offer was a tacit agreement to accept Solidarity in some form, and the talks were predicated on Wałęsa's ability to bring the remaining strikes to an end, which he did with some difficulty.[46]

While the regime's proposal to negotiate with the opposition was a dramatic departure from previous policy, it coincided with analogous political changes in the Soviet Union. For three years, Gorbachev had been encouraging his East European allies to respond to their domestic conditions, and this position had been stated most forthrightly in Yugoslavia in

---

40. Ost, *Solidarity and the Politics of Anti-Politics*, p. 183.

41. Lech Wałęsa, *The Struggle and the Triumph: An Autobiography* (New York: Arcade Publishing, 1991), pp. 152–59.

42. Osiatynski, "The Roundtable Talks in Poland," pp. 58–59.

43. Ibid., pp. 23, 28.

44. "It's Wałęsa Again," *Economist*, September 3, 1988, p. 45–46.

45. This was the first time the Round Table terminology was used in connection with a discussion between regime and opposition in Eastern Europe.

46. Wałęsa, *The Struggle and the Triumph*, pp. 157–160; and Osiatynski, "The Roundtable Talks in Poland," p. 28.

March 1988.[47] Jaruzelski had also apparently discussed the political changes he was considering with Gorbachev in July 1988 during Gorbachev's visit to Poland, and Gorbachev had expressed only enthusiasm.[48] This made the initiation of discussions with the opposition less of a gamble.[49]

The entire Polish government resigned during the parliamentary session in September, apparently due to its failure to solve the country's economic and political problems. The appointment of Mieczysław Rakowski as the new prime minister on September 26, however, raised concern about whether the government intended to follow through on the proposed discussions with the opposition. While Rakowski was viewed outside the country as one of the reformers within the Party leadership, he had been the government's negotiator with Solidarity in 1980 and was an outspoken opponent of the union. He also loathed Wałęsa, and was clearly against holding official talks with Solidarity.[50] Though talks with

---

47. While touring Yugoslavia in the spring, Gorbachev stressed the diversity of socialism and the right of each nation to pursue independent development, emphasizing that outsiders lacked "any claim to impose their own ideas about social development upon anyone else whomsoever." His emphasis on internal autonomy was accompanied by comments that suggested a similar change in Moscow's view of international relations. Gorbachev noted that "every country has its voice in the general chorus of the community of nations. . . . The time has passed when a handful of big states made decisions for the whole world and divided it into spheres of influence according to the law of might is right." See Mikhail S. Gorbachev, "Address to the Federal Assembly," from Belgrade Home Service, March 16, 1988, in *BBC Summary of World Broadcasts: Eastern Europe* [hereafter *SWB:EE*], March 18, 1988; and "USSR-Yugoslav Joint Declaration," *Pravda*, March 19, 1988, in *SWB:EE*, March 21, 1988.

48. Shakhnazarov, *Tsena Svobodii*, p. 117; Medvedev, *Raspad*, pp. 89–91; and Jacques Lévesque, *The Enigma of 1989: the USSR and the Liberation of Eastern Europe* (Berkeley: University of California Press, 1997), p. 112.

49. By the summer of 1988 Gorbachev was moving toward the introduction of partially free elections in the Soviet Union itself. At the 19th Party Conference in June and July 1988, a new Congress of People's Deputies was proposed. It was to be made up of a new legislative body and a smaller version of the existing Supreme Soviet. Elections for the legislative body would be competitive—meaning more candidates would run than the number of available seats, though they would be chosen from lists nominated by the Communist Party and other approved groups and organizations, such as the Academy of Sciences. Legislation amending the constitution to legalize this new body, and voting procedures for it, were passed by the existing Supreme Soviet on December 1, 1988. On the 19th Party Conference, see Archie Brown, *The Gorbachev Factor* (Oxford: Oxford University Press, 1996), pp. 175–184.

50. Rakowski's behavior was complex. While he closed the Lenin shipyard in Gdansk, which at the time appeared to be a deliberate assault on Solidarity, he also was remarkably candid in some circles about the dangers if the Party was unable to re-

official and unofficial groups were scheduled to begin in October, they were delayed by disputes between the different groups. The regime accused the opposition of obstructing the process by setting conditions for the beginning of negotiations. Disagreements arose over both the composition of Solidarity's delegation in the talks, and whether Solidarity should be legalized prior to any negotiations.[51]

The regime committed a major blunder, however, in allowing a debate between Wałęsa and Alfred Miodowicz, head of the official trade union set up to counter Solidarity in 1982, to be televised live throughout the country in early December. All commentators, including government ones, agreed that Wałęsa "won" the debate by eloquently presenting Solidarity's point of view.[52] Yet regime and opposition were unable to get to the negotiating table in 1988, and the economy continued to deteriorate.

THE ROUND TABLE NEGOTIATIONS AND THEIR AFTERMATH

The stalemate over negotiations was broken in January 1989, for two reasons. First, at a private meeting between Wałęsa and General Czeslaw Kiszczak, the government's negotiator, that was mediated by the Church at Magdalenka, Wałęsa accepted that Solidarity's legalization could be the result of the talks, rather than a precondition.[53] Second, also in January the Party agreed to the legalization of the union after a heated internal debate during the second session of the 10th Plenum of the PUWP.[54] Jaruzelski's insistence on this move was apparently decisive; he put the issue of political and union pluralism on the agenda for the plenum, and at a closed session on this question, Jaruzelski and several others in the

---

solve the country's problems. More clearly than most, he also laid out the danger to the Party's authority should it lose the support of its Soviet patron: "But what if that 'somebody,' bearing in mind his own interests, does not want to intervene?" Quoted in Timothy Garton Ash, "Reform or Revolution?" *New York Review of Books,* October 27, 1988; see also "Statement by Premier Mieczysław Rakowski," Polish TV and Warsaw Home Service, October 13, 1988, in *SWB:EE,* October 17, 1988; Barclay and Ware, "Background Paper: Reforming Poland," p. 10; and Stokes, *The Walls came Tumbling Down,* p. 123.

51. Wałęsa, *The Struggle and the Triumph,* pp. 159–167; and Osiatynski, "The Roundtable Talks in Poland," p. 29; Letter from A. Stelmachowski to Józef Glemp, Primate of Poland, 24 October 1988," in *CWIHP Bulletin,* Issue 12/13 (Fall/Winter 2001) pp. 107–108.

52. One pertinent comment came from Miodowicz; see "Rakowski 21 December 'Closed Door' Speech Cited," *Suddeutsch Zeitung* (West Germany), January 7–8, 1989, in *FBIS:EEU,* January 10, 1989.

53. Osiatynski, "The Roundtable Talks in Poland," p. 29.

54. The first session was held on December 17 and 18.

Politburo submitted their resignations to the meeting should this policy not be endorsed.[55]

Round Table discussions began in February. Negotiations centered in three areas: trade union pluralism; political reforms; and social and economic reforms, with a myriad of smaller issues relegated to smaller negotiating groups.[56] The pace of dialogue accelerated quickly, if not always smoothly,[57] over the next month. Though the negotiations were conducted in a closed forum, Solidarity spokesmen were careful to stress that whatever agreement was reached must be made public, to prevent post-facto efforts to tamper with the results of the discussions. Each day's negotiation ended with a press conference, and Solidarity's leaders also held weekly meetings open to the public to discuss the process, to ensure that the population would not perceive the eventual agreement as secret or an elite bargain.[58] Neither Jaruzelski nor Lech Wałęsa were involved in daily negotiations.[59]

The Round Table discussions culminated on April 5, 1989. The negotiators agreed to a power-sharing formula for the existing house of the

---

55. A vote of confidence on Jaruzelski's leadership passed, and was followed by a "unanimous" vote of approval for "the stand of the Central Committee on political pluralism and union pluralism." See "Closed Session on Pluralism," Warsaw Domestic Service, January 17, 1989, in *FBIS:EEU,* January 18, 1989; and "Jaruzelski Vote of Confidence," Warsaw PAP, January 18, 1989, in *FBIS:EEU,* January 18, 1989. On Jaruzelski's outlook on pluralism, see "Speech by Wojciech Jaruzelski," Warsaw Home Service," January 16, 1989, in *SWB:EE,* January 18, 1989. See also William Pfaff, "Poland: An Uncertain Path, but the Only One," *International Herald Tribune* [hereafter *IHT*], February 3, 1989; and Michael Simmons, "Party Hardliners Rattle Jaruzelski," *The Guardian,* January 19, 1989. The issue of pluralism was also reported in the Soviet Union; see Jan Lysek and Ryszard Najderski, "Country on a Hairpin Bend," *New Times,* No. 5, 1989, p. 28.

56. In addition, the earlier discussions at Magdalenka were continued. These provided an important venue where the top negotiators could resolve impasses that had developed in the process. For a detailed overview of the Round Table negotiations in Poland, see Osiatynski, "The Roundtable Talks in Poland," pp. 21–59.

57. High-level Solidarity officials have noted that the PUWP accepted the union's demands on the first day of negotiations, which then led to some scrambling to see what more might be possible. From author's interviews in Warsaw, April 1991.

58. Osiatynski, "The Roundtable Talks in Poland," p. 32. This did not eliminate disagreement within different factions of Solidarity. See "Letter from Andrzej Słowik to "Roundtable" Chair Władysław Findeisin, 12 February 1989," in *CWIHP Bulletin,* Issue 12/13 (Fall/Winter 2001), pp. 109–110.

59. Jaruzelski clearly helped shape the PUWP's negotiating position, and Wałęsa worked with General Kiszczak in the Magdalenka discussions. For one analysis of Jaruzelski's role in the negotiations, see Jackson Diehl, "Jaruzelski Seeks Image Shift: Tough Party Boss to Statesman," *IHT,* March 21, 1989.

Sejm, in which 65 percent of the seats would be allotted to the PUWP and its "coalition" partners, the United Peasant's Party and the Democratic Party. The remaining 35 percent of the seats would be filled in free elections. A new post of president was established with a six-year term, which the PUWP insisted on controlling for the first term. The new position appeared to be designed for Jaruzelski, to give him a way to end his career with dignity. The opposition's quid pro quo was the creation of a new and freely elected upper chamber of the Sejm.[60] The Round Table agreement also legalized Solidarity as a trade union,[61] accepted the legal right of an opposition media to exist, and granted legal status to the Church for the first time under communist rule.[62] The weakest part of the Round Table accord lay in the failure to agree on how to solve the country's economic problems, and the provisions for dealing with this issue were therefore vague.[63]

Elections for the Sejm were held on June 4, 1989, and the PUWP was rejected decisively. Only 2 of the party's slate of 33 candidates who ran unopposed, and 5 of the candidates for the 299 communist-controlled seats contested only by party members, received enough votes even to gain a seat in the Sejm.[64] Solidarity candidates, in contrast, won an

---

60. The idea of a new chamber for the parliament was broached in the fall, but the possibility of free elections to fill it was not. According to reports that appeared after the Solidarity government was installed, the agreement on free elections grew out of an off-the-cuff comment made by a junior member of the PUWP's delegation, which was seized upon by Solidarity's negotiators. See Jackson Diehl, "Poland: `Free Elections,' the Irretrievable Words," *IHT*, January 15, 1990; "Jerzy Urban's 13 September Press Conference, *Rzeczpospolita* (Poland), September 14, 1988, in *FBIS:EEU*, September 20, 1988.

61. Solidarity's status as a political "party" was not clarified. Indeed, the various groups within Solidarity did not agree on whether the union should take on the role of political party. By early 1991, two factions of Solidarity had split apart and created separate and specifically political groupings, while the union had reaffirmed its role as a trade union. See, for some examples, Stephen Engelberg, "Solidarity is Uniting Behind Wałesa," *New York Times*, November 30, 1990; and Engelberg, "Poland Agrees to IMF Aid and Asks Solidarity's Help," *New York Times*, February 25, 1991.

62. Jackson Diehl, "Agreement Legalizes Solidarity," *IHT*, April 6, 1989.

63. Ironically, the officially sanctioned trade union headed by Miodowicz complicated the search for economic solutions because it demanded the indexation of wages to inflation, a major concern of the workers, in an effort to woo support from Solidarity's traditional constituency. "Agreement Legalizes Solidarity," *IHT*, April 6, 1989.

64. The Party had blundered badly in the way it set up the election process, whereby even unopposed candidates for safe seats had to receive 50 percent of the votes cast in order to win a seat in the parliament. Ash described what he calls "the glorious work of deletion": voting was done with great gusto by crossing out unfavored candidates.

overwhelming victory, garnering 99 percent of the seats that they contested.

The Party acknowledged its loss within days of the tabulation of votes, and even conceded that this defeat reflected its estrangement from the population.[65] Party spokesmen almost immediately broached the creation of a coalition government to lead the country, and called on the opposition to join it.[66] Solidarity was equally surprised by its victory, and initially was concerned that the Party's disastrous showing could have negative consequences for the process as a whole. Solidarity spokesmen were careful to reassure the Party that it could fill its seats in the Sejm as it chose, which would preserve the power balance brokered in the spring.[67] Yet Solidarity rejected the call for a coalition.[68]

The Party's control of the presidency, however, came into question at the first session of the new Sejm in July, accompanied by demands for the formation of a Solidarity government. The PUWP's bargaining position with the new opposition was complicated by the increasing efforts of its former client parties, the Peasants and the Democrats, to disassociate themselves from their previous alliance with the PUWP. Despite objections from the floor to holding a one-candidate election, Jaruzelski was elected president on July 19. His election was based partly on his promise to resign his position as party leader; this post went to Mieczysław Rakowski.

Timothy Garton Ash, *We the People: The Revolution of 1989 Witnessed in Warsaw, Budapest, Berlin and Prague* (Cambridge: Granta Books, 1990), pp. 27–28.

65. Lévesque notes that Jaruzelski met with the Central Committee in two groups, so that a vote of confidence in him would not be possible. See *The Enigma of 1989*, p. 118; and "Jaruzelski Chairs 12–13 June Party Meetings," Warsaw PAP, June 13, 1989, in *FBIS:EEU*, June 14, 1989.

66. The coincidence in timing with the crackdown by the Chinese Communist Party on the democracy demonstrations in Tiananmen Square may have given the Polish leadership additional incentive to make its support for the election results clear. On Jaruzelski's efforts to make his endorsement of the process clear, see "Monopoly Rule has Ended, Jaruzelski Says," *IHT*, June 30, 1989; "[Jaruzelski] Interviewed on Election," London ITV Television Network, June 10, 1989, in *FBIS:EEU*, June 12, 1989; "Jaruzelski Praises Wałęsa on French Television," PAP, June 12, 1989, in *FBIS:EEU*, June 13, 1989; and "Jaruzelski Speaks at Brussels Foreign Institute, PAP, June 12, 1989, in *FBIS:EEU*, June 13, 1989.

67. "Election Results: Solidarity to Follow Agreement," Warsaw Domestic Service, June 6, 1989, in *FBIS:EEU*, June 7, 1989.

68. "Party, Solidarity View Results," Warsaw Television Service, June 5, 1989, in *FBIS:EEU*, June 6, 1989; and "Solidarity Rules out Coalition," Paris AFP (Agence France Presse), June 6, 1989, in *FBIS:EEU*, June 6, 1989.

There was growing resistance within Solidarity, however, to any prospect of joining a communist-led coalition government after winning so decisively in the spring elections.[69] Jaruzelski wanted Solidarity to join a communist-led coalition, and Rakowski, still acting as prime minister until a new government was formed, recommended General Kiszczak for this post on August 1. Even though Kiszczak had behaved honorably during the Round Table negotiations, Solidarity considered him unacceptable due to the role he had played in the imposition of martial law and to his association with the previous regime.[70] On August 8, Wałęsa proposed a coalition with the Democrat's and Peasant's parties, without Communist Party participation.[71] In mid-month, Kiszczak resigned his candidacy for the prime ministership, proposing the chairman of the Peasant's Party, while on August 17 Wałęsa reiterated his offer of a Solidarity-led coalition, but this time suggested PUWP participation in such a government. Jaruzelski accepted this proposal on August 18, and the following day designated Tadeusz Mazowiecki, a staunch Catholic and long-time adviser to Solidarity, to be prime minister.[72] The PUWP continued to insist that it have several ministerial posts, including the ministries of the interior, communication, and defense. Mazowiecki was elected prime minister on August 24, making the new Polish government the first noncommunist-led government in the Eastern bloc in forty years; his list of cabinet nominations was submitted to the Sejm on September 8, and was approved a few days later. Communist Party members retained the key defense and interior portfolios, and the PUWP pledged its support of the new government, and that it would not be a "destructive force" in the state.[73] Despite the only partially free character of the elections, the new government clearly had the mandate of the population.

---

69. "Michnik for Party President, Solidarity Premier," Warsaw PAP, July 3, 1989, in *FBIS:EEU*, July 3, 1989.

70. "Gang of Three," *Economist*, August 5, 1989, pp. 40–41; "Anti-Kiszczak Election Mutiny," Paris AFP, August 1, 1989, in *FBIS:EEU*, August 2, 1989; and Osiatynski, "The Roundtable Talks in Poland," p. 55.

71. "Wałęsa Proposes SD-ZSL Coalition Government," Paris AFP, August 7, 1989, in *FBIS:EEU*, August 8, 1989; and Stokes, *The Walls Came Tumbling Down*, p. 129.

72. "Wałęsa Foresees Continuing Communist Role," Paris AFP, August 17, 1989, in *FBIS:EEU*, August 18, 1989; and "Jaruzelski to Designate Solidarity Candidate," Warsaw PAP, August 17, 1989, and "[Jaruzelski] Offers Premiership to Mazowiecki," Paris AFP, August 18, 1989, both in *FBIS:EEU*, August 18, 1989; and "Communique Names Mazowiecki Premier," Warsaw PAP, August 19, 1989, in *FBIS:EEU*, August 21, 1989.

73. "Cabinet Installed in Poland," *IHT*, September 13, 1989.

The PUWP, which had clearly underestimated both its own lack of support and Solidarity's popularity, faced a severe crisis as a result of these dramatic changes. At a party congress held in January 1990, the PUWP followed the Hungarian party's example and dissolved itself. It created a new socialist party called the Social Democratic Party of the Polish Republic (SDRP) in an effort to gain more national support, and appointed a relative unknown, Aleksander Kwasniewski, as the new party's head.

Measuring the Regime's Attitude Toward Reform

I have proposed that the PUWP regime's outlook on two crucial issues was critical to its decision to introduce reforms relatively early in the transformation that eventually enveloped the Warsaw Pact. These issues are the regime's recognition of the need for political changes, and the regime's confidence that it can survive in a more open political climate. This section evaluates the first of these two factors; the next section evaluates the second.

A regime would recognize the need for reform if it was aware of the urgency of economic repairs, and was cognizant that economic reforms without political reforms would be unlikely to succeed. To measure these I examine four intermingled variables: the magnitude of the problems facing the state; the nature of previous reform efforts in the state, particularly before Gorbachev came to power in 1985; the degree of socialist "orthodoxy" of the state's economic and political structure, and the ties its leaders made in Moscow; and the regime's apparent willingness to use the opportunity presented by Gorbachev to introduce reforms.

THE MAGNITUDE OF POLAND'S ECONOMIC PROBLEMS
Poland's economy was in disastrous condition in the early 1980s. The economy deteriorated badly during the late 1970s, and then worsened in the Solidarity period. Martial law compounded the situation further. The ambitious economic reforms begun in January 1982 were constrained by the simultaneous militarization of the economy, as officers were given oversight of industries. Additionally, the state's distribution system was not changed in the 1982 reforms; even with self-management, factories depended on supplies of raw materials whose delivery they could not guarantee, while they still had to meet productivity requirements set by central plan guidelines.[74] Moreover, the economic apparatus of the social-

---

74. Barclay and Ware, "Background Paper: Reforming Poland," pp. 6–7.

ist state obstructed efforts to introduce reforms, due to the bureaucracies' suspicion of the changes proposed.[75] Added to the problems posed by the bureaucracy, the way that reforms were implemented tended to make them less effective. Prices were increased in early 1982, for example, but they were still changed periodically, rather than being made elastic so that they could respond to market demand.[76]

As a result, the economy continued to deteriorate rather than improve. Food prices increased 305 percent over three years, while investment spending fell by 12.1 percent overall between 1980 and 1985. Manufacturing output was 10.9 percent lower in 1985 than it had been in 1979, the last year before the Solidarity crisis began.[77] Agriculture fared somewhat better in the early 1980s than it had at the end of the 1970s. Nonetheless, the national income per person in Poland in 1985 was 20 percent lower than it had been in 1973.[78] As an indication of the difficulties the regime faced in resolving the country's problems, its policies tended to work at cross purposes. Both the Party and industrial managers tended to buy the acquiescence of the population by increasing wages, for example, rather than enacting reforms to improve production. This added to inflationary pressures.[79]

Poland's economy also suffered because its foreign debt skyrocketed during the early 1980s, reaching $39 billion in 1988. The imposition of sanctions by the West in response to martial law hurt the country's ability to service its debt, and its Eastern bloc allies could offer little direct financial support.[80] The regime's cognizance of the staggering economic

---

75. Kaminski, *The Collapse of State Socialism*, p. 218.

76. Cezary Jozefiak, "The Polish Reform: A Tentative Evaluation," in Hubert Gabrisch, ed., *Economic Reforms in Eastern Europe and the Soviet Union* (Boulder, Colo: Westview Press, 1989), pp. 142–143.

77. Ekiert, *The State Against Society*, p. 293; and *Eastern Europe and the USSR: Economic Structure and Analysis*, p. 153.

78. The net national income at constant prices in 1986 was 1 percent above the 1980 level. See Barclay and Ware, "Background Paper," p. 6–7.

79. *Eastern Europe and the USSR: Economic Structure and Analysis*, p. 149.

80. In 1981 Poland had received $670 million in Western food credits, and $70 million of surplus food. Its debt repayment of $80 million to Western lenders had been rescheduled. The impact of Western sanctions on the Polish economy is evident in the decline of trade with the West, from $7.5 billion in 1980 to roughly $1 billion in 1983. Ekiert, *The State Against Society*, pp. 301–302. Stokes has also pointed out that Western sanctions forced Poland to reorient its economy toward the Soviet bloc, after having worked in the 1970s to expand its ability to export to Western markets. This hindered efforts to improve the efficiency of various industries. See *The Walls Came Tumbling*

problems the debt burden created was evident in its efforts to work toward lifting martial law, which would make the lifting of Western sanctions more likely.[81] Indeed, the government succeeded in reestablishing its relations with Western banks in 1985, and Poland was allowed back into the International Monetary Fund (IMF) in June 1986.[82] Its efforts to introduce reforms and to stabilize economic and political conditions in the country in order to alleviate the ongoing crisis leave little doubt that the regime was aware of the country's dire economic condition.

PRIOR REFORM EFFORTS IN POLAND

Poland's economic and political malaise in the 1980s was perhaps the most deep-seated in the bloc, and was of long standing. The imposition of communist control after World War II and Stalin's emphasis on developing heavy industry created dissatisfaction with economic hardships and political conditions in Poland that surfaced as early as 1956, during the "Polish October." The PUWP was able to win approval from the population in October 1956 by standing up to Moscow on the issues of greater autonomy in policy and in leadership choices.[83] Immediately after the Polish October, collectivization of agriculture was essentially abolished, to the delight of the peasants. Yet this concession was offset over time by the regime's refusal to invest in agriculture, stymying any hope of improving or modernizing farming. Similarly, in 1958, Party leader Wladislaw Gomulka reverted to the previous Stalinist reliance on rapid industrialization, and made extensive investments in heavy industry.[84] Over the next few years, any hope of serious reform of the system in Poland dissipated, and with it the Party's short-lived popular approval.

Down, pp. 118–119. On the extent of Poland's debt, see Terry, "The Future of Poland," pp. 203–204.

81. Ekiert, *The State against Society*, pp. 292–294, 302–303.

82. *Eastern Europe and the USSR: Economic Structure and Analysis*, p. 139.

83. On the imposition of communist control, see Brzezinski, *The Soviet Bloc*, pp. 9–14; on the Gomulka period, see Brown, *Eastern Europe and Communist Rule*, pp. 160–168. On Polish history more broadly, see Norman Davies, *God's Playground: A History of Poland*, 2 vols. (Oxford: Clarendon Press, 1981).

84. Wladislaw Gomulka was a staunch communist of long standing who had been the underground head of the Polish Worker's Party, and a member of the Politburo from 1945–48. He was imprisoned during a purge of those suspected of holding deviant views in the East European communist parties, and released after Stalin's death in 1953. See Brzezinski, *The Soviet Bloc*, pp. 10, 62, 96.

By the second half of the 1960s, it became increasingly clear to some in the Party that economic factors were crucial to the political stability of the regime in Poland, as its attempts to reform the economy in 1968 showed.[85] Yet the regime again concentrated on heavy industry at the expense of other economic sectors, which did little to mitigate the problems of the centralized economy.

Economic conditions in Poland improved in the early 1970s, somewhat mitigating popular discontent with the regime. The economic growth during this period was due primarily to massive injections of foreign aid, a byproduct of strengthened Western ties made possible by the détente in U.S.-Soviet relations, and the signing of the Helsinki Accord in 1975. By 1976, conditions in the state were again deteriorating. Notably, fuel prices in Eastern Europe increased dramatically after the price indexing system used within the Council of Mutual Economic Assistance (CMEA) was modified to reflect the oil shocks of 1973–74, and the costs of Western technology, critical to the modernization of the Polish economy, rose dramatically as the impact of the oil crises hit the West.[86] Compounding these problems, the Polish government squandered the Western aid and credits it received on grandiose schemes that did little to improve the economy. Meanwhile, the level of corruption in the government skyrocketed, and the government made no effort to modify the country's centralized planning system.[87]

The economic reforms introduced in Poland in the early 1980s were among the most extreme in the Eastern bloc in moving away from the socialist command system. The most notable of the reform efforts, introduced at the 9th PUWP Congress in July 1981, was entitled "Directions of Economic Reform" and was intended to give state enterprises more autonomy, and provided for de facto autonomy of trade unions.[88] This was meant to be the "first stage" of a larger campaign of reforms. Although

---

85. Korbonski notes that "despite impressive progress in industrialization and economic development, the living standard of the Polish population has been growing at a rate slower than in most of the other people's democracies, contributing still further to economic and political discontent." Korbonski, "Poland," p. 55.

86. The pricing structure for oil was switched to a five-year moving index based on world market prices. For details on the price indexing system used by the CMEA, see Paul Marer, "East European Economies: Achievements, Problems, Prospects," in Teresa Rakowska-Harmstone, ed., *Communism in Eastern Europe* (Bloomington, Ind.: Indiana University Press, 1984), pp. 304–305.

87. Brown, *Eastern Europe and Communist Rule*, pp. 176–182; and Barclay and Ware, "Background Paper: Reforming Poland," pp. 5–6.

88. Jozefiak, "The Polish: Reform," p. 133.

some measures were initiated in January 1982 in spite of the imposition of martial law, these reforms failed to revise the structure of the economy. The government followed the 1982 reforms with a three-year stabilization program to cover 1983–85, intended to ensure sufficient resources for consumption and export goods, rather than investment. Had the 1981 program gone into effect as planned, it would have led to more economic decentralization, and toward self-management and worker participation. This would significantly have weakened the central planning structure of the state, a clear indication that the Party acknowledged the need to change the economic structure.

THE NATURE OF THE STATE'S ECONOMIC AND POLITICAL STRUCTURE

Economic reforms in Poland in the early 1980s were explicitly tied to the political structure of the state, and the need to address political as well as economic problems. The ongoing crisis of the state caused by the rise of Solidarity and its demand for trade union pluralism and other concessions led the PUWP bluntly to concede in its economic program of July 1981 that the success of economic reforms required changes to the institutional system of the state.[89]

By the early 1980s, Poland's economic, political, and social structure had drifted quite far from the "orthodox" model of socialism favored by Moscow as the regime tried to address the prolonged economic crisis. For example, at the height of Solidarity's popularity in the early 1980s, the Party acknowledged the need to accept greater pluralism in society. Rakowski himself, then a mediator between the PUWP and the union, suggested that "We are witnessing the end of an epoch, the end of [the PUWP's] monopoly of power. In its place there is only a prospect, for the Party must remove any barriers . . . before it recognizes the new unions as an equal partner."[90]

At least some members of the Party recognized the need for greater pluralism even prior to the emergence of Solidarity. A discussion club organized in the late 1970s, made up of intellectuals and Party members, proposed a greater division of power between the Party and the state. Some argued for broadening political discussions to include groups outside the PUWP.[91]

---

89. Jozefiak, "The Polish Reform," p. 134.

90. As cited in Syrop, "Warsaw Unpacked."

91. Raymond Taras, "The Crisis of Ideology and the Ideology of Crisis: Marxist Critiques of the Polish Socialist System 1956–90," in Michael E. Urban, ed., *Ideology and*

"Orthodox" Communist Party rule was not restored after martial law was declared in December 1981. Instead, control resided with the military, in a sharp break with socialist methods. Moreover, in its efforts to "normalize" the situation, the Party did not try to revert to the previous system of rule, but instead tried to move to a new type of structure. Notably, the regime abandoned Marxist rhetoric and adopted nationalist symbols in an effort to elicit popular support. Since national symbols had been central to Solidarity's stand, as well as a mainstay of the Catholic Church in Poland, the Party appeared determined to wrest these symbols from Solidarity. This further downplayed the socialist basis of the PUWP's authority.[92]

As the regime struggled to "normalize" its relations with society, it lifted restrictions on censorship, with the result that the official press became the most open in the bloc by the mid-1980s. Over time, this undermined the flourishing underground press, because people were able to publish so freely in official mediums.[93] This indicates the distance between an "orthodox" Marxist-Leninist system, with its exhortation of strict control over media, and the situation in Poland in the 1980s.[94]

Of course, not all of the Party leadership favored the weakening of socialist methods. The hard-line element of the Party favored a far more severe crackdown on Solidarity after the imposition of martial law, and a return to stricter discipline and centralized control of the economy rather than significant reforms. This faction appeared to be on the ascendance in the first half of the 1980s, acting at times in open defiance of Jaruzelski.[95] This faction enjoyed considerable support from some elements in the Soviet leadership between Brezhnev's death and Gorbachev's appointment as General Secretary, underlining the vulnerability of the moderate forces in the PUWP. The hard-line elements in the PUWP were able to exploit the conservatives' predominance in the Kremlin even during Andropov's temporary leadership. This evidence of external support from the Soviet leadership is a sign of both the continuing influence of the Soviet Union

---

System Change in the USSR and East Europe (New York: St. Martin's Press, 1992), pp. 172–173.

92. Ekiert, *The State Against Society,* pp. 296–300.

93. Ost, *Solidarity and the Politics of Anti-Politics,* pp. 172–178; and Stokes, *The Walls Came Tumbling Down,* p. 116.

94. Jeremy D. Popkin, ed., *Media and Revolution: Comparative Perspectives* (Lexington, Ky.: University Press of Kentucky, 1995), p. 10.

95. The most notable example of this defiance was the murder of Father Jerzy Popieluszko. See Brown, "Poland Since Martial Law," pp. 7–8.

on domestic political developments in Eastern Europe, and the long history of cross-border influence in the region.

SEIZING THE OPPORTUNITY TO INTRODUCE REFORMS

The regime's recognition of the need for political and economic changes was evident in its response to Gorbachev. For example, at the first meeting of the Political Consultative Committee (PCC) of the Warsaw Pact after Gorbachev's appointment as General Secretary, Jaruzelski apparently detailed the problems confronting Poland in frank terms after Gorbachev called for an open discussion of conditions within the bloc.[96] Jaruzelski and Gorbachev developed a warm working relationship from early on. As Gorbachev began to introduce changes in the Soviet Union, the Jaruzelski regime cautiously followed suit, a process that eventually led to the Round Table negotiations.

In the area of economic reform, the Polish regime proposed its own package of economic reforms in October 1986, following Moscow's call for change at the 27th Party Congress in February 1986. Moreover, it accepted the public objections to the economic reforms it proposed, and withdrew the package for reconsideration.[97] By doing so, the regime tacitly acknowledged that it needed to consider a broader array of options than it had in the past. The radical nature of the changes proposed by the PUWP indicates that Poland's continued economic malaise was forcing the Party to attempt increasingly unorthodox methods to deal with the situation. Interestingly, the measures proposed at the 10th PUWP Congress tacitly addressed political and cultural issues as well as economic problems, indicating the regime's appreciation of the connections between economic and political concerns in Poland.

In 1987, the regime submitted a new reform package for consideration, and held a public referendum asking for popular acceptance of these reforms. This reform package was similar to the reforms proposed but not fully implemented in 1981. It included significant steps away from a socialist economy, such as the acceptance of private employment.[98]

The government announced a full amnesty of all political prisoners in the fall of 1986, as part of the regime's longer term effort to "normalize" relations with society. While this move cannot be traced to Gorbachev's influence, Jaruzelski could count on Gorbachev's support for this move, in the face of potential opposition within the PUWP and

---

96. Gorbachev, *Zhizn' i Reformi*, p. 314.

97. Kaminski, *The Collapse of State Socialism*, p. 225.

98. *Eastern Europe and the USSR: Economic Structure and Analysis*, p. 145.

from other East European regimes.[99] The regime also allowed the legalization of a variety of independent clubs beginning in 1987, which led to
a wide expansion in the number of officially sanctioned independent organizations.[100]

By 1988, the Polish regime also acknowledged the need for discussions with the opposition if the country's economic and political problems were to be addressed, the process that led eventually to the Round
Table. This was a bigger step than had been taken up to that point in the
Soviet Union, which had no similarly well-organized opposition movement. But at the same time, Jaruzelski's actions paralleled moves
Gorbachev was taking. In the summer of 1988, the CPSU 19th Party Conference approved the establishment of the Congress of Peoples' Deputies
(CPD), to replace the Supreme Soviet, and with it the call for multicandidate elections, with some seats reserved for representatives of
officially accepted groups within the state. Moreover, it appears that during the summer of 1988 Jaruzelski discussed similar measures with
Gorbachev, who responded positively.[101]

SUMMARY

This evaluation suggests that the Polish regime was well aware of the
need for political as well as economic change. The regime's previous reform efforts, which attempted to introduce market mechanisms, clearly
went beyond the confines of socialist economics. Similarly, the economic
and political structure that existed in Poland when Gorbachev came to
power showed a weak ideological grounding in socialism. Instead, the regime had turned to statist rhetoric in its effort to ameliorate popular opposition to communist rule. Finally, the leadership seized the opportunity
presented by Gorbachev to show even greater flexibility in addressing
the country's problems. This helps explain the Polish regime's decision to
introduce early reforms.

Judging the Regime's Ability to Survive

The regime's judgment of its own ability to survive in a more open political climate is difficult to measure, because a regime could take similar ac-

---

99.   Gorbachev faced a similar challenge regarding the release of dissidents in the Soviet Union, such as Andrey Sakharov, who was freed from internal exile in December
1986.

100.   Mason, Nelson, and Szklarski, "Apathy and the Birth of Democracy," p. 209.

101.   Wałesa, *The Struggle and the Triumph,* pp. 159–167; and Osiatynski, "The
Roundtable Talks in Poland," p. 29.

tions for a variety of reasons. For example, conflict within a regime over substantive policy choices could lead one faction to look for support from outside the ruling party. This could lead it to undertake reforms designed to coopt the opposition into backing this faction's policies, thereby giving the regime enough support to rule, and possibly leading it—or part of it—to conclude that it could survive in a freer political climate. Alternately, if the regime perceived that it had achieved a reasonable degree of legitimacy in the eyes of the population then it might risk tolerating challenges to its political authority, again allowing greater participation by the opposition in the political arena.

The degree to which the regime, or some part of it, felt sufficiently legitimate to risk political changes can be measured by looking for indications of conflict within the regime; examining statements by regime members about how they perceive the legitimacy of the regime; and by looking at the degree of repression in the state. This last variable is the most difficult to evaluate; low degrees of repression can imply either that the regime feels relatively secure, or that it has lost control over society. To understand the significance of the level of repression, it is also important to examine the status of the opposition in the state. These points are discussed below.

CONFLICT WITHIN THE REGIME

There is ample evidence of conflict within the leadership of the PUWP in the 1980s, and between the reformist leadership and the Party and government bureaucracy. Conflict between the reformist leaders and the ranks of the bureaucracy was one reason the economic reforms introduced in the 1980s, after martial law, failed. Obstruction by local officials, who felt threatened by the changes proposed, substantially derailed the reform effort.[102] This problem continued well into 1989, and during the Round Table negotiations the obvious divide was not between regime and the opposition, but within the "government-coalition" side of the talks. Indeed, throughout the negotiations, those representing the Party and government bureacracy strongly opposed the changes being suggested. The result was a shift in the center of conflict, with the reformers on both sides of the negotiations finding themselves aligned against the Party and government bureaucrats.[103]

---

102. Jozefiak, "The Polish Reform," pp. 140–141.

103. Indeed, some participants note that the government team eventually adopted the opposition's language in the way it referred to the apparatus, as well as the perception of "us" versus "them." See Wałęsa, *The Struggle and the Triumph*, p. 179; and Osiatynski, "The Roundtable Talks in Poland," p. 59.

Conflicts within the leadership led moderate reformers to initiate a dialogue with the opposition. It is clear that in the early 1980s Jaruzelski faced opposition within the Party leadership for his efforts to introduce political and economic reforms. The differences within the PUWP centered on the evident need for reform versus the importance of maintaining a rigidly orthodox system. Jaruzelski himself was essentially a moderate, who aligned himself with the liberals in the PUWP. This faction of the party believed that serious economic reforms were needed, and it also recognized that the government would probably have to make some political concessions to the population in order to gain some support, which was vital if changes were to succeed. In allying with this faction, Jaruzelski appears to have hoped to play a role similar to that of Party leader János Kádár in Hungary, who managed to elicit support for the regime and its policies by demonstrating that he was trying to improve the lot of the people while working within the limits set by Soviet expectations. (See Chapter 4.) To this end, Jaruzelski purged the party of both Solidarity sympathizers and hard-liners, as well as those who had proven corrupt or incompetent.[104] He also advocated a policy of "renewal" as a way to improve the economic and political mechanisms of the state. While a far cry from meaningful liberalization, which was probably impossible at the time due to Moscow's opposition, Jaruzelski's efforts were a cautious attempt to elicit goodwill from the population.

The divisions that arose within the Party over the initial decision to negotiate with Solidarity in 1980 continued after martial law, with the more conservative forces on the ascendant. This division was due both to the crackdown on the opposition and concern about the Soviet response to developments in Poland. The most visible sign that intragovernmental rivalry continued in the mid-1980s was the murder of a Catholic priest, Father Jerzy Popieluszko.[105] Popieluszko was an active and outspoken supporter of Solidarity and its aims, in contradiction to the Church leadership's more pragmatic position of working for dialogue.[106] His murder

---

104. J.F. Brown, "Poland Since Martial Law," RAND Note N-2822-RC, December 1988, pp. 5–6. On continuing dissension within the party, see also Janusz Bugajski, "The Party in Crisis," in Mastny, ed., *Soviet/East European Survey, 1983–4*," pp. 206–210.

105. Ost, *Solidarity and the Politics of Anti-Politics*, p. 159.

106. Opinions differ about the Church's role. Most analysts credit it with trying to reconcile regime and opposition, and it undoubtedly played an important role in supporting Solidarity both by assisting people during martial law and by providing a conduit for outside aid. Yet some scholars argue that Cardinal Glemp took the regime's side, with the aim of preserving the Church's broader mission in Poland. See Stokes, *The Walls Came Tumbling Down*, pp. 112–114.

was widely believed to be a hard-line plot, and it seems clear that Jaruzelski and Interior Minister General Kiszczak had nothing to do with it. The Jaruzelski regime insisted on trying the priest's accused killers in order to convince the population that the murder had not been sanctioned by the government.[107] Jaruzelski also used the Popieluszko scandal as a pretext for removing several officials who opposed his policies, thereby improving his control over the Party.

Finally, divisions within the Party were evident after the referendum on the regime's 1987 economic reform proposals. What was striking was that the referendum failed even though the regime wanted it to pass. As noted earlier, the opposition concluded from this that a reform group might exist within the leadership, with which negotiations could be possible.[108]

LEGITIMACY

The question of the degree to which members of the Polish leadership perceived their rule to be legitimate is complex, and the evidence is contradictory. There is strong evidence to suggest a lack of legitimacy, or limited legitimacy. Four factors in particular stand out. First is the rise of Solidarity, and the massive public support it elicited. This was a clear rejection of Communist Party rule. Second is the Party's inability to regain the public's trust despite significant endeavors. These efforts included tolerance of a relatively open press and travel restrictions that were relaxed by Warsaw Pact standards, as well as notable events like the trial of Father Popieluszko's killers.[109]

Third, support for the Party and its rule was clearly low. Party membership among the country's youth in particular was low in the 1980s.[110]

---

107. Ibid., p. 114–115.

108. By this point the opposition recognized that the country's problems, and the opposition's inability to rally the population decisively to support it against the regime meant that compromise was probably the only viable solution.

109. The Party leadership was well aware of societal disillusionment in spite of its efforts at liberalization. See "A Synthesis of the Domestic Situation and the West's Activity," in *CWIHP Bulletin*, Issue 12/13 (Fall/Winter 2001), pp. 98–101.

110. The Union of Polish Socialist Youth, one of the officially recognized youth organizations, lost one third of its membership by May 1981, after Solidarity's emergence. Independent youth organizations emerged during the Solidarity period, but went underground when martial law was declared. Communist Party membership went from a high of 3,158,000 in September 1980 to just over 2,000,000 in May 1988. See Richard F. Staar, *Communist Regimes in Eastern Europe*, 5th ed. (Stanford, Calif.: Hoover Institution Press, 1988), pp. 156, 175.

The population in general showed little interest in official institutions, despite their importance in a socialist state; there was little interest in politics, and low voter turnout after 1981, something that had not been tolerated earlier.[111] Finally, in its effort to generate public trust, the regime embraced national and state symbols, rather than Communist Party rhetoric. This indicated that its attempts to establish legitimacy based on socialist ideology had failed. This last factor is particularly significant because it reveals the leadership's recognition of the problem. Jaruzelski's speech just prior to the June elections reflected this trend; in addition to crediting the Party for taking the risk of elections, he stressed that "its supreme goal is the nation's prosperity. We stretch out a hand to everyone who truly has the good of the country at heart. With this in mind, I call for a broad, post-election coalition, a kind of pact to promote economic reforms, to enrich democracy, to strengthen the state, to develop Poland." Socialist goals were notably absent.[112]

Evidence suggesting the regime had some popular legitimacy also can be found. The waning of Solidarity's support base in the mid-1980s, lasting until 1989, provides indirect evidence of legitimacy.[113] This was due in part to the regime's success in its initial crackdown against the union, and also to the moderate nature of its repression against the union and its supporters.[114] There was mixed public support for both the opposition and the regime in 1987, with the majority willing to give the government the benefit of the doubt in its efforts to improve the economy and living standards.[115] While popular apathy and exhaustion explain this position as well as anything else, it can also be read as evidence of at least partial legitimacy of the regime—within the confines of the Soviet-led system that existed. Finally, the regime did receive considerable popular support for the referendum on its economic policies in 1987. Though it failed, the referendum does appear to have been part of an on-

---

111. Mason, Nelson, and Szklarski, "Apathy and the Birth of Democracy," pp. 217–218.

112. "Jaruzelski Addresses Nation," Warsaw Television Service, June 2, 1989, in *FBIS:EEU,* June 5, 1989; see also Ekiert, *The State Against Society,* pp. 297–300.

113. Solidarity's popular support was measured at about 25 percent in 1988. Brumberg, "Poland: The New Opposition."

114. Though thousands of Solidarity activists were jailed under martial law, repression was moderate in comparison to other periods of repression in Eastern Europe, such as those in Hungary in 1956 and Czechoslovakia in 1968. See Ekiert, *The State Against Society,* p. 289; and Terry, "The Future of Poland," pp. 198–201.

115. Brumberg, "Poland: The New Opposition"; see also Mason, Nelson, and Szklarski, "Apathy and the Birth of Democracy," pp. 211–213.

going campaign by Jaruzelski to obtain, in essence, a vote of confidence for his policies.[116]

The regime also tried to expand its popular approval by raising the issue of "blank spots" in Soviet-Polish history. From Moscow's perspective, the reevaluation of history was necessary if serious changes in the Soviet system were to emerge, and Soviet–East European ties must be examined if better relations were to develop with the East European states.[117] The Polish regime hoped that a discussion of the history of Soviet-Polish relations might provide an opportunity at least to acknowledge that errors had been made in past policies, and that the Polish regime was on the same side of the issue as the population. Though it was unclear just how far this reevaluation might go, the opening of such a discussion might gain the regime credibility with a population that nursed bitter grievances against the Soviet Union.

There is also direct evidence that the regime felt itself sufficiently legitimate to risk reforms. Rakowski evidently believed that the regime could resolve the country's economic problems and thus gain popular support without negotiating with the opposition.[118] Jaruzelski noted that "we were sincerely convinced that we would win the June [1989] elections."[119] Another participant in the Round Table negotiations noted that the regime would never have begun the process if it had suspected it might lose: "If the Party leadership realized how weak it was, there would never have been the Round Table talks and peaceful change."[120]

---

116. As Brown has pointed out, "economic improvement. . . . is impossible without a degree of political legitimacy enabling the regime not only to harness the national effort, but also to ride out the unpopularity of the hard measures necessary for effective reform." "Poland Since Martial Law," p. 24.

117. On the Soviet attitude toward an examination of earlier Soviet–East European relations, see "East-West Relations and Eastern Europe (An American-Soviet Dialogue)," *Problems of Communism*, Vol. 37, Nos. 3–4 (May–August 1988); Quentin Peel, "Moscow Admits Policy Errors," *Financial Times*, June 27, 1988; and Paul Marantz, "Soviet `New Thinking' and East-West Relations," *Current History*, Vol. 87, No. 10 (1988). On the issue of Polish-Soviet relations, see Thomas Szayna, "Addressing "Blank Spots" in Polish-Soviet Relations," *Problems of Communism*, Vol. 37, No. 5 (November–December 1988) pp. 37–60; Andrzej Ajnenkiel, "Blank Pages in Polish History," *The Polish Review*, Vol. 33, No. 3 (1988), pp. 333–341; and "Report on a Working Visit of Wojciech Jaruzelski to Moscow," in *CWIHP Bulletin*, Issue 12/13 (Fall/Winter 2001), pp. 112–113.

118. Kaminski, *The Collapse of State Socialism*, p. 233.

119. Wojciech Jaruzelski, *Les Chaines et le refuge: Memoires* (Paris: Jean-Claude Lattes, 1992), p. 317, as cited by Lévesque, *The Enigma of 1989*, p. 110.

120. Aleksander Kwasniewski, as cited by Osiatynski, "The Roundtable Talks in Poland," p. 26.

Additional evidence of the regime's seeming legitimacy is the opposition's fear that it would not win sufficient seats in the June 1989 election to be a viable minority bloc in the new parliament.[121]

In retrospect, the regime's lack of legitimacy is obvious. It was not so obvious in 1989. The level of support for the 1987 referendum, Gorbachev's clear popularity throughout Eastern Europe, and the statements of Party leaders suggest that Jaruzelski and other reformers believed that they had sufficient backing to take the risk of opening the political process, with the goal restricted to sharing power with the opposition and with the PUWP's controlling position secure. That is, the goal was to expand the legitimacy of the new government, not to test the Party's legitimacy on an open playing field.[122] This highlights again the importance of perceptions; the Party evaluated its legitimacy within the constraints of communist and Soviet domination that it expected to persist.

REPRESSION

In December 1981, the Polish regime used repressive means to end the crisis caused by Solidarity's popularity and demands for reform. Martial law was harsh, but not as cruel as the crackdowns after earlier uprisings in Hungary and Czechoslovakia. The government was able to lift martial law in 1986 partly because much of the structure of martial law had been incorporated into the legal structure, so that the regime's authority and the restrictions on opposition groups stayed in place. Nonetheless, by the late 1980s, the Polish regime did not appear to be relying on repression to sustain its rule. Harassment of Solidarity and opposition figures continued, but, after martial law was lifted, there were more warnings than arrests as the regime made a deliberate effort to persuade people to avoid open defiance of the regime.[123] The regime's desire to avoid coercion was

---

121. Wałesa, *The Struggle and the Triumph,* p. 202.

122. Jaruzelski's defense of the decision to open talks with the opposition reflects both optimism (which might be forced) that the Party would survive, and a clear statement of the constraints of the liberalization envisioned: "It is not weakness, it is bold political thinking, not desperate measures but determination which brought us to [negotiations]. Our stance is clear: Truth—yes; Partnership—yes; Criticism—yes; Compromise—Yes; but undermining the constitutional order, drawing from alien sources, demagogy and pressure—no. . . . It is obvious, however, that the PZPR [or PUWP], by virtue of its role, defined by history and the system of government, will not relinquish—like every ruling party in authority—its influence over socioeconomic strategy." "Jaruzelski Asks Support," Warsaw Domestic Service, September 27, 1988, in *FBIS:EEU,* September 27, 1988.

123. Simultaneous with the lifting of martial law, around 3,000 activists were visited by Interior Ministry representatives, to make clear to them that their activities were known to the regime. Brumberg, "A New Deal in Poland?" p. 32.

evident as well in the Popieluszko trial, in which the regime tried to ensure its control of the security forces, and to convince the population of this aim. Censorship in Poland was the most lax in the bloc; by some measures, Poland had the most free and open society in Eastern Europe in the late 1980s.[124]

The state of repression in Poland appears to indicate one of two things. Either the regime was relaxing repression in an effort to improve its relations with society, or it was aware that measures such as censorship had simply failed, and stopped trying to enforce them.

SUMMARY

The regime's estimation of its ability to survive is somewhat unclear. Both before and after the June 1989 elections there was reason to conclude that the regime lacked sufficient legitimacy to rule in a more open political environment, due to the persistent popular rejection of the Party and the government. Yet there is evidence to suggest that Jaruzelski and his supporters believed they had sufficient support to survive, and even to enhance their authority, presuming as they did that Communist Party rule remained a given. The regime could look to Solidarity's decreasing support in the mid-1980s, as well as to the partial support it received for new economic reforms in the 1987 referendum. Statements by members of the leadership indicate that they had faith in their ability to endure. Moreover, this perception was clearly vital to the regime's decision to negotiate with the opposition.

In the end, the regime's misperception of its legitimacy may have been critical. Since there was conflict within the Party leadership, a sense of legitimacy would have helped to convince the moderates within the Party to attempt to coopt the opposition and initiate early reforms to improve their standing in the long run.

External Influences

In addition to the two domestic factors—the regime's recognition of reform and its assessment of its ability to survive—it is clear that the Soviet Union also affected Poland's reform process. Gorbachev's active encouragement of change in Eastern Europe, and his emphasis on the need for East European leaders to address the particular problems they faced at home, affected the political choices of all the East European leaders, whether they responded with reform or resistance to it. Moscow's

---

124. Brown, *Eastern Europe and Communist Rule*, pp. 197–198.

willingness to support the Polish regime's reform efforts was significant for several reasons. First, it was an early and important sign that the Soviet leadership was sincere when it claimed to have no intention of interfering in Eastern Europe, showing that the tenets of "new thinking" in Soviet foreign policy applied to Eastern Europe as well as to East-West relations. Second, Moscow's support encouraged experimentation with reform in the bloc as a whole, again reinforcing Moscow's claims that it backed such exploration by its allies. Third, developments in Poland were covered by official Soviet newspapers and journals, and since Soviet newspapers were available throughout most of Eastern Europe, information about reforms in Poland (and Hungary) was available even in more conservative states that refused to cover the changes.[125] Thus, Moscow broadcast the changes—and its own acceptance of them. Notably, throughout the fall of 1988 the Soviet government remained unruffled by the creeping expansion of reform emerging in Poland and Hungary, and the Soviet media provided frank coverage of developments in Poland. One notable example of Soviet equanimity toward the more radical steps being taken in Poland was the comment made in September 1988 by one of Gorbachev's advisers, Nikolai Shishlin, that the relegalization of Solidarity would not present a problem for the Soviet Union.[126]

More specifically, Gorbachev's call for the establishment of the Congress of Peoples' Deputies (CPD) in the Soviet Union coincided with the development of the idea of Round Table negotiations and partially free elections to the Sejm in Poland. It is not clear where the idea for the Round Table discussions originated.[127] But the process, a combination of elections and acceptance of greater societal representation, paralleled the format of the CPD. Thus, it was likely to be a safe option for the Polish regime. In terms of the outcome he wanted to achieve, Jaruzelski would ap-

---

125.   Indeed, the Soviet newspaper *Pravda* had begun selling out in East Germany, something unheard of prior to Gorbachev's rise to power.

126.   In another example, former Prime Minister Zbigniew Messner's fall was pronounced "justified" by the bad job he had done addressing the state's economic crisis. See Jackson Diehl, "East Europe Awaits Shock Waves," *IHT*, October 1, 1988; and "Throwing the Rascals Out," *Time*, October 3, 1988, pp. 14–15.

127.   Different people credit it to Rakowski, the Pope, U.S. President George Bush, and Jaruzelski. The establishment of an "anti-crisis pact" was proposed by Solidarity leaders in 1987 and early 1988. Shaknazarov also notes that Jaruzelski and Gorbachev discussed the idea of partially free elections for the Sejm in July 1988. See Shaknazarov, *Tsena Svobodii*, p. 117; Stokes, *The Walls Came Tumbling Down*, pp. 120, 123; Ost, *Solidarity and the Politics of Anti-Politics*, p. 181; and Wałęsa, *The Struggle and the Triumph*, p. 111.

pear, then, to be following the Soviet model more explicitly than did any other leader in the Eastern bloc.

Concern about the Soviet "threat" was also evident throughout much of the process. The Polish leadership was cautious, checking with Gorbachev and his associates in 1988 before starting negotiations with Solidarity. Regime representatives also visited Moscow during the negotiations, to ensure that their initiatives were understood and approved by the Soviet leadership.[128] The Soviet Union was also a tacit "third presence" at the Round Table talks. Both regime and Solidarity recognized the need for caution to avoid derailing the reform process.[129]

Interestingly, well before the proposal of negotiations in Poland, Polish opposition figures expressed concern that strikes or other anti-government actions in Poland might derail the Soviet reform process, which would be bad for Poland. For example, Adam Michnik noted in early 1988 that "the worst actions today would be those which blocked changes in the Soviet Union. There is a nineteenth century precedent for this in Poland. . . . Current developments in the Soviet Union offer a real possibility of changes for the better throughout the Communist bloc. Since we have helped stimulate these changes, and since their deepening is impossible without Solidarity, we do not want to frustrate them."[130]

---

128. Party representatives went to Moscow at the end of January to discuss the 10th PUWP Plenum's decision to establish a process of negotiations, and Jaruzelski himself visited Moscow at the end of April. Soviet reportage of the results of the Round Table negotiations, and Gorbachev's reception of Jaruzelski, pointed to continued Soviet equanimity about the progression of events in Poland. Again, this was probably due to the parallels in developments in the two states at that time. This is not to suggest that Moscow "approved" developments in Poland; as noted in Chapter 2, Gorbachev was careful to avoid giving the impression that he or other Soviet leaders had veto power over initiatives in Eastern Europe. See "Urban, Gerasimov, Hold Moscow News Briefing," *Trybuna Ludu,* January 25, 1989, in *FBIS:EEU,* January 30, 1989; "Reform is a Common Cause," Interview with Jerzy Urban, *New Times,* No. 9 (1989), p. 36–37; "Report on a Working Visit of Wojciech Jaruzelski to Moscow," pp. 112–113. On Moscow's coverage of developments in Poland, see "Agreement is Reached," *Pravda,* April 7, 1989; "Reforms break off the fetters: Poland's Economy on the Road to Renewal," *Pravda,* April 11, 1989; "Meeting with W. Jaruzelski," *Pravda,* April 26, 1989; and "Friendly Meeting," *Pravda,* April 29, 1989. On Gorbachev's policy toward Poland, see Medvedev, *Raspad,* p. 90.

129. Osiatynski, "The Roundtable Talks in Poland," p. 24; and Lévesque, *The Enigma of 1989,* pp. 113–114.

130. By "changes for the better" Michnik was referring to the 19th Party Congress in the Soviet Union, and to perestroika in general. Adam Michnik interview with Erica Blair, "Towards a Civil Society: Hopes for Polish Democracy," *Times Literary Supplement,* February 19, 1988.

The desire that reform in the Soviet Union should continue was evident in the opposition's insistence, throughout 1987 and 1988, that it was interested not in power, but in pluralism.[131] Thus, Solidarity made clear that it was not threatening Communist Party rule or Soviet control in Poland. This indicates that all sides in Poland believed that tacit limits to Soviet tolerance remained.

Indeed, the opposition was concerned about its resounding success in the June 1989 elections, fearing an increased danger of destabilization. In an ironic twist, the first Solidarity spokesmen publicly to assess the results of the elections were subdued rather than jubilant, and began by reassuring the regime that Solidarity would honor the Round Table accords.[132]

Caution about Soviet control was also evident in the absence of foreign policy issues from discussion at the Round Table negotiations. Even after their victory in the June elections, Solidarity spokesmen were scrupulous in stressing their interest in continued good relations with the Soviet Union throughout August and early September. Wałęsa himself, in calling for a Solidarity-led coalition, was careful to emphasize that none of the changes in Poland were meant to threaten the country's alliance ties with Moscow.[133] Mazowiecki reiterated this view in his earliest statements as prime minister, striving to make clear that he anticipated no change in Polish-Soviet relations.[134]

The Soviet Union's response to developments in Poland suggests both concern and a desire to avoid active involvement. Moscow had stressed the need for cooperation in its reportage of the June elections in Poland, and Soviet preference for continued communist rule of the government was evident during Jaruzelski's struggle to obtain Solidarity's

---

131. Wałęsa, *The Struggle and the Triumph,* p. 177; and Lévesque, *The Enigma of 1989,* p. 114. See also Jacek Kuroń, "The Round Table: Instead of Revolution," *Tygodnik Mazowsze,* March 8, 1989, reprinted in *East European Reporter,* Vol. 3, No. 4 (Spring–Summer 1989), pp. 32–34.

132. Gross argues that much of the population was furious that Solidarity did not begin by thanking the electorate for its stunning victory. See Jan T. Gross, "Poland: From Civil Society to Political Nation, " in Ivo Banac, ed., *Eastern Europe in Revolution* (Ithaca, N.Y.: Cornell University Press, 1992), p. 62.

133. "Statements By Lech Wałęsa on Formation of Government," Warsaw Home Service, August 15, 1989, in *FBIS:EEU,* August 17,1989. Solidarity's concern that it might push too hard is seen in internal discussions over formation of a government. "Minutes of the Meeting of the Presidium of the Citizens' Parliamentary Club, 1 August, 1989, 8 P.M.," in *CWIHP Bulletin,* Issue 12/13 (Fall/Winter 2001), pp. 118–122.

134. "Premier Mazowiecki on Avoiding PZPR Opposition to His Government," Warsaw Home Service, September 3, 1989, in *SWB:EE,* September 5, 1989.

participation in a communist-led coalition government in August.[135] The head of the Warsaw Pact, General V. N. Lobov, visited Warsaw on August 4, and Moscow implicitly warned Wałęsa against creating a "prolonged political crisis," noting that the desperate state of the Polish economy demanded that *all* political forces, including the Communists, join in a coalition.[136] These moves could have created the impression that the Soviet Union would not countenance the complete exclusion of the Communist Party from a governing role; as such, this may have influenced Solidarity's proposal of a coalition that included the PUWP. Yet once Wałęsa proposed such a coalition and Jaruzelski nominated Mazowiecki, the Soviet Union responded by declaring this "solely an internal political affair," in essence accepting the turn of events.[137] More importantly, the key factor that influenced the change in the Polish Communist Party's acceptance of this proposal was Gorbachev's telephone call to party leader Rakowski, in which he apparently pressed Rakowski to accept participation in a noncommunist-led government.[138] Coming in the wake of calls by both the Czechoslovakian and Romanian regimes for a reinstitution of the Brezhnev Doctrine in some form, Moscow's adamance clearly reflected Gorbachev's commitment to noninterference. Adding to the impression that business as usual would be maintained, the Soviet foreign minister, Eduard Shevardnadze, visited Poland on October 24, in what was depicted as a "necessary" visit to assess future cooperation between the two states, while Mazowiecki visited Moscow at the end of November.[139]

Of the other East European states, only Hungary was also implementing reforms early in 1989. The problems facing the two states and the solutions they were considering were very different, but it was important to each that it not be totally isolated within the Warsaw Pact. Negotiations between the Hungarian Communist Party and newly formed

---

135. "The Polish Election Results" reported in *Pravda*, June 9, 1989, in *SWB:SU*, June 12, 1989.

136. See V. Volkov, "What's Going On in the Government?" *Pravda*, August 14, 1989, p. 6; and "Siwicki Receives Warsaw Pact's Lobov," Warsaw PAP, August 4, 1989, in *FBIS:EEU*, August 14, 1989.

137. "Soviet Statement on Political Situation Cited," Warsaw Television Service, August 17, 1989, in *FBIS:EEU*, August 18, 1989.

138. "PZPR Spokesman on Rakowski-Gorbachev Telephone Conversation," Warsaw Home Service, August 22, 1989, in *SWB:EE*, August 24, 1989. Lévesque suggests that Rakowski initiated the phone call by requesting a visit to Moscow a week or so earlier. Nonetheless, the key factor appears to have been Gorbachev's recommendation that the PUWP accept a noncommunist-led government. *The Enigma of 1989*, p. 125.

139. "USSR Foreign Minister in Poland," Abstract of report, *SWB:EE*, October 27, 1989.

opposition parties were underway in Hungary by the summer of 1989, and it appeared that the opposition there would not concede to the Communist Party any of the perquisites that the PUWP had retained after Poland's Round Table negotiations. This probably stiffened Solidarity's resolve to demand political powers more in line with its electoral strength. Negotiations over the new government also coincided with the opening of the new Soviet CPD, the first meeting of which was held on May 25, 1989. The range of debate in this new body was stunning, indicating that the reforms in the Soviet Union were expanding in their scope, and were increasingly likely to be irrevocable. Jaruzelski himself noted the influence of the Soviet Union and Hungary, indicating external influence both from the Soviet Union, through its initiation of reforms, and from another East European state that had adopted Poland's own model, and then pushed it further: "Neither are we shutting ourselves away from the experiences of our friends in the Soviet Union and Hungary. We are opening to everything that is new, everything that is proving its worth."[140]

Poland was also feeling negative pressure from conservative states in the bloc. In July 1989 Jaruzelski defended Poland's reform process at a highly divisive Warsaw Pact meeting in Bucharest. Though it did not become public at the time, a heated debate developed at this meeting about the nature of the reforms Gorbachev was proposing.[141] In August 1989, Romanian leader Nicolae Ceauşescu called for an intervention by the Warsaw Pact in Poland, to defend the interests of socialism.[142] These indications of opposition to reform were clearly outweighed by Moscow's backing of Poland's reform process, but they underscored the perceived fragility of the reform process.

Western influence in Poland played an important, but ancillary role. The Polish Pope, John Paul II, was important both as a succor and an ad-

---

140. Interview with Wojciech Jaruzelski," *Konfrontacje*, reported in *Trybuna Ludu*, June 29, 1989, in *FBIS:EEU*, July 10, 1989.

141. Lévesque, *The Enigma of 1989*, pp. 119–121.

142. "*Scinteia* on the Situation in Poland," *Agerpres* (Romanian News Service), August 20, 1989, in *FBIS:EEU*, August 22, 1989. It has been suggested that Ceauşescu went so far as to send a delegation to Poland to press the Party to forestall the change in government, by force if necessary. PUWP members claimed that the RCP had expressed its "concern" with the situation in Poland, and proposed joint action by the communist states to "defend socialism and the Polish nation"—an offer which the PUWP refused. See *Radio Free Europe Weekly Record of Events*, September 29, 1989. See also Lévesque, *The Enigma of 1989*, p. 119; and Stokes, *The Walls Came Tumbling Down*, p. 130.

vocate for the population and opposition, as noted earlier.[143] Western support for Solidarity from the early 1980s on had helped the union survive during martial law.[144] The sanctions imposed by Western governments in response to martial law unquestionably affected the Polish economy, and the regime was well aware of the need to ease domestic restrictions so that sanctions could be lifted, and so that the government could negotiate debt relief from the West. Yet Western leaders were also cautious about pushing too far once the regime began to initiate reforms. In 1989, for example, U.S. President George Bush apparently helped to secure Jaruzelski's election as president when he emphasized the need for stability in the region during his visit to Poland.[145] It was clear that the United States did not want reforms in Eastern Europe to threaten the Soviet Union's own reforms.

Interestingly, some prominent members of Solidarity saw Spain as the model they hoped to emulate. Adam Michnik pointed to the rise of trade unions and political parties late in dictator Francisco Franco's rule, as well as the spread of cultural freedoms and the greater independence of the church during this period. His comments implied that Solidarity's leaders hoped that Spain might prove to be a useful model of how to move peacefully from dictatorship to democracy.[146]

Conclusions

The evidence presented in this chapter supports the conclusion that the Polish regime recognized the need for political as well as economic reforms, one of the factors that I argue is likely to stimulate the early introduction of reform. It is not surprising, then, that Poland was one of the leaders in the introduction of reform in Eastern Europe. The regime saw that political changes were vital if it was to overcome the estrangement of the population, which would be required for the country to address its serious economic problems. In particular, the regime saw a need to ex-

---

143. Wałęsa, for example, stresses the importance of both of the Pope's visits to Poland. *The Struggle and the Triumph,* pp. 112–121.

144. This was more of a grassroots effort than a government-sponsored one, though Western governments also supported Solidarity.

145. Lévesque, *The Enigma of 1989,* pp. 121–123.

146. Adam Michnik interview, "Towards a Civil Society," p. 198. Even after the June election, Solidarity did not foresee the extent of the political changes in Poland. "Minutes from a Meeting of the Presidium of the Citizens' Parliamentary Club, 15 July, 1989," *CWIHP Bulletin,* Issue 12/13 (Fall/Winter 2001), pp. 114–118.

pand the scope of political pluralism, both by legalizing Solidarity and by holding partially free elections. See Table 3.

The regime's perception of its ability to survive in a more open political climate is less clear. It is important to remember that the Polish regime intended to introduce limited pluralism, not a fully competitive political process; its perception of its own legitimacy must be judged within the constraints that it believed existed at the time, and that it expected to continue until a future round of elections. Given this restriction, three points are evident. First, reform was initiated from above, by the regime, though it is unlikely that the regime would have taken this step if it had not reached a stalemate with the opposition. Poland had the most vital opposition movement in Eastern Europe, and Solidarity played a critical role in stimulating the reform process that occurred. Reform was introduced from above, therefore, but with vital popular pressure from below. In the tables in Chapter 1, Poland falls near the divide between models A and C.

Second, the regime's leaders, including Jaruzelski, appear to have believed that the Party had sufficient legitimacy to survive within the new political structure that was being established. Since the Party had ensured, it believed, that it would have clear control in the new parliamentary structure through the voting procedures, as well as control over the new presidency, this seems a reasonable assumption. The regime's faith in its ability to compete in the restricted manner established for the June 1989 elections rested on indications of popular endorsement for its earlier reform proposals, voter turnout in the elections in 1987, and the decline in support for Solidarity that continued until the Round Table negotiations began. The fact that Solidarity was willing to negotiate a power-sharing agreement with the regime may also have encouraged some to believe that if Solidarity had accepted the need to work with the PUWP, the population would as well.[147]

Third, the regime's confidence probably was bolstered by popular enthusiasm within Poland for Gorbachev and the reforms he was introducing in the Soviet Union. The regime may have presumed it would gain similar approval by adopting similar steps. Moreover, both Party and Solidarity trod carefully in establishing their new relationship, due to apprehension about Moscow's reaction. So long as they believed that the Soviet Union retained the final say over the breadth of reform possible in the Eastern bloc, the regime was justified in believing that it would survive. This apparent faith in its ability to compete, accompanied by the

---

147. The regime may have thought it would improve its popular appeal simply by talking to Solidarity, as well.

Table 3. Indicators Measuring the Polish Regime's Attitudes in 1989.

EARLY REFORM

INDICATORS OF REGIME'S RECOGNITION OF NEED FOR REFORM

INDICATOR	POLAND	REGIME'S ATTITUDE
Previous reform efforts	Substantial economic reforms	Awareness of need for reform
Nature of state's economic and political structure	Weak adherence to Marxist-Leninist model	
Problems facing the state	Serious economic difficulties	
Response to Gorbachev	Positive	

INDICATORS OF REGIME'S PERCEPTION OF ITS ABILITY TO SURVIVE

INDICATOR	POLAND	REGIME'S ATTITUDE
Statements of legitimacy	No	Some perception of legitimacy
Intra-regime conflict	Yes	
Level of repression	Low	

state's urgent economic problems, helps explain its early introduction of reforms.

The Polish Party's faith in its endurance shows why the reform process in Poland was so important for the later reforming states. Only after Gorbachev had accepted Mazowiecki as prime minister, and indeed only after Mazowiecki was sworn in, was it evident that the Soviet Union would accept a noncommunist-led government in Eastern Europe. Soviet influence in this case, then, was critical in two ways: first, it catalyzed the process, and second, it sanctioned the outcome.

Chapter 4

Reform from Above: The Hungarian Gamble with Transformation

Hungary presents a clear case of reform initiated from above by the regime in power. The Hungarian leadership was one of the earliest in the bloc to introduce substantial changes, tackling both economic and political reforms, and the reformers within the Hungarian Party leadership were confident that they would continue to rule in the new structure they had established. Though their causes and trajectories differed, Hungary and Poland began to introduce substantial reforms at roughly the same time, late in 1988.

While the Hungarian leadership considered reforms necessary to address the country's economic problems, the extent of political reforms reflected the beliefs of only some of Hungary's leaders that substantial political reform was essential if economic reforms were to succeed. Disagreements within the top ranks of the Party led to conflict, paralysis, the search for outside allies, and the Party's eventual electoral defeat.

In this chapter, I first outline the course of reforms in Hungary and then measure the regime's recognition of the need for change and its assessment of its ability to survive. Following this, I examine external influences on the process and evaluate how well the hypotheses outlined here about early reforming states explain this case.

Hungary's Transition

In 1985, Hungary was one of the most western-oriented states in the Warsaw Pact, and one in which the communist regime appeared to enjoy genuine popular support. This was due to the efforts of János Kádár, the Hungarian Socialist Worker's Party's (HSWP's) leader since late 1956, to reach an accord with the population. Kádár was placed in power by the Soviet Union when it invaded Hungary to quell the revolution there in November 1956. Though he had been in the Politburo, and an active supporter of Premier Imre Nagy's policies during the early days of the revolution, in the aftermath of the revolution and the subsequent Soviet invasion Kádár was viewed by his countrymen as a traitor, the betrayer of the revolution.[1] However, Kádár's actions over the ensuing months and years gradually changed popular perceptions of his role and aims. By the mid-1960s, the Hungarian population was increasingly aware that Kádár was acting within constraints imposed by the Soviet Union, and even pushing the limits of Soviet toleration with his comparatively liberal domestic economic policies. The 1968 Soviet crackdown in Czechoslovakia reinforced the realization by the majority of the population that Kádár's rule was comparatively benign.[2] This made clear that communist rule in Hungary was the only option available, and Kádár was able to convince the population that he was striving to make domestic life as comfortable as possible.[3] Thus, the regime's credibility with the population was prob-

---

1. The opening of the Soviet archives has revealed new information about Soviet thinking during the crisis in Hungary in 1956. The Soviet leaders very nearly accepted a noncommunist system in Hungary, though they rejected this course in the end. Kádár also appears to have been less of a quisling than often believed, arguing strongly against the use of force. See Mark Kramer, "New Light Shed on 1956 Soviet Decision to Invade Hungary," *Transition*, November 15, 1996, pp. 35–40. For an overview of the Hungarian revolution and its aftermath see Ferenc A. Vali, *Rift and Revolt in Hungary* (Cambridge, Mass: Harvard University Press, 1961); and Tibor Meray, *Thirteen Days that Shook the Kremlin* (New York: Praeger, 1959).

2. Kádár worked both to mediate a political solution to the 1968 crisis and to minimize direct Hungarian involvement in this Warsaw Pact operation. See Jiri Valenta, *Soviet Intervention in Czechoslovakia, 1968: Anatomy of a Decision* (Baltimore, Md.: Johns Hopkins University Press, 1979), p. 27; see also Robin Alison Remington, *Winter in Prague: Documents on Czechoslovak Communism in Crisis* (Cambridge, Mass.: MIT Press, 1969).

3. Though he had carried out reprisals against revolutionary leaders, these were balanced by a purge within the party of the hard-liners who had most adamantly fought the reform process. And Kádár's famous slogan of 1961, "He who is not against us is with us," highlighted a fundamental ingredient of what came to be known as "Kádárization"; a marked absence of demands for active support of the government by the population, so long as there was not active dissent. As a result of Kádár's policies in the thirty years that followed the 1956 uprising, it could be said in 1985 that the Kádár regime was if not popular, at least "palatable." Charles Gati, *Hungary and the Soviet Bloc* (Durham, N.C.: Duke University Press, 1986), pp. 159–169, p. 174; *EIU Regional Review: Eastern Europe and the USSR, 1986* (London: Economist Intelligence Unit, Ltd., 1986), pp 68–69.

ably the highest of any state in the Eastern bloc aside from the Soviet Union itself.

In spite of Hungary's comparative stability, the Hungarian government was unwilling to attempt significant political reforms for several years after Mikhail Gorbachev came to power in the Soviet Union.[4] This was due in good part to Kádár. Though he had been a moderate and even a reform-minded communist during the previous twenty years, in his late seventies he was incapable of adjusting to a reinvigorated Soviet leadership calling for serious reforms.[5] His removal appears to have been necessary in order for Hungary to begin responding seriously to the possibilities of reform presented by glasnost and perestroika, suggesting that in this case, at least, conservatism born of age was critical to the old leadership's objection to reform.

Nonetheless, discussion of reform within the HSWP expanded in 1986, after Gorbachev introduced reform policies in the Soviet Union.[6] Enthusiasm for reforms was evident within the Party when Gorbachev visited Hungary in June 1986, and Imre Pozsgay, head of the Patriotic People's Front (PPF), the party's mass organization, launched a debate on reform in December 1986 by attacking the government's economic policy and presenting a commissioned report of the PPF entitled "Turnabout and Reform." This paper openly discussed Hungary's economic problems and advocated the introduction of the profit motive and the rule of law in Hungary as means to address the country's difficulties.[7] The report was initially suppressed by the Party; when it was eventually pub-

---

4. In 1983, the Hungarian government adopted a requirement that there be at least two candidates for each post in elections, but these were still to be Party-approved candidates. The first such elections were held in June 1985. See *EIU Regional Review: Eastern Europe and the USSR*, p. 69; and J.F. Brown, *Eastern Europe and Communist Rule* (Durham, N.C.: Duke University Press, 1988), pp. 221–222.

5. Iván T. Berend, *Central and Eastern Europe, 1944–1993: Detour from the Periphery to the Periphery* (Cambridge: Cambridge University Press, 1996), pp. 270–271; and Brown, *Eastern Europe and Communist Rule*, pp. 228–229.

6. Berend, *Central and Eastern Europe, 1944–1993*, pp. 271–272.

7. While a legal code existed under communism, people were not treated equally under the law and laws could change arbitrarily, by decree. Thus, adopting a law-based system would be a significant change. "Journal Reports PPF Economic Reform Article," Budapest MTI (Hungarian Telegraph Agency), June 23, 1987, in *Foreign Broadcast Information Service: Eastern Europe* [hereafter *FBIS:EEU*], June 30, 1987; Gale Stokes, *The Walls Came Tumbling Down: The Collapse of Communism in Eastern Europe* (New York: Oxford University Press, 1993), p. 91; and Rudolf L. Tökés, *Hungary's Negotiated Revolution: Economic Reform, Social Change, and Political Succession, 1957–1990* (Cambridge: Cambridge University Press, 1996), p. 203.

lished, it helped to inspire a broader discussion of reforms by both Party reformers and opposition figures.

Criticism of Kádár, and pressure from within the Party and government for him to resign, began to grow in 1987.[8] The regime did initiate some changes that year, and Kádár appointed Politburo member Károly Grósz prime minister in June 1987, giving him the difficult task of salvaging the economy.[9] As Grósz was considered his potential successor, Kádár may have intended to neutralize Grósz by giving him this job, since responsibility for the economy would make him accountable for its problems. However, Grósz used his position to initiate more economic changes and to begin cautious criticism of the earlier slow pace of change, and implicitly of Kádár himself. Grósz also tried to paint himself as the Hungarian Gorbachev—a progressive reformer who worked within the Party from a centrist position. He clearly favored maintaining a socialist system led by the HSWP.

Political debate began to spread outside the Party as well. Opposition to the regime in Hungary remained quite small well into 1989; there were perhaps 300 active dissidents in the country, fragmented into various groups, and they were generally tolerated by the regime so long as they remained "within system" critics. More active rejection of Communist Party policies began to appear in 1986, after Gorbachev introduced reform in the Soviet Union, and different opposition groups began to make greater efforts to work together—albeit with limited success.[10] The intellectual rumblings within the Party were evident in the participation of radical reformers from within the HSWP, including Pozsgay, at an "intellectuals' conference" in September 1987 at Lakitelek, which was attended by members of the populist opposition who later founded the Hungarian Democratic Forum (HDF).[11] Both Party members and popu-

---

8. See George Schöpflin, Rudolf Tőkés, and Ivan Volgyes, "Leadership Change and Crisis in Hungary," *Problems of Communism*, Vol. 37, No. 5 (September–October 1988), pp. 23–45.

9. Kádár took the same opportunity to elevate Janos Berecz, Grósz's main rival for the position of General Secretary, to the Politburo to keep these two from working together against him. See "Hungary: Change of Leadership," Background Brief from the Foreign and Commonwealth Office, London, August 1988.

10. For a detailed evaluation of different strands of the dissident movement in Hungary and their initial efforts to cooperate in the mid-1980s, see Tőkés, *Hungary's Negotiated Revolution*, pp. 168–197.

11. "Formal Founding of Hungarian Democratic Forum," Budapest Home Service, September 3, 1988, in *BBC Summary of World Broadcasts: Eastern Europe* [hereafter *SWB:EE*], September 6, 1988; and Alfred Reisch, "Democratic Forum Holds First National Congress," *Radio Free Europe Situation Report,* Hungary, No. 5 (March 31, 1989).

lists appeared interested in exploring the potential for cooperation or future alliance.[12]

On May 22, 1988, at a special Party conference, Kádár resigned, and the Central Committee appointed Károly Grósz as General Secretary of the HSWP. This was the beginning of serious political and economic changes in Hungary.[13] The conference was doubly significant, since the Party not only changed its leadership, but also put constitutional reform on its agenda. Several people who favored radical reforms were nominated to the Politburo, including Pozsgay and Rezsö Nyers, designer of Hungary's 1968 reform program (the New Economic Mechanism, or NEM) and a supporter of broad reforms of the system.[14] Changes in many aspects of the country's legal code were broached in the next few months, ranging from laws on associations and demonstrations to the need to regulate ownership, property, and wages.[15]

Startling modifications emerged by the fall. Grósz had proposed in May that the posts of Party General Secretary and prime minister not be held by the same person; he resigned the prime ministership in November. Miklós Németh was appointed to replace him in this post on November 24, 1988.[16] And on November 25, 1988, the National Assembly read and approved a radical reform program that laid out a timetable for draft legislation to be reviewed over the next two years. This proposal was pre-

---

12. Tökés points out that Pozsgay courted not only the populists, but virtually every independent movement in Hungary between 1982 and 1988, either to expand his own power base, or to garner greater support for reform efforts within the Party. *Hungary's Negotiated Revolution*, p. 199.

13. Kádár's removal was made possible by an "alliance of convenience" between Grósz and his main rival, Berecz. See "Hungary: Change of Leadership," p. 3.

14. Both enjoyed widespread popularity as a result of their reform orientation, and actively advocated steps toward "socialist pluralism." See Brown, *Eastern Europe and Communist Rule*, pp. 228–229; and Charles Gati, "Reforming Communist Systems," in William E. Griffith, ed., *Central and Eastern Europe: The Opening Curtain?* (Boulder, Colo.: Westview Press, 1989), p. 235–236.

15. *Europa World Yearbook, 1990*, Vol. 1 (London: Europa Publications Ltd., 1990), p. 1258.

16. Németh explicitly encouraged the division of labor between Party and government, both by resigning from his post as Central Committee secretary, and by moving to appoint a professionalized "government of experts" and distancing it from the mistakes of the Party. "Grósz, Nemeth Queried on Parliamentary Session," Budapest Television Service, November 26, 1988, in *FBIS:EEU*, November 29, 1988; "Karoly Grósz to give up Premiership: 'Magyar Hirlap' Interview, MTI, October 28, 1988, in *SWB:EE*, November 2, 1988; and Alfred Reisch, "Young Pro-reform Economist Replaces Karoly Grósz as Prime Minister," *Radio Free Europe Situation Report*, Hungary, No. 20 (December 15, 1988).

sented by Imre Pozsgay, and made clear that changes were forthcoming in the constitution, the electoral system, and opposition political parties, among other things. Though the proposal was easily approved, support for it was not unanimous—a sign that the Parliament had already begun to take its role more seriously.[17]

Equally significant, by the fall the question of adopting a multiparty political system in Hungary had been raised within the Party, and then spread to public discussion. This was perhaps the most hotly debated issue for several months. The opinions of different Central Committee (CC) and Politburo members suggested that a wide range of options was under discussion but that little consensus existed, and most individuals were unsure which policies they favored.[18] The possibility of pluralism "under a one-party system" was raised by the CC, while Grósz stated on November 7, 1988, that the HSWP would, in theory, accept defeat in elections.[19] Others, such as Nyers, acknowledged that a multiparty system was possible in principle but only in the future, stressing that "today Hungarian society is truly in the preparatory phase for this." He also pointed out that other parties were not sufficiently organized to clarify their own political and economic programs. Similarly, the relationship between any new parties that might form and the ruling HSWP was unclear; throughout the fall, party officials insisted that any new parties would have to embrace a "socialist" orientation in order to be legalized. Yet other commentators, such as Mihaly Bihari, pointed out that pluralism might have advantages for the HSWP, since this might push it "to become a democratic communist party, under the pressure of the multiparty system," and Nyers noted in February 1989 that "in the case of the parties, the only condition of operation should be acceptance of the Constitution. In my opinion, that is the limit of democracy."[20]

---

17. See Alfred Reisch, "National Assembly Approves Radical Reform Program," *Radio Free Europe Situation Report*, Hungary, No. 20 (December 15, 1988), p. 15.

18. In most communist-ruled states the General Secretary was first among equals of the Politburo, which for all intents and purposes ruled the country; the Central Committee was the broader Party body from which Politburo members were chosen, and which officially approved Politburo decisions. For an overview of how communist systems in the Soviet Union and Eastern Europe were governed, see Ronald J. Hill and Peter John Frank, *The Soviet Communist Party* (Boston: Allen & Unwin, 1986).

19. "New Rules to Play By," interview with Károly Grósz in *Time*, November 7, 1988, p. 14.

20. "Rezső Nyers and Mihaly Bihari on Possibility of Multi-Party System Evolving," Budapest Home Service, November 11, 1988, in *SWB:EE*, November 15, 1988. See also Report by Janos Berecz, MTI, November 2, 1988, in *SWB:EE*, November 4, 1988; "Min-

Disagreements within the Party about correct policy decisions arose openly at the November 1988 meeting of the CC.[21] The differences of opinion indicate that the Party was beginning to lose any sense of unity; moreover, arguments among the leadership hindered the Party's ability to adopt a coherent reform program quickly and decisively.

As a consequence, Hungary's tiny opposition gained valuable time in which to organize. In April 1988, before Kádár's retirement, several carefully apolitical "interest groups" had been formed, as had an independent trade union; the number of such groups mushroomed throughout the country over the summer.[22] The HDF was formally founded on September 3, 1988, as an "intellectual-political movement" since independent political parties were not yet legal.[23] Other groups declared their intention to become political parties once they could do so legally, and the Smallholder's Party, one of the country's prewar parties, announced the "resumption" of its activities, arguing that it had never been officially disbanded in the 1940s.[24]

In the first few months of 1989, the pace of change quickened dramatically. As part of the government's effort to improve the economic situation and move toward a market economy, the first of four major price hikes planned for 1989 was launched on January 8.[25] On January 11, 1989,

---

isters Answer Internal and Foreign Affairs Questions," Hungarian TV, September 22, 1988, in *SWB:EE,* September 26, 1988; and "Nyers on Social Democracy, 'Reform' Communism," MTI, February 20, 1989, in *FBIS:EEU,* February 21, 1989.

21. The leadership included reformers and more conservative politicians who differed on the direction and pace of reforms. While Grósz tried to maintain a centrist position, those favoring more radical reforms, notably Imre Pozsgay, pressed for a more rapid schedule for change. "Janos Berecz Interviewed on Central Committee Meeting," Hungarian TV, November 2, 1988, in *SWB:EE,* November 4, 1988. See also "Keynote Speech by Janos Berecz," Budapest Home Service, December 15, 1988, in *SWB:EE,* December 20, 1988; and Alfred Reisch, "Hard-Pressed Leader Launches Political Offensive," *Radio Free Europe Situation Report,* Hungary, No. 20 (December 15, 1988), p. 25.

22. Judith Pataki, "The Rebirth of Political Parties," and Edith Markos, "Hungary's First Independent Trade Union Holds Its Founding Congress," both in *Radio Free Europe Situation Report,* Hungary, No. 1 (January 12, 1989).

23. "Formal Founding of Hungarian Democratic Forum," Budapest Home Service, September 3, 1988, in *SWB:EE,* September 6, 1988.

24. Pataki, "The Rebirth of Political Parties," *Radio Free Europe Situation Report,* p. 1. On the fate of the Smallholder's Party in the 1940s, see Joseph Rothschild, *Return to Diversity: A Political History of East Central Europe since World War II* (New York: Oxford University Press, 1989), pp. 98–103.

25. Károly Okolicsanyi, "Massive Price Hikes Polarize Trade Unions and Government," *Radio Free Europe Situation Report,* Hungary, No. 2 (February 8, 1989).

rights of association and assembly were legalized by the National Assembly, the first major change in the constitution. New rules of procedure were passed for the Assembly, and serious debates over the new bills being presented became customary, as all sense of unanimity in the formerly rubber-stamp Assembly vanished.

These actions by the government were followed in February with startling moves by the HSWP. At a CC meeting in mid-February, the party accepted the goal of mixed ownership of the economy and acknowledged the need to create social welfare mechanisms to allay the upheavals this change might cause for the work force. Conceding after much debate that the country should aim for pluralism and the establishment of a multiparty system, within days the Party gave up its constitutional right to play the "leading role" in society. HSWP spokesmen insisted that Hungary would remain "socialist" and that the Party intended to continue to predominate in Hungarian politics, but that it would do so by demonstrating its competence to lead rather than by mandating its place in the constitution.[26] Yet Party spokesmen also warned of destabilization if the pace of political reforms accelerated too quickly. In early 1989, the HSWP was still talking about holding wholly free elections only in 1995, and again pointed to the unreadiness of other parties as a reason to maintain a calm pace and delay elections.

Disagreements within the Party grew increasingly acrimonious in early 1989, as the boundaries of reform began to be tested seriously. Imre Pozsgay, clearly a supporter of rapid and far-reaching reforms, announced at the end of January that a special commission of the CC had reevaluated the country's history under socialist rule, and concluded that the 1956 revolution had been a "popular uprising against an oligarchic rule that had debased the nation."[27] Beyond the obvious volatility

---

26. The CC communiqué noted that "the HSWP does not lay claim to the constitutional declaration of its leading role. However, it wishes to fulfill a determining role based on political work in the management of society." See MTI, February 22, 1989, in *SWB:EE*, February 24, 1989.

27. Party leaders also acknowledged that the introduction of a multiparty system was necessary due to the HSWP's mistakes. "Grósz Comments on State of One-Party System," Budapest Domestic Service, February 24, 1989, in *FBIS:EEU*, February 27, 1989; "Gyorgy Fejti and Mihaly Bihari on the New Political Parties," Hungarian TV, February 19, 1989, in *SWB:EE*, February 23, 1989; "Pozsgay on Nagy Reburial, Political Reassessment," Budapest Domestic Service, January 28, 1989, in *FBIS:EEU*, January 30, 1989; and Pozsgay Interview with Radio Budapest, February 2, 1989, in *Nepszabadsag*, February 3, 1989; as quoted by Alfred Reisch, *Radio Free Europe Research Report*, Hungary, No. 3 (February 24, 1989), p. 5. See also "Historical Sub-Committee's Report," Budapest Home Service, February 15, 1989, in *SWB:EE*, February 18, 1989.

of its content—Poszgay's aides expected condemnation from Moscow —Pozsgay's announcement was also evidence of the newly politicized climate in the country, and the increasingly public jockeying both for positions within the leadership during the power and policy struggles underway, and for public approval in a competitive political arena.[28] General Secretary Grósz's anger over this unexpected public reappraisal of such a sensitive historical issue reflected his conservative stand. Though he acquiesced to the initiation of a pluralist system, Grósz had insisted that a new constitution stipulate the perpetuation of a socialist system in Hungary. Grósz's reservations about allowing the formation of other parties were evident in his speeches at the end of 1988.[29] In spite of his efforts, by the spring the reformist wing in the Party leadership clearly had gained the upper hand, and in June the disagreement over reform policies led to a change in the entire structure of the Party's leadership. A four-man presidency was created, which included Grósz, along with Pozsgay and Miklós Németh, but Rezsö Nyers was chosen to head the collective presidency.[30]

Almost simultaneously with the reappraisal of the 1956 revolution, the government announced that it would allow the reburial of Imre Nagy, leader of the HSWP during the revolution, who was executed in 1958. Despite disagreement within the party, Nagy was rehabilitated as well, and when his funeral took place on June 16, 1989, he was accorded the honors of a national hero.[31] This was an effort by the HSWP to gain—or

---

28. Jacques Lévesque, *The Enigma of 1989: The USSR and the Liberation of Eastern Europe* (Berkeley, Calif.: University of California Press, 1997), pp. 129–130. Pozsgay made his announcement without the sanction of the Politburo or CC, but few in the Party were willing to reject the new interpretation. The exception was the hard-line element of the Party, which saw this reinterpretation as a betrayal. See "Interview with Robert Ribanski," *Magyar Hirlap*, reprinted in *World Affairs*, Vol. 151, No. 4 (1990), pp. 220–223.

29. Probably not coincidentally, Pozsgay made his announcement while Grósz was traveling outside the country. Grósz openly favored the continuation of socialism in some form, to be led by the HSWP. See, for example, "Károly Grósz at County Party Aktiv," Budapest Home Service, December 16, 1988, in *SWB:EE*, December 19, 1988.

30. Though the four leaders initially tried to stress the continued unity of the party, Grósz acknowledged defeat in July by announcing his intention to resign from the leadership prior to elections. See Leslie Colitt, "Hungarian Party Dilutes Grósz's Powers," *Financial Times*, June 26, 1989; and "Television Interview with New Four-Member HSWP Presidium," Hungarian TV, June 25, 1989, in *SWB:EE*, June 27, 1989.

31. Grósz was among those who expressed doubts about Nagy's rehabilitation. "Interview with Károly Grósz," Hungarian TV, May 30, 1989, in *SWB:EE*, June 2, 1989. See also "Reaction to Károly Grósz's Statement on Nagy's Rehabilitation," Budapest Home Service, May 31, 1989, in *SWB:EE*, June 3, 1989.

at least maintain—popular support, and also an attempt by the reforming party to distance itself from past Party actions.[32]

One of the factors that may have caused significant friction within the party and its leadership was the issue of opening discussions with opposition groups. Three-sided talks began on June 13, 1989, among the government, the Opposition Round Table—a loose coalition of opposition parties—and a "third side," made up of representatives of social organizations that had been satellites of the HSWP. The spread of "Round Table" negotiations across Eastern Europe is one of the clearest examples of diffusion. The possibility of a Round Table discussion was broached in Poland in August 1988, and discussions between regime and opposition began there in February 1989. In Hungary, "prenegotiations" between the regime and representatives of opposition groups began in March, and agreement to hold talks was reached on June 10, 1989.[33]

The regime had initially attempted to negotiate with new opposition groups independently, which would have enabled it to work with those more likely to cooperate, and to preclude the unification of the opposition movement. But in mid-March the main opposition parties, recognizing the need for unity, established the Opposition Round Table (ORT), and insisted that the government negotiate with this unified body.[34]

The regime and the ORT differed on the aims of Round Table discussions as well. The regime wanted wide-ranging talks on the political, economic, and societal problems facing the country, while the ORT wanted

---

32. Several reform communists, including Pozsgay and Nyers, participated in Nagy's reburial. Laszlo Bruszt argues that by doing so, they hoped to make clear that they were part of the "us" of the population, rather than the "them" of the discredited past of the Party. Bruszt, "1989: The Negotiated Revolution in Hungary," *Social Research*, Vol. 57, No. 2 (Summer 1990), p. 380.

33. One reason negotiations were necessary in Hungary (as well as Poland) was that no group in the Party was able to prevail in promoting its policies, and the opposition was too weak to force a solution on its own; only a negotiated solution could resolve this impasse. For detailed accounts of the Opposition Round Table and the Round Table process, see Bruszt, "1989: The Negotiated Revolution in Hungary," pp. 365–387; Andras Bozoki, "Hungary's Road to Systemic Change: The Opposition Roundtable," *East European Politics and Society*, Vol. 7, No. 2 (Spring 1993), pp. 276–308; Tőkés, *Hungary's Negotiated Revolution*; and Andras Sajo, "The Roundtable Talks in Hungary," in Jon Elster, ed., *The Roundtable Talks and the Breakdown of Communism* (Chicago: University of Chicago Press, 1996).

34. The efforts of Imre Konya, a lawyer not affiliated with any political party, were instrumental in achieving unity. Nine groups agreed to cooperate in the Opposition Round Table, including some with whom the regime had theretofore refused to open talks. Bozoki, "Hungary's Road to Systemic Change," p. 282; and Sajo, "The Roundtable talks in Hungary," pp. 72–74.

discussions to focus only on establishing the basis for free elections. The opposition was anxious to avoid being coopted into sharing responsibility for the mistakes made by the previous regime. The two also disagreed about who should participate in negotiations, and the status to be given to different groups.[35] And while the Polish Round Table provided an important example, the Hungarian opposition wanted to avoid the outcome of the Polish negotiations, which seemingly guaranteed the Communist Party a controlling majority in the new government.[36] In the end, agreement was reached to hold three-sided talks. Opposition spokesmen stated from the outset that their goal was the creation of a completely democratic, pluralist system: "The basis of power is the sovereignty of the people. . . . The people's will must be manifested in free elections . . . from which no party or political organization which accepts the principles of democracy and rejects the employment of violent means can be excluded."[37] While the opposition agreed to a wider range of topics than it originally preferred, the HSWP tacitly acceded to a peaceful change of the system through its acceptance of negotiations.

Negotiations did not remain within the carefully agreed bounds. The HSWP raised the issue of revising the constitution, and the ORT responded by raising sensitive issues such as the abolition of party organizations at the workplace, the status of the Worker's Guard (the Party's paramilitary organization), and removing any privileges for the HSWP from the constitution. The most contentious issues proved to be whether

---

35. This paralleled discussions in Poland; neither opposition group wanted to share its "side" of the table with groups long affiliated with the ruling party. Nor did they want the ruling party to be treated as one of many parties, since it had far more power and resources than the fledgling parties, and the opposition considered it the locus of power, not one actor among many. Bozoki, "Hungary's Road to Systemic Change," pp. 280–281; and Bruszt, "1989: The Negotiated Revolution in Hungary," pp. 370–371.

36. Ironically, Prime Minister Németh also emphasized the importance of holding fair and open talks, stating that "we cannot under any circumstances, accept the kind of agreement adopted by the Polish Round Table, that is where the proportions of seats in the parliament to be allocated after the elections was already determined in advance." See "Hungarian Premier's visit to Poland," dispatch by Gabor Nemes, Budapest Home Service, May 15, 1989, in *SWB:EE*, May 17, 1989.

37. These comments showed that the opposition would not accept strictures such as the acceptance of the "socialist" nature of the state. Imre Konya also stressed quite pointedly that "it is not our intention to share power with the present owners of power." See "HSWP-Opposition Round-Table Talks," speech by Imre Konya, Budapest Home Service, June 13, 1989, in *SWB:EE*, June 15, 1989; Agreement about the Commencement of Substantial Political Negotiations between the Hungarian Socialist Workers' Party, the Members of the Opposition Roundtable and the Organizations of the Third Side, 10 June 1989, *Cold War International History Project Bulletin* [hereafter *CWIHP Bulletin*], Issue 12/13 (Fall/Winter 2001), pp. 79–81.

the country would be defined as "socialist" in the constitution;[38] disclosure of the HSWP's assets; and the nature and timing of the presidential elections. This last issue led to a split in the ORT, as two of the nine parties refused to accept the HSWP's proposal of early presidential elections prior to elections to the National Assembly.[39]

After several months of bargaining, on September 18, 1989, an agreement was signed by the HSWP and some members of the ORT on six draft laws considered to be crucial to the creation of a new political structure: amendment of the constitution; establishment of a constitutional court; operation and management of parties; election of National Assembly deputies; amendment of the penal code; and amending the law on penal procedures.[40] The six bills accepted by the participants in the discussions were to be forwarded to the premier, so that he might submit them to the National Assembly, a procedure that had been agreed at the outset of the talks. The new laws went further than the agreements reached earlier in the year in Poland in that there was no provision for a special role for the HSWP; similarly, the legal revisions represented an additional separation of the Party from the state's legal apparatus. The only point on which the HSWP appeared to have gotten the upper hand was in the timing of the election of the president. An early election was presumed to give Pozsgay, the party's candidate, an advantage, since he was widely popular due to his championship of reform.

But by the fall of 1989, the HSWP's domestic standing was rapidly weakening. In by-elections held around the country in July and August, opposition candidates were allowed to participate for the first time, and the HSWP lost badly.[41] At the HSWP's 14th Congress, from October 6–9, 1989, the controversy over the future shape of the Party came to a head. The Reform Assembly platform, developed by the reform circles that had sprung up around the country, easily gained the most support, but it was

---

38. A compromise was eventually reached, with the following wording: "The republic of Hungary is an independent democratic rechtsstaat [right-based state] in which the values of bourgeois democracy and democratic socialism are realized equally." As cited in Tökés, *Hungary's Negotiated Revolution*, p. 345.

39. Bozoki, "Hungary's Road to Systemic Change," pp. 297–298, 305–307.

40. "Agreement Signed at Trilateral Coordination Talks," Budapest Home Service, MTI, September 18, 1989, in *SWB:EE*, September 20, 1989.

41. Candidates affiliated with the HDF won 60 to 70 percent of the votes. This led some HSWP officials, such as Nyers, to speculate that the HSWP would win at best one third of the votes in nation-wide elections. See "HSWP Chairman on Multi-Party Elections and Political Change," Austrian TV, August 14, 1989, in *SWB:EE*, August 17, 1989.

opposed by hard-line factions.[42] In the end, the HSWP was dissolved, and a "renewed" party, called the Hungarian Socialist Party (HSP) was created. Its members adopted the goal of working for democratic socialism by establishing a market-based economy. The new party also stated its willingness to cooperate with any "democratic political forces which feel responsibility for the future of Europe"—a dramatic change from a year earlier, when the HSWP had insisted that any opposing party adopt "socialist" values if it wanted to be recognized.[43] By November 1989 the new party's membership was only 15,000; the old HSWP at one time had a membership of 700,000.[44]

The Party Congress demonstrated that the socialist party had lost control of the process of reform. Its willingness to renounce virtually all the principles of socialism in order to maintain any standing in the country shows how defensive it had become over the course of the summer, and how dramatically the political climate had changed.

The conservative factions of the Party deplored almost all of the changes, and the "Marxist Unity" platform of the old HSWP subsequently formed a new "communist" party to uphold Marxist-Leninist values that it felt the HSP had abandoned. This group held its own 14th Party Congress in December, declaring that the HSWP had not ceased to exist. Grósz, by now clearly among the conservatives in the country and party, was chosen as president of the preparatory committee of this party.[45]

In a final blow to the Party's efforts to preserve a role in the new political system, in November 1989 the Alliance of Free Democrats, one of

---

42. Patrick O'Neil, "Revolution from Within: Institutional Analysis, Transitions from Authoritarianism, and the Case of Hungary," *World Politics*, Vol. 48 (July 1996), pp. 597–599.

43. "Manifesto of Hungarian Socialist Party," MTI, October 9, 1989, in *SWB:EE*, October 12, 1989.

44. One major dispute at the Congress concerned who among the previous membership ought to be allowed to join the new party; the reformists worried about opening the membership to all, since this might allow tainted members to remain and damage the new party's credibility. In the end, however, it was agreed that all members of the HSWP would have the right to join the new party if they chose, but all must reapply. The discharge of members appears to have been a significant tactical error, as Tökés notes. See *Hungary's Negotiated Revolution*, pp. 355–356; see also O'Neil, "Revolution from Within," p. 600.

45. The new HSWP was careful to stress that its goal was not the dictatorship of the proletariat, but that it did support the continuation of "democratic centralism," the party's term for Communist Party–led democracy. See "Fourteenth Congress of the HSWP," MTI, December 17–18, 1989, in *SWB:EE*, December 21, 1989.

the opposition parties that had refused to sign the Round Table agreement, forced a referendum on the timing of presidential elections, arguing that a new president should not be chosen until after a freely elected National Assembly was in place. The opposition view prevailed by a narrow margin in a referendum held on November 26, 1989, a positive sign for the credibility of the election process in Hungary and a setback to the HSP. For all its changes, it was unlikely to overcome the latent hostility to communism that had been reinvigorated by the changed political atmosphere, at least in the short run. Parliamentary elections would be held on March 25, 1990, and the new president chosen thereafter.[46] While analyses of the elections predicted various outcomes during the ensuing months, by the spring elections the HSP's support had dwindled further. The HSP won 8 percent of the vote in the March 1990 elections, ensuring it representation in the National Assembly, but far from a controlling voice. The HDF won the elections, but only as part of a coalition called the United Democratic Front, and a new government with an HDF prime minister, Jozsef Antall, was inaugurated on May 24, 1990.

Measuring the Regime's Attitude Toward Reform

In a state that chose to introduce reforms relatively early, we should find evidence that the regime recognized the need for political as well as economic changes to resolve the country's problems; and that it felt that it could survive in a more open political environment. This section evaluates the first of these two factors by looking at prior reform efforts, the nature of the system, and the regime's response to Gorbachev.

PRIOR REFORM EFFORTS IN HUNGARY
In contrast to Poland, reforms in Hungary focused relatively little on the linkage between economics and politics. In fact, Kádár explicitly denied such a linkage, though others in the Party leadership clearly recognized its importance as early as 1966.[47] Yet the Hungarian regime introduced more market elements into the economy than did the Poles, thus moving the state further from a true socialist economic model and tacitly rejecting the ideology on which centrally planned economies were based.

---

46. The debate about how to elect the president did not end here; at least once more in the following months, votes were taken on whether the president should be elected directly by the population or chosen by the new National Assembly.

47. Brown, *Eastern Europe and Communist Rule*, pp. 219–223. Tökés also notes that theoreticians in the Party noted the need for political reforms as part of any reform package as early as 1965–1968. Tökés, *Hungary's Negotiated Revolution*, p. 180.

Under Kádár, there was a clear intention to mitigate the hardships of the Stalinist economic model to the degree possible. This was part of Kádár's effort to court popular acceptance, which required maintaining a reasonably good standard of living in the country. The two most notable indications of this trend were the expansion of contacts with the world market, and the introduction of market elements in domestic production in Hungary.

The New Economic Mechanism (NEM), introduced in Hungary early in 1968, incorporated both of these factors. The NEM was developed because the regime recognized that it needed to shift from the extensive emphasis on heavy industry common to Stalinist systems, replacing this with intensive development and a focus on light industry and consumer goods.[48] The NEM limited central planning and delegated more power to enterprise managers as a way to compel them to be responsive to market forces. As part of the program, Hungary's economy was also opened somewhat to the world market.[49] The NEM also made more provisions for privatization. In agriculture, for example, there was broad scope for private initiative and individual profit-making, and as a result, agriculture became the most efficient and effective part of the Hungarian economy.

The program introduced in 1968 was intended to be the first stage of a new economic program, but the later stages were never enacted. The Hungarian government came under pressure from the Soviet Union and conservatives within the HSWP leadership in 1972–1973 to end these reforms; the NEM was halted in 1974 and new restrictions were put on profit-making and decentralization.[50] However, some of the reforms of the NEM were reinstated in 1977–1978.[51] New price reforms introduced in 1979 and 1980 included a reduction of subsidies for consumer goods. In January 1980, competitive wholesale prices were instituted in industry;[52] a year later, in an effort to improve the economy's efficiency, several branch ministries were abolished and a single ministry for industry was

---

48. Bill Lomax, "Hungary, the Quest for Legitimacy," in Paul G. Lewis, ed., *Eastern Europe: Political Crisis and Legitimation* (London: Croom Helm, 1984), p. 89.

49. Istvan Magas, "Reforms Under Pressure: Hungary," *East European Quarterly*, Vol. 24, No. 1 (March 1990), pp. 68–71.

50. Brown, *Eastern Europe and Communist Rule*, pp. 210–214.

51. The Hungarian government also declared its intention to shift to greater emphasis on exports late in 1977. Forty to 50 percent of the state's national income came from foreign trade. Ibid., p. 214.

52. Berend, *Central and Eastern Europe, 1944–1993*, pp. 268–269; and *EIU Regional Review: Eastern Europe and the USSR*, p. 68.

formed in their place, as an effort to break down the entrenched bureaucratic links that had developed between particular ministries and industries.[53] Import curbs were adopted in 1982, and some investment bonds were issued in 1983, with the aim of breaking the monopoly of the Hungarian National Bank on issuing credits to industry.[54] Enterprises were also given more latitude to conduct direct foreign trade.[55] A bond market was established in 1983 and a bankruptcy law was passed for the first time, though it was rarely enforced.[56] While piecemeal, these reforms again pushed away from the socialist model by introducing elements of a market system.[57]

Reforms in the 1980s also established greater toleration for private business. The private sector gained increasing support from official sources during the early 1980s; Kádár himself acknowledged the importance of the "second economy," as it was called, as a significant asset.[58] The long-standing toleration for private agricultural activity was extended into industrial enterprises at the end of the 1970s. Individuals and groups were encouraged to carry out "autonomous economic activity" either within their workplaces or as separate enterprises. The "second economy" grew signficantly in the 1980s; in 1983 about 33 percent of

---

53. *The Europa World Yearbook 1990,* vol. 1 (London: Europa Publications Ltd., 1990), p. 1257.

54. See Ralph Kinnear, "Creeping Capitalism in Hungary?" *Soviet/East European Survey: Selected Research and Analysis from Radio Free Europe/Radio Liberty* (Durham, N.C.: Duke University Press, 1985), p. 291. Two new banks were also established in 1985, to encourage competition. Brown, *Eastern Europe and Communist Rule,* p. 220.

55. The number of enterprises doing so initially rose slowly, since their faith that the regime would tolerate such activity grew only by watching other successful enterprises. Wim Swaan and Marie Lissowska, "Capabilities, Routines, and Eastern European Economic Reform: Hungary and Poland before and after the 1989 revolutions," *Journal of Economic Issues,* Vol. 30, No. 4 (December 1996), p. 1043.

56. Prior to establishing a bankruptcy law, enterprises could not go bankrupt regardless of how inefficient they were. *Eastern Europe and the USSR: Economic Structure and Analysis* (London: Economist Intelligence Unit, 1988), p. 116.

57. As one indication that the Soviet Union recognized the direction of Hungary's reforms, one Soviet economist at a conference in 1985 asked the Hungarians there, "Comrades, could you just answer me one question? In your country, is it still the plan which determines the market or is it now the market which determines the plan?" As cited by Gati, *Hungary and the Soviet Bloc,* p. 175.

58. Kádár noted that "during their spare time a certain percentage of the workers participate in work that is useful to the national economy and to the individual. This is a supplementary source of our development that . . . enhances the growth of the nation's wealth." Stokes, *The Walls Came Tumbling Down,* p. 84.

Hungarians were working in the private sector, and by 1988 one-fifth to one-fourth of the state's output came from private sources.[59]

The regime's willingness to accept private enterprise, albeit on a limited scale, and its efforts to push state enterprises to be more responsive to competition indicate that it clearly recognized the need to move away from a purely socialist economic model and to incorporate market elements. While this did not translate into political reforms before 1985, the abdication of control over significant elements of the economy by the Party was in fact a political move, diluting as it did the Marxist-Leninist ideology.

THE NATURE OF THE HUNGARIAN SYSTEM

A second measure of the regime's recognition of the need for change is the nature of the state's political and economic structure prior to Gorbachev's accession. Almost from the outset, Kádár's rule broke with the standards accepted within the Soviet bloc. The fragile legitimacy that Kádár built for the Hungarian Socialist Worker's Party during the 1960s was based on the tacit bargain he made with the population; in return for a reasonable standard of living and minimal interference in daily life, the population accepted that it could have essentially no political voice. This contradicted the Soviet model in two ways; it diverged from the insistence on mobilization of the population in support of the regime, and it emphasized consumerism.[60] Because he could point to the need to pacify the population after 1956, Kádár was able to continue this policy for most of his rule, though the divergence of Hungary's economic policies sometimes caused tension either within the HSWP or with Moscow. For example, the NEM was put on hold in 1974, and its main architects, Rezsö Nyers and Lajos Feher, were dismissed from their posts.[61]

The Hungarian regime also made an effort to coopt intellectuals and experts into the Party, though it maintained the distinction between "red"

---

59. Yanqi Tong, "State, Society, and Political Change in China and Hungary," *Comparative Politics*, Vol. 26, No. 3 (April 1994), p. 336; and Janos Kornai, "Individual Freedom and Reform of the Socialist Economy," *European Economic Review*, No. 32 (1988), p. 243.

60. To be sure, other communist-ruled states relaxed their efforts to mobilize the population after Stalin's death. Yet the combination of low mobilization and consumerism was unique to Hungary. This contrasted sharply with the traditional insistence by ruling communist parties on popular mobilization in support of communist ideals. See, for example, Alexander Dallin and George Breslauer, "Political Terror in the Post-Mobilization Stage," in Chalmers Johnson, ed., *Change in Communist Systems* (Stanford, Calif.: Stanford University Press, 1970), pp. 191–214.

61. *EIU Regional Review: Eastern Europe and the USSR 1986*, p. 68.

and "expert" in the jobs to which people were assigned, with intellectuals generally assigned to state rather than Party posts. But as Hungary faced increasing economic difficulties over the years, the HSWP tended to devolve the responsibility for economic issues to the government and away from close Party control.[62] Again, this diverged from the norm of Party control over important aspects of the economy.

One notable consequence of the inclusion of intellectuals in the party was that by 1984, before Gorbachev came to power, reform-minded critics from within the system dominated theoretical discussions of the country's political choices.[63] This indicates a broad awareness within the Party ranks that political reforms were a prerequisite for economic health.

By the mid-1980s, the Party leadership included a mix of reformers and conservative thinkers. That reformers were gaining strength was evident in the Party's acceptance of wider forms of ownership and in its positive discussion of "pluralism." The Party also moved to accept the need for political competition in a limited way in 1983, by passing a law mandating multicandidate elections for some posts. While this competition was still carefully regulated, and all candidates had to endorse the platform put forward by the Patriotic People's Front, it nonetheless represented a break with traditional Party appointments.[64]

Notably, clear generational divides existed between the reformers and the conservatives.[65] While Kádár had been one of the most "liberal" leaders in the bloc, by 1985, he was among the conservatives in the Politburo, due to his unwillingness to contemplate radical change. His conservatism could be seen in the way the regime responded to criticism; calls for change within the system were tolerated, but change *of* the system remained unacceptable.[66]

USE OF THE OPPORTUNITY TO EXPAND REFORMS

The regime's recognition of the need for change was evident in its positive response to change in the Soviet Union. This positive response was

---

62. Tökés, "Hungary's Political Elites," p. 54.

63. Tökés, *Hungary's Negotiated Revolution*, p. 193.

64. Some independent candidates managed to survive the process and win election to the National Assembly in 1985. Competitive elections also had the effect of making the elections focus on issues, something that had not been necessary in single-candidate competitions. Ibid., pp. 264–265.

65. In terms of the post-Stalin leadership, six "generations" of leaders within the Party were represented within the leadership at this point. Ibid., pp. 213–215.

66. Gati notes that Kádár distinguished between what the regime would "support," "tolerate," or "prohibit." *Hungary and the Soviet Bloc*, p. 162.

due initially to Hungarian support for the Soviet Union's changed foreign policy line under Gorbachev, and the easing of tensions with the West.[67] However, while Gorbachev's call for reform was welcomed since it gave sanction to Hungary's less-than-orthodox position within the bloc, until Kádár's forced retirement in 1988 government efforts to promote reform moved slowly.

A serious discussion of economic reforms began in 1986, when Pozsgay attacked the economic program the government had proposed in March 1985. This attack built on the long-running discussions of reform in party and intellectual journals, and the PPF-commissioned paper "Turnabout and Reform." Discussion at this point focused on the type of reform the country needed; the question of whether reforms per se were needed was taken for granted.[68]

Personnel changes were made within the CC economic branches beginning in 1986, with younger experts appointed to run leading economic agencies. In addition, more responsibility for the economy was shifted from the Party to the government, and the Party candidly admitted the depth of the economic problems facing the country.[69]

Indeed, the state's economy suffered during the 1980s.[70] To sustain its policy of importing Western goods, which kept the population content, the regime had borrowed from the West. With millions of "petro-dollars"

---

67. Hungary had been lukewarm at best in its support for Soviet foreign policy in the early 1980s, when Moscow's relations with the West deteriorated. Hungary offered late and tepid support for Moscow's invasion of Afghanistan in December 1979. After the Soviet Union shot down Korean Airlines (KAL) Flight 007 in 1983, the Hungarian government expressed sympathy for the victims of this tragedy, rather than mimicking Moscow's anti-American condemnations. The Soviet decision to deploy intermediate-range nuclear weapons in East Germany and Czechoslovakia as "countermeasures" to balance NATO's deployments of Pershing II missiles in Western Europe met with equally lukewarm support, while Hungary also made efforts to maintain good relations with Western states. See Alfred Reisch, "Openings to the West," *Soviet/East European Survey*, p. 211–216.

68. Stokes, *The Walls Came Tumbling Down*, p. 91.

69. Tökés, *Hungary's Negotiated Revolution*, p. 275.

70. In 1985, the year Gorbachev came to power, Hungary had the lowest growth rate in the Eastern bloc. The state's gross national product (GNP) grew slowly, at an average annual rate of 1.6 percent over the period 1980–88, while the consumer price index (CPI) soared due to rising food prices and rents and decreasing subsidies. In comparison, real income grew very slowly in 1980–87, so that living standards dropped for the average citizen. For example, by April 1984, the CPI had risen 9.3 percent, while wages increased by only 3 percent in 1983, indicating a substantial decline in real wages for blue-collar workers. *The Europa World Yearbook*, p. 1260; and William F. Robinson, "Hungary in 1983: Rising Expectations, Declining Economy," *Soviet/East European Survey*, pp. 220–221.

available for loans and credits as newly rich OPEC countries deposited dollars in the Western banks, East European borrowing from Western institutions had flourished in the mid-1970s, encouraged by the new political climate of détente. This borrowing, however, came at the expense of investment in or modernization of Hungary's industrial base, limiting the state's ability to export as much to the West as it imported. Mandatory exports to the Council for Mutual Economic Assistance (CMEA) states also hurt the state's ability to balance its trade with the West. The system remained heavily centralized, and the reforms that had been attempted in the early 1980s did little more than tinker with the edges of the problem. The government introduced austerity measures in 1987, and income tax and value-added taxes in 1988.[71] Meanwhile, Hungary's hard currency debt doubled during the 1980s, rising from $9.1 billion in 1980 to $20 billion in 1989. This was the highest external debt in the bloc both per capita and per unit of GNP.[72]

Economic reforms expanded after Karoly Grósz's appointment as prime minister, and within a few months the Party announced its "Economic and Social Program for Development." The goal of this program was to stablize the economy in order to control the country's indebtedness, and to follow with economic reforms that would lead to stable growth.[73] The regime also reorganized the Council of Ministers in December, merging the ministries of foreign and internal trade. Banking and tax reform measures were implemented in 1987–1988, and a law was passed allowing the formation of corporations. Grósz also worked to strengthen his own image as a pragmatist who was the right person to lead the country.[74]

---

71. Schöpflin, Tökés, and Volgyes, "Leadership Change and Crisis in Hungary," p. 25.

72. The official estimate in 1988 was $18.6 billion, but an additional $2 billion debt was "discovered" in 1989, adding to this total. Gati, *Hungary and the Soviet Bloc*, pp. 228–229; Lincoln Gordon, *Eroding Empire: Western Relations with Eastern Europe* (Washington, D.C.: Brookings Institution, 1987), p. 331, appendix table A-2, as cited in Brown, *Eastern Europe and Communist Rule*, pp. 504–505, Table 14; and *The Military Balance 1989–90* (London: International Institute for Strategic Studies, 1989), p. 48.

73. Károly Grósz acknowledged the economy's disastrous condition and the difficulties it presented: "on the one hand, in a stagnating economy marked by deteriorating living conditions it requires much more effort from the party to formulate the correct answers and have it accepted, on the other hand, a certain loss of intellectual orientation, lack of information and confused approach to the new phenomena can be experienced." See interview with Károly Grósz, MTI, December 24, 1988, in *SWB:EE*, December 29, 1988.

74. Ibid., p. 277.

As a further indication of the changing climate in the state, a hundred intellectuals sent a letter to Parliament in September 1987, protesting that the government's economic program would not solve the country's problems. They objected to Grósz's promise of economic but no political reforms, and the indication that he was unwilling substantially to change the political structure of the state.[75] While political reforms might not yet be on the table, the economic debate had broadened considerably.

Only after Kádár's removal from power in May 1988 did serious discussion of political as well as economic reforms begin. In June 1988, the Party established four task forces to construct guidelines for the Party's future; one of the questions confronted was whether and how to accept other political groups or parties.[76] The extent of change remained most evident in the economic sphere, with Politburo members stating that Hungary wanted "a genuine market economy, without any qualifying adjectives."[77] Such a rejection of the planned economy could not fail to have political reverberations, and the Hungarian leadership acknowledged that a market economy required at least partial separation of the party and state apparatus. Grósz had been working to focus responsibility in the government since 1987; Németh furthered this process in 1989, establishing a "government of experts" that by May had greater control in Hungary than did the HSWP.[78]

The regime thus took significant advantage of the opportunity to introduce reforms. By 1989 the goal was a market economy, and Németh's government was chosen for its expertise, rather than its Party standing. Significant reforms did not begin until well into 1988, however, after the generational change in Hungary's Party leadership.

SUMMARY

A substantial part of the HSWP leadership recognized two things: first, that economic reforms well beyond the constraints of the socialist model were needed to fix the state's economic problems; and second, that political reforms must accompany economic changes if they were to succeed. Hungary's economic system had already strayed significantly from the

75. Jason McDonald, "Transition to Utopia: A Reinterpretation of Economics, Ideas, and Politics in Hungary, 1984 to 1990," *East European Politics and Society,* Vol. 7, No. 2 (Spring 1993), p. 218–225.

76. Tőkés, *Hungary's Negotiated Revolution,* p. 286.

77. Timothy Garton Ash, "Hungarian Rhapsodies: The Avant-Garde of Communist Reform," *The Spectator,* reprinted in *World Press Review,* Vol. 35, No. 11 (November 1988).

78. Tőkés, *Hungary's Negotiated Revolution,* pp. 326–327.

socialist model in 1985; Gorbachev's introduction of reform energized those who wanted to address the political problems that had weakened earlier reform efforts.

Judging the Regime's Ability to Compete

A regime that believed it had some real popular support would be more likely to risk greater political competition. Alternately, conflict within the regime over policy choices could lead some groups to search for allies outside the ruling party, especially if these groups believed they could survive in a liberalized political arena. In Hungary, the HSWP had enjoyed reasonably high support from the population. Yet competition within the HSWP for control overshadowed regime efforts to take advantage of its relative popularity and ensure the Party's position in the new political system it was trying to establish. Kádár's succession was unresolved, and the major figures in the Party were focused on the competition for the leadership, sometimes at the expense of the Party—certainly at the cost of Party unity—and often by discrediting the Party's past and trying to distance themselves from past mistakes and abuses of power.[79] As a result, the HSWP did little to bolster its standing or popularity; instead, leaders juggled for power. The Party was immobilized, which allowed opposition groups to seize the initiative and change the terms of the political debate. This change significantly weakened the HSWP's relative legitimacy and its ability to compete.

LEGITIMACY

Many in the Party leadership appear to have believed that the Party could preserve its role in a more open political environment. As one analyst has noted, "None [of the leadership] doubted that the HSWP would remain the largest party, or at least would become the dominant force in a coalition government after the next elections."[80] This belief reflected the leaders' perception of the political climate when they began to introduce significant political changes, rather than the changed political climate that existed by late 1989. The Party's confidence is an important indication of why it took the steps that it did.

This faith was based on several factors. First, during the Kádár period, the majority of the population appeared to accept that Kádár was

---

79. Kádár was unable or unwilling to tackle personnel decisions, including the inevitable need to find his successor. Tökés, *Hungary's Negotiated Revolution*, pp. 23, 213–215.

80. Tökés, *Hungary's Negotiated Revolution*, p. 315.

doing his best to shield them from the worst excesses of a Stalinist system. Their recognition of this, combined with cognizance that the Soviet Union would not countenance a different political and economic system in Hungary, gave Kádár some genuine popularity as a leader.

Second, while Round Table discussions were underway in the summer of 1989, the Party appeared to have a strong popular base, with 36–40 percent of the population supporting it.[81] With such backing, the Party would easily be competitive in a broader political environment, even if it might have to share power. The HSWP's confidence in its position was probably bolstered by the disunity of the new political parties. Opposition to the regime was fragmented; moreover, the disagreements among opposition groups were in some cases as severe as their objections to the ruling party. Membership in opposition political groups was less than half of 1 percent of the population at the beginning of 1989, and remained under 1 percent in September 1989, when the Round Table accord was signed.[82] This figure is somewhat misleading, of course, due to the distrust of political parties common in East European states; most people rejected party affiliation in the early 1990s because the idea of party membership had been discredited by the single party state. Nonetheless, the apparent fragmentation of the opposition made it appear unlikely, in early 1989, that these parties could challenge the degree of support the HSWP enjoyed.

Third, Imre Pozsgay, the Party's leading reformer and presumed presidential candidate, was genuinely popular in the country.[83] He was also far better known than any representatives of the opposition. Since he was expected to be elected the country's new president prior to new elections for the National Assembly, the reformed HSWP would be in a good position to compete for seats, and to play an active role.[84]

Added to this, various Party officials expressed their belief that the HSWP would continue to lead, though they disagreed about the type of political system the state should have. Late in 1988, General Secretary Grósz best expressed the Party's nervousness about the dangers that a truly pluralist political system and new parties could present to the HSWP's plans:

---

81. Lévesque, *The Enigma of 1989*, p. 135.

82. Bruszt, "1989: The Negotiated Revolution in Hungary," p. 369.

83. For example, it was "taken for granted" during the Round Table discussions that he would be elected president. Sajo, "The Roundtable Talks in Hungary," p. 81; and Tökés, *Hungary's Negotiated Revolution*, p. 292.

84. This was precisely why some opposition parties rejected the early elections for the presidency.

Our political opponents strive for power sharing, and then for taking power over. This has its logic. A political force wants to enter power not so to remain second fiddle; it wants to enter so that afterwards, from within, it would obtain absolute power. Well, there are a huge number of examples of the history of this in politics. We, therefore, do not want to share power . . . what we want is to draw the various forces into the exercise of power.[85]

This is perhaps the clearest statement made about the ruling party's desire to coopt segments of the population into acceptance of a reformed, but not completely changed, system.

Evidence that Party leaders believed the Party would sustain its hold on power can be seen in statements they made in 1988 and 1989. After his appointment as prime minister, Németh broached the possibility of a multiparty system, maintaining that "if we communists manage to adopt correct stances with regard to a multiparty system, I am not afraid of our losing power in an open competition. This process and the climate of open competition will release new energies and new forces within society and the party."[86] At the same time, he stressed the importance of the Party's renewal to achieve support: "If the HSWP does not discuss its past with self-criticism and in the light of the criticism of others, then we are actually speaking of a party and government unable to keep in step with events. This might cause the Party to lose its legitimacy and public confidence for good."[87] Grósz also confirmed his belief in the Party's continued domination, stating that "it is my conviction, that the HSWP will be capable of safeguarding its leading role amidst the agreement between the parties, and then amidst the relations of open competition."[88] This combination of a recognition of the need to adjust to the new political situation with faith in the Party's continued role suggests that members of the leadership were confident the Party would continue to be a major political actor in Hungary in a more open system.

The HSWP also worked to bolster its legitimacy by emphasizing the Party's role as initiator of the reforms. Party leaders insisted that there were no alternate political forces in the country "that would have a coher-

85. "Károly Grósz at County Party Aktiv." See also "Berecz Speaks on Domestic, Political Issues," Budapest Domestic Service, November 30, 1988, in *FBIS:EEU*, December 1, 1988.

86. "Németh Interviewed on Democratization Issue," *La Repubblica* (Italy), November 27–28, 1988, in *FBIS:EEU*, November 29, 1988.

87. "Németh Holds Discussions while Touring District," MTI, February 16, 1989, in *FBIS:EEU*, February 17, 1989.

88. "'Excerpts' of Grósz CC Speech," MTI, February 13, 1989, in *FBIS:EEU*, February 14, 1989.

ent program even for solving the current problems," thus emphasizing the HSWP's efforts to develop solutions to the country's crisis.[89] Officials such as Grósz claimed credit for allowing even the possibility of reform:

The reform movement which has begun today in Hungary was not forced upon us from outside, it was not invented by the alternative movements, it was not forced out of us by opposition and the enemy, but we recognized that we must take steps and act. We ourselves stood, as so often at other times during the past decade, in the vanguard of renewal, and we want to remain in the vanguard too.[90]

Notably, the Party's belief in its ability to survive was gauged in a climate in which the Party had control and the opposition was at a clear disadvantage. Party leaders who expected a pluralist system to develop also expected that the transition to such a system would be gradual, taking "a couple of years."[91] Opposition leaders, as well, believed the Party would survive in power, if only because the opposition was too weak to challenge it at that time.[92] This helps explain why parties such as the HDF, which appeared to be gaining strength during the summer of 1989, were willing to accept the HSWP's insistence on early presidential elections; they expected Pozsgay to win, and felt that compromise was necessary in order to achieve other, more realistic goals.

CONFLICT WITHIN THE REGIME

Disagreements within the regime were severe by 1989, and these were critical to the outcome of the transition. Differences within the Party over the direction of reforms led to a search for outside partners, primarily by Pozsgay in his courting of the HDF, which began as early as 1987. Disagreements also paralyzed the Party at times when it needed to take the initiative in attempting to control the transition process. Finally, Party disputes demoralized a significant portion of the rank and file, who left

---

89. "Interview with Károly Grósz," MTI, December 24, 1988, in *SWB:EE,* December 29, 1988. Coupled with these claims, of course, the Party had to issue disclaimers of responsibility for having gotten the country into its economic mess.

90. "Károly Grósz at County Party Aktiv."

91. Janos Berecz also noted the problems for the opposition in preparing for power: "let us be frank, the overwhelming majority perhaps have not even reached the stage of thinking about one or more parties, or alternative organizations, or such expressions." "Berecz Interview on Alternative Groups," Budapest Television Service, January 10, 1989, in *FBIS:EEU,* January 11, 1989; and "Németh Interviewed on Democratization Issue."

92. Bruszt, "1989: The Negotiated Revolution in Hungary," p. 370.

the Party; the Party thus lost what had been a strong potential base of support. At least some Party leaders were aware of the dangers that the fissures within the Party presented, yet they were unable to resolve them.[93]

Divisions within the Party existed at several levels. First, reformers and conservatives were split within the CC and Politburo. Their differences represented more a spectrum than a neat division into a few groups: Janos Berecz, at the conservative end, referred to himself as "Hungary's Ligachev" (at least until Ligachev, a member of the Soviet Politburo favoring greater worker discipline rather than the democratization Gorbachev favored, lost power), while Grósz was more stolidly pragmatic; Németh and Nyers favored substantial economic changes and controlled political reforms; and Pozsgay was considered a radical reformer, advocating major political as well as economic changes.[94] These actors disagreed both on policy and on who should rule. Moreover, their personal political ambitions at times overwhelmed their ability to cooperate to develop a coherent strategy for political reform if they intended to expand the political arena. This clearly set the stage for the reformers' search for external allies that took place from 1987 to 1989.

A second level of division was between intellectuals and the apparatus. For example, intellectuals were relegated to government rather than Party positions, as a way to channel the intellectuals away from decision-making positions. The divide was most obvious outside Budapest, where regional Party leaders controlled virtual fiefdoms, and Party intellectuals found themselves shut out of the lines of patronage. Disillusionment with this system led intellectuals in Szeged to create a "reform cell," which they hoped would generate a political movement within the Communist Party and link reformers horizontally across the country.[95] What

---

93. Rezsö Nyers, for example, noted in July 1989 that the three things that could defeat the Party were its past, its disintegration, and paralysis of the rank-and-file. "Memorandum of a Conversation between President Mikhail Gorbachev, President Rezsö Nyers, and General Secretary of the Hungarian Socialist Worker's Party (HSWP) Károly Grosz, Moscow, 24–25 July 1989," *CWIHP Bulletin*, Issue 12/13 (Fall/Winter 2001), pp. 83–84.

94. For a careful overview of the development of the positions of Berecz, Grósz, and Pozsgay, see Tökés, *Hungary's Negotiated Revolution*, pp. 217–248.

95. The first reform circle declaration, announced on November 29, 1988, advocated comparatively radical reforms including reintegration with the world economy, a multiparty system, and dialogue both within and outside the Party aimed against Party hard-liners. The group was attacked by Grósz, but it reemerged in support of Pozsgay in early 1989, backing him in his evaluation of 1956. For a detailed discussion of the rise and fall of the reform circle movement, see O'Neil, "Revolution from Within," pp. 579–603.

were referred to as reform circles had formed across much of the country by March 1989 and began forming connections that led to both informal and formal meetings to discuss policy goals.[96] They were also instrumental in pushing for the extraordinary Party Congress that took place in October, and they put together the Reform Alliance platform that became one of the main pillars for planning the reformed Hungarian Socialist Party. The emergence of this movement illustrates the disillusionment of many of the intellectuals with the Party leadership; reform circles were organized to push the Party in the direction of reform, but they were not sufficiently strong or organized to overcome the tendencies pulling the party apart.[97]

Finally, the rank and file were dissatisfied with the direction the Party leadership was taking. This was most evident in the mass resignations from the HSWP beginning in 1988. By one estimate, 120,000 members had left the Party by the spring of 1989. In addition, mass organizations affiliated with the Party were falling apart by 1989. The Young Communist's League (YCL), for example, lost half of its membership by the spring of 1989.

These divisions were important because, by the late 1980s, they revolved around questions of policy and reform. In comparison to most other states in the bloc (particularly the more conservative ones), the disagreements were tolerated within the Party, but they prevented the Party from developing a clear strategy for competing in the new system the regime was designing.

REPRESSION

The level of repression in Hungary was lower than in much of the Eastern bloc. It is clear that the Hungarian regime's tolerance for a wide range of groups, and for at least muted criticism, was comparatively broad well into the 1980s. Intellectuals were free to critique the system so long as they made calls for change only within the existing system, rather than change of the system altogether. Some harsher measures to curb dissent were taken in 1981, showing that limits to the regime's tolerance remained, but in the mid-1980s a comparatively wide range of non-Party

---

96.   The first meeting took place in April, followed by a formal meeting of reform circle representatives in May 1989. By then, 110 reform circles had been formed in over half the counties in Hungary. O'Neil, "Revolution from Within," pp. 593–594; and Tőkés, *Hungary's Negotiated Revolution,* p. 319.

97.   Many members of the reform circles wanted simply to leave the Party and join the Opposition Round Table, but opposition groups urged them to remain and work for reform from within the Party.

dominated activity was accepted.[98] Travel to the West was also relatively easy, and 665,000 Hungarians travelled West in 1985; the figure went up to 7.2 million in 1987.[99]

Limits to the Party's tolerance appeared in 1988, when the regime broke up demonstrations organized by opposition groups to commemorate heavily symbolic anniversaries such as the revolution of 1848 in March, Nagy's execution in June, and the 1956 uprising in October. The HSWP's reaction to demonstrations on symbolic national holidays points to its fear that the past might be a potent weapon against the Party, and its desire to prevent opposition groups from appropriating these dates to rally the population against the regime—or the Soviet Union, in the case of the October uprising. Pozsgay eventually addressed this issue head-on, by announcing the Party's reevaluation of the events of 1956. Pozsgay apparently recognized that the only way to neutralize the power of the past as a weapon against the regime was to acknowledge the mistakes of the past publicly and to stress the differences between the Party of the past and the present—or at least its reform wing.[100] In 1989, the regime not only allowed organized marches on these dates but organized its own observances in an effort to garner popular support.[101] Reformers like Pozsgay hoped that both the reevaluation of 1956 and the reburial of Nagy would allow them to align themselves with the population and the nascent opposition groups and to put distance between their position and the hard-liners remaining in the HSWP.

Party leader Grósz appears to have considered the use of force to support the regime at several points during his tenure. After he became prime minister in 1987, he apparently made plans to deal with economic collapse, the regime's political collapse, and the possibility of martial law. These plans, which remained incomplete, envisaged drawing on the

---

98. Lomax notes that the regime suppressed expressions of discontent by workers far more harshly than it did intellectuals. "Hungary: The Quest for Legitimacy," p. 82.

99. Of those travelling in 1987, 6.5 million were tourists. Kornai, "Individual Freedom and Reform of the Socialist Economy," p. 253; and "Rezso Nyers on Reforms, Ties with Italy," *Avanti,* January 15–16, 1989, in *FBIS:EEU,* January 26, 1989.

100. Interestingly, Kádár's main concerns before he agreed to step down were about his past actions; he wanted guarantees that he would not be persecuted for his part in the trial and execution of Laszlo Rajk, the events of 1956, and the restriction of reforms in the 1970s. Tőkés, *Hungary's Negotiated Revolution,* pp. 283–284.

101. The Party had limited success in distancing itself from its past actions. Far more people attended the opposition-sponsored rally on March 15 than that organized by the HSWP, but the reburial of Imre Nagy, organized by the government rather than the Party, with the participation of prominent reformers from the HSWP, did become a moment of national reconciliation.

Party's Worker's Guard and riot police, among other forces. Later, in September 1988, Grósz asked the minister of the interior, Istvan Horvath, if it would be possible to authorize the use of arms against environmental demonstrators outside the Parliament building.[102]

On November 29, 1988, Grósz gave a speech in which he decried the possibility of counterrevolutionary forces emerging and threatened to use any force necessary against this "white terror," warning that the HSWP "will conduct an open political battle against the extremist, right-wing, reactionary forces."[103] He again raised the possibility of a state of emergency in April 1989—an option that Prime Minister Németh promptly and publicly rejected.[104]

These incidents indicate the nervousness of at least some elements of the Party with the processes underway, and a desire to keep reforms under control by the Party. They also hint at the conservatives' inability to accept a lessening of political control, which may have generated a knee-jerk response of turning to force, with the expectation that opposition groups would back down before such threats. Finally, Grósz's willingness to make such threats suggests that he may have assumed he would have Soviet backing for sustaining the HSWP's position.

Thus, while government repression certainly existed in Hungary, it was far more innocuous than in many of Hungary's counterparts in Eastern Europe. Few if any Hungarians were executed or deported for expressing dissenting political beliefs; even imprisonment was rare. There are different ways to view this. Possibly it was part of the regime's bargain with society; the regime tolerated a wider range of "opposition" activities in return for general acquiescence by the population in its rule. Low repression may also have indicated the regime's confidence that it need not resort to repressive means to maintain order. Alternately, the regime could be seen as better at calibrating the necessary level of repression, using repressive means more efficiently than some others in the bloc, with little excess. The level of repression in Hungary was low in

---

102. Tökés, *Hungary's Negotiated Revolution*, pp. 296–297.

103. Grósz later claimed that it was obvious at that point that some form of pluralism was inevitable, and that his speech was meant as a warning of what was to come. "Grósz Addresses Budapest Party Activ 29 November," Budapest Domestic Service, November 29, 1988, in *FBIS:EEU*, November 30, 1988; and Tökés, *Hungary's Negotiated Revolution*, p. 297.

104. "Grósz Urges 'Economic State of Emergency,'" Budapest Domestic Service, April 22, 1989; "Németh Denies Emergency Plans," Budapest Domestic Service, April 24, 1989; and "Németh 'Opposes' Measure," Budapest Television Service, April 22, 1989, all in *FBIS:EEU*, April 24, 1989.

the 1980s, but in the absence of legal guarantees against regime abuses, the threat of repression remained constant. Moreover, having proved its willingness to take harsh measures after 1956, the regime did not need to use such a heavy hand.[105]

SUMMARY
The Hungarian case shows both strong evidence of the leadership's confidence in the HSWP's legitimacy relative to its circumstances, and of intra-regime conflict. The low level of repression in the state supports the impression that the regime was reasonably confident of its position. There is also evidence that some members of the regime looked outside the regime for new allies to support the political reform process. Party Leader Grósz's contemplation of police measures may indicate his residual fear of system change. His concern may also have been provoked by the growing differences of opinion within the Party leadership over the nature of reform. Thus, it is not surprising that the Hungarian regime was one of the first in the Eastern bloc to initiate substantial political reforms.

External Influences in Hungary

As in Poland, external influences shaped developments in Hungary in 1989. While the Soviet leadership appears to have disavowed the right to a say in internal political decisions within Eastern Europe fairly early in Gorbachev's tenure, it took a while for this to sink in, and East European leaders continued to ask for and expect Soviet guidance.

For example, when Soviet President Andrei Gromyko, the former foreign minister, visited Hungary early in 1988, he and Kádár discussed when Kádár should retire.[106] This indicates both the Hungarian leader's continued belief that the Soviet Politburo had a say over the succession process in its satellite states, and infighting within the Soviet Politburo itself; Gromyko's visit came at a point when the conservatives within the Politburo were attacking Gorbachev's reform programs. As another example, Grósz also felt obliged to visit Moscow shortly after his appointment as prime minister in 1987, to ensure that he had the approval of the

---

105. This latter view is the argument of some Hungarian analysts, who contend that what Western scholars perceive as "legitimacy" was more aptly considered "passivity," out of recognition by society that the regime would use coercion if necessary. Lomax, "Hungary: The Quest for Legitimacy," p. 69.

106. Schöpflin, Tökés, and Volgyes, "Leadership Change and Crisis in Hungary," p. 36.

Soviet leadership. When the makeup of the Hungarian Politburo changed in May 1988, the Party leadership again conferred with Moscow before announcing its new appointments.[107]

Late in 1988 and in 1989, the Soviet policy of noninterference was more apparent. In spite of Moscow's increasingly hands-off approach to developments in Hungary, both regime and opposition in Hungary clearly believed well into 1989 that Soviet interests must be factored into their political calculations. Efforts to get Moscow's endorsement—or at least acquiescence—took two forms in the fall of 1988. First, Grósz carefully underscored Hungary's support for the Soviet Union's peace policy, emphasizing the synergy of Hungary's and Moscow's policies.[108]

Second, the Soviet leadership was consulted fairly regularly about the reforms under consideration in Hungary. This was apparent from the visits made by high-ranking Soviet officials to Hungary, and vice versa, and the statements of Soviet officials that affirmed Moscow's approval for and noninterference in the developments in Hungary. In response to the expanding discussions of a multiparty system, for example, Soviet Politburo member Aleksander Yakovlev avouched Moscow's willingness to accept Hungarian decisions, stating that "the CPSU and the HSWP determine their policy independently and bear the responsibility for their actions first and foremost before their own peoples."[109]

When tensions began to rise within the Hungarian leadership, Imre Pozsgay apparently met with Aleksander Yakovlev to ask for Moscow's support in his struggle with Grósz; but the Soviet leadership refused to get involved in intraparty disputes. Yakovlev did, however, stress to Pozsgay the importance of uniting behind the Party leadership.[110]

---

107. This led to embarrassment, because TASS announced the changes in Hungary's leadership before these had been officially announced in Hungary, clear proof that Moscow had been consulted. Ibid., p. 39.

108. "Károly Grösz: Setting the Stage for Further Advance," interview in *New Times*, No. 21 (1988).

109. Soviet Foreign Minister Eduard Shevardnadze also stated that he was satisfied with "the cooperation in socialist construction" (meaning work toward the building of socialism) in Hungarian-Soviet relations. "Shevardnadze on Troop Withdrawal Issue in Interview for Hungarian Foreign Ministry Weekly," MTI, November 4, 1988, in *SWB:EE*, November 8, 1988. See also "Hungarian Interviews with Vadim Zagladin," Hungarian Television, September 11, 1988, in *SWB:EE*, September 21, 1988; and "Aleksandr Yakovlev in Hungary," Abstract of Reports, in *SWB:EE*, November 15, 1988.

110. Pozsgay apparently tried at least twice to get Moscow's backing, with limited success. Pozsgay met with Yakovlev in Rome in March 1989, and requested an invitation to Moscow, arguing that Gorbachev should back him as the more reform-minded

Pozsgay and his aides also expected Soviet condemnation of his announcement regarding the reevaluation of 1956, but the Soviet leadership accepted this as an internal matter.

Hungarian concern for Soviet sensitivities was also evident just before and during the Round Table discussions. HSWP spokesmen pointedly reminded the population in March 1989 that pushing reforms too quickly could have negative repercussions:

We should always reckon with and keep in mind that there is, here, next door to us, an enormous country, a world power, the Soviet Union. . . . If we have no confidence in the Soviet Union, it is unfortunate but does not have any special importance. But if the Soviet Union has no confidence in us, this endangers the free and smooth development of Hungary.[111]

Such reminders were undoubtedly intended to remind the opposition groups that attempting to maneuver within the constraints of the Soviet alliance—an attachment that was not then open to question—was a very delicate process. HSWP leaders continued throughout the summer to remind the population of the geopolitical realities of Hungary's position, and stressed that Hungary was not, in any case, trying to cut its ties to the East: "our top historical priority is to preserve close allied relations with the Soviet Union because they guarantee the stability of our progress and lend weight to the Hungarian policy of reform."[112] This reassurance became tinged with concern, as signs of anti-Soviet sentiment in Hungary mounted in the summer. Even such radical reformers as Pozsgay reminded the population that Moscow's reforms provided the

---

leader in the HSWP. Though he eventually received an invitation, Yakovlev stressed the need to support the Party's leader, and Grósz managed to deflect the proposed visit when it was offered. Tőkés, *Hungary's Negotiated Revolution*, p. 320.

111. "Hungary's Mátyás Szűrös on Relations with the USSR, CMEA," Budapest Home Service, March 4, 1989, in *SWB:EE*, March 7, 1989.

112. Foreign Minister Gyula Horn also emphasized the realities of Hungary's position when he commented in July 1989 that Hungary did not want to distance itself from the Soviet Union and its Warsaw Pact allies, but "to modernize the system of relations that connect us to these states" while also expanding ties to the West. Similarly, Geza Kotai noted the need for some kind of regional guarantees for Hungary in the future, rather than a choice to simply cut existing ties. See "Hungary and the Warsaw Treaty," *SWB:EE*, May 22, 1989; "Foreign Minister on the U.S. President's Visit and Romania," MTI, July 10, 1989, in *SWB:EE*, July 13, 1989; "Foreign Ministry Secretary on Foreign Policy, MTI, July 21, 1989, in *SWB:EE*, July 25, 1989; and "Hungarian View of Marshal Akhromeyev's Remarks on Neutrality," Budapest Home Service, July 29, 1989, in *SWB:EE*, August 1, 1989.

context within which it was possible to initiate substantial changes in Hungary.[113]

This suggests that, despite the absence of public objections from Moscow, the Hungarian leadership remained unsure of the Soviet Union's actual preferences for the outcome of a reform process. The official Soviet response throughout the year was to reiterate Moscow's policy of noninterference; indeed, Gorbachev insisted in the spring that even the creation of a multiparty system was "the private affair of every party, the internal affair of every country."[114] Yet Gorbachev also stressed the importance of socialism and maintaining stability in his private meetings with Hungarian leaders, while at the same time disavowing foreign intervention.[115]

Opposition figures too worried about Moscow's attitude toward changes in Hungary, and thought that limits existed. This was evident in the widely shared popular expectation that Pozsgay would be the next president, due to the need to ensure Moscow's support for Hungary's political reforms. Indeed, one of the members of the ORT argued in September 1989 that the opposition needed to agree to early presidential elections in order to keep the Russians calm.[116]

The process of reform in Poland also had a significant impact on Hungary. Discussions about creating a Round Table process in Hungary began within a month of the announcement of Round Table talks in Poland. The agreement eventually reached in Poland was seen as a model of a negotiated settlement, which the Hungarians also had in mind. Yet the outcome of the Polish talks alerted the Hungarian opposition to the dangers of such a negotiated outcome; they explicitly wanted to avoid the kind of partial solution that Solidarity agreed to, which seemed to give the Communist Party a dominant influence in the new Parliament. This led to the Hungarian opposition's insistence during the prenegotiation phase of talks that nothing short of free elections would be acceptable. This demonstrates the learning process that went on during the course of

---

113. See Pozsgay's comments in "Television Interview with New Four-Member HSWP Presidium."

114. "Meeting of M.S. Gorbachev with M. Németh," *Pravda*, March 4, 1989, p. 1; Editorial Report on Károly Grósz's visit to Moscow, in *SWB:EE*, March 27, 1989; and Gerasimov: "The Fate of Every Country Is In Its Own Hands," *SWB:SU*, March 8, 1989.

115. "Memorandum of a Conversation between M.S. Gorbachev and HSWP General Secretary Kárely Grósz," in *CWIHP Bulletin*, Issue 12/13 (Fall/Winter 2001), p. 78.

116. Bozoki, "Hungary's Road to Systemic Change," p. 295.

1989, as a model was transmitted from one country to the next, and then improved.[117]

Hungary was also influenced by the West in a variety of ways. First, Hungary's debt burden gave Western bankers and the International Monetary Fund some leverage over Hungary's economic policies, particularly by 1989. By this point it seemed likely that Western creditors would insist on more market-oriented policies, regardless of the nature of the government.[118] Second, in 1989 Hungarian foreign policy decisions were increasingly justified by reference to Hungary's "Europeanness." This reflected a deep-seated sentiment within Hungary that the country shared the West's cultural and religious traditions, rather than the Byzantine traditions of the East.

Hungary's interest in becoming "a European country in every respect" was also evident in its decision in the spring of 1989 to dismantle the barbed wire barriers on its border with Austria.[119] Since Hungarian citizens could already travel to Austria and the West fairly freely, this was largely symbolic, and a clear sign of Hungary's efforts to improve its relations with the West.[120] However, a few months later increasing numbers of East German citizens vacationing in Hungary tried to slip across the open border into Austria, and from there to West Germany. To allow this

---

117. By 1989, the other East European states were openly hostile to the reform processes in Hungary, Poland, and the Soviet Union. Tensions with Romania were of the greatest concern for Hungary, due to their shared border and the ethnic Hungarian minority in Transylvania. The Hungarian government was also concerned about a military threat from Romania, particularly after Ceauşescu implied that he might have nuclear weapons. Grösz confirmed in later interviews that such threats were made, which prompted him to move troops to Hungary's border with Romania in 1988. On the issue of nuclear weapons, see Jonathan Eyal, "Looking for Weapons of Mass Destruction," *Jane's Soviet Intelligence Review*, Vol. 1, No. 8 (August 1989); and James F. Burke, "Romanian and Soviet Intelligence in the December Revolution," *Intelligence and National Security*, Vol. 8, No. 4 (October 1993), both cited in Lévesque, *The Enigma of 1989*, p. 133; see also "Foreign Minister Horn on the U.S. President's Visit and Romania," MTI, July 10, 1989, in *SWB:EE*, July 13, 1989.

118. Bruszt, "1989: The Negotiated Revolution in Hungary," p. 382.

119. On Hungary's European orientation, see "Hungary's Mátyás Szürös on Relations with USSR, CMEA"; and "Foreign Ministry Secretary on Foreign Policy," MTI, July 21, 1989, in *SWB:EE*, July 25, 1989.

120. Indeed, the Hungarian premier, Miklós Németh, presented U.S. President George Bush with a piece of the barbed wire removed from the Austrian-Hungarian border when Bush visited Hungary, the first U.S. president to do so, in July 1989. See *Foreign Affairs Chronology, 1978–1989* (New York: Council on Foreign Relations, 1990), p. 387.

to continue would violate Hungary's treaty with East Germany, which stipulated that citizens of either state would not be permitted to travel to third countries without proper visas; the Hungarian government was therefore obliged to try to stop these would-be escapees. This created a refugee problem in the country, as East Germans chose to remain in Hungary hoping to slip past the border guards, rather than return to East Germany. In the face of the continuing refusal or inability of the East German government to reach an agreement with West Germany on how to deal with the refugees in Hungary, the Hungarian government chose to honor its international human rights obligations, and opened its border to East German citizens.[121]

This move toward a "European" perspective on security and human rights is one manifestation of Western influence on the process of change in Eastern Europe. That it would help Hungary achieve better trade and aid relations with the West made the move toward Western norms a smart one; it would also promote Hungary's acceptance into the Western community of nations.

Some Western leaders were concerned at the rapid pace of reform in Hungary in 1989, and continued to advocate gradual change. The most prominent of these was U.S. President George Bush, who visited the region in the summer of 1989. He was more impressed by the reformers within the HSWP than he was with the opposition representatives he met, and stressed to the latter that "your leaders are moving in the right direction. Your country is taking things one step at a time. Surely that is the prudent thing to do."[122] This reflected Western, and particularly U.S., concern that the Soviet Union might be provoked to react if the process of reform went too far, as well as Bush's personal discomfort with the opposition spokesmen he met.

---

121. Government spokesmen announced that: "The (Hungarian) government decided temporarily to suspend the relating paragraphs of the intergovernmental agreement signed by Hungary and the GDR in 1969, and make it possible for the GDR citizens staying in Hungary and refusing to return home to leave for any country which is prepared to let them through or receive them." "Authorized Statement," MTI September 10, 1989, in *SWB:EE*, September 12, 1989. On Hungary's efforts to reach an agreement with East Germany, see "Hungarian Foreign Minister Discusses Refugee Problem," Hungarian TV, August 26, 1989, in *SWB:EE*, August 31, 1989; and "Hungarian Foreign Minister's Visit to the GDR," MTI, August 31, 1989, in *SWB:EE*, September 2, 1989. The Hungarian leadership also consulted with Moscow before opening the border. See Sajo, "The Roundtable Talks in Hungary," p. 91.

122. Michael R. Beschloss and Strobe Talbott, *At the Highest Levels: The Inside Story of the End of the Cold War* (Boston: Little, Brown, 1993), p. 92.

SUMMARY

External factors played three important roles in Hungary. Since regime and opposition both believed that Soviet concern about reforms mandated caution, some of the decisions of the Round Table negotiations were tempered. The reforms underway in Poland provided both a model for the Hungarian regime's efforts to draw the opposition into power-sharing discussions and some shelter from criticism by the hard-liners in the Eastern bloc. Finally, Western influences mattered both because of Hungarians' desire to be part of Europe and because Hungary's financial straits and indebtedness to Western institutions obliged the regime to consider more radical economic reforms.

Conclusions

Hungary's decision to introduce reforms comparatively early can be explained by the indicators examined here. The Hungarian regime was well aware of the need for economic reform, as evidenced by previous experimentation with market mechanisms, the degree of openness to the international market, and the range of debate about reform prior to 1985. The Party leadership had a long history of divergence from the Marxist-Leninist economic model in an effort to preserve domestic acquiescence to continued communist rule. Moreover, by 1985, the country faced serious economic difficulties. While Kádár rejected the necessity of political reforms to bolster economic reforms, many in the Party ranks recognized that political reforms must accompany economic reforms if they were to operate effectively. The Party leadership was also confident that it could survive in a more open political setting. Both comparatively radical reformers and conservatives in the Party leadership expressed their faith that the Party would continue to lead in a multiparty setting. Opinion polls also supported the perception that the Party would continue to be a major political force in the state, while the bargain it negotiated with opposition groups over the summer of 1989 appeared virtually to ensure the Communist Party candidate the presidency in the reformed political system.

Early reform in Hungary, initiated by the ruling party, was the logical choice of a regime that was cognizant of its dire economic straits and confident of its ability to preserve its power. (Table 4 lays out the indicators examined here.) Yet in spite of apparent indications of domestic support, the Party failed to sustain its relative popularity and fared poorly in the March 1990 elections. Two factors help explain this. First, the conflict within the regime prevented the Party leadership from working together to save or sustain its position. Several prominent figures, notably Grósz

Table 4. Indicators Measuring the Hungarian Regime's Attitudes in 1989.

EARLY REFORM

INDICATORS OF REGIME'S RECOGNITION OF NEED FOR REFORM

INDICATOR	HUNGARY	REGIME'S ATTITUDE
Previous reform efforts	Substantial economic reforms	Awareness of need for reform
Nature of state's economic and political structure	Weak adherence to Marxist-Leninist model	
Problems facing the state	Serious economic difficulties	
Response to Gorbachev	Positive	

INDICATORS OF REGIME'S PERCEPTION OF ITS ABILITY TO SURVIVE

INDICATOR	HUNGARY	REGIME'S ATTITUDE
Statements of legitimacy	Yes	Perception of rule as legitimate
Intra-regime conflict	Yes	
Level of repression	Low	

and Pozsgay, were more concerned about their own ambitions, and the Party failed to keep the leadership's disagreements to itself, or to formulate a unified strategy for competition in the new political system it helped to design. It can be argued that the HSWP lost its position due to its paralysis and internal divisions. This is particularly notable with regard to Pozsgay, who did little to rally the party or to fight for his own political career in the fall of 1989.[123]

Second, the impact of external influences on domestic Hungarian politics changed dramatically during the summer and fall of 1989, making Hungary the first case in which a diffusion of ideas from outside changed popular perceptions. In the spring of 1989, Hungary adopted the Polish model of negotiations, with modifications, as a way for regime and opposition to agree on the rules for a new political structure. The opposition was careful not to mimic the Polish process too closely, however; it rejected the prospect of negotiating a power balance in advance of elections. By September, when the Hungarian Round Table agreement was signed, the political climate in Hungary had changed, due to Soviet acceptance of a Solidarity prime minister in Poland. Both Poland and the

123. Tőkés, *Hungary's Negotiated Revolution*, pp. 364–365.

Soviet Union were important as external influences—Poland by the steps it took, and the Soviet Union by the actions it did not take. In combination with the Communist Party's fragmentation that followed in October, this made the opposition more willing to adopt an anticommunist stance, which helped pare the reformed HSP's support. Moreover, popular cognizance that Moscow's tolerance extended to a rejection of Communist Party control dissolved the bounds of the system within which the HSWP's calculations of legitimacy had been made. This change was underscored by the successive collapse of the other Warsaw Pact regimes by the end of 1989.

Chapter 5

Reform from Below: Popular Protests and Regime Collapse in the German Democratic Republic and Czechoslovakia

East Germany and Czechoslovakia are the first two cases of late reforming states. Communist Party rule in East Germany and Czechoslovakia was carefully maintained and adhered closely to the prescribed socialist model during the 1970s and 1980s. Both regimes vigilantly suppressed their critics, and they were considered among Moscow's more loyal allies before Gorbachev took power. This loyalty reflected the historical vulnerabilities of each regime, and their positions on the front line of the divide between the Communist bloc and the West. The regimes in these states responded to the introduction of reforms in the Soviet Union and then in Eastern Europe by rejecting the option of initiating reform. In neither state did a substantial opposition movement exist at the beginning of 1989. Yet when they did occur, changes were impelled from below by spreading popular protests that, in November 1989, triggered the fall of the Berlin Wall in East Germany and the Velvet Revolution in Czechoslovakia.[1]

The East German and Czechoslovakian cases are examined together because they are examples of the same pattern of transition. The variables examined here play out in similar ways in both cases. The communist regimes could not—or would not—acknowledge the need for reform, and change occurred when growing popular protests compelled the regimes to concede the need for reform.

---

1. Czechoslovakia's opposition coined the term "Velvet Revolution" to describe its peaceful revolution against the state. The adoption of the term may also be explained by the fact that Václav Havel was a great fan of the pioneering 1960s rock band, the Velvet Underground.

Regimes that did not choose reform early either did not accept the need for reform or did not feel that they had sufficient legitimacy to risk reforms. In earlier periods of the Cold War, East European regimes tended, sometimes reluctantly, to adopt policies similar to Moscow's. But the East German and Czechoslovakian regimes chose not to do so in 1988–1989, in spite of the acceleration of reforms in the Soviet Union and the initiation of reform measures in Poland and Hungary. One reason to stall on reforms was the hope that Gorbachev might fall from power and that the Soviet Union would return to business as usual. But regime leaders also appear not to have recognized how profoundly the situation around them was changing, and what these changes meant in terms of continued Soviet support and popular acquiescence to continued communist rule. I argue that cognitive processes can help explain why regime leaders were unable to perceive their changed circumstances for so long and continued to reject reforms. As discussed in Chapter 1, people use a variety of simplifying "knowledge structures" to help interpret the world. Analogies, one of these structures, represent the lessons people learn from their experiences, and they are used to make future judgments. People tend to assume that the analogy that comes to mind first is the correct one for the new situation, and they then make assumptions about the current situation that accord with their expectations. And since people are most likely to notice information that confirms their beliefs, these beliefs persevere.

It is not easy to measure cognitive factors. We can, however, look for evidence of whether the regime's attitude toward reforms changed in the late 1980s. If the regime continued to resist change and to profess faith in the existing system of rule, this would suggest that its leaders' attitudes remained unchanged in spite of the events in neighboring states—and at home. If the regime highlighted the danger of reforms, this would indicate the regime's concern about processes underway elsewhere, and its fear of introducing changes at home. Finally efforts to quell reform would indicate the regime's continued insistence that changes were unnecessary.

As Chapter 1 discusses, I argue that a demonstration effect triggered the growing protests by previously quiescent populations. The behavior of elites and populations in the early reforming states acted as a "decision cue" for people in the later reforming states and also shaped their behavior. These external influences could affect both regime and population; they would be a factor if there was communication between populations in different states, or if people in one state knew about developments elsewhere. The demonstration effect is most apparent if groups in one state mimic the patterns in other states—for example, if regimes call for negotiations with the opposition, or if populations call for changes similar to those taking place in neighboring states or adopt comparable forms of protest.

The next section describes East Germany's and Czechoslovakia's processes of reform and the capitulation of their regimes. I then examine why these regimes rejected the option of early reform and the variables influencing the process of reform that was impelled from below in these states.

The Transition in East Germany and Czechoslovakia

OBSTACLES TO REFORM

The German Democratic Republic and Czechoslovakia faced singular challenges in responding to perestroika. In East Germany's case, the problem was its fragile claim to statehood, while the legacy of the Soviet invasion of Czechoslovakia in 1968 had severely damaged the ruling party's relations with Czechoslovakian society.

The Socialist Unity Party's (SED's) hostility to reform grew out of the circumstances that surrounded East Germany's formation. While a separate East German state was established with Moscow's support after World War II, the Soviet Union endeavored for several years after the war to gain greater influence throughout the whole of Germany by bargaining away full control over the eastern zone in return for political concessions in the western zone of the defeated state. The Soviet Union's efforts continued even after East Germany was founded as a separate state on October 12, 1949. Only in 1955, when the Federal Republic of Germany (FRG [West Germany]) was admitted into the North Atlantic Treaty Organization (NATO), did Moscow end its efforts to gain greater influence throughout Germany.[2]

Once the socialist German state was established, the new government had to find a way to justify the division in terms other than pure Great Power politics. To do so, the regime embraced the Marxist-Leninist ideology promulgated by the Soviet Union to a degree unmatched elsewhere in Eastern Europe. Yet the government had little success in creating a separate sense of national identity and convincing the population of the benefits of their separate socialist course; a continuing stream of citizens left East Germany through West Berlin, which was their only way out of the state after 1952.[3] Not until the Berlin Wall was erected on Au-

2. See Adam Ulam, *Expansion and Coexistence: Soviet Foreign Policy, 1917–73* (New York: Holt, Rinehart, and Winston, 1973), p. 455, and chap. 10; and David Childs, *The GDR: Moscow's German Ally* (London: George Allen and Unwin, 1983), chap. 2.

3. The June uprising of workers in Berlin that followed Stalin's death in 1953 gave

gust 13, 1961, closing this last escape route to the West, did the majority of the population come to terms with the inevitability of its socialist existence.

The building of the Wall solved the problem of keeping people in East Germany, but it did not resolve the issue of the state's status in the international arena. Nor did it completely assuage the regime's concerns about external pressures, primarily from West Germany, on the domestic stability it was struggling to maintain. East Germany did not receive international recognition as an independent state until ten years after the Wall was built, when relations between East and West Germany were "normalized" following the signing of the Basic Treaty in 1972.[4] The treaty made possible greater contact across the inner-German frontier, especially for divided families. Moreover, along with a series of East-West agreements intended to reduce tensions and expand contacts across Europe's ideological divide, the Basic Treaty allowed the entry of both German states into the United Nations, giving East Germany the international recognition that had previously been denied to it by the West.

By mandating greater contact between the citizens of the two states, the Basic Treaty exacerbated the SED's long-standing concern about the dangers of external influence, which it perceived as a particular threat. Party leader Erich Honecker therefore adopted a policy of *Abgrenzung*, or demarcation. This was an effort to keep the population politically neutralized by raising the standard of living—a step made possible because of the state's growing prosperity—while leaving people little room for independent views. The regime maintained rigid control over the press,

---

evidence of the regime's problems establishing the separate state, and the fact that the regime had to call in Soviet tanks to crush the demonstrations did little to enhance its standing with the citizenry, or its sense of an independent identity. Afterwards, measures were taken to secure the inner-German frontier in 1952 by placing fences and watchtowers along the border. Childs, *The GDR: Moscow's German Ally*, pp. 29, 37.

4. Interestingly, normalization was the issue that led then Party leader Walter Ulbricht to break ranks with Moscow, after years as Moscow's most loyal ally. Moscow's revision of its policy toward the West, and in particular toward West Germany, raised strong objections from Ulbricht, for whom East-West detente represented too great a danger to the domestic stability he had achieved in East Germany. This was one of the factors leading to Ulbricht's replacement by Erich Honecker in May 1971. See Ulam, *Expansion and Coexistence*, pp. 745–756; Arthur Hanhardt, Jr., "The German Democratic Republic," in Teresa Rakowska-Harmstone, ed., *Communism in Eastern Europe* (Bloomington, Ind.: Indiana University Press, 1979, 1984), pp. 149–151; and J.F. Brown, *Eastern Europe and Communist Rule* (Durham, N.C.: Duke University Press, 1988), p. 90. On Honecker's efforts to gain popular support, see A. James McAdams, *East Germany and Detente: Building Authority after the Wall* (Cambridge: Cambridge University Press, 1985).

and was harshly intolerant of alternate views within the Party, or of dissent outside it.[5] High levels of ideological schooling were also required of the population, to guard against infection from the West. However, the transmission of West German television to virtually all of East Germany made it impossible for the government to isolate its population, or to hide the growing disparity between the two Germanys. Thus, by the end of the 1970s, East Germany presented the dichotomy of a tightly structured, socialist country whose citizens were able to opt out to the West via the air waves.

*   *   *

Prior to 1968, the Communist Party of Czechoslovakia (CPCZ) was one of the few in the bloc that could claim any popularity among its citizenry. There was comparatively little hostility toward the Russians or the Soviet Union in Czechoslovakia; indeed, traditional ties and the wartime experience of Soviet liberation from the Nazi occupation had generated goodwill toward the Russians.[6] Sympathy for the socialist ideals of Marxism-Leninism also existed in Czechoslovakia, particularly in Bohemia and Moravia.[7] In spite of the genuine sympathy of socialist ideals, the process of Stalinization after 1948 was particularly harsh in Czechoslovakia, where the massive purges and liquidations within the Party ranks decimated the intelligentsia, while the population was cowed into quiescence by widespread repression.[8] And unlike other countries in Eastern

---

5.   The East German secret police, or Stasi, was among the largest and most efficient of such agencies in the bloc. On *Abgrenzung,* see Herman Weber, "The Socialist Unity Party," in David Childs, ed., *Honecker's Germany* (London: Allen and Unwin, 1985), p. 12.

6.   The Soviet Union owed its image as liberator of Czechoslovakia partly to an agreement between the Allied Forces in World War II about how far each army would advance across Europe in pursuit of the retreating German army. The United States and the Soviet Union agreed that U.S. troops would not go beyond Plzen in Bohemia, leaving the liberation of most of Czechoslovakia to the Red Army. See H. Gordon Skilling, "Czechoslovakia Between East and West," in William E. Griffith, ed., *Central and Eastern Europe: The Opening Curtain?* (Boulder, Colo.: Westview Press, 1989), p. 244.

7.   As a result, the Communists won 38 percent of the vote in free elections held in 1946, in marked contrast to the poor showing of the Communists in other East European countries during the same period. In Hungary, for example, the Communists gained only 17 percent of the vote in elections held in November 1945. See Balogh, *Parliamentary and Party Struggles in Hungary, 1945–47,* p. 98, as cited in Charles Gati, *Hungary and the Soviet Bloc* (Durham, N.C.: Duke University Press, 1986), p. 70.

8.   As in other parts of Eastern Europe, those suspected of supporting "national" communism were particularly suspect; indeed, Gustáv Husák, head of the Communist Party in Slovakia and later secretary general of the Czechoslovak Party, was tried in 1953 on this charge. See Skilling, "Czechoslovakia Between East and West," p. 245.

Europe and even the Soviet Union, Stalinist-style rule in Czechoslovakia was not relaxed after the Soviet dictator's death, but continued unabated even after the East-West détente in the mid-1950s.

Liberalization began under Party First Secretary Alexander Dubček's leadership in 1968. The aim of the reforms proposed during the Prague Spring was to make the existing system more democratic without endangering socialism, and to address the country's economic problems. That a blueprint for change was initiated by reformist elements within the Communist Party gained the party a good measure of public approval and support for its platform. Early proposals for reform focused on economic problems, but the discussion of political issues within the party soon questioned the basic tenets of Marxism-Leninism, existing control mechanisms such as censorship and Party control, and even issues of military doctrine.[9] This was too much for the Soviet leadership to accept, and in August 1968 the Soviet Union led its Warsaw Pact allies—except Romania—in an invasion to halt the Czechoslovak reforms.[10] The justification for this move was explained in the "Brezhnev Doctrine," by which the Soviet Union arrogated to itself the right to intervene in any socialist country to "defend the achievements of socialism" if it felt the indigenous communist party was not doing so, since "the sovereignty of individual socialist countries cannot be counterposed to the interests of world socialism and the world revolutionary movement."[11]

---

9. This is of course a very sketchy appraisal of the issues involved on both the Czechoslovak and the Soviet sides in 1968. For some comprehensive accounts of the Czechoslovakian crisis, see Mark Kramer, *Crisis in Czechoslovakia, 1968: The Prague Spring and the Soviet Invasion* (Oxford: Oxford University Press, 2001); Jiří Valenta, *Soviet Intervention of Czechoslovakia: Anatomy of a Decision* (Baltimore, Md.: Johns Hopkins University Press, 1979); Philip Windsor and Adam Roberts, *Czechoslovakia, 1968: Reform, Repression and Resistance* (London: Chatto and Windus for the International Institute for Strategic Studies, 1969); Zdeněk Mlynár, *Nightfrost in Prague: The End of Humane Socialism* (New York: Karz, 1980); Vladimir V. Kusin, *The Intellectual Origins of the Prague Spring: The Development of Reformist Ideas in Czechoslovakia 1956–1967* (Cambridge: Cambridge University Press, 1971); and Robin Alison Remington, ed., *Winter in Prague: Documents on Czechoslovak Communism in Crisis* (Cambridge, Mass.: MIT Press, 1969).

10. There had been serious disagreements within the CPCZ about the reforms under consideration in 1968. Not only did this lead to the issuing of an appeal for aid against the danger of a reactionary coup by some members of the Communist Party leadership—one of the public justifications used by the Soviet Union for its decision to intervene—it also provided Moscow with a local cadre willing to reassert Moscow's interests. On the existence and makeup of an "antireform coalition," see Valenta, *Soviet Intervention in Czechoslovakia, 1968*, particularly pp. 36–39, 137–138.

11. S. Kovalev, *Pravda*, September 26, 1968; and Leonid Brezhnev, "The Brezhnev

The Soviet-led invasion shattered Czechoslovakia's favorable attitude toward the Soviet Union. Even in the Communist Party, there was widespread disillusionment with Moscow; political opposition and resistance to the installation of a Soviet-backed government from within the Party continued for almost seven months. By the spring of 1969, Dubček had been replaced by Gustáv Husák, who proceeded to dismantle the reforms initiated during the Prague Spring. During the process of "normalization," Husák reimposed a political model similar to that which had existed during the 1950s and 1960s. As part of this process, an extensive and vindictive purge of the Communist Party itself was begun in 1970 under the direction of Milos Jakeš.[12] The new government was also forced to accept the imposition of a permanent Soviet military presence.

The role of the conservative members of the Party's leadership in the Soviet invasion destroyed whatever legitimacy the Communist Party had regained during the Prague Spring; the CPCZ never recovered this support. There were no significant changes in the party leadership over the next two decades; in the late 1980s, the Czechoslovakian government and CPCZ leadership remained rigidly conformist and hard-line.

OPPOSITION TO COMMUNIST RULE

Although the East German regime proved reasonably successful in constricting popular sentiment against the regime, some dissenting voices existed.[13] The regime was able to restrict the development of a significant opposition movement by expelling the most troublesome dissidents to West Germany—an escape valve that other East European countries did not share. The option of expulsion was a consequence of the Basic Treaty with West Germany; by the mid-1980s, as part of the inner-German détente, West Germany had developed a practice of essentially exchang-

---

Doctrine," in Gail Stokes, ed., *From Stalinism to Pluralism: A Documentary History of Eastern Europe since 1945*, 2nd ed. (Oxford: Oxford University Press, 1996), pp. 132–134.

12. About a third of the Party's membership was purged, particularly those with higher education or in positions of authority. Otto Ulc, "Czechoslovakia," in Teresa Rakowska-Harmstone, ed., *Communism in Eastern Europe*, 2nd ed. (Bloomington, Ind.: Indiana University Press, 1979, 1984), p. 126.

13. Indeed, in the 1960s and 1970s, several former Party members who had become estranged from the SED expressed grievances that fell within the realm of Marxist thought; writers such as Stephan Heym reiterated their identity of *values* with the regime, while disagreeing with the means by which the Party was trying to reach its goals. Such disagreements between Party and intellectuals occurred in many countries in the Eastern bloc. See Robert Sharlet, "Human Rights and Civil Society," in William E. Griffith, ed., *Central and Eastern Europe: The Opening Curtain?* (Boulder, Colo.: Westview Press, 1989), pp. 156–177.

ing political prisoners in East German jails for hard currency. In spite of the protests it occasionally provoked, this practice had the useful effect, from the SED's perspective, of simply removing from the state any opposition leaders who looked capable of fomenting a serious challenge to the regime.[14]

One source of support for opposition in East Germany was the evangelical church. Though its efforts were small in comparison to that of the Catholic church in Poland, the East German evangelical church consistently supported pacifism and conscientious objection. It did not directly confront political issues or oppose government policies. As a result, it had been tolerated by the SED.[15] Yet tensions developed both within the church and in its relations with society during the early 1980s over questions raised by the growing peace movement in East Germany, and the role that the church should play in this process.[16] There was an increasing sense of disaffection among East Germany's youth, many of whom had turned to the peace movement harbored by the church as an outlet for their objections to the state's political system.[17]

---

14. The withdrawal of singer Wolf Biermann's citizenship in 1976 was a particularly egregious example of East Germany's expulsion of dissidents, a practice that provoked protests in both East and West Germany. On the expulsion of East German intellectuals, see Brown, *Eastern Europe under Communist Rule*, pp. 254–255.

15. The government even made additional concessions to the church in 1978, probably to allay the societal strains that had emerged at about the time of the Biermann episode. The fact that the church had in general been so quiescent was one reason the regime could afford to grant it more leeway; there was reason to expect that the church would continue to operate within self-imposed limits in its ministerings. See Vladimir Tismaneanu, "Nascent Civil Society in the German Democratic Republic," *Problems of Communism*, Vol. 28, Nos. 2–3 (March–June 1989), pp. 96–97.

16. A prominent minister, Rainer Eppelmann, issued what came to be known as the Berlin Appeal in 1981, which was a condemnation of all weapons, and thereby a rejection of the SED's contention that the correct ideological stand could serve as a justification for Soviet arms. The Berlin Appeal, and the support it received from at least some members of the clergy, became a major impetus for the development of an independent and self-conscious peace movement in East Germany. The church also rejected the increasing militarization of society. On this, see Damon A. Terrill, "Tolerance Lost: Disaffection, Dissent and Revolution in the German Democratic Republic," *East European Quarterly*, Vol. 28, No. 3 (September 1994), pp. 360–363.

17. The church's caution created strains with these groups, and also led to strains between older and younger priests, since the latter shared the frustration engendered by the regime's restrictions on society. A particularly notable example of popular frustration with the church's caution is seen in a comment made in a meeting in 1982; "I am 19 years old and nevertheless have nothing to lose. You talk and talk behind safe doors. Do you intend to keep putting us off until doomsday? What about the shining

*   *   *

In Czechoslovakia, the events of 1968 shaped the opposition that emerged in the mid-1970s. The intervention of 1968 caused widespread disillusionment with the Soviet Union in both Party and the general populace, and many Party members quit the CPCZ after the invasion. The Party purges carried out in the early 1970s also removed much of the remaining intelligentsia from the party. These two factors created a wellspring of intellectuals outside the regime, which provided the basis for dissenting views in Czechoslovakia. Indeed, Charter 77, the first opposition group formed in the Eastern bloc (in 1977), was founded by reform-minded communists who had left the Party or had been purged from it after 1968, together with members of the intellectual community who had supported the Prague Spring. Its aim was the promotion of civil and human rights in Czechoslovakia.[18]

At the same time, the oppression and pervasive fear created by police intimidation that followed the Prague Spring seriously demoralized the population, which led to almost nationwide apathy and unwillingness to take any interest or participate in public or political affairs.[19] This apathy was particularly widespread among the industrial working class, which the regime made a special effort to mollify through consumerism and perks like vacations. As a result, the opposition groups that did emerge in the late 1970s were unable to gain broad backing, but instead remained small and isolated from the mainstream of society.

RESISTANCE TO REFORM

Honecker's initial response to Gorbachev's introduction of reforms was lukewarm at best. While applauding the Soviet Union's decision as a timely and necessary action for the Soviet Union, the SED leadership took pains in 1986 to illustrate the health of East Germany's economy and the technological advances it had made over the past few years, and avoided

city on the hill?" See Tismaneanu, "Nascent Civil Society in the German Democratic Republic," pp. 96–97.

18.   This aim was an explicit response to the Helsinki Final Act. This was evidence that the West played an important role by presenting an alternative model. Though the government was successful in marginalizing Charter 77 by repressing its activities and jailing its members, in general it did not expel these dissidents from the state; this proved important to later political efforts in the country. See "Charter 77 Declaration," Prague, January 1, 1977, in Vojtech Mastny, *Helsinki, Human Rights, and European Security: Analysis and Documentation* (Durham, N.C.: Duke University Press, 1986), pp. 103–105.

19.   Vladimir V. Kusin, "Husák's Czechoslovakia and Economic Stagnation," *Problems of Communism*, Vol. 31, No. 3 (May–June 1982), pp. 26–28.

any acknowledgment that changes might be relevant at home. Change in the Soviet Union alone was unlikely to be sufficient to convince Honecker and his colleagues to adopt reforms of a similar nature in East Germany.[20] This initial response continued well into 1987. East Germany also began in 1987 to block external sources of information about reforms—sources from the East, not the West. The regime stalled on its coverage of the changing Soviet line; even Gorbachev's speeches, as they grew increasingly radical by East German standards, were not reported in full in the East German press.[21] Simultaneously, the regime tried to limit access to Soviet publications.[22]

Only when the Soviet leadership specifically objected did Gorbachev's speeches begin to receive complete coverage. Yet when discussing its own economic and political conditions, the regime talked of "perfecting" and "renewal," rather than restructuring or reform. The leadership also began more adamantly to stress that glasnost and perestroika were strictly Soviet ventures that East Germany need not copy, leading to such famous comments as that by Politburo member Kurt Hager: "Just because your neighbor is repapering his house doesn't mean that you have to do the same."[23] Honecker's own comment about reform in East Germany was even more telling: "When we say that we need democracy as we need the air to breathe, then we obviously do not mean the bourgeois but the socialist democracy."[24] His explicit use—and reinterpretation—of one of Gorbachev's rallying cries made his rejection of any such claim quite plain.

---

20. The fact that this tacit rejection of glasnost and perestroika took place in Gorbachev's presence, since he attended the 11th SED Congress, reinforced the regime's opposition to any adoption of such policies at home.

21. Dirk W. Rumberg, "Glasnost in the GDR? The Impact of Gorbachev's Reform Policy on the German Democratic Republic," *International Relations,* Vol. 9, No 3 (May 1988), pp. 204, 213.

22. This took place at one of the few times when Soviet newspapers were genuinely popular in East Germany. Prior to this point, only Party members had much interest in reading the Soviet press, but with the changes in the Soviet Union, newspapers such as *Pravda* and *Izvestiya* began selling out, with people lining up to buy the increasingly limited numbers available.

23. Kurt Hager, in an interview with *Der Stern,* April 9, 1987, later reprinted by *Neues Deutschland,* April 10, 1987. As quoted in Griffith, "The German Democratic Republic," in William E. Griffith, ed., *Central and Eastern Europe: The Opening Curtain?* (Boulder, Colo.: Westview Press, 1989), p. 322.

24. Quoted in Karl-Heinz Baum, "Ein Hauch von Glasnost ist zu spuren," in *Frankfurter Rundschau,* May 29, 1987, as cited by Rumberg, "Glasnost in the GDR?" p. 214.

In late 1987, a crackdown on dissent began within the state, and continued in 1988. The first sign of the crackdown came in November 1987 with a police raid on the Church of Zion in East Berlin, which was active in the peace movement; this was followed by the arrests of demonstrators during unofficial marches commemorating the murders of Rosa Luxemburg and Karl Leibknecht, German socialist leaders killed in the 1920s, in January 1988.[25]

*   *   *

The Czechoslovak regime also had no enthusiasm for the policies Gorbachev promoted during the early years of his tenure. Like the East German SED, the CPCZ stressed Czechoslovakia's economic achievements and denied that the country needed to introduce reforms. The CPCZ gave only minimal lip service to the ideas of glasnost and pere--stroika, while prominent figures in the Party were openly hostile to many of the basic reform concepts emanating from Moscow. Beyond accepting the concept of "acceleration," an exhortation used by Gorbachev in 1985 to encourage workers to achieve greater productivity, little happened to suggest that the regime intended to enact any programs at home similar to the reforms in the Soviet Union.[26]

Only in 1987 was any discussion of reforms begun in Czechoslovakia; the need for economic changes was broached at a Central Committee (CC) meeting that January, and Husák acknowledged the need for "democratization" as well as economic reform in March.[27] But this was accompanied by a hardening of opposition to reform within the Czechoslovak leadership. This resistance was spurred in good part by the increasing number of comparisons being made, by journalists and politicians, between Gorbachev's experiments in the Soviet Union and the events in Czechoslovakia in 1968. The existing leadership of the CPCZ, which had demolished the Czechoslovakian reform program, was particularly sensitive to any suggestion that this might, in fact, have been the correct policy to follow. Vasil Bilak, one of the more conservative members of Czechoslovakia's Politburo at the time, cautioned against making

---

25. Griffith, "The German Democratic Republic," p. 331; and Tismaneanu, "Nascent Civil Society in the German Democratic Republic," pp. 106–111.

26. At one point Husák did mention "reform," a taboo concept in Czechoslovakia since 1968, in a speech toward the end of 1986. On the CPCZ's hostility to reform, see Karen Dawisha, *Eastern Europe, Grobachev, and Reform: The Great Challenge* (Cambridge: Cambridge University Press, 1988), pp. 167–170.

27. Brown, *Eastern Europe and Communist Rule*, p. 305.

such parallels, stating that this implied an effort to "dismantle" social-ism.[28]

Husák's removal as Party leader and reappointment to the ceremonial post of president in December 1987 suggested that some movement toward reform might begin in Czechoslovakia; the appointment of Milos Jakeš as General Secretary implied the opposite. Like Husák, Jakeš came to power after the Soviet invasion, and he was staunchly opposed to reform. And though some officials who were thought to favor reforms remained in the Politburo, the balance clearly favored the conservatives, making the chances of reform slim.[29]

Under Jakeš' leadership, the Czechoslovak government became more vocal in its rejection of change in 1988. Conservatives within the CPCZ leadership began openly to side with the hard-line elements in the Kremlin. Thus, there appeared to be genuine support in the Czechoslovak government for the views expressed in the "Andreyeva Letter," which attacked Gorbachev's reforms, and Eva Fojtikova, wife of the CPCZ's leading ideologist, published an article that denounced glasnost as similar to "counterrevolution".[30]

By 1988, the persistence of reform in the Soviet Union led to tentative stirrings among the Czechoslovak population. Charter 77 began to broaden its focus beyond human rights to address directly other political freedoms. Additionally, the number of young people willing to participate in demonstrations, while still a tiny portion of the population, rose considerably in 1988, particularly around the twentieth anniversary of

---

28.   Dawisha, *Eastern Europe, Gorbachev and Reform*, p. 169.

29.   The removal in November 1988 of Lubomir Strougal, one of the most candid advocates of reforms in the Czechoslovak Politburo, was a sign that under Jakeš opposition to reforms was likely to continue. Some observers have argued that Gorbachev made a mistake in not supporting Strougal's bid for the Party leadership in 1987; had he been willing to back Strougal, the CPCZ might have adopted policies similar to perestroika under his leadership. See Jacques Lévesque, *The Enigma of 1989: The USSR and the Liberation of Eastern Europe* (Berkeley, Calif.: University of California Press, 1997), pp. 59–64. On Strougal, see Vladimir V. Kusin, "Reform and Dissidence in Czechoslovakia," *Current History*, Vol. 86, No. 523 (November 1987), p. 383.

30.   The "Andreyeva Letter," published by an influential Soviet newspaper, criticized the reappraisal of Stalin because it threatened the ideological foundations of the Soviet state. For an analysis of the Andreyeva letter and its impact on Gorbachev's political position, see Archie Brown, *The Gorbachev Factor* (Oxford: Oxford University Press, 1997), pp. 172–175; and Michael Tatu, "The 19th Party Conference," *Problems of Communism*, Vol. 37, Nos. 3–4, (May–August 1988), pp. 1–15. On the Czechoslovak response, see Vladimir V. Kusin, "Thinly Veiled Criticism of Soviet Glasnost by Czechoslovak Hardliner," *Radio Free Europe Background Reports*: Czechoslovak Situation Report, No. 13, September 1, 1988.

the Warsaw Pact invasion.[31] The government tried to prevent any commemoration of the Soviet intervention, and it brutally suppressed the demonstrations that did occur on the August anniversary.

In 1989, the Czechoslovakian Party reluctantly acknowledged that some restructuring was necessary, but continued throughout much of 1989 to distinguish between political and economic reforms. Some plans for change began to appear, but the implementation of many of the measures proposed continued to be put off, while the nature of the changes under consideration remained narrowly constricted. For example, the regime authorized a commission to write a new constitution; work began in January 1989. While the CPCZ could thus claim to be adopting a reform program, it was merely mimicking developments in the Soviet Union. In contrast with the constitutional committee in Hungary, only approved members of the CPCZ were involved in the commission, which meant the new version was unlikely to accommodate any alternative views. Multicandidate elections were held on a local level in the spring —but only Party members were allowed to vie for positions.[32]

The regime was also increasingly defensive in its justifications of its own policy choices and in its attitude toward what was going on around it. As a result, though it was beginning to abandon its outright rejection of reform, the Party was adamant that any changes remain within the confines of "socialism." Party ideologues acknowledged the need to "renew" socialism, but contended that only by maintaining the Marxist-Leninist character of the regime could an acceptable outcome be found.[33] The CPCZ also remained exceptionally hostile to any reconsideration of the past.

CURRENTS OF OPPOSITION IN 1989

A change in the popular mood in 1989 was seen in the notable rise in the number of public demonstrations and protests against government pol-

---

31. This reflected both disaffection from the society in which they lived and the apathy and demoralization of most adults. Bernard Wheaton and Zdenéc Kavan, *The Velvet Revolution: Czechoslovakia, 1988–1991* (Boulder, Colo.: Westview Press, 1992), p. 25.

32. "Run-Up to First Multicandidate Election Outlined," *Rude Pravo*, March 25, 1989, in *Foreign Broadcast Information Service: Eastern Europe* (hereafter *FBIS:EEU*), March 30, 1989.

33. "Party Ideological Commission Meets 31 Jan," Prague Domestic Service, January 31, 1989, in *FBIS:EEU*, February 6, 1989; "Fojtík Views Reform, Rejects Brzezinski Comments," *Rude Pravo*, September 5, 1989, in *FBIS:EEU*, September 8, 1989; and "Legalization of Opposition Ruled Out," *Tribuna*, May 17, 1989, in *FBIS:EEU*, May 26, 1989.

icy. The first demonstration, organized by dissidents and human rights supporters in January 1989 to commemorate the self-immolation of Jan Palach twenty years earlier—though tiny compared to Polish strikes—was a tangible sign that the opposition in Czechoslovakia was growing.[34] The government's repression of this protest stimulated a week of additional protests. Human rights demonstrations also emerged at the official May Day parade and after the crackdown in Beijing's Tiananmen Square, while Charter 77 objected to the planned visit of Romanian Party leader Nicolae Ceauşescu in May as an "embarrassment" in view of his human rights record.[35] Another round of demonstrations took place around the anniversary of the 1968 invasion, and demonstrations continued sporadically during September and October. Notably, the spring demonstrations attracted an estimated 1,000 people, while by October 3,000–5,000 people were willing to participate.[36]

On January 24, Charter 77 asked the CPCZ to open a dialogue about the problems facing the country and the need for political change, a development that echoed trends elsewhere in Eastern Europe. This proposal appeared less than two weeks after the announcement that negotiations between the Polish regime and Solidarity were to begin.[37] Building on the precedent of attempting to engage the regime, a number of petitions appeared during the year that called on the regime to implement changes. Hundreds of cultural figures signed a petition early in the year demanding the release of several of the dissidents arrested during the January 1989 demonstrations—one of the first times that people in positions that required official sanction had been willing to risk their standing with the

---

34. Palach took this action in protest against the Soviet invasion in 1968 and the subsequent rollback of reforms in Czechoslovakia.

35. "Protesters, BBC Journalist Arrested," Paris AFP, May 1, 1989, in *FBIS:EEU,* May 1, 1989; "Vatican Says Human Rights March Held in Prague," Vatican City International Service, June 21, 1989, in *FBIS:EEU,* June 22, 1989; "Charter 77 Protests Ceauşescu's Visit to Prague," Budapest Domestic Service, May 16, 1989, in *FBIS:EEU,* May 16, 1989; and "Charter 77 Protests Visit," Paris AFP, May 17, 1989, in *FBIS:EEU,* May 17, 1989.

36. See "Opposition Members Reportedly Arrested," Budapest Home Service, August 20, 1989, in *FBIS:EEU,* August 21, 1989; "Vienna Reports Police Intervention," Vienna Television Service, August 21, 1989, in *FBIS:EEU,* August 22, 1989; "Prague Police Break Up Environmental Protest," Budapest Domestic Service, September 13, 1989, in *FBIS:EEU,* September 14, 1989; and "Prague Demonstrators Call for Reform, Arrests Made," *FBIS:EEU,* October 30, 1989.

37. "Charter 77 Asks CPCZ to Open Dialogue," Vatican City International Service, January 24, 1989, in *FBIS:EEU,* January 25, 1989.

regime.[38] This was followed by an open letter to the regime entitled "A Few Sentences," which appeared in late June; despite police harassment of some of the signatories, 40,000 people had signed this document by October. More than a hundred official Czechoslovak journalists signed another petition in October calling for the legalization of the most prominent samizdat journal, *Lidove Noviny*.[39] This was the first time in twenty years that official journalists had publicly supported an opposition publication. Additionally, a petition circulated by the Catholic Church requesting greater religious freedom received 600,000 signatures.

The changing public mood was also seen in an increase in the number of independent groups that emerged. In February 1989, an organization called Obroda (Renewal) was created by former communists, with the goal of "socialist renewal."[40] Another notable arrival was the reformed International PEN Club, which had been disbanded twenty years earlier. This was significant because it was the first organization that had as members both writers who were officially sanctioned and writers who were proscribed by the regime.[41]

The regime responded to growing opposition with greater coercion. Police brutality during demonstrations in January 1989 was quite severe, with many arrests and some injuries reported. While the regime's reaction to the sporadic demonstrations that arose over the next few months

---

38. Twelve hundred people had signed a petition for Havel's release by February 7. See "Cultural Workers Call for Release of Protesters," Vienna Domestic Service, February 1, 1989, in *FBIS:EEU*, February 3, 1989; and "Artists Call for Release of Václav Havel," Vienna Television Service, February 7, 1989, in *FBIS:EEU*, February 8, 1989.

39. Samizdat refers to self-published underground literature, generally of a political nature that could not be published in official mediums. See Jiří Pehe, "Journalists Appeal in Behalf of Prosecuted Editors of *Lidove Noviny*," *Radio Free Europe Czechoslovak Situation Report*, No. 22, October 27, 1989, pp. 21–23. For an early analysis of "A Few Sentences" and the regime's reaction to it, see Jiří Pehe, "Dissidents Joined by Cultural Figures in a Demand for Democratization" and "Petition Calling for Democracy Angers Regime," both in *Radio Free Europe Czechoslovak Situation Report*, No. 15, July 14, 1989, pp. 19–23. See also Wheaton and Kavan, *The Velvet Revolution*, pp. 28–29.

40. Not only serious groups emerged at this point; an absurdist group, called the Society for Merrier Present Times, appeared in May 1989 and proceeded throughout the summer to ridicule and confound the regime and the police. See Jiří Pehe, "Absurd Protests Ridicule Prague Regime," *Radio Free Europe Czechoslovak Situation Report*, No. 19, pp. 13–15. On Obroda's goals and organization, see Pehe, "'Obroda: A Club For Socialist Restructuring' Publishes its Program and Holds a Meeting in Prague," *Radio Free Europe Czechoslovak Situation Report*, No. 14, July 5, 1989, pp. 11–15.

41. Jiří Pehe, "The Czech Branch of the International PEN Club is Revived," *Radio Free Europe Czechoslovak Situation Report*, No. 17, August 18, 1989, pp. 21–23.

was more muted, the government stiffened sentences for breaches of order in mid-February, while many of those arrested during the January demonstrations were still awaiting trial.[42] By August, the Western media was following developments in Czechoslovakia closely; this probably explains the mixed police response to the situation at the West German embassy in Prague, which was by then overflowing with refugees from East Germany. Some days the police were quite brutal in their efforts to keep would-be refugees away from the embassy and to keep Czechoslovak citizens out of the area in general; other days, policemen simply looked the other way as East Germans climbed the embassy's fence.[43] Yet the police showed little hesitation in quelling the demonstrations on the anniversary of the 1968 invasion.

*　　*　　*

Within East Germany, pressure for reform was still coming from only a tiny percentage of society at the beginning of 1989. One estimate suggested that there were about 500 independent groups in East Germany in early 1989, with perhaps 20 members each.[44] Interestingly, some of the earliest calls for reform in 1989 came from groups that were responding to, or at least were influenced by, external developments. For example, the unofficial demonstrations accompanying the official commemoration of Rosa Luxemburg's death contained appeals for perestroika, in a reminder to the regime that even its patron state, the Soviet Union, had opted for change. Shortly thereafter, 171 different peace and human rights groups held a demonstration urging the release of Václav Havel, then Czechoslovakia's most famous dissident, who had been arrested earlier that year.[45]

While sporadic protests appeared throughout the spring, demonstrations directly protesting against the regime began in earnest in May. On May Day, protesters demanded the right to emigrate; demonstrations for greater human rights followed. Five people were arrested at the Berlin

---

42. "Laws to Maintain Law, Order Strengthened," Prague CTK, February 17, 1989, in *FBIS:EEU*, February 21, 1989.

43. For all its hostility toward Western interference, and particularly at a time when it was under increasing pressure to reform, the Czechoslovak government was sensitive to accusations that it could only keep control by repressive means; this probably helps explain the lack of clarity about how to deal with the East German refugee crisis. Moreover, individual policemen undoubtedly responded differently.

44. R. Asmus, J. F. Brown, and K. W. Crane, *Soviet Foreign Policy and the Revolutions in Eastern Europe*, RAND Report R-3903-USDP, 1991.

45. "Human Rights Groups Demand Havel's Release," Cologne Deutschlandfunk Network, February 27, 1989, in *FBIS:EEU*, February 27, 1989.

Wall on May 7, while a silent protest march was held in Leipzig.[46] Demonstrations swelled after the elections on May 7, 1989, when it became clear that the results announced by the regime were fraudulent.[47] Even larger protest demonstrations were held throughout the country following the crackdown in Beijing's Tiananmen Square; these continued for several weeks.

Additionally, the church became more politically active in the spring. The evangelical church reacted to the evidence of deceit in the May elections with a public protest against the election fraud. This was followed by an appeal to the regime from a prominent church leader for dialogue with the citizens, and an open admission that the church was obligated to play a role in this rather than keep itself apart from the political process.[48]

At the end of May 1989, Hungary dismantled the "iron curtain"—the fences along its border with Austria. Hungarian citizens could already travel freely to Austria, but East German citizens could not. By the end of the summer vacation season, thousands of East German citizens had fled to Hungary to try to escape across the loosely guarded frontier. The numbers of citizens trying to leave was a scathing disavowal of the regime's claims that it had gained broad popular support for the socialist state it had created. It also showed the dissemination of outside information into East Germany, since the source of information about the opening of the border was either Western media (primarily television) or Soviet or other East European sources.

The East German regime remained intransigent in the face of the growing exodus. By early August, refugees had overrun West German embassies in Budapest, Prague, and East Berlin in an effort to gain asylum in the West, and the Hungarian government was constructing camps

---

46. See "Arrests at Leipzig Rally," Hamburg DPA, May 7, 1989, in *FBIS:EEU*, May 8, 1989.

47. Independent action groups in East Berlin, for example, reported that 3 to 20 percent of the voters interviewed had voted no in the elections, yet the official returns listed a 97 to 99 percent vote in favor of most candidates nationwide. Similarly, the official returns claimed that 97 to 99 percent of the population had voted in the elections, while the independent tallies estimated that under 90 percent of the population had voted. Honecker called the official results a "convincing reflection" of the people's faith in the country's leadership. See "Opposition Cited on `Rigging,'" Hamburg DPA, May 8, 1989, in *FBIS:EEU*, May 8, 1989; and "Honecker Say Elections Demonstrate Unity," ADN (East German) International Service, May 11, 1989, in *FBIS:EEU*, May 12, 1989.

48. "Bishop Appeals for Survey of Vote Discrepancies," Cologne Deutschlandfunk Network, June 9, 1989, in *FBIS:EEU*, June 9, 1989; and "Stolpe Speaks on Domestic, Foreign Issues," *Frankfurter Rundschau*, June 15, 1989, in *FBIS:EEU*, June 20, 1989.

to house its swelling numbers of refugees.[49] The regime responded to this exodus with repressive measures at home, refusing to offer any guarantees of change or a loosening of travel restrictions to convince citizens to return to East Germany other than freedom from punishment for having attempted to leave.[50] Honecker condemned those fleeing, stating that "nobody is going to weep" for them.[51] The SED also attacked West Germany for interfering in East Germany's domestic affairs, and for "subversive" actions within the refugee camps in Hungary. Thus, it transferred all blame for the situation to external sources, notably the West, rather than acknowledge that there might be domestic explanations for this situation.[52]

The increasing flight of citizens to Hungary stimulated expanding protests against the lack of reform in East Germany by citizens wishing to stay. A demonstration was held at the Berlin Wall on August 7, 1989, and by the beginning of September demonstrations protesting an ever broader scope of issues, and involving increasing numbers of participants, began to emerge around the country. Several hundred people took part in a demonstration in Leipzig on September 4, the first of many weekly protests that were to prove particularly crucial.[53]

Two important developments for the growth of opposition were the church's expanding role, and the almost simultaneous emergence of viable opposition groups outside of it. By September 1989, in a departure from their earlier nonpolitical stance, church leaders appealed to both the

---

49. On August 3, the number of refugees in West German missions was 80 in East Berlin; 20 in Prague; 130 in Budapest, and the Hungarian government was constructing refugee camps. See "Number of Refugees in FRG Missions Rising," Hamburg DPA, August 3, 1989, in *FBIS:EEU,* August 4, 1989.

50. By August some 2,500 people had been imprisoned in East Germany for trying to escape to Hungary. See "2,500 Imprisoned in GDR for Trying to Escape," *Bild,* August 8, 1989, in *FBIS:EEU,* August 9, 1989; and "Krolikowski Reaffirms Stance," ADN International Service, August 18, 1989, in *FBIS:EEU,* August 21, 1989. See also "FRG `Campaign' on Asylum-Seekers Criticized," *Neues Deutschland,* August 10, 1989, in *FBIS:EEU,* August 17, 1989.

51. Igor Maximychev, "End of the Berlin Wall," *International Affairs* (Moscow), No. 3, March 1991, p. 102.

52. East Germany pressured Hungary in private, but directed much of its public ire at West Germany.

53. Western reports suggested that this demonstration was "crushed" by the regime. See "Police `Brutally Crush' Leipzig Demonstration," Vienna Domestic Service, September 5, 1989, in *FBIS:EEU,* September 5, 1989; see also "At Least 40 People Arrested in Alexanderplatz," Hamburg DPA, September 7, 1989, in *FBIS:EEU,* September 8, 1989.

state and the Party to make changes in East Germany, to hold public discussions with the population, and to end the "rigidity" that existed so as to allow change in society. It also appealed to the people not to emigrate, but to stay and work for East Germany's future.[54]

The emergence of "New Forum," founded by a group of artists and intellectuals who had disagreed with the regime's policies for years, was also significant. New Forum did not advocate the adoption of a Western democratic system, but instead favored a "third way" between capitalism and socialism, incorporating the best values of each system. The group urged substantial revision of East Germany's political and economic system. Though New Forum's application for official status as an independent group was summarily rejected by the regime and its members harassed, the group continued to maintain a public stance and fight for legal recognition.[55]

The greater willingness of groups like New Forum to take a public stand opposing the regime was probably a response to three factors. First, and perhaps most immediate in September, was the inauguration of a Solidarity prime minister in Poland—evidently with the blessing of the Soviet Union. Second, the expanding flow of émigrés from East Germany, and the significant attention devoted to this in the Western media, made the widespread discontent of East Germany's population palpable to all viewers, shattering the enforced silence that had prevented East Germans from recognizing that they were not alone in their distaste for their system. Third, the almost total hostility expressed by the government toward any calls for change even after this hemorrhage began could give both the population and the opposition no hope that the system would reform itself. It also angered many citizens that representatives of the regime called those who had fled "dirtbags"—at a time when much of the

---

54. "Church Appeals to People not to Emigrate," Hamburg DPA, September 8, 1989, in *FBIS:EEU*, September 11, 1989; and "Church Plans to Request Swift Changes," Hamburg DPA, September 5, 1989, in *FBIS:EEU*, September 6, 1989.

55. New Forum's application was rejected on the grounds that "the goals and matters of concern expressed by those who applied are in contradiction with the GDR constitution and represent a platform hostile to the state." See "'New Forum' Application Rejected," ADN International Service, September 21, 1989, in *FBIS:EEU*, September 22, 1989. The SED also rejected the evangelical church's calls for greater discussion of the state's problems. See "SED Rejects Dialogue," *Die Welt*, September 16–17, 1989, in *FBIS:EEU*, September 19, 1989; and "Opposition 'New Forum' Founders Discuss Goals," Vienna Television Service, September 14, 1989, in *FBIS:EEU*, September 19, 1989. On the emergence of the opposition, see also Gale Stokes, *The Walls Came Tumbling Down: The Collapse of Communism in Eastern Europe* (New York: Oxford University Press, 1993), pp. 138–140.

population was stunned and dismayed by the flight of so many people, so many of them young.[56]

The Hungarian government's decision on September 9, 1989, to open its border with Austria to East German citizens wishing to go to the West brought a harsh response from the SED leadership.[57] The government restricted travel to Hungary, but the emigration problem did not abate. Instead, the number of East Germans seeking refuge in West German embassies in Prague and Warsaw skyrocketed, forcing the East German leadership finally to "expel" these citizens, and permit them to travel to West Germany only days before East Germany's fortieth anniversary celebration in October. The regime then suspended visa-free travel to Czechoslovakia on October 3, leaving East German citizens increasingly sequestered within their borders.

Concurrent with the swelling numbers of refugees, demonstrations for change within the state expanded. On September 24, 8,000 people marched in Leipzig; by October 9, the number of demonstrators had grown to 50,000, a figure unheard of in this regimented state.[58] And violent protests broke out in Dresden when the police tried to seal off the train stations as trainloads of refugees from Prague and Warsaw passed through East Germany to West Germany. Calls mounted for a national dialogue and reform of the state's rigid system, with one reform group going so far as to write a letter to Gorbachev on the eve of the fortieth anniversary celebration, imploring his aid in initiating reform.[59]

---

56. Norman M. Naimark, "'Ich will hier raus': Emigration and the Collapse of the German Democratic Republic," in Ivo Banac, ed., *Eastern Europe in Revolution* (Ithaca, N.Y.: Cornell University Press, 1992), p. 85.

57. The SED sharply criticized both Hungary and West Germany for this move, with its strongest attacks aimed at West Germany.

58. The regime apparently ordered security forces to respond to the October 9 demonstration with force; troops were massed near the city, hospitals were emptied, and blood supplies were rushed to Leipzig. While Politburo member Egon Krenz takes credit for countering the order, it was the efforts of local officials and leaders of the peace movement, including conductor Kurt Masur, that resulted in an agreement not to use force against marchers. See Naimark, "'Ich will hier raus,'" p. 91; "50,000 Join Peaceful Protest," Hamburg DPA, October 9, 1989, in *FBIS:EEU*, October 10, 1989; Stokes, *The Walls Came Tumbling Down*, p. 140; Charles S. Maier, *Dissolution: The Crisis of Communism and the End of East Germany* (Princeton: Princeton University Press, 1997), p. 156; and Elizabeth Pond, *Beyond the Wall: Germany's Road to Unification* (Washington, D.C.: Brookings Institution, 1993), p. 117.

59. "Reform Group Sends Open Letter to Gorbachev," Hamburg DPA, October 5, 1989, in *FBIS:EEU*, October 6, 1989; "'Many' Arrested at Dresden Train Station," Hamburg DPA, October 4, 1989, in *FBIS:EEU*, October 5, 1989; "'Many' Injured in Dresden Violence," Hamburg DPA, October 5, 1989, in *FBIS:EEU*, October 6, 1989.

Honecker continued to reject calls for reform, including Gorbachev's most pointed suggestion to date in his speech at the fortieth anniversary of the founding of East Germany on October 7, 1989. But while the anniversary celebration in East Berlin took place under tight police control, protest demonstrations throughout the country increased in size and frequency. In response, government spokesmen began comparing the situation to that in China earlier in the year, an implicit warning that the demonstrators could face a brutal crackdown.

THE REGIMES CAPITULATE

A sea change in the East German regime's attitude toward reform appeared on October 11, 1989, less than a week after East Germany's fortieth anniversary. A special meeting of the Central Committee of the SED, which continued for several days, started on that date. One faction of the Party leadership, led by Egon Krenz and Gunter Schabowski, put forward a proposal for reform that was accepted over Honecker's doubts.[60] These two, and Erich Mielke, head of the Stasi (the East German secret police), met on October 8 and formulated a draft acknowledging the flight of East German citizens and promising reforms.[61] In the first official acknowledgment that the socialist system in East Germany had problems that must be addressed, the SED admitted, in an editorial in the official party newspaper, the need to make socialism "attractive" to all, and that the state had a need for all of its citizens.[62] Yet Honecker continued to insist that the "socialist" nature of the state remained incontestable.

Over the next two months, three trends emerged in the SED's actions. The first was a spreading wave of personnel changes in the Party and government. Honecker resigned on October 17, and was replaced by Krenz, a Politburo member long presumed to be his heir apparent. Honecker's resignation was not entirely voluntary, and he later referred to Krenz and the Politburo as "traitors";[63] his wife, Margot, resigned her

---

60. Condoleezza Rice and Philip Zelikow, *Germany Unified and Europe Transformed: A Study in Statecraft* (Cambridge, Mass.: Harvard University Press, 1995), p. 85.

61. Maximychev, "End of the Berlin Wall," p. 103.

62. The absence of a monopoly on truth by the Party was conceded as well, and Honecker himself urged an "open dialogue" with society in another editorial. See "SED Politburo Statement on Disturbances and Emigration," ADN, October 11, 1989, in *FBIS:EEU*, October 13, 1989; "Honecker says `Open Dialogue' Planned," ADN, October 13, 1989, in *FBIS:EEU*, October 16, 1989; and "Gerlach Says Party `Has No Monopoly on Truth,'" *Der Morgen*, October 13, 1989, in *FBIS:EEU*, October 18, 1989.

63. Maximychev, "End of the Berlin Wall," p. 104. For an extensive discussion of the effort to oust Honecker, see Pond, *Beyond the Wall*, pp. 102–129.

post as education minister on November 2. Local officials, confronted by spreading protests, independently began opening negotiations with pro-testers in different cities around the state.[64] Resignations of local officials snowballed around the country in late October and early November, as party officials were unable to convince the citizenry that they were truly willing to implement reforms, or to overcome their previous negative reputations. The Cabinet resigned on November 7; the SED Politburo fol-lowed suit the next day. This led to the Party's nomination of Hans Modrow, a reform-minded party leader from Dresden, to be prime minis-ter. And as allegations of corruption by the Party leadership spread in late November, the entire SED leadership, including Krenz, resigned on December 6.

The second trend was the SED's almost desperate affirmation throughout the fall of its bonds with the Soviet Union. Within days of his appointment as Party Secretary in October, Krenz spoke with Gorbachev and acknowledged for the first time that the recent experiences of the So-viet Union were relevant to East Germany. He visited the Soviet Union at the end of October, and emphasized the continuing importance for East Germany of its friendship with the Soviet Union.[65] This affirmation was repeated by other prominent SED officials, and underlined the regime's clear dependence on the Soviet Union.[66]

Third, the leadership made an ever-expanding series of political con-cessions in an effort to satisfy the opposition's demands. The regime al-lowed greater freedom of the media, as seen by the growing frankness of reportage in the official press, and acceptance of more independence for domestic and foreign journalists.[67] The regime also conceded the legiti-

---

64. The first negotiations between a local government and opposition took place in Dresden, in response to the riots prompted as thousands of citizens tried to board sealed trains passing from Czechoslovakia and Poland to West Germany. Elizabeth Pond, "A Wall Destroyed: The Dynamics of German Unification in the German Demo-cratic Republic," *International Security*, Vol. 15, No. 2 (Fall 1990), p. 43.

65. "Egon Krenz Speaks on Telephone with Mikhail Gorbachev," ADN, October 21, 1989, in *BBC Summary of World Broadcasts: Eastern Europe* (hereafter *SWB:EE*), October 23, 1989; "Gorbachev's Meeting with Krenz," Tass, November 1, 1989, in *SWB:EE*, No-vember 3, 1989.

66. Krenz stressed East Germany's dependence in his discussions with Gorbachev in Moscow, noting that "the GDR is in a certain sense the child of the Soviet Union, and one must acknowledge paternity for his children." Rice and Zelikow, *Germany Unified and Europe Transformed*, pp. 87–88.

67. On October 20, the regime announced the reissuing of *Sputnik*, a Soviet journal it had banned in 1988 because an issue contained articles questioning aspects of history that the East German regime felt were too sensitive. See "*Sputnik* Magazine to Return

macy of opposition groups by recognizing New Forum on November 8, 1989.

In a particularly significant concession, the regime announced in late October that it would legislate changes in the state's travel laws. Restrictions on travel to Czechoslovakia were lifted on November 1. Within a week, on November 9, 1989, the leadership announced the removal of all travel restrictions and in a moment of drama that captured the world's attention, it opened the Berlin Wall. In fact, the opening of the Wall appears to have been unintended, or at least its timing was. The Party's press spokesman, Gunter Schabowski, announced new travel guidelines at a news conference that evening, but he did not read the full text of the Party's decision, and ignored the notation that this would take effect on November 10. He announced that travel would be allowed virtually on request, and eliminated the need for exit permits. This led thousands of East Berliners to go to the Wall to find out if restrictions had in fact been lifted, and, in the face of huge crowds and no orders, the border guards eventually opened the Wall to all.[68] By November 18, a commission was given the task of revising the state's election laws, and the temporary government had announced that the constitution would be studied and revised. Charges of government corruption would be investigated, and the command structure of the army would be made separate from that of the Party.[69] Finally, in the ultimate admission of the mistakes of the past, by the end of November it was acknowledged that a radical reshaping of the SED itself was necessary.

Yet the expanding scope of concessions from the regime did not end the demonstrations, nor did it satisfy popular demands for structural change. Instead, the public's demands intensified as the regime compromised, and the level of protests increased. The size of the demonstrations skyrocketed throughout October; on October 15 about 120,000 people marched in Leipzig—a remarkable figure, but one that was soon dwarfed by a demonstration of 500,000 in Berlin on November 4. Demonstrations

---

to Circulation", ADN, October 20, 1989, in *FBIS:EEU*, October 23, 1989. See also Ingomar Schwelz, "Print Media Sound Note of Criticism," *Hannoversche Allgemeine*, October 12, 1989, in *The German Tribune*, October 22, 1989.

68. See Maximychev, "End of the Berlin Wall," pp. 107–108; and Pond, "A Wall Destroyed," pp. 48, 123–133; and Hans-Hermann Hertle, "The Fall of the Wall: The Unintended Self-Dissolution of East Germany's Ruling Regime," in *Cold War International History Project Bulletin* [hereafter *CWIHP Bulletin*], Issue 12/13 (Fall 2001), pp. 131– 164.

69. "People's Chamber Holds Session," ADN, November 17, 1989, in *FBIS:EEU*, November 20, 1989.

were held protesting Krenz's election to the state leadership on October 24, an extraordinary protest against single-party rule. And in a particularly telling indication of the complete loss of faith in the leadership, Party members held a demonstration calling for "credible renewal" of the leadership on November 8.[70]

And still the flow of people leaving the state continued. The vast majority of those who visited the West in the first few days after the Wall was opened returned to East Germany.[71] At the end of the year, however, East Germans were continuing to move West at the rate of 1,000 per week, and the SED appeared to be unable to staunch this flow by addressing popular demands. Moreover, popular demonstrations in East Germany were increasingly being marked by banners and slogans favoring unification, thus changing the tenor of the domestic political debate. Calls for unification did not surface in any meaningful way until after the Berlin Wall was opened; almost immediately afterwards the tone of the demands at demonstrations such as those in Leipzig changed dramatically.[72] This change in tone undermined the regime's efforts merely to liberalize—or indeed to find any solution short of unification that would pacify popular demands.

Though the Communist Party was rapidly deteriorating due to the combination of internal differences and the weight of popular disapproval, the inchoate character of the opposition in East Germany remained a major obstacle to political reform in late 1989 and early 1990. A critical problem shared by the numerous opposition groups in East Germany was a lack of capable leaders due to Honecker's earlier tactic of exiling prominent dissidents to the West. New Forum, which gained widespread support as a rallying point during the demonstrations, refused to become a political party because it rejected the existing political system; as in other East European countries, the concept of political parties had been discredited during the communist period. Moreover, New Forum reflected a wide range of views, and neither it nor any other group had presented an explicit catalogue of demands for change, other than calls for free elections and the removal of travel restrictions. Similarly, none of the opposition parties was sure how to address the issue of unification, though they clearly recognized it as an important issue. Only in Decem-

70. "Thousands of Party Members Demonstrate", ADN, November 8, 1989, in *FBIS:EEU*, November 9, 1989.

71. In the first few weeks, 11,000,000 visas were issued to a population of 17,000,000.

72. Timothy Garton Ash, *We The People: The Revolutions of 1989 Witnessed in Warsaw, Budapest, Berlin and Prague* (Cambridge: Granta Books, 1990), pp. 69–75.

ber did the opposition groups agree to work together through negotiations with the government, in a Round Table discussion modeled on those in Poland and Hungary. This collection of groups reluctantly agreed to join a nonaffiliated coalition government with the renamed socialist party—now the Socialist Unity Party-Party of Democratic Socialism (SED-PDS)—on January 28, 1990, and free elections were set for March 18, 1990.[73] By this point, the newly formed Social Democratic Party (SDP), with links to West Germany's SDP, had emerged as a feasible challenger to the SED-PDS, and was the fastest growing party in East Germany.[74]

In the end, East Germany's attempt to reform was subsumed by Germany's unification. Alarmed by the continued flow of refugees, West German leaders concluded that the only way to staunch the flight to the West was to unify the two states. Free elections in East Germany in March 1990 were dominated by pressures for unification. A coalition of East German parties aligned with the West German Christian Democratic Union (CDU) won the elections, signaling Eastern support for unification. The "two plus four" negotiations between the two Germanies and the four powers controlling Berlin—the United States, Great Britain, France, and the Soviet Union—began on May 5, 1990, and led to Germany's unification on October 3, 1990, less than a year after the Wall fell.[75]

*   *   *

In Czechoslovakia, the regime's continued inflexibility and the people's general sense of discontent metamorphosed into wave after wave of mass demonstrations, beginning in November 1989. The exodus of East Germans through Hungary (via Czechoslovakia) had been visible proof that reforms were having a profound impact on other conservative states in the bloc. Not only was the West German embassy in Prague overrun, but few could miss the abandoned East German cars in Prague and elsewhere, evidence that East German citizens were fleeing from their conservative regime.[76] The mass demonstrations in East Germany were surpris-

---

73. "East Germans Form Coalition, Advance Vote," *International Herald Tribune* [hereafter *IHT*], January 29, 1990.

74. The SPD was overtaken by the Christian Democratic Party by the time elections were held in May. See Serge Schmemann, "Coalition Planned in Berlin," *IHT,* January 27–28, 1990.

75. On the unification of Germany, see Pond, *Beyond the Wall;* Rice and Zelikow, *Germany Unified and Europe Transformed;* and Maier, *Dissolution.*

76. See Owen V. Johnson, "Mass Media and the Velvet Revolution," in Jeremy D. Popkin, ed., *Media and Revolution* (Lexington, Ky.: University Press of Kentucky, 1995), p. 228.

ingly successful by November, leading to the opening of the Berlin Wall. Since much of Czechoslovakia could receive West German or Austrian television, the government could not hide these developments from the population. The government had also stopped jamming Radio Free Europe in January 1989.[77]

Finally, widespread outrage at police brutality during a student demonstration in Prague on November 17 provoked a growing number of protests throughout the country.[78] The November 17 demonstration had been officially sanctioned and was organized to commemorate the execution by the Nazis in 1939 of a number of students who had opposed the Nazi takeover of Czechoslovakia. It was unclear whether anyone died as a result of police actions, but several dozen people were hospitalized after the demonstration.[79] Within days of the November 17 demonstration, crowds of up to 300,000 people were protesting against the regime in Prague. Two days after protests began in November, opposition leaders came together with student groups in a loose grouping called Civic Forum. A similar organization, the Public Against Violence (PAV), was established in Bratislava, the Slovak capital, at roughly the same time, and coordinated its actions with Civic Forum.

Though the protest movement that swept Czechoslovakia began spontaneously and was organized mostly by students, the ability of the fragmented groups of protesters to organize quickly, to coordinate with the existing opposition groups, and to gain the support of important groups such as workers throughout the country, gave it a singular advantage in its negotiations with the CPCZ.[80] In addition, prominent figures

---

77. Lévesque, *The Enigma of 1989*, p. 182.

78. One of the government's early concessions in negotiations with the opposition was its agreement to investigate the police actions of November 17.

79. The secret police apparently tried to fake at least one death, in order to expose it later and discredit the opposition. One of the reports commissioned on the use of force by the regime against the demonstrators on November 17 concluded that the extreme use of force (given the nonviolent nature of the demonstration) was intended to bring down the leadership of the Communist Party. This was subsequently discredited, since the commission that wrote the report included several secret police agents. The most extensive discussion in English of the events surrounding November 17 and the generation of protests throughout the state is Wheaton and Kavan, *The Velvet Revolution*, chaps. 3 and 4. See also Theodore Draper, "A New History of the Velvet Revolution," *New York Review of Books*, January 14, 1993.

80. One factor promoting unity among diverse groups that distrusted each other to some extent was their shared fear that the regime would quickly decide to crack down and end their efforts. A significant problem in trying to reach the workers was that once the protests began, the police blocked access to factories to nonworkers. Student groups managed to circumvent this by having medical students enter the factories un-

were willing and able to lead the opposition movement. These included Václav Havel, a playwright and the country's best known dissident—though relatively unknown within the state at the start of the revolution—and Alexander Dubček, the Party leader during the Prague Spring.[81] Within days, Civic Forum had presented a list of demands to the government, and had begun discussions with Prime Minister Ladislav Adamec.

It is also notable that the Socialist Youth Union, an officially sanctioned organization, participated in the November 17 demonstration and protested against the police use of force; other Party-affiliated groups distanced themselves from the use of force shortly thereafter, and even objected to it. Similarly, some of the official media chose to ignore the party's restrictions on the press, and reportage of the events of November 17 and after was detailed and frank.[82]

The Party leadership seemed surprised by the protests, and appeared divided about how to respond. Conflicting statements were made by different spokesmen during the initial week of protests. On November 20 the Czech, Slovak, and federal governments issued a statement warning that they were prepared to "defend the interests of the socialist state with all energy," and the Politburo attempted to mobilize both police units and people's militia units to quell the demonstrations.[83] On November 21

---

der the guise of running health and safety meetings, which allowed them to present their grievances to the workers, and thereby gain their support. The participation of the official Socialist Union of Youth in both the November 17 demonstration and subsequent efforts to protest against the regime's response also boosted efforts to contact the workers, because the official youth organization had branches in factories. It was more difficult to spread information about developments to the countryside, since newspapers were confiscated and police would not allow cars with Prague license plates to leave the vicinity during this period. Apparently, some Prague residents convinced relatives with license plates from other regions to ferry newspapers from the cities to the countryside. Based on author's private conversations in Prague, May 1991; see also Wheaton and Kavan, *The Velvet Revolution*, pp. 66–67.

81. The Party had endured Dubček's partial return to the public debate earlier in the year, with his open support for Gorbachev's reform program and criticism of the Party's repressive policies. See Robin Gedye, "Call by Dubček for Trials to Be Stopped," *Daily Telegraph*, February 21, 1989; his interview on Hungarian Television of April 28, 1989; and his interviews with *L'Unita* (Italy).

82. Vladimir Kusin, "Despite Pressure, Authorities Remain on Slow and Hesitant Reformist Course," *Radio Free Europe Czechoslovakia Situation Report*, No. 24, December 8, 1989, p. 22; and Jan Obrman, "Leadership Sends out Mixed Signals," *Radio Free Europe Czechoslovak Situation Report*, No. 24, December 8, 1989, p. 26.

83. Remarkably, they had little success, as one Party organization after another rejected the leadership's demands. The security police insisted that the top Party leader-

Jakeš appealed to society to show "civic responsibility," yet simultaneously Prime Minister Adamec held a meeting with student representatives and Civic Forum, and called for a dialogue with opposition forces.[84] Within a week, the Party leadership had resigned en masse. A relative newcomer, Karel Urbánek, was appointed to be its head, as the old guard was completely purged from the Politburo and Central Committee. The new Central Committee resolved that a party congress would be convened sooner than planned, and it pledged to begin a dialogue with citizens who supported the constitution. Yet it proposed only minor adjustments to the constitution, which would leave the Communist Party firmly in control of the political system.[85]

This did not satisfy the opposition, which had already called for a nation-wide strike on November 27. The strike received overwhelming support, and as planned, it paralyzed the country for two hours.[86] Within days, the government yielded and Adamec endorsed far-reaching reforms, including the immediate acceptance of noncommunist participation in a new government. However, Civic Forum rejected the first cabinet proposed by Adamec, which would have been dominated by CPCZ members with only token participation by opposition groups. That the Party proposed such a cabinet indicates that it still hoped for liberalization, not democratization, and wanted to preserve its dominant role. Finally, in mid-December a new cabinet was announced; the new premier, Marián Čalfa, was a Communist, but thirteen of the twenty minis-

---

ship take responsibility before it would act, and several militia units simply balked—or disbanded. On November 24 the regime tried to turn to the army for support, but the option was narrowly rejected by the Politburo. Wheaton and Kavan, *The Velvet Revolution*, pp. 65–72; and Draper, "A New History of the Velvet Revolution," p. 15.

84. Jan Obrman, "Leadership Sends Out Mixed Signals," p. 27–28.

85. Adamec, in his negotiations with the Civic Forum, insisted on the importance of maintaining the "rule of law" in any changes of leadership. See "Resolution" of the Extraordinary Session of the Central Committee, November 25, 1989, in *SWB:EE*, November 27, 1989; and Milos Calda, "The Round Table Talks in Czechoslovakia," in Jon Elster, ed., *The Roundtable Talks and the Breakdown of Communism* (Chicago: University of Chicago Press, 1996), pp. 135–177.

86. About three-fourths of the population supported the strike in some form. The decision to limit the strike to two hours was meant to show that the Civic Forum did not want to injure the state's economy, while at the same time showing its strength. Students even volunteered to work full shifts without pay in many factories, to ensure that the economy did not suffer. This indication of the students' resolve was apparently an important factor in breaking through much popular apathy. Many adults expressed shame that "the children" must be the ones taking the moral stance to try to change things. Wheaton and Kavan, *The Velvet Revolution*, pp. 76–77.

ters named were not. Čalfa also announced his intention to resign from the Party. Jirí Dienstbier, a founding member of Charter 77 who was employed as a stoker after 1968, was named foreign minister.[87] Husák's resignation as president followed, and, after negotiations between Party and Civic Forum representatives, an agreement was reached whereby free elections for the Parliament would be held in June 1990. In December 1989, the interim National Assembly elected Alexander Dubček as its head and Václav Havel as president of the Czechoslovak republic.

Explaining the Regimes' Rejection of Early Reform

In both East Germany and Czechoslovakia reform emerged relatively late and was initiated from below rather than directed from above by the ruling regime. To understand why the transitions in these two states took this form, we must first explain why the states rejected the option of early, regime-directed reform. A regime's decision to reject reforms was shaped by two factors: whether it recognized the need for reforms, and whether the regime believed it could survive in a more open political environment. In states where the regime was cognizant both of its own economic shortcomings and of the crucial linkages between economic and political reform in the search for solutions to the country's problems, it saw that the need for reforms was urgent. The regime's perception of its ability to remain in power was colored primarily by its appreciation of its own legitimacy, or lack of it. This section briefly examines the East German and Czechoslovak regimes' attitudes toward reform, and their calculation of their ability to survive should they introduce reforms.

The East German government appeared reasonably confident of its position in 1985, when Gorbachev came to power, mainly because it had made real achievements in economic development since it had undertaken a substantial organizational restructuring of the economy in the 1970s. The resulting system of partially decentralized industrial units, in which several enterprises in a production chain were grouped into units with broad competence for decision-making and negotiating trade agreements, proved effective in promoting economic growth.[88] As a result, by

---

87. Ján Carnogurský, one of the deputy premiers, had been in prison only three weeks earlier. Čalfa and two others resigned from the Party after their appointments to the new government.

88. On the different phases of East Germany's economic planning, see Arthur Hanhardt, Jr., "The German Democratic Republic," in Teresa Rakowska-Harmstone, ed., *Communism in Eastern Europe* (Bloomington, Ind.: Indiana University Press, 1979, 1984), pp. 147–155; and Brown, *Eastern Europe and Communist Rule*, pp. 245–251.

the 1980s East Germany had attained the highest standard of living in the Eastern bloc, and it was ranked among the top ten to fifteen industrialized countries in the world.[89] It therefore faced no immediate pressure to change its economic policies, and when Gorbachev began to encourage reforms, the regime even used the argument that it had already carried out a policy of restructuring in the late 1970s.[90] After the Soviet Union, East Germany was also the main trading partner of all other members of the CMEA, specializing in high-technology goods.

However, the state's economy was not healthy, and by the late 1980s it clearly was starting to falter. The state's continued dependence on Soviet oil, and the highly centralized structure of its economy, meant that there would inevitably be limits to how far productivity could be raised in the absence of substantial structural reforms.[91] Moreover, East Germany was increasingly falling behind the West in high-technology production, and its trade deficit with West Germany, an indication of East German dependence on inter-German trade, grew from 1985 on.[92] After the communist regime collapsed, it became clear that the East German economy was in a far worse state than had been recognized; by November 1989 the state was on the verge of insolvency, having lived beyond its means for years.[93]

An equally important element of East Germany's economic stability was the normalization of relations with West Germany, which gave the regime access to trade credits and technology, and, more lucratively, to the European Community's (EC) Common Market. Because West Germany refused to recognize East Germany as a separate country, relying

---

89. Brown, *Surge to Freedom:* The End of Communist Rule in Eastern Europe (Durham, N.C.: Duke University Press, 1991), pp. 128–131.

90. Asmus, Brown, and Crane, *Soviet Foreign Policy and the Revolutions in Eastern Europe,* p. 116.

91. Indeed, the early benefits from the introduction of the decentralized industrial units were largely one-time advances, and the problems of inefficiency confronting such monopolistic structures had not been taken into consideration. See Thomas A. Baylis, "East Germany's Economic Model," *Current History,* Vol. 86, No. 523 (November 1987), pp. 379, 394.

92. Griffith, "The German Democratic Republic," p. 328.

93. Gunter Mittag, an economic advisor to Honecker, had for years manipulated information about East Germany's economy. Karl-Dieter Opp, Peter Voss, Christiane Gern, *Origin of a Spontaneous Revolution: East Germany, 1989* (Ann Arbor: University of Michigan Press, 1995), p. 50; see also Rice and Zelikow, *Germany Unified and Europe Transformed,* p. 187; Pond, "A Wall Destroyed," p. 53; and Hertle, "The Fall of the Wall," pp. 132–135.

instead on the formula of "two states in one nation," East Germany became a de facto member of the EC, able through its intra-German trade to gain access to the Community without paying import duties. Thus, though it opposed the contact that the Basic Treaty gave the West to the East German population, East Germany did not object to the economic advantages it gained.[94] The disadvantage of this was that East Germans compared their situation not with their Eastern European neighbors, but to West Germany, and the gap in living standards between the two states was increasing.[95]

By the early 1980s, it would have been extremely difficult politically for any West German politician to allow the ties to East Germany to be broken.[96] West German interest in East-West ties was an element East Germany could exploit, at least temporarily. The East German regime's confidence that it could manipulate this relationship was founded on its belief that East Germany's backing by the Soviet Union was inviolable, setting clear parameters for both sides.

The ideological orthodoxy on which East Germany's leadership based its rule was a factor in both its rejection of economic reform, and its attitude toward change. That the East German regime embraced Marxist-Leninist orthodoxy more strictly than other states in the Eastern bloc was evident in its adherence to central planning, and the rejection of market elements in the East German economy. The leadership also explicitly rejected potential links between economic and political reforms.[97] This ideological orthodoxy provided the rationale East Germany needed to perpetuate a separate German state. This was one reason why the East

---

94. In fact, the "trade" in East Germans that evolved from East Germany's policy of expelling dissidents proved lucrative; between 1963 and 1989, East Germany may have gained DM 1 billion this way. Naimark, "'Ich will hier raus,'" p. 79. See also Thomas A. Baylis, ed., "East Germany, West Germany and the Soviet Union: Perspectives on a Changing Relationship," Cornell University Center for International Studies Occasional Paper No. 18, 1986.

95. By 1988, the gross national product (GNP) per capita in East Germany was about half of that of West Germany, while East German employees earned about 47 percent of what comparable workers made in the West. Rumberg, "Glasnost in the GDR?" p. 207.

96. This became clear in the wake of the Soviet invasion of Afghanistan and the implementation of martial law in Poland; Kohl's efforts to avoid destroying the inter-German relationship made clear that, at this level at least, détente was important to West Germany. See A. James McAdams, "Inter-German Detente: A New Balance," *Foreign Affairs*, Vol. 65 (Fall 1986), p. 141–143.

97. Baylis, "East Germany's Economic Model," pp. 378–379.

German leadership rejected Gorbachev's calls for reform so bluntly; diluting the ideological basis of its rule would threaten the very basis for the separate German state.[98]

In sum, the East German regime appears clearly to have rejected the need for reform to improve its economy. Moreover, the ideological orthodoxy on which the East German regime based its rule meant that reforms would threaten the very basis for a separate German state. Additionally, Party leader Honecker appears to have been confident of the Party's ability to rule—so long as the Soviet Union did not abandon it. This combination of factors helps explain why the regime rejected the option of early reform.

*   *   *

In 1985, Czechoslovakia's economy was far from healthy, but was not under sufficient strain to force the regime to make substantial changes. Czechoslovakia, like East Germany, was one of the most industrially advanced states in the Eastern bloc in the 1980s, and was an important trading partner to the Soviet Union. It had benefited from a strong industrial base and comparatively little industrial damage at the end of World War II.[99] Czechoslovakia had avoided the debt spiral into which several of its neighbors fell by the end of the 1970s, so that its living standards were higher than in states burdened with massive debt. But the greater costs of energy resulting from the oil shocks of 1973 and 1975 made the inefficiency of the state's industry increasingly painful, and hindered the country's ability to compete in the world market.[100]

There was certainly recognition within the Party that changes in economic policies were necessary; minor modifications were made in the economic planning system in 1981, and again in 1983. These allowed for some decentralization of decision-making in both industry and agriculture, and the changes did lead to some improvement in the economy. Yet the inherent conservatism of the CPCZ leadership made it impossible for the regime to adopt the sorts of systemic reforms that even Communist Party economists considered necessary. Instead, the regime responded to

---

98.   Lévesque also argues that Honecker recognized that Gorbachev's European policy threatened East Germany's existence; ending the division of Europe called its separate state into question. *The Enigma of 1989*, p. 144.

99.   In the long run this became a liability, since little was done over the next few decades to modernize the industrial plant, leaving the country with outmoded, inefficient and very energy-intensive factories. Ulc, "Czechoslovakia," p. 115.

100.   Lubomir Strougal apparently commented that "if things go on this way, we'll have to put up signs on the frontier, 'Entering Czechoslovakia, the museum of an industrial society.'" In David Binder, "Czechoslovakia, the East's New Economic Disaster," *New York Times*, November 8, 1981, as quoted in Ulc, "Czechoslovakia," p. 132.

increasing economic difficulties by focusing blame for its problems on external causes and relying on ideological arguments to justify its opposition to reform.[101]

The Czechoslovak regime had reason to worry about its ability to survive should it begin to introduce reforms. Husák illustrated the Party's hesitation in 1985 when he stated: "We will not take the road of any of the market-oriented concepts that would weaken the system of socialist collective property and the party's leading role in the economy. We have had bad experience with that kind of thing."[102] As early as 1987, commentators were drawing parallels between Gorbachev's reforms and the Prague Spring of 1968—reforms the current Czechoslovakian leadership was responsible for dismantling. The regime could not risk introducing new reforms without delegitimating the previous twenty years of their rule. This led the Czechoslovak regime to avoid reforms.

SUMMARY

In both East Germany and Czechoslovakia, the ruling regime denied the need for reform well into 1989. Each contended that its economy did not need the kind of overhaul that Gorbachev had advocated. Each also dismissed economic and political reforms on the grounds that this would erode the ideological foundations of the state's system. Both regimes had reason to worry about their legitimacy in changed political circumstances. East Germany's very existence as a separate state was premised on its socialist nature. The Czechoslovakian leadership had ruled the country since the Soviet intervention in 1968, and this association compromised its authority to rule—or any prospect of significant reform.

Late Reform

Despite their rejection of early reform, by the end of 1989, the regimes in East Germany and Czechoslovakia had conceded the need for change

---

101. Indeed, the word "reform" was taboo in Czechoslovakia during this period; "intensification" was preferred by the leadership as a way to push for better productivity but not reforms. By 1985, some in the Party clearly recognized the need for elemental change; for example, Prime Minister Strougal and Leopold Ler, the finance minister, had both acknowledged that the 1981 reforms were not sufficient to address the country's problems. Professional economists in the Party, most notably at the Institute for Economic Forecasting, were even more frank in advocating structural change. See Asmus, Brown, and Crane, *Soviet Foreign Policy and the Revolution in Eastern Europe,* pp. 145–149; Kusin, "Husák's Czechoslovakia and Economic Stagnation," pp. 35–37; and Ulc, "Czechoslovakia," pp. 133–134.

102. As quoted in Kusin, "Reform and Dissidence in Czechoslovakia," p. 383.

and fallen from power. In each state, popular protests led to regime capitulation. To understand why regime change—and with it, change of the political system—happened in this way, it is necessary to look at leaders' and populations' perceptions. The two tools I use to do so are cognitive processes and the demonstration effect.

Cognitive processes help explain the leaderships' unwillingness to recognize the need for change, and the widespread popular quiescence. Though cognitive processes are difficult to measure precisely, some indicators—among them a regime's denial that change was necessary, arguments by the regime about the danger of change of the sort taking place elsewhere, and efforts to stop reforms, possibly by force—reveal the attitudes of particular leaders or regimes.

The lessons East German and Czechoslovakian leaders learned during the Cold War militated against recognizing the changes in the Soviet Union's attitude toward its allies. We can conjecture that the most important lessons in East Germany and Czechoslovakia were that liberalization was dangerous, difficult to control, and might make matters worse. This would be especially deeply felt by the Czechoslovakian regime, after Czechoslovakia's experiment with reforms during the Prague Spring led to the Soviet invasion. Additionally, Soviet toleration for reform had been limited in the past, and at the beginning of 1989 its newly professed tolerance had not been severely tested. Only as events progressed during the year was Moscow's changed attitude confirmed. Finally, it seems likely that the regimes believed that Moscow would not countenance the collapse of socialism in Eastern Europe, particularly in these two states, which sat on the divide between East and West. Soviet control and a commitment to sustain the regimes was presumed to be a given. These lessons matter because they would have made it virtually inconceivable to the leaders of these states that Gorbachev would really let their regimes collapse. This undoubtedly colored their perceptions and behavior during 1989. This section examines the regimes' rejection of change for indications that leaders' attitudes had not changed. It looks for similar indications in the regimes' efforts to quell the spread of reforms within their own states.

REJECTION OF CHANGE

Erich Honecker's tight control in East Germany, and his opposition to change, are central to an understanding of the regime's intransigent opposition to reform. Honecker limited internal debate within the SED, so that alternate views within the Party were far more limited than in other East European communist parties. Some SED members, notably Hans

Modrow, did support reform in the late 1980s, but the few openly reform-minded thinkers were in general excluded from the regime's top bodies. As in the Soviet Union, power was highly concentrated. Only a few people had real decision-making power, and Politburo meetings tended to approve rather than debate decisions. Moreover, disagreements were not raised in Politburo sessions. There was little dissension within the Politburo over Honecker's rejection of Gorbachev's reform policies. Gorbachev himself was rarely mentioned.[103]

In 1989, Honecker appeared to be strongly committed to the perpetuation of socialism in East Germany, and confident of his ability to continue to lead the country. This is evident both in his statements and in efforts of others to convince him of the need for change. Early in 1989, Markus Wolf, head of the Stasi, urged Honecker in a private meeting to introduce reforms.[104] In a speech in May 1989, Honecker insisted that the Wall would remain for a hundred years, an indication of his rejection of reform.[105] And as late as October 1989, when Gorbachev stressed the need for reforms in his visit to East Germany, Honecker did not respond. Instead, he continued to stress East Germany's achievements—and to attack West Germany, a common thread in Honecker's speeches that year. In his first speech in early 1989, Honecker castigated West Germany for its "anti-détente" attitude, and accused the West German leadership of hypocrisy and of trying to interfere in domestic politics in East Germany through its calls for greater human rights and reform.[106] The East German regime was particularly harsh in its attacks on West Germany over the refugee crisis, particularly after Hungary opened its border to all East German citizens.

Honecker's obduracy was particularly noteworthy once other members of the leadership became uncomfortable with the flight of East Germans through first Hungary and then Czechoslovakia. The Stasi held a

---

103. Opp, Voss, and Gern, *Origins of a Spontaneous Revolution*, p. 15; and A. James McAdams, "The GDR Oral History Project," *Cold War International History Project Bulletin*, No. 4 (Fall 1994), pp. 35–44.

104. Lévesque, *The Enigma of 1989*, p. 151.

105. Maximychev, "End of the Berlin Wall," p. 100.

106. Similar attacks on West Germany's interference, sometimes accompanied by condemnations of U.S. militarism, continued throughout the spring, particularly during the campaigning prior to the local elections held in May. "Honecker on the Berlin Wall and Protecting the State," ADN, January 19, 1989, in *SWB:EE*, January 23, 1989; and "Tisch Addresses 'Militant' May Day Rally," East Berlin Television Service, May 1, 1989, in *FBIS:EEU*, May 2, 1989.

high-level meeting to discuss the exodus, and Erich Mielke, the minister for state security, noted that "this is no isolated group" leaving the state, but members of mainstream society.[107] Both the exodus and the growing demonstrations were brought up at Politburo meetings in the fall, though with no immediate effect on policy. Indeed, Honecker made the decision to tighten travel restrictions to Czechoslovakia to stop the accelerating flow of would-be refugees, rather than accepting the need for policy changes at home.[108] Honecker's response was that "nobody is going to weep over those who are leaving," a comment that raised the ire of both the population and significant numbers of Party members.[109] Honecker's refusal to acknowledge the need for reforms during Gorbachev's visit in October 1989 led Krenz to note to one member of the Soviet delegation as it departed, "Your man [Gorbachev] said all he needed to say. Ours didn't understand anything."[110] Honecker's inability to adjust to the rapid pace of change in the Eastern bloc and to recognize that rejection was no longer an option was noted by Gorbachev in a conversation with Krenz in early November 1989, "He [Honecker] did not really perceive anymore what was actually going on."[111] Indeed, in 1989, Honecker told one foreign visitor that efforts to change the course he had set in East Germany were "nothing more than Don Quixote's futile running against the steadily turning sails of a windmill."[112]

Honecker's faith in the persistence of socialism was evident as well in the defense of socialism found in official newspapers and the statements of other Party leaders. As reforms were initiated in Poland, Honecker stressed the importance of advancing "socialist construction," while Party ideologues called for an increase in the role of the SED.[113] The SED also more openly began to state its support for separate roads to so-

---

107. Naimark, "'Ich will hier raus,'" p. 85.

108. Pond, *Beyond the Wall*, pp. 100–102.

109. Maximychev, "End of the Berlin Wall," p. 102.

110. Lévesque, *The Enigma of 1989*, p. 155.

111. "Memorandum of Conversation Between Egon Krenz, Secretary General of the Socialist Unity Party (SED), and Mikhail S. Gorbachev, Secretary General of the Communist Party of the Soviet Union (CPSU) November 1989," in *CWIHP Bulletin*, Issue 12/13 (Fall/Winter 2001), p. 142.

112. Craig R. Whitney, David Binder, and Serge Schmemann, "The Opening of the Berlin Wall," in Gail Stokes, ed., *From Stalinism to Pluralism: A Documentary History of Eastern Europe Since 1945*, 2nd ed. (Oxford: Oxford University Press, 1996), p. 245.

113. See, for example, "Dolhus Speaks at Secretaries Conference," *Neues Deutschland*, May 29, 1989, in *FBIS:EEU*, June 2, 1989.

cialism. In a clear declaration of his lack of interest in initiating change, Honecker insisted that there was no reason that East Germany should copy other fraternal countries in their efforts to reform. Margot Honecker underlined this by stressing that each state must find its "own path, that corresponds with national conditions."[114]

The regime increasingly began to defend the Wall itself.[115] This was coupled with heightened insistence on the uniqueness of East Germany, and a renewed stress on the importance of maintaining the socialist character of the state.[116] Otto Reinhold, a member of the SED's Central Committee, even went so far as to note that East Germany "is only conceivable as an anti-fascist and socialist state, a socialist alternative to the FRG. What right would a capitalist GDR [German Democratic Republic] have to exist alongside a capitalist Federal Republic of Germany?"[117] The defense of socialism included occasional comments about the reform process in other states. The SED pointedly noted that "peaceful change can never mean ideological coexistence," a veiled warning against changes in the structure of the government in Poland.[118] It also criticized the Hungarian regime for tolerating blatant expressions of anticommunist sentiment by opposition spokesmen.[119]

This defense of socialism and the Wall reflected the regime's inability to imagine the loss of the ideological foundation for its rule. At the same time, the defense was a tacit reminder to the Soviet Union of the East Germany's importance to it, suggesting that it appears to have been incom-

---

114. Margot Honecker, "Defend Socialism with Weapons," *Neues Deutschland*, June 14, 1989, in *FBIS:EEU*, June 20, 1989.

115. Indeed, an escape attempt at the Wall was foiled in early February. This was the last attempt prior to the opening of the Wall in November. For examples of the regime's defensiveness about the Wall, see "Honecker on the Berlin Wall and Protecting the State."

116. "GDR-Polish Friendship is a strong pillar of our peoples' joint welfare," Interview of Erich Honecker by the Warsaw weekly *Polityka*, in *Foreign Affairs Bulletin* (GDR), Vol. 29, No. 26, September 12, 1989. See also "Honecker Grants Interview to Youth Journal," *Neues Deutschland*, February 9, 1989, in *FBIS:EEU*, February 13, 1989.

117. As quoted by Jurgen Engert, *Rheinischer Merkur*, September 1, 1989, in *German Tribune*, September 17, 1989, p. 5.

118. See "Erich Honecker on GDR-Polish Relations and the "GDR Model" in Europe," ADN, September 6, 1989, in *SWB:EE*, September 8, 1989; and "Hermann Delivers Report," Eighth SED Central Committee Session, ADN, June 22, 1989, in *FBIS:EEU*, June 23, 1989.

119. Aleksander Kondrashov, "On the Reburial of Imre Nagy," TASS editorial published in *Neues Deutschland*, June 21, 1989, in *FBIS:EEU*, June 22, 1989.

prehensible, particularly to Honecker, that the Soviet Union would let socialism fall.

*   *   *

The actions and statements of the Party leadership in Czechoslovakia do not reveal whether the regime rejected reforms out of conviction or paralysis. However, the CPCZ's rejection of change was persistent, suggesting an inability to grasp that the ground rules were inexorably changing.

The regime's antagonism toward reform appears to have been primarily motivated by its fear of any reevaluation of the past. The regime's resistance to reevaluation was evident in its rejection of parallels between Soviet reforms under Gorbachev and those in Czechoslovakia in 1968. The Party leadership was also quick to remove those few members of the Party leadership with leanings toward reform, notably Lubomir Strougal and Bohuslav Chnoupek.[120] The depth of the Party's preoccupation was evident in Party leader Jakeš' comments immediately after a meeting in which Gorbachev pressed him on the importance of reform, including a reappraisal of 1968; Jakeš explicitly rejected any reassessment of the past, and claimed to have Gorbachev's support in this, noting that "no revision of the Party's policy on the subject of the events of 1968, no rehabilitation of Dubček and his friends was envisaged."[121] The Party's sensitivity to this issue appears to have grown from a desire to sustain the basis for the regime's rule, which was premised on the correctness of the Soviet invasion to halt the reform process in Czechoslovakia.[122] This preoccupation appears to have immobilized the regime, preventing its leaders from recognizing the need to address domestic discontent.

In early 1989, when the regime made some concessions to the need for restructuring, the Party leadership was careful to assert that the centralized economic structure of the state must be preserved, a clear indication of resistance to basic structural changes in economics, much less politics.[123] The leadership continued to reject any substantial economic

---

120. Wheaton and Kavan, *The Velvet Revolution*, p. 35.

121. Lévesque, *The Enigma of 1989*, p. 180.

122. Dubček himself drew increasing fire from the CPCZ both for his greater outspokenness and for having made the "wrong" decisions in 1968. "Fojtík offers comments on Charter 77," Vienna *Volksstimme*, February 15, 1989, in *FBIS:EEU*, February 17, 1989; and "Dubček 'Cheating' Public," *Rude Pravo*, April 22, 1989, "Attack on Internationalism," Bratislava *Pravda*, April 22, 1989, both in *FBIS:EEU*, April 25, 1989.

123. "Editorial Stresses Importance of Strong Center," *Rude Pravo*, March 2, 1989, in *FBIS:EEU*, March 8, 1989.

reforms by insisting that the "real values" of socialism must not be weakened by reform, and to defend the "Leninist" character of the state.[124]

The Party's antagonism toward reform was also seen in its attacks on the reforms in other East European states. While the reforms being undertaken elsewhere in Eastern Europe were covered by the official Czechoslovakian media, unlike in some other states, the Czechoslovakian media attacked Solidarity for breaking its word in the Round Table discussions, for trying to obstruct the agreement reached at the Round Table, and for undermining socialism.[125] Cross-border ties between East European opposition groups were also condemned as anticommunist, particularly as the opposition in Hungary and Poland gained legitimacy and strength, and as their connections with the Czechoslovakian opposition became more public in mid-summer.[126] After Tadeusz Mazowiecki's nomination as prime minister in Poland, one Czechoslovakian analysis virtually invoked the Brezhnev Doctrine, arguing that "whoever endangers the character of socialist development" was essentially endangering the whole community, which ought not to be tolerated.[127] This analysis indicated the regime's inability to accept the dramatically changing political climate in Eastern Europe, and its reliance on the previous constraints that had existed in the bloc suggests the regime's incomprehension that these might have changed.

---

124. "Jakeš Addresses Ranking Media on Role in Restructuring," Prague Domestic Service, February 9, 1989, in *FBIS:EEU*, February 10, 1989; "Fojtík, Lenart, Address Communist Deputies," *Rude Pravo*, April 26, 1989, in *FBIS:EEU*, April 28, 1989; and Vladimir Kusin, "Fojtík Defines CPCS Stand on Reform," *Radio Free Europe Czechoslovak Situation Report*, No. 19, September 20, 1989, pp. 3–5.

125. "'Decisive Majority' for Solidarity Reported," *Rude Pravo*, June 6, 1989, in *FBIS:EEU*, June 8, 1989; "PZPR Cannot be Loser of Polish Elections," *Prace*, June 10, 1989, in *FBIS:EEU*, June 14, 1989; "Commentary on Mazowiecki's Appointment," *Rude Pravo*, August 25, 1989, in *FBIS:EEU*, August 28, 1989; "Polish Solidarity Trying to Discredit Rakowski," Prague International Service, August 3, 1989, in *FBIS:EEU*, August 7, 1989; "Solidarity Going against Roundtable Conclusions," Prague Domestic Service, August 10, 1989, in *FBIS:EEU*, August 11, 1989; and "Credibility of Wałesa, Solidarity Questioned," *Rude Pravo*, August 17, 1989, in *FBIS:EEU*, August 18, 1989.

126. See, for example, "Cooperation of Czech, Polish Dissidents Viewed," *Tribuna*, No. 17, April 26, 1989, in *FBIS:EEU*, May 10, 1989.

127. The full quote, aimed at both Poland and Hungary, is "Wałesa and those like him in Hungary must be told that whoever endangers the character of socialist development in individual countries, also endangers the whole community and above all peace and security in Europe and in the world." "Czechoslovak Call for Unity amongst Socialist Countries," in Prague Home Service, August 27, 1989, in *SWB:EE*, August 31, 1989.

The CPCZ's attitude toward the Hungarian socialist party also hardened. CPCZ ideologist Jan Fojtík condemned the handling of Imre Nagy's reburial in Hungary, and warned of an imminent counterrevolution in Hungary.[128] This followed the government's expression of support for the Chinese government in the aftermath of the Tiananmen Square debacle in June, and praise for its efforts to quell what was termed a "counterrevolution."[129] As it became clear that the reformist wing of the HSWP had prevailed in the Hungarian Party's internal power struggle, increasingly blunt criticism of its policies appeared in Czechoslovakia. But the CPCZ's most emphatic objections followed the Hungarian decision to allow the East German refugees to leave Hungary on September 9. Hungary was censured for violating its treaty obligations, and for not properly defending socialism.[130] By the time the HSWP dissolved itself in October, the CPCZ was openly opposed to the new socialist party and its platform, as well as to the opposition parties in Hungary.[131]

The inability of the Party leadership to grasp the depth of change was most apparent during negotiations between the regime and Civic Forum

128. "Pluralism in Hungary Examined," Bratislava *Pravda,* January 3, 1989, in *FBIS:EEU,* January 6, 1989; "15 March Celebrations in Budapest Noted," Bratislava *Pravda,* March 16, 1989, in *FBIS:EEU,* March 20, 1989; "Opposition Accused of "Orchestrating' Anniversary," *Rude Pravo,* October 24, 1989, in *FBIS:EEU,* October 27, 1989; "Nagy Funeral 'Stage-managed' by Opposition," Bratislava *Pravda,* June 19, 1989, in *FBIS:EEU,* June 21, 1989; and "Fojtík Fears 'Counterrevolution' in Hungary," Prague Domestic Service, June 16, 1989, in *FBIS:EEU,* June 19, 1989; see also "Correspondent Criticizes Hungarian Opposition," Bratislava *Pravda,* August 5, 1989, in *FBIS:EEU,* August 8, 1989.

129. "Reaction to Continuing Violence in China Reported," in *FBIS:EEU,* June 8, 1989; "Continuing PRC Unrest Termed 'Internal Matter,'" Prague Domestic Service, June 11, 1989, in *FBIS:EEU,* June 12, 1989; and "Events in China Termed 'Internal Affair,'" *Rude Pravo,* June 14, 1989, in *FBIS:EEU,* June 16, 1989.

130. "Hungarian Decision 'Violation' of Agreement," Prague Domestic Service, September 11, 1989, in *FBIS:EEU,* September 12, 1989; "Lenart: Socialism in Poland, Hungary Threatened," Bratislava *Pravda,* September 21, 1989, in *FBIS:EEU,* September 25, 1989; "Czechoslovak View of GDR Refugees Leaving Hungary," in *SWB:EE,* September 13, 1989; and "Activation of MSZMP 'Left-Wing' Welcomed," *Rude Pravo,* September 4, 1989, in *FBIS:EEU,* September 25, 1989.

131. Yet while the CPCZ condemned the Hungarian parliament for "rejecting" Marxism-Leninism, it nonetheless continued to report on controversial Hungarian actions such as the government's "disassociation" with the events of 1968, rather than simply ignoring these moves. See "MSZMP Congress to view 'disintegration.'" *Rude Pravo,* October 4, 1989, in *FBIS:EEU,* October 6, 1989; "HSP's Platform 'Abandons' Marxism-Leninism," *Rude Pravo,* October 13, 1989, in *FBIS:EEU,* October 17, 1989; "CTK Reacts to Hungarian Statement on August 68," Bratislava *Pravda,* September 29, 1989, in *FBIS:EEU,* October 4, 1989; "Hungarian Decision 'Rejects' Marxism-Leninism," *Rude Pravo,* October 4, 1989, in *FBIS:EEU,* October 30, 1989.

in November and December 1989. The negotiations differed from those in earlier reforming states in that there was no official Party participation in the negotiations. Instead, the government conducted the talks. The Party's refusal to participate indicated its difficulty in accepting what was happening in the state. The Party's inability to comprehend the situation was also evident in its castigation of Adamec as the "liquidator of socialism" when he undertook talks with the opposition.

Even after negotiations had begun, Party and government leaders seemed unable to recognize the extent of change that had taken place within the Eastern bloc, as well as within Czechoslovakia. Even government officials like Adamec, who were involved in the negotiations, appeared unable to grasp the changes. For example, though he accepted the need for reforms, Adamec insisted that discussions remain within the framework of the rule of law based on the existing order, rather than conceding that far broader changes were required.[132] Similarly, Karel Urbánek, who was chosen to lead the Party after the entire Politburo resigned in early December, publicly insisted that the opposition's demands in the negotiations, such as the disbanding of the people's militias and party organizations in factories, were "unacceptable."[133]

Party spokesmen were also unable to comprehend the untenability of their situation. For example, Miroslav Štěpán, in attempting to rally workers behind the regime, insisted that the Party would not be dictated to "by children," indicating his continued rejection of the need for political change.[134] Taken together, these statements by regime members indicate an inability by the CPCZ leaders to come to terms with the changed environment in which they were operating by November 1989.

EFFORTS TO PREVENT CHANGE

The East German regime attempted to prevent change in East Germany in several ways. First, as best it could, the regime suppressed news of developments in both the Soviet Union and Eastern Europe, in keeping

132. Draper, "A New History of the Velvet Revolution," pp. 16–17; and Milos Calda, "The Roundtable Talks in Czechoslovakia," p. 137. Internal documents from this period also illustrate the Party's inability to grasp its changed circumstances. See Oldrich Tuma, "Czechoslovak November 1989," in *CWIHP Bulletin*, Issue 12/13 (Fall/Winter 2001), pp. 181–186.

133. In the negotiations with Civic Forum, Urbánek was more reasonable, stating that "you have put the things on the move, you have the full right to set the conditions, it is your right." Milos Calda, "The Round Table Talks in Czechoslovakia," p. 149; see also Wheaton and Kavan, *The Velvet Revolution*, p. 100.

134. Workers responded by shouting "we are not children"; he was unable to finish. Weaton and Kavan, *The Velvet Revolution*, p. 80.

with East Germany's long-standing fear of infection. While it limited access to some Soviet publications it deemed improper, the regime could do little to restrict exposure to Western television. Eighty-five percent of East German citizens could receive West German broadcasts.[135] Second, during the summer of 1989, the regime arrested people trying to flee to West Germany via Hungary. In October, the regime also strove to prevent people from reaching the trains that were transporting East German citizens from Czechoslovakia and Poland to the West via East Germany.

Third, Honecker apparently was willing to authorize the use of "any force necessary" to quell a peaceful demonstration in Leipzig on Monday, October 9. Police had battled crowds attempting to board trains heading West and had broken up demonstrations with force, early in October.[136] Prior to the October 9 demonstration, police and army forces were massed near the city and hospitals apparently prepared for a deluge of casualties. Violence was avoided by the efforts of opposition leaders and local government officials. Honecker's willingness to use force also indicates his inability to comprehend the depth of changes underway throughout the bloc.[137] Honecker was furious when, at a Politburo meeting on October 10–11, other members of the Party leadership argued against the use of force, and for the need to examine the causes of youth discontent in the country.

*   *   *

The Czechoslovak regime attempted to obstruct change first by blocking the flow of information about reforms. This was notable in its coverage of Gorbachev's speeches after he introduced perestroika; foreign policy changes were covered, but Gorbachev's ideas about restruc-

---

135.   Indeed, the East German government had to install cable near Dresden to attract workers there, since it could not receive West German broadcasts. See Stephen D. Krasner, "Global Communications and National Power: Life on the Pareto Frontier," *World Politics,* No. 43 (April 1991), p. 347; see also Hans-Dietrich Genscher, *Rebuilding a House Divided* (New York: Broadway Books, 1998), p. 264.

136.   Mielke apparently urged brutality to quell demonstrations on October 7, saying "give those pigs a good beating." Naimark, "'Ich will hier raus,'" p. 90. See also Maximychev, "End of the Berlin Wall," p. 102.

137.   One recent analysis of the collapse of East Germany suggests that Honecker was not, by October 9, sufficiently firm in his resolve to demand the use of force that day; instead, local leaders in Leipzig had to reach their own decision without clear guidance from Berlin. Another suggests that the option of violence remained salient in the Politburo even after October 9. Maier, *Dissolution,* p. 156; Hertle, "The Fall of the Wall," p. 134.

turing were not always reported.[138] The regime's efforts to obstruct the flow of information continued after the Velvet Revolution began; the Party blocked the distribution of newspapers outside the capital in an effort to keep rural workers and those in other cities from finding out about spreading protests in Prague.[139]

Second, the Czechoslovak regime attempted to use force to end the expanding demonstrations in Prague, without success. Party leader Jakeš ordered the mobilization of militia units to break up the demonstrations that followed the November 17 incident, but his order was ignored. Over the next few days, several militia units voluntarily disbanded themselves. Military units near Prague were confined to their bases and denied access to newspapers, radio, and television to prevent them from learning about the growing protests, and the defense minister, Milan Vaclavik, proposed using the army to quell the demonstrations on November 24.[140] Though his proposal was defeated, the regime's willingness to contemplate force suggests that it truly did not recognize the depth of the changes in the bloc and the changing mood within its own state.

SUMMARY

The rejection of reform by the leadership in East Germany and Czechoslovakia indicated an inability to grasp the significance of the changes in the Eastern bloc, or to adjust their policies to this new situation. This inability to recognize the significance of the differences in policy emanating from the Soviet Union and, by 1989, from other East European states as well, is not surprising. Western leaders also had trouble adjusting their views of the Soviet Union. Since evidence that does not conform to expected patterns of behavior tends to be discounted or ignored, and evidence supporting deeply held beliefs is magnified or enhanced, the leaders of East Germany and Czechoslovakia discounted the implications of the spread of reforms in Eastern Europe. This helps explain the continued rejection of reform. Finally, regime efforts to prevent change suggest that even when confronted by substantial evidence that their current policies were untenable, these regimes (or their leaders) were unable to envision new or different means of dealing with the population. Instead, they turned to the conventional repertoire of options available, and attempted to use force to quell popular demonstrations.

---

138. When protests began in Czechoslovakia, the Party leadership was openly criticized for this. Wheaton and Kavan, *The Velvet Revolution*, p. 70.

139. Ibid., pp. 65–67; and author's interviews in Prague, May 1990.

140. Wheaton and Kavan, *The Velvet Revolution*, pp. 70–71.

It is notable both that the leaderships in both of these states used low levels of force and contemplated much greater reliance on repression to quell the reform process. The willingness of the top leaders to rely on force indicates their inability to recognize or reassess the rapidly changing situation both within their states and in the Eastern bloc; that others blocked a greater resort to force suggests that some officials in each state were being influenced by developments around them.

The Impact of Change Elsewhere in Eastern Europe

The events and reforms in Poland and Hungary had a signficant influence on the timing and shape of reforms in East Germany and Czechoslovakia. People can be spurred into action by the "demonstration effect," by seeing an example of a desired action somewhere else. The changes in Poland and Hungary, together with their own leaders' continued rejection of reforms, helped to catalyze the mass-based protests that pushed reform in East Germany and Czechoslovakia.

It is possible to determine whether information about events in neighboring countries was readily accessible by looking at whether citizens had access to media from other states, whether print, radio, or television, and by looking at their behavior. Mimicry of events in other reforming states indicates direct or indirect cross-border influences. The demonstration effect can also help explain a regime's response to growing protests; for example, a regime may react by proposing negotiations with opposition groups similar to those other governments used. To assess the impact of changes in other East European states, I look at communication and knowledge about other East European developments and evidence of change in popular attitudes toward the regime. I also examine Soviet influences in East Germany and Czechoslovakia to assess distinctions between change in Eastern Europe and Moscow's attitude toward reform in the Eastern bloc.

COMMUNICATION AND KNOWLEDGE OF CHANGE IN EASTERN EUROPE
Knowledge of Gorbachev's reforms was evident in Esat Germany early in his tenure. Cross-border ties between dissident groups resulted in the publication of the "Joint Declaration from Eastern Europe" in October 1986; the document, a response to Gorbachev's calls for reform, was a public resolution to struggle for political democracy in the region.[141] In 1987, peace groups within East Germany quoted Gorbachev's admoni-

---

141. Tismaneanu, "Nascent Civil Society in the GDR," pp. 103–104.

tions for reform in their protests against the regime's intransigence.[142] The shouted appeals to Gorbachev—as well as some denouncing the Wall—from East German youths trying to hear a rock concert across the Wall in West Berlin in June 1987 also indicated that external factors were influencing some portions of the population.[143]

Some of the earliest calls for reform that surfaced in 1989 showed clearly that domestic groups in East Germany were influenced by developments within Eastern Europe. This was seen in the appeals for perestroika at demonstrations accompanying the official commemoration of Rosa Luxemburg's death, and in the demonstration urging Havel's release from prison. Calls from church and opposition groups for a dialogue with the regime also mirrored the process underway in other East European states during the summer. The clearest indication of awareness of external developments, though, was the exodus of East German citizens to Hungary in order to escape East Germany.

*   *   *

In Czechoslovakia, awareness of the reform process in neighboring states was evident shortly after Gorbachev introduced perestroika in the Soviet Union. Charter 77 sent an appeal to Gorbachev requesting that he address the malaise caused by the events of 1968 and encourage democratization in Czechoslovakia.[144] This petition is important proof that external influences were penetrating Czechoslovakia's borders.

Charter 77's appeal to the regime to begin a dialogue with societal groups in January 1989 indicated the influence of external developments in prompting calls for reform. By this point, aspiration for change was spreading beyond the dissident community, as was evident in muted comments supporting independent literature and ideas that began to appear in the spring of 1989.[145] In July, both Charter 77 and a group called the Movement for Civil Liberties also advocated the writing of a new constitution, one that would include provisions for broad political freedoms and democratization, as well as changes in the state's economic structure.[146] This echoed the constitutional changes underway in the

---

142. Rumberg, "Glasnost in the GDR?" p. 211.

143. Griffith, "The German Democratic Republic," p. 322.

144. Skilling, "Czechoslovakia Between East and West," p. 257.

145. Ordinary citizens were more willing to express interest in censored literature and in learning about Havel, who until that point was almost unknown within his own country. See Jirina Siklova, "The 'Gray Zone' and the Future of Dissent in Czechoslovakia," *Social Research*, Vol. 57, No. 2 (Summer 1990), p. 356; and Johnson, "Mass Media and the Velvet Revolution," fn. 19, p. 228.

146. Clearly, these groups did not expect the version being revised by the regime to

early reforming states—a sign of external influences on the opposition. Havel also called publicly for changes like those in Hungary, a clear indication that opposition figures saw these as a model.[147]

The opposition in Czechoslovakia also had increasingly visible contacts with newly legalized opposition groups from other East European countries during 1989. Meetings between Polish and Czechoslovak dissidents had been taking place for years on the border between the two states, but Solidarity's triumph and the legalization of alternate political parties in both Poland and Hungary changed the nature and scope of contacts among opposition groups. The successes in Poland and Hungary led joint meetings to concentrate more on the importance of pressing for reform in Czechoslovakia.

In July, representatives of Charter 77 met in Prague with Solidarity spokesmen who were now members of the Polish parliament. The Polish visitors issued a communiqué expressing their support for Czechoslovak dissident groups and calling on the Czechoslovak regime to begin a process of dialogue with these groups.[148] Shortly thereafter, Democratic Initiative and the Hungarian Democratic Forum established a "Joint Committee for Czechoslovak-Hungarian Democratic Cooperation," an organization intended to help coordinate efforts to bring about democratic change.[149] Less official contacts occurred with representatives of groups such as Hungary's Federation of Young Democrats (FIDESZ), and some of its members apparently participated in several demonstrations in Czechoslovakia during that summer.[150]

A more widespread effect on the population in Czechoslovakia came from the exodus of East German citizens. From August to October, the West German embassy in Prague repeatedly was overrun by East Ger-

---

respond to their concerns. See Jan Obrman and Jiří Pehe, "Two Independent Groups Publish Proposals for a New Constitution," *Radio Free Europe Czechoslovak Situation Report*, No. 18, August 24, 1989, pp. 35–38.

147. Lévesque, *The Enigma of 1989*, p. 183.

148. "Czech Dissidents Meet Solidarity MPs, Talk," Paris AFP, July 24, 1989, in *FBIS:EEU*, July 25, 1989; and Jan Obrman, "A Visit by Polish Members of Parliament and Solidarity Representatives," *Radio Free Europe Czechoslovak Situation Report*, No. 17, August 18, 1989, pp. 7–9.

149. Jiří Pehe, "Joint Committee Founded by Czechoslovak and Hungarian Opposition Groups," *Radio Free Europe Czechoslovak Situation Report*, No. 19, September 20, 1989, pp. 11–12.

150. The regime was well aware of these cross-border contacts. "Czechoslovak Regime Documents on the Velvet Revolution," in *CWIHP Bulletin*, Issue 12/13 (Fall/Winter 2001), esp. pp. 194–199.

mans seeking refuge; streams of East Germans were later allowed passage to West Germany via Czechoslovakia. It was impossible for the regime to hide this development from the population; though it tried to block access near the West German embassy, the cars that the East Germans abandoned were harder to hide. This visible rejection of East Germany's political system by so many citizens apparently had a profound impact on the Czechoslovak citizenry.[151]

The influence of Eastern Europe was also clearly seen in the progress of the revolution in Czechoslovakia. The organization of peaceful demonstrations echoed the process under way in East Germany; the unwillingness of the police and militia to crush these protests indicates the demoralization caused by both the failures of the Czechoslovak regime and the delegitimation of neighboring regimes.

The Round Table negotiations themselves showed the extent to which change in Eastern Europe had permeated borders. Rather than negotiating a power-sharing agreement to be codified in future elections, from the outset the Civic Forum proposed a coalition government with strong opposition representation to govern in the interim before completely free elections. This showed how the pace of reforms accelerated in response to the successful demonstration of reforms across the region.

CHANGING POPULAR ATTITUDES

The East German exodus showed two important things: the population's access to information about developments in Eastern Europe, and its belief that change was not possible within East Germany. The primary motivation for flight from East Germany was the pervasive sense that the only way to gain political freedoms was to leave. As one refugee noted, "if you put a bird in a cage and give it something to eat, it still doesn't feel free."[152] The perception that East Germany would not change was fed by comments, like Honecker's, that the Wall would remain, as well as the continued repression of demonstrations and attempts to leave the state.[153]

---

151. Johnson, "Mass Media and the Velvet Revolution," p. 228; and Alexander Dubček, *Hope Dies Last,* ed. and trans. by Jiri Hochman (New York: Kodansha International, 1993), p. 269.

152. Another refugee, asked about East Germany, responded, "GDR? Never heard of it." This typified the strong anti-SED, anti-East German sentiment among many that fled the country. Naimark, "'Ich will hier raus,'" p. 86.

153. By August 1989, 1.5 million East German citizens had officially applied for exit visas, according to the *New York Times*. As noted by Naimark, "'Ich will hier raus,'" p. 83.

The East German flight played a critical role in stimulating efforts by opposition groups to convince people to stay, primarily by pressing the government for reforms. Honecker's dismissal of those fleeing by saying "no tears will be shed" over them also catalyzed a strong reaction. Many in the population were outraged that the Party leadership could dismiss those leaving so easily at a time when many were deeply disturbed by this loss. This may have compelled people to participate in protests. Indeed, one notable early statement of protest, made by actors in the State Theater of Dresden on October 4, 1989, emphasized the impact of popular flight:

We're stepping out from behind our roles. Under the current conditions in our country, we have no choice. A country which cannot keep its youth jeopardizes its future. A government which does not speak to its people is not trustworthy. A party leadership which does not adapt its principles to new realities is doomed to fall. A people forced into silence will begin to become violent. The truth must be told. We have built this country. We won't let this country be destroyed.[154]

Moreover, the success of the early demonstrations themselves, and particularly the regime's failure to use force at the October 9 demonstration in Leipzig, apparently convinced more citizens that popular protest could have an effect on the political situation.[155] Indeed, the Stasi and other security forces in East Germany were apparently demoralized by the exodus of refugees and the growing protests in the fall.[156]

*   *   *

The swelling number of demonstrators in the November protests in Czechoslovakia was the clearest indication of change in popular attitudes in late 1989. The protests were begun by youth; student groups worked hard to persuade the adult population to support and participate in the protests. This "shamed" people out of their apathy into support of the students' protest against the regime. A second critical factor in shaping popular attitudes was, apparently, the East German exodus. This provided important proof both of the far-reaching effects of reforms and of the widespread discontent with the communist-ruled system. But the Czechoslovak population had no escape valve, leaving protest against

---

154. Opp, Voss, and Gern, *Origins of a Spontaneous Revolution*, p. 13.

155. Ibid., p. 13

156. The effective network of Stasi informers ensured that it knew the level of dissatisfaction in the country. Maier, *Dissolution*, pp. 149–152.

the regime as the only option. The rapidity of the shift from apathy to demonstrations is an indication that the population was swayed by the kind of "tipping" behavior posited in Chapter 1. Demonstrations mushroomed from a few hundred people on November 17, 1989, to around 300,000 three or four days later. By November 26, a rally organized by the opposition attracted 750,000 people, and three-fourths of the state's population supported a strike called by Civic Forum on November 27.

SOVIET INFLUENCE ON THE INTRODUCTION OF REFORMS

The influence of the Soviet Union in both East Germany and Czechoslovakia changed over time. The Soviet desire to sustain its policy of noninterference was evident in Gorbachev's encouragement of reform during visits to both states, but without insistence that these states follow Moscow's lead. The Soviet leadership also made few public statements that challenged or criticized either state's regime. This was especially obvious in the case of Czechoslovakia. During a visit to Czechoslovakia in April 1987, Gorbachev carefully supported the existing government, and publicly endorsed the regime's stand against a reappraisal of 1968, stating that Czechoslovakians had learned the "correct" lessons from this experience. His reluctance to take on historical issues at that point probably reflected the CPSU leadership's cognizance that an examination of the past in Eastern Europe was fraught with dangers, both for Soviet control of the region, and for the continued stability of at least some regimes in power there. In private, though, Gorbachev encouraged the Party leadership to do its own public assessment of 1968 as part of a broader reform package.[157] This caution notwithstanding, the April visit to Czechoslovakia was also Gorbachev's clearest advocation of reform in Eastern Europe to date, evidence of his support for self-generated reforms. In addition to promoting perestroika, he noted the importance of responding to domestic problems, emphasizing the government's "responsibility to its people."[158] This combination of encouragement and noninterference typified Gorbachev's effort to persuade the East European regimes to take on the task of reform.

At the same time, by 1989 Gorbachev was frustrated with the failure of the nonreforming states to act. In private, Gorbachev pushed these

---

157. Lévesque, *The Enigma of 1989*, p. 178.

158. Gorbachev also stated that "minor repairs will not be enough. Overhauling is in order." Gorbachev, *Pravda*, April 11, 1987, as quoted in Dawisha, *Eastern Europe, Gorbachev and Reform*, p. 170.

leaders harder, and argued that the better economic circumstances of both East Germany and Czechoslovakia meant that they would weather the process of reform far better than Poland or Hungary and reap the benefits more quickly. In public and private, Gorbachev warned that avoiding change would not succeed in the long run. Gorbachev did this most pointedly while visiting East Germany for its fortieth anniversary celebration on October 7, 1989, in a meeting with the full Politburo. In Moscow in April 1989, he encouraged Czechoslovak leader Jakeš to accept the need for change, and warned not to wait too long.[159] This message was repeated more directly in November at a Kremlin reception, where Gorbachev pointedly reiterated the message he had given Honecker in October, again warning the Czechoslovak regime to act.[160] Shortly thereafter Moscow warned the Czechoslovak regime that the Soviet Union would shortly change its public assessment of significant events like the Prague Spring.[161] Within days of the start of demonstrations, Gorbachev responded to a query about the situation in Czechoslovakia by noting that communist leaders must move quickly in implementing changes in order to make up for lost time. His public use of a variant of the most famous catchwords of the Prague Spring, "socialism with a human face," a week after demonstrations spread across Czechoslovakia, was a stark indication to both the government and population of exactly where he stood.[162] Thus, Gorbachev urged, but did not demand reforms.

Soviet inaction had a significant impact on developments in these two states as well. The withdrawal of military backing for the East European regimes was one type of inaction. Having publicly announced in December 1988 that it planned to withdraw 50,000 troops from Eastern Europe, Moscow made clear to its allies in July 1989 that it would not back these regimes with force. In October, Soviet concern about being drawn into any conflict led the Soviet ambassador to East Germany to order all Soviet troops to stay in their barracks as protest demonstrations

---

159. Georgii Shakhnazarov, *Tsena Svobodii: Reformatsiya Gorbacheva Glazami evo Pomoshchnika* [The value of freedom: Gorbachev's reforms through the eyes of his aide] (Moscow: Rossika * Zevs, 1993), pp. 108–109.

160. Lévesque, *The Enigma of 1989* , pp. 179–180, 184.

161. R.W. Apple, Jr., "Prague Gets the Word From Moscow: It's Time to Ease Up," *IHT*, November 17, 1989; and Lévesque, *The Enigma of 1989*, p. 184.

162. He referred to the "new face" of socialism, not an exact parallel, but certainly an analogous concept. See "The Socialist Idea and Revolutionary Reform," *Pravda*, November 26, 1989, p. 1.

spread across the country, to ensure that they would not be pulled into any melee.[163]

The Soviet Union also refused to intervene in leadership decisions in these states. One notable example of this noninvolvement was Gorbachev's refusal to endorse Strougal's bid to lead the CPCZ in 1987, when he was clearly the candidate most likely to initiate some reforms in Czechoslovakia. Again in November 1989, Gorbachev refused to take sides in the CPCZ's leadership dispute.[164] During the negotiations, Gorbachev refused even to accept a telephone call from Prime Minister Adamec, to avoid the impression that he backed the Prime Minister.

Finally, Moscow's refusal to block Hungary's decision to open its borders to East Germans was probably its most consequential non-action in 1989.[165] The impact of this move on East Germany and Czechoslovakia was profound, as has been noted. Gorbachev may have hoped to jolt Honecker or his assistants into acting, but the refusal to interfere also fit with his long-standing policy of noninterference.

One consequence of the Hungarian decision to open its borders was that Yegor Ligachev, one of the conservative members of the Soviet Politburo, visited East Germany to show his support for the regime in September 1989. Indeed, Ligachev announced Gorbachev's intention to attend the fortieth anniversary celebrations during this visit, a clear sign of support for the regime.[166] Ligachev's visit illustrated another side of Soviet policy toward Eastern Europe during this period: support for nonreforming states from the conservative members of the leadership. So long as the conflict continued within the Soviet Politburo, the East European conservative leaders had allies who insisted that they not be forced to change.[167] This probably sustained the hope by leaders like Honecker and Jakeš that they could hold out against reform.

---

163. Lévesque, *The Enigma of 1989*, p. 155.

164. Ibid., pp. 59–64, 106–107.

165. Shevardnadze apparently played a critical role in finding a solution to the problem caused by East German refugees in the FRG's embassies in other East European states later that month; he allegedly agreed to help convince the East German regime—as well as that of Czechoslovakia—to allow these refugees to leave for West Germany. See "Shevardnadze's Help Seen," *Frankfurter Allgemeine*, October 2, 1989, in *FBIS:EEU*, October 2, 1989; and Genscher, *Rebuilding a House Divided*, pp. 268–270.

166. "Yegor Ligachev in the GDR," ADN, in *SWB:EE*, September 16, 1989; see also Lévesque, *The Enigma of 1989*, pp. 154–155.

167. See Chapter 2.

Conclusions

The strongest explanation for the refusal of the East German and Czechoslovak regimes voluntarily to introduce reforms is their top leaders' perception that they would be unlikely to survive politically in a broader political arena. In East Germany, the absence of legitimacy was due to the
artificiality of the separate German state; its only durable source of authority was its Marxist-Leninist ideology. The regime in power in
Czechoslovakia was responsible for dismantling the reforms of 1968, and
as a result it was utterly discredited in the eyes of the population. Thus,
both states fall into category D of the matrix presented in Chapter 1. At
the same time, regime leaders in both states appear to have felt comfortable rejecting reforms, confident that the constraints of the Soviet-
dominated system in Eastern Europe were not open to question. Within
this framework, they felt no need to change their behavior.

The regime's behavior and statements by their leaders during 1989
suggests one of two things. First, they may indicate an inability to perceive how dramatically the changes outside their states were influencing
developments within. Second, they may suggest paralysis by the regimes, an inability to change behavior despite some awareness of
changed and fluid circumstances. If the latter is the case, the regimes or
leaders may have been unable to envision any new strategy for dealing
with the new situation; old policies were continued simply because
leaders could perceive no options.[168] Either of these is possible, and elements of both are likely.[169] The absence of legitimacy and the inability to
recognize the dramatic nature of the changes in the bloc combined to prevent these regimes from acting until it was too late.

This conclusion is supported by the behavior of opposition groups
and the population in East Germany and Czechoslovakia during 1989. In
neither state did a strong opposition exist that was capable, in early 1989,
of compelling the regime to negotiate or capitulate. The population in
both states was relatively apathetic, unwilling at the start of the year to
object to the ruling regime's stasis. In neither state did the population expect the regime to introduce reforms, or to loosen its grip on society. This

---

168.   Recent historical analyses confirm this possibility in East Germany. Maier, *Dissolution*, pp. 153–156.

169.   At the same time, however, the Polish example suggested a model by which regimes could have tried to establish power-sharing. Since neither East Germany nor
Czechoslovakia had a vibrant opposition movement like Poland's, a regime aware of
the need for adjustments might have risked such a plan.

lack of hope for reform, together with external developments, critically shaped the protests that ensued.

The East German exodus—an indication of the hopelessness of large segments of the population—was the first sign of action taken by regular East German citizens. This public step had a snowballing effect, goading others to take similar action. This in turn triggered a rise in demonstrations at home. The demonstrations within East Germany grew out of a sense of hopelessness and pain over the loss of so many neighbors fleeing west, and despair at the regime's refusal, or inability, to respond.[170] As restlessness grew, the regime's failure to crush the demonstrations made more and more citizens willing to join in the protests. The East German population was aware of the flood of refugees and subsequent demonstrations because of West German television and its impact on East German media, which grew increasingly open in its coverage of demonstrations during October and November 1989.

In Czechoslovakia, students and artists spread the message of protest most effectively, while it slowly spread to the state's official media. The "tipping" of the working class, and their decision to support or join demonstrations, appears to have been stimulated by the example of the students and their willingness to try to provoke change when the older generation had no hope. (See Table 5.)

Some distinction is necessary between the top leaders and the regimes in these two states, and particularly in East Germany. Honecker and Jakeš both remained steadfast in their rejection of reform. They fit the model of leaders constrained by the lessons learned from the past, unable to comprehend the depth of the changes in the Eastern bloc. Honecker, moreover, remained convinced of his right to rule the state in the same manner as before. However, by the fall of 1989, at least some members of the top leadership in these states were concerned about the continued rejection of reform. Nonetheless, the nature of the governments in these two states meant that change did not emerge until propelled by popular protests, and in East Germany's case, even hesitant reforms had to wait for Honecker's removal from office. This illustrates both the strong con-

---

170. Around 5,000 East German citizens fled East Germany via Hungary in August 1989. After Hungary officially opened its border on September 11, 6,500 more left immediately. A total of more than 30,000 escaped through Hungary. Seven thousand were allowed to go from the West German embassy in Prague to the West on October 1. By one calculation, 344,000 East Germans left East Germany in 1989. Whitney, Binder, and Schmemann, "The Opening of the Berlin Wall," p. 245; Naimark, "'Ich will hier raus,'" p. 84; and *The Hutchinson Dictionary of World History* (ABC-CLIO, 1993), pp. 232–233.

Table 5. Indicators Measuring the East German and Czechoslovakian Regimes' Attitudes in 1989.

EARLY REFORM

INDICATORS OF REGIME'S RECOGNITION OF NEED FOR REFORM

INDICATOR	EAST GERMANY	REGIME'S ATTITUDE
Previous reform efforts	Limited reform	Rejection of need for reforms
Nature of state's economic and political structure	Marxist-Leninist model	
Problems facing the state	Some economic difficulties	
Response to Gorbachev	Negative	

INDICATOR	CZECHOSLOVAKIA	REGIME'S ATTITUDE
Previous reform efforts	Limited reform	Rejection of need for reforms
Nature of state's economic and political structure	Marxist-Leninist model	
Problems facing the state	Some economic difficulties	
Response to Gorbachev	Lukewarm to negative	

INDICATORS OF REGIME'S PERCEPTION OF ITS ABILITY TO SURVIVE

INDICATOR	EAST GERMANY	REGIME'S ATTITUDE
Statements of legitimacy	Some	Low perception of legitimacy; top leader convinced of right to rule
Intra-regime conflict	Low	
Level of repression	Medium	

INDICATOR	CZECHOSLOVAKIA	REGIME'S ATTITUDE
Statements of legitimacy	No	Low perception of legitimacy
Intra-regime conflict	Some	
Level of repression	Medium	

Table 5. Continued

UNDERSTANDING LATE REFORM

COGNITIVE PROCESSES: INDICATORS OF REGIME'S RESISTANCE TO CHANGE

INDICATOR	EAST GERMANY	REGIME'S ATTITUDE
Resistance to need for reform	Yes	Resistant to change
Statements of faith in system	Yes	
Statements of legitimacy	Yes	
INDICATOR	CZECHOSLOVAKIA	REGIME'S ATTITUDE
Resistant to need for reform	Yes	Resistant to change
Statements of faith in system	Some	
Statements of legitimacy	No	

EVIDENCE OF THE DEMONSTRATION EFFECT

INDICATOR	EAST GERMANY	EFFECT WITHIN THE STATE
Communication of developments elsewhere	Yes	Strong evidence of demonstration effect
Mimicry	Yes, by opposition	
INDICATOR	CZECHOSLOVAKIA	EFFECT WITHIN THE STATE
Communication of developments elsewhere	Yes	Strong evidence of demonstration effect
Mimicry	Yes, by opposition	

trol these men exercised over their governments, and their personal inability to recognize and accept that change was inevitable.

External influence on the process of reform is evident in several ways. Opposition groups in both states called for dialogue with the regime once the Round Table began in Poland, and again when the Hungarian negotiations were underway. Expressions of support for the dissidents in other states also showed that some of the population was aware of developments in neighboring states. Added to this, the calls for change that emerged in the protests, and demands such as those for constitutional revisions, mirrored earlier reforms in Poland and Hungary.

The spread of protest marches in October was evidence of mimicry across East Germany itself, which then flowed into Czechoslovakia. Even the emergence of calls for a "third way" in East Germany indicates an awareness of external events, since the roadmarks delineating the path between capitalism and socialism had been set in the earlier processes of reform in Poland and Hungary. Finally, the Round Table negotiations that sprung up in each state were convincing proof that by the fall of 1989, a clear model had been established for the rejection of the old system and negotiation of a new one.

The differences in the course of discussions in the Round Tables in East Germany and Czechoslovakia, compared to those in Poland and Hungary, reveal the acceleration of the reform process from state to state. Round Table discussions in East Germany and Czechoslovakia agreed on free elections as the goal from the outset, following the Hungarian model, but in both of these states there was also agreement on negotiated governments to govern in the interim. This was absent in the earlier reforming states, and shows the rapid collapse of the old regimes once the process of reform had begun. Finally, the accelerating pace of the process indicates that as the model for reform emerged, the end result was achieved more quickly, with less need to grope for solutions. Thus, external influences strongly shaped the nature of the reform process in these states.

If anything, the Soviet Union was more hands-off in East Germany and Czechoslovakia than it had been in the earlier reforming states, though its inaction had a profound impact. While Gorbachev called the Polish Communist Party leader to urge him to accept a noncommunist prime minister, Gorbachev refused to accept a call from Czechoslovakian leader Adamec when the latter was trying to rally the Czechoslovakian Communist Party to reorganize in November. Soviet tolerance for developments in Poland and Hungary indicated Moscow's acceptance of a new arrangement in Eastern Europe. This affected populations, by making them realize a unique opportunity existed to push for change, which they did. It also affected regimes, by paralyzing some, and convincing other members of the leadership that they must address the crisis, though they proved to be too late.

Gorbachev remained sanguine as these regimes swayed and fell, with the notable exception of his concern over the prospect of rapid German unification. Though Gorbachev clearly opposed this outcome, he did not get involved in East German politics even in his efforts to prevent it. His concern focused more on West German Chancellor Kohl's behavior, and Gorbachev looked to U.S. President Bush and other European leaders to ensure that there would be no change in the European structure, rather than attempting to bolster the East German regime.

Chapter 6

Late Reform from Above: Bulgaria Switches Course

Bulgaria's transition was remarkably uneventful in comparison with the upheavals in neighboring countries at the time. The Bulgarian Communist Party's (BCP's) rule was virtually unquestioned, and the regime had enjoyed close ties with conservative forces in Moscow for decades. Popular opposition to the regime, though growing by 1989, was not strong enough seriously to threaten the Party's controlling position. Party leader Todor Zhivkov's tepid response to Gorbachev's call for reforms, and the accelerating pace of change throughout the Eastern bloc in 1989, led others in the Party leadership to decide to remove Zhivkov in November 1989 and introduce reforms from above, while the Party enjoyed comparatively wide popular support.

In theoretical terms, however, the Bulgarian case is notable because it is an example of a late reforming state in which changes were initiated from above, by a ruling party that had unquestionably maintained both its conservative views and its control of the state. Since Bulgaria reformed late, we can assume that it rejected reforms earlier because the regime either did not accept the need for reforms, or did not feel sufficiently legitimate to risk them. I examine how top members of the leadership responded to changes in the Eastern bloc to help explain why the regime did not recognize the nature of the process underway in Eastern Europe, and continued to resist reforms. (See Chapter 1 for an outline of the psychological theories I use here.) External influences from other East European states as the reform process progressed help explain the eventual decision of the regime to change policies. In Bulgaria, both regime and population were influenced by the demonstration effect; but due to its commanding position, the regime's changed behavior shaped the introduction of reforms in Bulgaria.

In this chapter, I examine the process by which reforms were introduced in Bulgaria. I then evaluate why the Bulgarian leadership rejected early reforms, and the variables influencing the process of reform that was introduced by members of the Bulgarian regime late in 1989.

The Transition in Bulgaria

The right of the Bulgarian Communist Party to rule was not seriously questioned for forty years once it had solidified its grasp on power after World War II. In spite of its suppression by the Bulgarian government during the war, the BCP was the strongest party left when Bulgaria shifted its loyalties from the Axis to the Soviet Union. It was the dominant party within the Fatherland Front, a group of four opposition parties that seized power in Sofia in 1944.[1] Between 1944 and 1949, the Communists gradually and ruthlessly eliminated the other political parties in the country, or reduced them to puppet parties backing the Communists' policies. The Fatherland Front became a mass association encompassing the entire population, and the BCP was left firmly in control of Bulgaria.[2]

Todor Zhivkov initially emerged as one of the BCP's leaders in 1954, and became the preeminent Party leader by the late 1950s by eliminating his opponents. Over the next thirty years, Zhivkov adopted a policy of almost complete compliance with Soviet wishes and policy, including a pattern of mimicking the policies introduced by Soviet leaders. The historic ties between the two countries, and their "traditional friendship," were continually emphasized.

Zhivkov's rule was personalistic in nature as Stalin's had been, and was based on tight control over Party and society. Under Zhivkov's rule, the BCP continued its reliance on repression to safeguard social order in Bulgaria. The strict enforcement of political control kept the population

---

1. Guerrilla activities in Bulgaria took place on a far smaller scale than in neighboring countries such as Yugoslavia, but Joseph Rothschild has pointed out that this was largely because the government in Bulgaria was far more stable, and therefore capable of repression, than in many of the other Balkan states. King Boris's government suppressed the communist party in the later years of the war, which weakened it. See Joseph Rothschild, *Return to Diversity: A Political History of East Central Europe Since World War II* (New York: Oxford University Press, 1989), pp. 68, 114.

2. For details on the BCP's use of terror and accumulation of power, see Zbiegniew K. Brzezinski, *The Soviet Bloc: Unity and Conflict*, rev. and enl. ed. (Cambridge, Mass.: Harvard University Press, 1967), pp. 15–16; and Rothschild, *Return to Diversity*, pp. 115–119.

quiescent; additionally, Zhivkov managed to preserve either sufficient support or fear within the Party leadership to enable him to eliminate any potential rivals for the top position in the Party. While Zhivkov managed to adapt to the prevailing political climate emanating from Moscow over the years, he did little to change the Stalinist character of the state, which had been put in place in the late 1940s.

Zhivkov's political conservatism made him slow to endorse the reforms that were launched in the Soviet Union in 1986.[3] Nonetheless, his habitual allegiance to the Soviet policy line and the undeniable economic shortfalls Bulgaria suffered in the mid-1980s led Zhivkov to fall more in step with Gorbachev's policies shortly thereafter. The need for changes was publicly accepted in January 1987, and in July 1987 a series of reforms was announced by the Party leadership. These reforms were intended to reshape electoral policies and the role of the Communist Party in the political system, to allow more industrial self-management, and to reorganize drastically both state and local governmental structures. Numerous economic reforms were proclaimed in 1986 and 1987 as well. The sweeping nature of these proposals, known as the "July concept," made them—on paper—more far-reaching than the reforms in the Soviet Union at the time.[4] The Bulgarian government also announced its decision to create a committee to revise the state's constitution in August 1987.[5]

Had the reforms been implemented, they would have been the most radical in the Eastern bloc. While some of the proposed political reforms were introduced, such as widespread dismissals in some branches of the Party bureaucracy, the flurry of economic decrees created confusion, and had little obvious impact on economic practices.[6] Similarly, while elections were held in Bulgaria in February 1988, they did not involve multiple candidates competing for positions. And though the Party put forward additional proposals for political change in 1988, Zhivkov also dismissed three purported reformers, including his presumed successor, Chudomir Alexandrov, from the Party leadership in July 1988.

---

3. Karen Dawisha, *Eastern Europe, Gorbachev, and Reform: The Great Challenge* (Cambridge: Cambridge University Press, 1988), pp. 39, 165–166.

4. For a broader discussion of Bulgaria's policies, see J.F. Brown, *Eastern Europe and Communist Rule* (Durham, N.C.: Duke University Press, 1988), pp. 316–335.

5. By January 1989, however, no meetings of this committee had been held.

6. "Bulgaria," in *Eastern Europe and the USSR: Economic Structure and Analysis* (London: The Economist Intelligence Unit, 1988), p. 59; Ilse Grosser, "Economic Reforms in Bulgaria," in Hubert Gabrisch, ed., *Economic Reforms in Eastern Europe and the Soviet Union* (Boulder, Colo.: Westview Press, 1989), pp. 99–108.

Alexandrov's removal coincided with Gorbachev's solidification of his own power in Moscow, and with indications that Moscow disapproved of Zhivkov's style of rule. It is possible that Zhivkov chose to remove Alexandrov and the others to ensure that he had no obvious successors. His ability to remove Alexandrov is evidence of Zhivkov's continued firm control over the Party leadership. Indeed, Zhivkov apparently offered his own resignation shortly thereafter, but Politburo members viewed this as an attempt to root out any lack of support within their ranks, and unanimously supported his continued rule.[7]

By the end of 1988, few reforms had been enacted in Bulgaria despite the massive changes recorded on paper. Instead, through consolidating his control of the party, Zhivkov had taken steps that in essence blocked the implementation of serious reforms. The regime's treatment of the opposition at this point also hinted at its lack of sympathy for significant change; during 1987–1988, the government broke up the few opposition groups that began to emerge, arresting or expelling their members.

Criticism of the regime was evident from late 1987 on, but only by a small fraction of the population. At several points between late 1987 and mid-1989, a handful of Party members, professors, or students criticized the regime or particular policies. In all cases, the regime responded promptly with intimidation and expulsions from the Party or university.

Nonetheless, a few small groups arguing for independent perspectives formed. In November 1987, the Discussion Group on Glasnost and Perestroika was established in Sofia. A group called the Independent Association for the Defense of Human Rights was formed in January 1988. The first independent trade union in the country, Podkrepa, was formed in February 1989. And, though there had been almost no sign of an independent press in Bulgaria in earlier decades, two samizdat magazines started publication in the spring of 1989.[8] These groups, and the editors of the magazines, were harassed by the police, but this did not stop their efforts to press for change.

The most successful of the early groups focused on ecological themes. The first organized group that focused on the environment was the Ruse Defense Committee (RDC), set up in February 1988. This group arranged an exhibit showing the damage caused to the environment

7. Jacques Lévesque, *The Enigma of 1989: The USSR and the Liberation of Eastern Europe* (Berkeley, Calif.: University of California Press, 1997), pp. 168–169.

8. Simon Simonov, "Independent Literary Publications in Bulgaria," *Radio Free Europe Bulgarian Situation Report*, No. 10, December 5, 1989, pp. 23–29.

around the city of Ruse, and the health problems that pollution and environmental degradation in the region had created; the appalling conditions illustrated provoked outrage and widespread concern. The regime responded by disbanding the group within a month. A year later, in March 1989, several former members of the original RDC established Ecoglasnost, a second attempt to focus attention on environmental problems.[9]

An additional source of protest was Bulgaria's ethnic Turkish population. In November 1988, ethnic Turkish leaders established the Democratic League for the Defense of Human Rights, a group that intended to work for a multiparty system in Bulgaria as well as defending the Turkish minority's interests. Almost immediately the group began to protest against the government's assimilation policies, since in the spring of 1989 the Bulgarian regime had renewed its pressure on the ethnic Turkish minority to conform. The Democratic League organized mass demonstrations in eastern Bulgaria to protest this policy.[10] The Bulgarian government responded by smashing these demonstrations, apparently killing people in the process.[11] This repression, coinciding with announced changes in the state's travel laws that made it easier for ethnic Turks to travel to Turkey, led over 300,000 ethnic Turks to flee Bulgaria by August 22, 1989, either out of fear for their safety or because they were forced to emigrate by Bulgarian authorities.[12]

The emergence of new voices for change—however small their beginnings—suggests that the Bulgarian population was aware of the new currents of reform in the Soviet Union and beyond. Similarly, it showed that for all Zhivkov's tight control and the appearance of stability, there was some sentiment in the population favoring change.

---

9. Richard Crampton, "The Intelligentsia, the Ecology and the Opposition in Bulgaria," *The World Today*, February 1990, p. 25.

10. Stephen Ashley, "Ethnic Turkish Refugees Describe their Movement for Human Rights and Democracy," *Radio Free Europe Research Situation Report*, No. 6 (July 3, 1989), as cited in Michael Shafir, "Xenophobic Communism—the Case of Bulgaria and Romania," *The World Today*, December 1989, p. 209.

11. "32 Ethnic Turks Reportedly Killed," Paris Agence France Presse (AFP), May 25, 1989, in *Foreign Broadcast Information Service: Eastern Europe* [hereafter *FBIS:EEU*], May 26, 1989; and "Emigres Claim 7 Killed in 27 May Turk Protest," Paris AFP, May 28, 1989, in *FBIS:EEU*, May 30,1989.

12. In June and July 1989, 121 Bulgarian opposition intellectuals signed a statement that blamed the Bulgarian leadership for the ethnic Turkish exodus, and appealed for the protection of minority rights in Bulgaria. A second statement, criticizing the re-

REGIME CHANGE AND THE BEGINNINGS OF REFORM

The BCP's lukewarm attitude toward reform gave way abruptly in November 1989. Zhivkov resigned at a Central Committee (CC) meeting on November 10, and Foreign Minister Petŭr Mladenov was named head of both the Party and the state. Mladenov promised to implement a far-reaching reform program, including greater separation of state and Party, and greater freedom of expression in society.[13]

Zhivkov's ouster was orchestrated by several members of the Politburo. Mladenov, Deputy Prime Minister Andrei Lukhanov, Defense Minister Dobri Dzhurov, Central Committee Secretary Dimitar Stanichev, and possibly Prime Minister Georgi Atanasov, began discussing the need to remove Zhivkov if real reforms were to be implemented during the summer of 1989; some discussion of this prospect may even have occurred in 1988, when Alexandrov was removed from office.[14] Zhivkov's tight control of the regime, and their long-standing obedience to Moscow, led the group to look for Soviet support of their intentions. Mladenov apparently broached the issue with Gorbachev in July 1989.[15] Zhivkov was not removed until the fall because those opposing him were looking for a pretext, which came in late October, and they remained uncertain of the Soviet position.[16] Once they decided to act, they began to lobby other

---

gime's failure to respond to the first appeal, appeared on August 6. Other opposition groups also declared solidarity with the ethnic Turkish minority. This was an important change, since animosity between these groups had made them suspicious of each other for a long time. Kjell Engelbrekt, "Intellectuals Stand up for Ethnic Turks," *Radio Free Europe Bulgarian Situation Report*, No. 8, September 1, 1989, pp. 9–13; Stephen Ashley, "Discussion Club Criticizes the Government for Creating a National Crisis," *Radio Free Europe Bulgarian Situation Report*, No. 8, September 1, 1989, pp. 15–18.

13. Zhivkov's formal resignation followed his ouster at a Politburo meeting the night before. Jordan Baev, "1989: Bulgarian Transition to Pluralist Democracy," *Cold War International History Project Bulletin* [hereafter *CWIHP Bulletin*], Issue 12/13 (Fall/Winter 2001), pp. 165–167.

14. Different accounts suggest that different people were involved in the early stages of discussions. Some place Atanasov among the group, while others do not, but include Stanichev. Gail Stokes, *The Walls Came Tumbling Down: The Collapse of Communism in Eastern Europe* (New York: Oxford University Press, 1993), pp. 147–148; and Lévesque, *The Enigma of 1989*, pp. 170–171.

15. In keeping with his policy of noninterference, Gorbachev was supportive but stressed that "we sympathize with you, but it's your business." Lévesque, *The Enigma of 1989*, p. 171.

16. The pretext was Zhivkov's peremptory order to Mladenov regarding how he should handle a meeting with the U.S. ambassador. "Letter from Foreign Minister Petar Mladenov to the BCP CC, 24 October 1989," in *CWIHP Bulletin*, Issue 12/13 (Fall/Winter, 2001) pp. 169–170.

members of the Politburo to support Zhivkov's removal, and Defense Minister Dzhurov moved several loyal army units to the capital as insurance against efforts to prevent a smooth transfer of power.[17]

The process of change that followed Zhivkov's ouster in Bulgaria was neither as rapid nor as dramatic as those that occurred in East Germany and Czechoslovakia. This was because throughout, the Communist Party remained firmly in control, which the East German and the Czechoslovakian communist parties did not. The new BCP leadership began implementing changes in the government before it was forced to do so by opposition forces, giving the Party leadership more control over the degree and pace of changes that were accepted. Indeed, negotiations with the opposition did not begin for two months after the changes at the top of the Party and government.

The new leadership moved quickly to capitalize on its endorsement of reform, and thus to maintain its grasp on the reform process. Personnel changes in the National Assembly and the Politburo followed within weeks of Zhivkov's resignation, and at a hastily scheduled plenum of the BCP, Mladenov announced major revisions in the form of the state's governance. He pledged to abolish the BCP's leading role in the state, to hold free elections by June 1990, and to open negotiations with the democratic opposition. Simultaneously, the Party announced that a special BCP congress would be held in March 1990 to address the changes in Bulgarian society.[18] This was a far more radical reform plan than observers had expected.

The BCP also made a scapegoat of Zhivkov. Though several other Politburo members were also removed within the first few weeks of the transition, the remaining members of the Party leadership blamed Zhivkov for failing to initiate substantial reforms. This ability to discredit a single figure was not available in the other conservative states, except in Romania a few weeks later.[19]

---

17. Stokes, *The Walls Came Tumbling Down*, p. 148.

18. "11th Session of Ninth National Assembly of Bulgaria: Proceedings," November 17, 1989, in *BBC Summary of World Broadcasts: Eastern Europe* [hereafter *SWB:EE*], November 20, 1989; Stephen Ashley, "Mladenov's Speech to the BCP CC Plenum," *Radio Free Europe Bulgarian Situation Report*, No. 11 (December 15, 1989), in *Radio Free Europe Report*, December 1989; pp. 41–45; "Radio Free Europe Weekly Record of Events, December 7 to 13, 1989," in *Radio Free Europe Report*, December 1989; "Arrangements for Special January Congress," BTA (Bulgarian Telegraph Agency), December 29, 1989, in *SWB:EE*, January 1, 1990; "Debate on Abolishing Leading Role of Party," Sofia Home Service, January 15, 1990; and "Constitutional Guarantee of BCP Leading Role Repealed," BTA, January 15, 1990, both in *SWB:EE*, January 17, 1990.

19. While Egon Krenz tried to focus blame on Honecker in the GDR, by the time the

The Bulgarian leaders did not, however, immediately relinquish power or move to share it with new groups, as had happened elsewhere in Eastern Europe by this point; Party spokesmen stressed that Bulgaria would follow the Soviet model of restructuring. Even after it held the special party congress in February 1990, changed the leadership of the party again (appointing Aleksandur Lilov as the new Party president), and set a date for free elections in May, the Party proposed a cabinet composed solely of members of the renamed Bulgarian Socialist Party (BSP), using the fact that it "has the majority of seats in the present National Assembly" as justification.[20]

One reason the new regime was able to maintain greater control over the process of change was that the opposition simply was not strong enough in November 1989 to press for a more rapid or far-reaching set of reforms. Furthermore, the scope of reforms initiated by the regime in November and December—before any attempt to hold negotiations with opposition groups—may have met the opposition's initial demands before it could make them.[21]

More independent organizations were founded in the first few weeks after Zhivkov's ouster, and Ecoglasnost received legal recognition from the Bulgarian government on December 11, 1989.[22] Demonstrations spread around the country and their size grew remarkably in a short

leadership changed in East Germany, protests against the Party were too widespread, and indications of its misdeeds and corruption too evident, for this to succeed. To some degree, the reform wing of the Hungarian Party had followed the same path as the BCP, by discrediting Kádár after his removal in 1988. Yet this process was neither so rapid nor so vindictive as the accusations that were hurled at Zhivkov almost immediately after his resignation.

20. "Premier Lukhanov Proposes New Government: Text of Unscheduled Live Broadcast," Sofia Home Service, February 8, 1990; in SWB:EE, February 10, 1990.

21. For a discussion of the Round Table negotiations in Bulgaria, see Rumyana Kolarova and Dimitr Dimitrov, "The Roundtable Talks in Bulgaria," in Jon Elster, ed., The Roundtable Talks and the Breakdown of Communism (Chicago: University of Chicago Press, 1996), pp. 178–201.

22. Some of the new organizations were the Union of Free Democrats, formed on November 27; an "Initiative Committee" made up leaders of eighteen independent groups, formed on December 8; a Democracy Club, set up at Sofia University on November 23; the Bulgarian Social Democratic Party in exile, which announced its reactivation at the end of November; a Committee for the Defense of Equal Rights of Turks, which appeared on December 12; and the Union of Democratic Forces, an umbrella of twelve independent groups, created on December 7. See also J.F. Brown, Surge to Freedom: The End of Communist Rule in Eastern Europe (Durham, N.C.: Duke University Press 1991), p. 191.

time; Ecoglasnost, the largest independent group, was able to organize an opposition rally of 50,000 people in Sofia without police interference within a week of the change of leadership. Yet rallies were also held in support of the new Communist regime and Mladenov, which suggested that the new Communist Party leadership continued to enjoy substantial support in Bulgaria.[23]

The mixed reaction of the population to the proposed changes was probably a sign of the greater conservatism of the Bulgarian population. It may also have been evidence that there was less hostility to Communist Party rule in Bulgaria than existed elsewhere in Eastern Europe, even if the country's ties with the Soviet Union were not as popular as the previous regime had portrayed them to be. This was underscored by the reformed BSP's solid victory in elections for a new parliament held in June 1990.

The BSP won almost 53 percent of the vote. But the newly formed Union of Democratic Forces (UDF), a coalition of opposition groups, won 36 percent of the vote and their leader, the philosopher Zhelyu Zhelev, was chosen as the country's president in August 1990. Mladenov was forced to relinquish his positions after a videotape showing him calling for the use of tanks against opposition demonstrators in December 1989 was aired publicly during the election campaign.[24] The first elected government fell in late 1990 after a nation-wide general strike. The BSP and opposition groups struggled for control of the parliament, and over the implementation of reform until April 1997, when the UDF gained decisive control over the parliament and government.

Explaining the Regime's Rejection of Early Reform

Reform in Bulgaria emerged relatively late in the process, initiated almost entirely by the ruling regime. To understand why the Bulgarian regime first rejected and then endorsed the option of reform, we must examine first why it disdained early reforms. A regime's rejection of reforms was

---

23. On December 13, for example, between 100,000 and 200,000 people demonstrated in support of the BCP government; 150 ethnic Turks apparently also demonstrated in support of Mladenov on December 2. And according to figures cited in *Moscow News*, arguably a biased source, 48 percent of the population thought the BCP could solve the country's problems. See "Radio Free Europe Weekly Record of Events," December 7 to 13, 1989; and Ventsel Raichev, "Ever Thus to Tyrants: How it was in Sofia," *Moscow News*, No. 1, 1990, pp. 14–15.

24. Rothschild, *Return to Diversity*, p. 253.

shaped by whether it recognized and accepted the need for reforms, and whether the regime believed it could survive in a more open political climate. States where the regime was aware both of its own economic shortcomings and of the linkages between economic and political reforms came to recognize the urgency of reform. The regime's perception of its ability to remain in power was shaped by its sense of its own legitimacy or its lack of legitimacy. This section briefly assesses the regime's attitude toward reform and its calculation of its ability to survive in a more open climate.

In Bulgaria, the top leader of the Party and regime had paramount sway over his colleagues. This strongly influenced the course of reform in the state, because while by 1988 at least some members of the Politburo recognized the need for substantive changes, Zhivkov rejected the need for reforms. Those who later overthrew Zhivkov apparently recognized the need for reforms in the state's economic structure, particularly in agriculture. To the degree that they were aware of the need for a change in leadership, Politburo members such as Mladenov and Lukhanov were cognizant of the link between economic and political reforms.[25]

Zhivkov and the Bulgarian regime were reasonably confident of their position when Gorbachev came to power because the Bulgarian economy was relatively healthy in the early 1980s. Bulgaria was not badly hurt by the debt crisis that hit the other East European states toward the end of the 1970s. The government had not borrowed too heavily from the West, and since the majority of its trade was in long-term contracts with the Soviet Union, other CMEA countries, and the Third World, it was less affected by fluctuations in the international market. Bulgaria also had good terms of trade with the Soviet Union, and it was the most subsidized country in the Eastern bloc in 1985.[26] The Bulgarian government had also had the foresight to invest in Western microchips that would run computers needed for engineering functions, rather than microchips for simple calculating functions favored by other Eastern bloc states at the same time. As a result, though Bulgaria was still reliant primarily on agricultural products for trade in the 1970s, it was capable of manufacturing export-quality goods, notably in microelectronics and robots.[27] Bulgaria

---

25. It was clear to members of the Soviet Central Committee that there was a growing interest in democratization among Bulgarian intellectuals and elites. V.A. Medvedev, *Raspad: Kak On Nazreval v "Mirovoi Sisteme Sotsialisma"* [Collapse: How it developed in the world Socialist system] (Moskva: Mezhdunarodnie Otnoshenia, 1994), p. 81.

26. *Eastern Europe and the USSR*, pp. 59–66; and Lévesque, *The Enigma of 1989*, p. 165.

27. See Angela Stent, "Technology Transfer to Eastern Europe: Paradoxes, Policies,

also had a thriving arms trade, which by the early 1980s was a major source of hard currency earnings.[28]

Nonetheless, the Bulgarian economy was clearly experiencing problems in the early 1980s. In the 1970s, agro-industrial complexes had been promoted in the countryside.[29] The regime's recognition that these efforts had not resolved the state's economic problems was evident when it implemented a New Economic Mechanism, which introduced new measures to promote efficiency in agriculture in 1978, and then was extended to other sectors of the economy in 1982.[30] The later reforms included less centralization of planning, profit sharing, and economic accountability of firms, among other things; this had the desired result of raising living standards, at least temporarily. Yet an impressive streak of bad weather in 1984–1985, which damaged the state's agricultural output, and the reforms introduced in 1982 suggested that the economy was faltering in the absence of real structural reforms. Moscow also cut its oil deliveries to Bulgaria in mid-1985, which hurt both the state's economy and its ability to produce better quality goods.[31]

Zhivkov's solution to the challenge to reform presented by Gorbachev was to introduce changes similar to those in the Soviet Union. He professed support for Gorbachev and his policies, as he had for earlier Soviet leaders. Yet Zhivkov's reforms largely remained on paper, and the sheer volume of continued changes led to confusion, as the system was unable to absorb them.[32] Moreover, while asserting his support for glasnost and perestroika, Zhivkov was careful to note that the new openness

---

Prospects", in William E. Griffith, ed., *Central and Eastern Europe: The Opening Curtain?* (Boulder, Colo.: Westview Press, 1989), pp. 90–91,

28. Alex Alexiev, "Demystifying Bulgaria," *Problems of Communism*, Vol. 34, No. 5 (September–October 1985), p. 91.

29. This was not the first time that economic reforms were broached in Bulgaria. Zhivkov had proposed a broad program of reforms in 1968, which would have significantly reshaped the state's economy. He withdrew this program, however, a month before the Soviet invasion of Czechoslovakia in August 1968, in an astute reading of the prevailing winds in the Kremlin. See Brown, *Eastern Europe and Communist Rule*, pp. 325–326.

30. Dawisha, *Eastern Europe, Gorbachev, and Reform*, p. 149.

31. This reduction may have been meant to show Soviet dissatisfaction with developments in Bulgaria and, together with the signs of a chill in Gorbachev's attitude toward Todor Zhivkov, gave the impression that Gorbachev favored a change in the BCP's leadership in late 1985. Part of Gorbachev's dislike for Zhivkov appears to have stemmed from his impressions during a visit he made to Bulgaria in 1984. See Brown, *Surge to Freedom*, pp. 185–186.

32. *Eastern Europe and the USSR*, p. 56.

was not meant to provide a "subjective mirror of those . . . not on the right track;"[33] glasnost was to remain carefully contained. The combination of Zhivkov's largely paper policies and continued firm hold on society suggests that he did not seriously intend to implement reforms similar to those in the Soviet Union or the early reforming East European states.

The regime's ability to survive did not appear to be under threat even in 1989. The conflict within the regime was carefully masked until late 1989, due to Zhivkov's control over the Party. The Sixth Department of the National Security Service monitored thousands of members of the political elite and nomenklatura, bolstering Zhivkov's control over the Party and bureaucracy.[34] This created a pervasive sense of fear in both Party and society. Critics within the Party were expelled, as were those whom Zhivkov perceived as potential threats to his position. Thus, there was little open disagreement over policies. Interestingly, one source of resentment against Zhivkov (in addition to concern that he would continue to stymie reforms) was his effort to promote his son in the Party leadership. This became a factor within leadership circles in late 1988, after Alexandrov's removal.[35]

Repression under Zhivkov was quite effective, if less harsh in the 1980s than it had been earlier. The regime promptly intimidated or expelled dissidents, and quickly spotted and quelled the formation of independent groups in the state. As a result, few sources of ideas existed outside of the Party.[36] At the same time, because of the absence of independent groups and the Party's widespread sway, reform-minded thinkers remained quietly within the Party. This worked to the Party's benefit later, when it began to introduce reforms.

This combination of strong control over Party and society, and the lack of opposition within the state, suggests that the Party was strong enough to fare well in a more open political climate. Indeed, the reformed BSP won the first open elections in June 1990. One notable sign of the Party's ability to survive—if not of its outright legitimacy in the eyes of much of the population—was that after Zhivkov was removed, several of those who had been expelled from the Party for criticizing it, and who

33. As quoted by Stokes, *The Walls Came Tumbling Down*, p. 142, fn. 37.

34. Kolarova and Dimitrov, "The Roundtable Talks in Bulgaria," p. 182.

35. Ibid., p. 183.

36. Luan Troxel, "Bulgaria," in Zoltan Barany and Ivan Volgyes, eds., *Legacies of Communism in Eastern Europe* (Baltimore, Md.: Johns Hopkins University Press, 1995) pp. 230–31.

had struggled to establish independent groups in the state, once again joined the Party to push the reform program within it.[37]

SUMMARY

The Bulgarian regime's rejection of reform prior to 1989 resulted from Zhivkov's denial of the need for substantial economic and political change, and his tight control over the government. Zhivkov initiated paper reforms that mimicked Gorbachev's, a pattern he had adopted with earlier Soviet leaders. Yet in practice little changed, because Zhivkov did not want real changes. Nonetheless, the Bulgarian regime does not appear to have been concerned about its ability to survive—indeed, the Party remained in power even after free elections in June 1990. The rejection of early reform, then, was the result of the regime's denial of the need for reforms similar to those introduced by Gorbachev.

Understanding Late Reform

The regime in Bulgaria enjoyed relatively strong legitimacy, stronger than that of most of its neighbors. It faced little opposition from the population before and during 1989. Moreover, the state's economy was not in particularly bad condition. Bulgaria rejected early reforms because Zhivkov, for all his rhetoric of perestroika, refused in practice to accept that political and economic reforms were necessary. Why, then, did reforms occur in 1989? The strongest explanation lies in the demonstration effect, which led Party members to challenge Zhivkov, and stimulated greater—though small—stirrings of popular discontent. Cognitive factors can help explain Zhivkov's unwillingness to introduce new policies; though aware of developments in other states, he appears to have been reluctant to change course, or to relinquish his grasp on power. This may have been due to his age, a factor in János Kádár's case as well. Instead, in 1989 Zhivkov chose to emphasize Bulgarian nationalism, and to stress those aspects of Gorbachev's policies that supported his rule, such as noninterference in other states' affairs. This section examines indications of the regime's—and particularly Zhivkov's—resistance to change, and arguments expressing faith in the existing system and against reform. Evidence of the communication of ideas across borders and knowledge of developments in other states by both elites and population is also assessed.

---

37. Kolarova and Dimitrov, "The Roundtable Talks in Bulgaria," p. 186.

RESISTANCE TO CHANGE

The policies implemented in Bulgaria under Zhivkov indicated that he was unwilling to adapt to the changes in the bloc. Instead, Zhivkov continued to operate using his accustomed methods, continuing to affirm the shared views and unity within the socialist camp, and especially with Gorbachev. His insistence that he and Gorbachev agreed about the importance of reforms suggested a perpetuation of his long-standing subservience to Soviet dictates. Thus, the impetus for the changes that appeared on paper probably came from a desire to preserve good relations with Moscow, rather than a sincere belief in the wisdom of such steps.[38]

Well into 1989, Zhivkov was also unwilling to acknowledge openly the growing divergences within the Eastern bloc. Instead, he continued to emphasize the similarities in the reforms underway. The BCP was thus in the paradoxical position of claiming that Bulgaria's reforms and those of both Czechoslovakia and Poland were "fundamentally the same" as the Soviet Union's reforms. Yet unease with the nature of reforms in different states, and with the growing disagreements within the bloc was evident in the BCP's emphasis on the importance of "unanimity" in working for "socialist construction."[39]

Resistance to substantive reforms was accompanied by a reaffirmation of the state's core values: the importance of socialism and Leninism. Any discussion of pluralism in Bulgaria, for example, was carefully placed within the confines of "socialist pluralism" as the only acceptable option; the "socialist" approach to human rights was also stressed. And more than its neighbors, Bulgaria continued to celebrate its ties with the Soviet Union.[40] This again indicates Zhivkov's effort to preserve his traditional strategies within the Soviet bloc.

---

38. See Zhivkov's interview on Soviet television, June 23, 1989, in *SWB:SU*, June 27, 1989.

39. How this could be possible when these states could find virtually no areas of common ground was not explained. See, for comparisons, "Polish Foreign Minister Concludes Talks, Departs," BTA, February 28, 1989 and March 1, 1989, in *FBIS:EEU*, March 6, 1989; "Mladenov, CSSR's Johanes Hold Official Talks," BTA, March 29, 1989, in *FBIS:EEU*, March 30, 1989. See also "Atanasov Visit to Poland, Czechoslovakia Viewed," *Rabotnichesko Delo* (Bulgaria), June 10, 1989, in *FBIS:EEU*, June 13, 1989.

40. The anniversary of Lenin's birthday, for example, received great fanfare in Bulgaria in 1989, as did Bulgarian-Soviet friendship month. See Velichko Dobriyanov, "Socialist Pluralism," *Rabotnichesko Delo*, April 1, 1989, in *FBIS:EEU*, April 10, 1989; "Leaders Attend Lenin 119th Anniversary Meeting," *Rabotnichesko Delo*, April 22, 1989; "Petur Dyulgerov Speaks at Lenin Anniversary," Sofia Domestic Service, April 21, 1989, both in *FBIS:EEU*, April 25, 1989; and "Month of Bulgarian-USSR Friendship Noted," *Rabotnichesko Delo*, October 9, 10, 1989, in *FBIS:EEU*, October 13, 1989.

As the reform process expanded in Poland and Hungary in 1989, Zhivkov bluntly ruled out similar measures for Bulgaria. Shortly after the announcement of negotiations in Poland in January 1989, Zhivkov flatly declared that there could be no questioning of the Party's leading role in the state in Bulgaria. The BCP also stated that no changes in the Communist Party's rules could be considered until the next party congress in 1992; the Party banned anonymous complaints as well.[41] Thus, despite his declarations of support for reform, Zhivkov resisted the kinds of changes occurring in other East European states.

The Bulgarian regime's unease with the changes underway in Hungary and Poland was also apparent. BCP spokesmen began to emphasize the importance of using "common sense" in carrying out restructuring, and criticized unspecified "distortions" of glasnost.[42] Yet the tone was not openly critical of the processes underway in these states, and the BCP continued to claim that similarities existed at least in the goals of the East European states.[43] This indicated Zhivkov's unwillingness publicly to acknowledge the level of disagreement becoming obvious in the Eastern bloc. Zhikov was more forthright in his concern about these reforms in private; at the July Warsaw Pact meeting in Bucharest he warned of destabilization and stressed the importance of maintaining the "fundamental principles and ideals" of socialism during the process of renewal.[44]

The Bulgarian regime also continued to support the communist parties in the early reforming states. It supported the conservative wing of the HSWP, and accepted Károly Grósz's analysis of the Hungarian situation, noting that the Party wanted changes to progress slowly in Hungary under the leadership of the Communist Party.[45] Outright criticism of the

---

41. "Zhivkov Interviewed on Staff Reductions, USSR," *Le Monde* (Paris), January 18, 1989, in *FBIS:EEU*, January 23, 1989; and "BCP Bans Anonymous Complaints from Citizens," BTA, March 8, 1989, in *FBIS:EEU*, March 10, 1989.

42. Simeon Manolov, "Let Us Apply Common Sense in Our Thoughts and Wisdom in Our Decisions," *Rabotnichesko Delo*, August 18, 1989, in *FBIS:EEU*, August 24, 1989.

43. For example, the regime continued to claim that there was "identity in principle of the aims of restructuring and renovation of socialism in Bulgaria and Poland with the restructuring in the Soviet Union." "Zhivkov Receives Olechowski," BTA, February 28, 1989, in *FBIS:EEU*, March 1, 1989.

44. "Memorandum from Petar Mladenov to the Politburo of the Central Committee of the Bulgarian Communist Party, 12 July 1989," in *CWIHP Bulletin*, Issue 12/13 (Fall/Winter 2001), pp. 167–169.

45. Since this view was expressed at the time when the Hungarian Party leadership had announced that it would relinquish its leading role, it was a clear sign of criticism of the direction being taken by the majority of the Hungarian Communist Party. Bul-

reforms underway in Hungary appeared only after the HSWP reformed itself and split from the conservatives in October 1989.[46] Similarly, serious criticism of Solidarity and the direction of Poland's reforms came only after the controversy over the choice of a prime minister in Poland became acute in August 1989. The BCP then attacked Solidarity for threatening the results of the Round Table agreement, accused it of using demagogy to attain power, and suggested that the new president, Wojciech Jaruzelski, might consider declaring a state of emergency to preserve order. The BCP also issued reminders about the importance of peace and stability in the region, and the need for communist participation in the government of Poland.[47]

As reforms expanded in Eastern Europe, the BCP also increased its efforts to quell nascent opposition groups and dissent in Bulgaria. This indicated Zhivkov's unwillingness to countenance change or opposition within society. The regime suppressed opposition demonstrations with differing levels of force; it also continued to arrest or expel members of these emerging groups.[48] As opposition activities began to spread in the spring, however modestly, the regime also launched a massive propaganda campaign against these groups. It attacked the character and motives of individual leaders, and accused the new organizations they were establishing of being anticommunist fronts for the CIA, and inciting "mistrust" of the regime.[49] It specifically castigated Radio Free Europe for trying to interfere in Bulgaria.

---

garia's support for the conservatives was also seen in the number of visits by Party members such as Károly Grósz, soon to be the loser in the power struggle within the Hungarian leadership. See "'Hot Political Period' in Hungary Analyzed," *Narodna Mladezh* (Bulgaria), March 13, 1989, in *FBIS:EEU*, March 15, 1989.

46. [Hungary's Károly Grósz] "Continues Talks with Zhivkov," BTA, April 17, 1989, in *FBIS:EEU*, April 18, 1989; "Paper Reports on Zhivkov-Grósz 17 April Talks," *Rabotnichesko Delo*, April 18, 1989, in *FBIS:EEU*, April 20, 1989; and "Pangelov Assesses Hungarian Socialist Party," *Rabotnichesko Delo*, October 14, 1989, in *FBIS:EEU*, October 17, 1989.

47. This was similar to the line taken by Czechoslovakia at the same time, though less heated; the Czechoslovak government called for a renewal of the Brezhnev Doctrine. See Ventseslav Karaivanov, "Between Demagogy and Sincere Concern," *Otechestven Front* (Bulgaria), August 18, 1989, in *FBIS:EEU*, August 22, 1989.

48. The timing of some of these arrests is interesting. A few days prior to French President François Mitterrand's visit to Bulgaria in January, for example, several prominent dissidents were jailed in Sofia. See "Dissidents Arrested Prior to Mitterand's Visit," Paris *Liberation*, January 13, 1989; "Regime Pressured by Intelligentsia, Dissidents," *Le Monde*, January 17, 1989, both in *FBIS:EEU*, January 24, 1989.

49. For some examples, see "Human Rights Activists Tomov, Minev Denounced," *Trud* (Bulgaria), January 13, 1989, in *FBIS:EEU*, January 17, 1989; "Who is Struggling

In the spring of 1989, Zhivkov also renewed pressure on the ethnic Turkish minority to assimilate. When this led to an exodus of refugees to Turkey, the government blamed the rise in tension on external forces, and organized rallies protesting Turkish interference in its domestic affairs. The regime also deported some Turkish activists as the protests against the government's assimilation policy expanded in the late spring. Why Zhivkov chose to renew this campaign in 1989 remains a mystery, but he may have hoped to rally support by presenting himself as a defender of Bulgarian nationalism.[50]

Finally, Zhivkov's resistance to change was evident in the enthusiasm with which he endorsed Gorbachev's policy of noninterference in other state's affairs. The BCP supported this policy toward other states in the bloc, even where the Bulgarian regime opposed the reforms being introduced.[51] This was particularly evident during a visit of the Hungarian foreign minister to Bulgaria in mid-July 1989; at a time when East Germany, Czechoslovakia, and Romania were attacking Hungary's reforms, Zhivkov told Gyula Horn that he considered it interference to criticize developments in other states.[52] Bulgaria also applied the Warsaw Pact's July 1989 pronouncement on noninterference in other state's affairs to its relationship with Turkey, not just to relations within the socialist community at which it was clearly aimed.[53] This was further evidence that Zhivkov did not want to face pressure to change his methods of rule.

ASSERTIONS OF LEGITIMACY

As noted earlier, the Bulgarian regime could reasonably argue in 1989 that a substantial portion of the population considered its rule legitimate.

---

for Human Rights in Bulgaria, and How?" *Rabotnichesko Delo*, February 7, 1989, in *FBIS:EEU*, February 13, 1989; "And Let No Unworthy Deeds . . ." *Literaturen Front*, February 9, 1989, in *FBIS:EEU*, February 14, 1989; and "Futile Efforts," *Rabotnichesko Delo*, October 21, 1989, in *FBIS:EEU*, October 24, 1989.

50. Under Zhivkov's rule, the BCP had relied heavily on nationalism as a tool in both foreign and domestic politics. Early in his tenure, nationalism and ideology were closely linked in Party doctrine. Zhivkov's daughter, Ludmilla Zhivkova, had also promoted Bulgarian nationalism, organizing exhibits intended to increase Bulgarian pride by celebrating Bulgaria's distinct cultural history and achievements.

51. There was little public comment from other Eastern bloc states about Bulgarian conduct, and the regime no doubt wanted this to continue.

52. See "Horn Sums Up Talks," Budapest MTI (Hungarian Telegraph Agency), July 18, 1989, in *FBIS:EEU*, July 19, 1989; and "'German Question' Raised Again with Refugees," *Rabotnichesko Delo*, September 19, 1989, in *FBIS:EEU*, September 21, 1989.

53. "Joint Actions in the Name of Peace," *Rabotnichesko Delo*, July 10, 1989, in *FBIS:EEU*, July 12, 1989.

The BCP faced no notable opposition to its rule, and there was little domestic pressure for reform. This was due in good part to the regime's effective control mechanisms, which inhibited the spread of alternate viewpoints. The regime had sufficient sway during 1989 to generate or coerce demonstrations of support for policies such as its attacks on the ethnic Turkish population. A mass meeting of ethnic Turks was held during the summer of 1989 supporting the regime's assimilation policy, while the main Muslim religious council in the state declared in August 1989, after the wave of emigration, that there were no constraints on Islam in Bulgaria.[54] Opposition demonstrations prior to Zhivkov's ouster remained small; the largest opposition demonstration was held on November 4, and consisted of about 4,000 people.

Even after Zhivkov's fall from power, the Communists were viewed by many as "omniscient."[55] While this fed the sense of fear that continued to affect the country during the election campaign in 1990, it also helps explain why many opposition intellectuals rejoined the Party after Zhivkov's fall, when the Party began to introduce reforms.

These factors help explain why Zhivkov may have continued to believe that he could avoid the introduction of tangible reforms in Bulgaria. His emphasis on the importance of noninterference, and the BCP's continued strong hold over the state, suggest that Zhivkov did not want real change, and the lack of a groundswell for change in the state meant that he had no reason to fear that pressure for reforms would come from below in the foreseeable future.

KNOWLEDGE OF CHANGE IN EASTERN EUROPE

What is notable in Bulgaria is that, while the demonstration effect influenced the population, its most significant impact was on members of the regime. The combination of changes in Eastern Europe and Moscow's tolerance of these changes appears to have galvanized the actors who removed Zhivkov from power. This section examines indications of the demonstration effect in Bulgaria; the next focuses on the interaction of Soviet and East European influences on the Bulgarian leaders.

Less information was available about developments in other Eastern bloc states in Bulgaria than in several other East European states. The Bulgarian press was heavily censored, and the regime maintained control over access to information. There was also relatively little contact with

---

54. Sabrina Petra Ramet, *Social Currents in Eastern Europe: The Sources and Consequences of the Great Transformation* (Durham, N.C.: Duke University Press, 1995), pp. 282–286.

55. Ibid., p. 287.

the West or western media.[56] However, Soviet television and journals were as readily available in Bulgaria as were Bulgarian journals; the regime could not curtail the spread of information about developments in the Soviet Union unless it opted to ban Soviet publications and media, as East Germany did with *Sputnik* magazine in December 1988.[57] Indeed, Soviet newspapers became increasingly popular during this period as the changes in the Soviet Union accelerated.[58] Compounding this wave of information from the East, Bulgaria stopped jamming Western radio broadcasts into the country in 1988 as part of its acceptance of the Helsinki accords.[59]

An awareness of external developments could be seen in several forms of mimicry in Bulgaria. First, Zhivkov himself was clearly mimicking Gorbachev's policies of glasnost and perestroika in the reforms he introduced between 1987 and 1989. In contrast, the other East European states that adopted early reforms were responding to domestic conditions, rather than mimicking Soviet practices.

Second, Zhivkov's successors clearly copied the model of developments elsewhere in Eastern Europe. They changed the Party's role in the state and promised multiparty elections and a revised political system. Further, two months after the change in leadership in Sofia, the new government agreed to hold Round Table discussions with opposition forces. The Round Table discussions in Bulgaria played a different role than they had in states where they had previously appeared, but this is further evidence that Round Table discussions had gained acceptance as a fundamental part of the "model" by which to change regimes in Eastern Europe. In other states, the Communist Party and opposition forces negotiated either power-sharing or the transfer of power from the Communists; the Round Tables signaled the diminishment or outright loss of power by the Communists. In Bulgaria, while the initiation of a Round Table discussion was in part an effort by the ruling party to ensure that the opposition shared responsibility for difficult economic choices ahead, the Round Table did not indicate or provoke a change in the Communist Party's power. Instead, it reflected the relative strengths of the different parties at the time. The Communist Party managed to avoid significant concessions in the negotiations by making changes outside the Round Ta-

---

56.   Ibid., pp. 280–281.

57.   On the abundance of Soviet journals in Bulgaria, see Alexiev, "Demystifying Bulgaria," pp. 90–91.

58.   Stokes, *The Walls Came Tumbling Down,* p. 146.

59.   Brown, *Surge to Freedom,* p. 189.

ble format (such as the change in the Party's official role in the state) while creating the impression that it was conceding points for the good of the state. The balance of power in the state did not change during the course of the negotiations or in the subsequent elections.[60]

Third, the growth of the opposition, however small, and the timing of its emergence indicated knowledge about the reform process elsewhere. Some change in attitudes was evident in 1987, when protests against human rights abuses occurred in Bulgaria and domestic groups sent letters protesting these abuses to the CSCE. In 1988, some major newspapers began to report on corruption among Bulgaria's elite. This was particularly aggravating to the regime, because those mentioned in the stories were known to have connections to Zhivkov's son.[61] Both domestic protests and greater frankness in reporting were responses primarily to the introduction of glasnost and perestroika in the Soviet Union. Interestingly, new groups that emerged in Bulgaria were careful to stress that they did not mean to oppose the Party. This indicated an unwillingness directly to address political issues, or to challenge the BCP's control.

The tactics used by Bulgarian opposition groups such as Ecoglasnost and Ruse showed parallels with the strategies adopted by other opposition groups in Eastern Europe, showing their awareness of outside events despite the limited access to information. Following the increasingly common trend throughout Eastern Europe, various opposition groups organized demonstrations in Bulgaria in 1989. The most notable were those organized in May and June by the Democratic League, which were combined with hunger strikes to protest the assimilation campaign against the Turks. This was followed in August by a series of demonstrations by the Pomaks, a group of ethnically Bulgarian Muslims, to protest the government's refusal to grant them passports.[62] Demonstrations in support of civil rights appeared during the CSCE meeting in October, and Ecoglasnost organized a demonstration calling for greater political freedoms on November 4. The timing of these later demonstrations suggests that they were influenced by the spread of demonstrations in East Germany in October 1989.

Several Bulgarian opposition groups also tried to establish links with other dissident groups in Eastern Europe in 1989. Contacts were estab-

---

60. Kolarova and Dimitrov, "The Roundtable Talks in Bulgaria," pp. 188–196.

61. Stokes, *The Walls Came Tumbling Down*, pp. 144–145.

62. At this point, the state's travel law had been altered only for the ethnic Turkish population. Brown, *Surge to Freedom*, p. 195.

lished with the opposition in Poland, while groups such as Ecoglasnost exhibited their support for the dissident movement in Czechoslovakia by backing calls for Václav Havel's release from prison in February 1989.[63] Both the demonstrations and efforts to contact other opposition groups mimicked the policies adopted by opposition movements in other East European states, albeit on a far smaller scale.

In addition to their weakness due to their small size, opposition groups in Bulgaria were handicapped by their isolation from the West. Few people had a good understanding of how liberal democracies worked, making it harder to argue for alternative models. Additionally, the lack of exposure to the West appears to have left the Bulgarian population lagging behind those of other East European states in their expectations; in early 1990, the population appeared ready to support glasnost and perestroika, while the majority of the Eastern bloc had moved beyond this and wanted western-style democracy.[64]

SOVIET INFLUENCE ON BULGARIA'S REFORM

Moscow's relations with Bulgaria were important, but not central to the process of reform. Yet Moscow's acceptance of change in Eastern Europe had a significant impact on the change of leadership in 1989.

When Gorbachev came to power in 1985, it was evident that he disapproved of Zhivkov and his methods of rule; Moscow's subsidies to Bulgaria dropped shortly thereafter. Though Gorbachev encouraged the East European leaders to adopt their own reform processes after he introduced reforms in the Soviet Union, the Soviet leadership did not approve of the program Zhivkov initiated in 1987. Gorbachev and his advisors admonished Zhivkov against going too far with any reform program in October 1987, when his decrees appeared likely to overwhelm the system, and counseled him to moderate his approach.[65]

By 1988, it appears that members of the Bulgarian Politburo knew that Gorbachev wanted Zhivkov to be replaced. Yet in keeping with his policy of noninterference, Gorbachev did nothing specific to push for this

---

63. Stephen Ashley, "Dissident Groups Forge Foreign Contacts," *Radio Free Europe Bulgarian Situation Report*, No. 10 (December 5, 1989), pp. 11–15.

64. Ramet, *Social Currents in Eastern Europe*, pp. 287, 344.

65. Soviet officials worried that perestroika would be discredited by the way it was being implemented in Bulgaria, and pointed their concerns out to Zhivkov. See "Gorbachev Meets with Bulgaria's Zhivkov," *TASS* (Moscow), October 16, 1987, in *FBIS:SU*, October 19, 1987. This pull-back by the Soviet Union is noted by Brown, *Surge to Freedom*. See also Medvedev, *Raspad*, pp. 57–66.

replacement. This affected the process of change in Bulgaria, because Gorbachev's support was clearly an important issue for those who removed Zhivkov from power. For example, when Mladenov asked for his backing at the Warsaw Pact meeting in July 1989, Gorbachev refused to take a stand, insisting this was Bulgaria's business. Mladenov and his colleagues were discouraged, and put off action to remove Zhivkov until the fall. Notably, Gorbachev's acceptance of developments elsewhere, and in particular his equanimity with the process of change in East Germany, appears to have helped convince Mladenov and his colleagues that they could safely force Zhivkov from power without meeting Soviet opposition.

It appears that the Soviet leadership was aware of the process by which Zhivkov was removed from power. Early reports suggested that Mladenov stopped in Moscow on his return from China in early November 1989 to consult with the Soviet leadership. Mladenov denies that this took place.[66] Lukhanov, however, spent about two weeks in Moscow at the end of October, discussing economic reforms with his counterparts in the Kremlin.[67] Mladenov apparently sent a copy of his letter attacking Zhivkov to Moscow with Lukhanov, to keep the leadership there informed. As in other East European states, Moscow's lack of a warning against action served as implicit support. Moreover, the Soviet Ambassador to Bulgaria, Victor Sharapov, and his deputy may have actively supported the efforts of the Party members working to remove Zhivkov.[68]

Zhivkov was apparently also in communication with the Soviet leadership during his final weeks in power. He was in close contact with the Soviet ambassador to Bulgaria, and requested that he be allowed to visit Moscow to consult with Gorbachev when his rule was clearly under threat. Gorbachev refused, recognizing that Zhivkov would use this as proof that Gorbachev supported him in the power struggle.[69] Thus, Gorbachev again implicitly influenced the process in Bulgaria.

---

66. "Mladenov Tells Workers How Zhivkov Was Replaced," BTA, November 20, 1989, in *SWB:EEU*, November 22, 1989. See also Charles Gati, *The Bloc that Failed: Soviet-East European Relations in Transition* (Bloomington, Ind.: Indiana University Press, 1990), pp 182–183.

67. "Lukhanov meets Voronin, Ministers in Moscow," *Rabotnichesko Delo*, October 17, 1989, in *FBIS:EEU*, October 18, 1989; and "Lukhanov Meets Politburo Member in Moscow," Sofia Domestic Service, October 28, 1989, in *FBIS:EEU*, November 3, 1989.

68. Baev, "1989: Bulgarian Transition to Pluralist Democracy, " p. 166.

69. Lévesque, *The Enigma of 1989*, pp. 172–174; see also Kolarova and Dimitrov, "The Roundtable Talks in Bulgaria," p. 184.

SUMMARY

Reforms in Bulgaria were introduced from above, in spite of Zhivkov. Though aware of and uneasy about the acceleration of reforms in the Eastern bloc, Zhivkov was unable to respond with changes in his policies. His inability to adjust may have been due to his age, or simply his long years in power, which made him incapable of shifting course. Reforms in Bulgaria were introduced after members of the leadership, emboldened by the changes in Eastern Europe and the Soviet Union's acceptance of these changes, ousted Zhivkov and introduced policies similar to Gorbachev's. Their actions show the demonstration effect at work on the leadership, as well as on the population.

Conclusions

Reforms in Bulgaria were introduced by the regime in power, with no significant pressure from below. They were introduced comparatively late in the transition process in Eastern Europe, making this a case of late reform from above, B in the model presented in Table 2 in Chapter 1.

Early reforms were rejected in Bulgaria because Todor Zhivkov, the predominant leader of the BCP, rejected the introduction of economic and political reforms. Instead, he responded to the changes introduced by Gorbachev with the mirage of reforms, and little real change. At the beginning of 1989, there was little evidence of opposition to the regime in Bulgaria. The regime's repressive measures clearly played a role in keeping any opposition to the regime at a minimum. Yet popular acquiescence to continued Communist Rule was probably also due to the fact that unlike in either East Germany or Czechoslovakia, there was no major source of illegitimacy hurting the BCP and its claims to deserve power. Overall, the BCP's rule appeared to be secure, and there was no evidence that this was likely to change. Though there are indications that the Party's strength was at least partly based on continued fear and passivity among the population, the Party's hold on power could nonetheless be considered to be relatively legitimate, as shown by the reformed BSP's success in the 1990 elections. That many of those who had left or been expelled from the Party rejoined it after Zhivkov's removal also indicates a perception that the Party was a legitimate force in the state, and the body most likely to succeed in implementing reforms at that time.

Zhivkov responded to Gorbachev as he had to previous Soviet leaders, by adopting policies that appeared similar to those of the Soviet Union, and continuing to be subservient to what he saw as Soviet wishes. He appears to have done so on the assumption that this would satisfy the

Soviet leadership. Though he was clearly uneasy about the direction of reforms in Eastern Europe in 1989, Zhivkov was unable or unwilling to adjust his policies to address the particular problems Bulgaria faced, rather than simply mirroring Soviet policies. See Table 6.

The demonstration effect helps explain Zhivkov's removal from power. Change in Eastern Europe was an important stimulus to the Bulgarian leadership; it indicated Soviet tolerance for change. This helps explain the timing of Zhivkov's ouster. Moscow's acceptance of developments in Poland and Hungary during the summer was particularly telling, since this made Soviet acquiescence to even the Communist Party's removal from power quite obvious. If this were not sufficient, the Soviet Union's refusal to support the hard-line regime in the GDR against massive internal protests was a sign that the previous foundations of power for a Communist regime in the Eastern bloc were clearly open to discussion. The changes in Moscow's attitude only became clear during this period; indeed, had Poland and Hungary not pressed the limits of Soviet tolerance, the degree to which the Soviet Union was willing to accept change in Eastern Europe might have remained cloudy for some time.

This clarity was important because Bulgaria's leaders appear to have been less willing to act independently of the Soviet Union than many East European leaders. While the other late reforming regimes rejected calls to reform, Zhivkov embraced them on paper. Moreover, his successors remained concerned with ensuring Soviet support for their actions. This is natural to some degree, since Bulgaria's was one of the few Communist parties to continue in power in Eastern Europe after 1989. The interaction of East European reform and the Soviet response thus had a significant effect on the elites' behavior.

Though conflict within the regime was not visible during Zhivkov's tenure, discomfort with Zhivkov's rule and his refusal to change policies led to Zhivkov's removal by his colleagues. Some members of the Politburo appear to have recognized that real changes were needed to resolve the state's economic problems, and to the degree that they understood that this would not happen while Zhivkov was in power, they recognized the need for political as well as economic changes.[70] Zhivkov's persecution of the ethnic Turkish population in Bulgaria, which led to international censure by the fall of 1989, may also have swayed those members

---

70. It should be noted that their understanding or ability to implement substantial economic reforms remained limited. It took several years after the 1990 elections for a changed Bulgarian leadership to introduce reforms that seemed likely to resolve the country's continued economic difficulties.

Table 6. Indicators Measuring the Bulgarian Regime's Attitudes in 1989.

EARLY REFORM

INDICATORS OF REGIME'S RECOGNITION OF NEED FOR REFORM

INDICATOR	BULGARIA	REGIME'S ATTITUDE
Previous reform efforts	Some reforms	No need for significant reforms
Nature of state's economic and political structure	Marxist-Leninist model	
Problems facing the state	Some economic difficulties	
Response to Gorbachev	Lukewarm	

INDICATORS OF REGIME'S PERCEPTION OF ITS ABILITY TO SURVIVE

INDICATOR	BULGARIA	REGIME'S ATTITUDE
Statements of legitimacy	Some	Perception of rule as legitimate
Intra-regime conflict	Low	
Level of repression	Medium	

UNDERSTANDING LATE REFORM

COGNITIVE PROCESSES: INDICATORS OF REGIME'S RESISTANCE TO CHANGE

INDICATOR	BULGARIA	REGIME'S ATTITUDE
Resistance to need for reform	Yes	Resistant to change
Statements of faith in system	No	
Statements of legitimacy	Some	

EVIDENCE OF THE DEMONSTRATION EFFECT

INDICATOR	BULGARIA	EFFECT WITHIN THE STATE
Communication of developments elsewhere	Yes	Evidence of the demonstration effect
Mimicry	Yes, by both opposition and regime	

of the Party leadership interested in improving Bulgaria's international image to support an attempt to remove him. Mladenov made this an issue in his attack on Zhivkov in October 1989.[71]

Because the regime's repressive mechanisms remained effective, pressure for change was not likely to come from below. This illustrates the difficulty of determining the relationship between repression and legitimacy: the Bulgarian regime's continued use of repression, in combination with its apparent stability, suggests that repression reflected the regime's perceived legitimacy, rather than indicating uncertainty. This is reinforced by the regime's willingness to introduce reforms and open the political system in the absence of acute pressures to do so.

Change in Eastern Europe had less direct impact in Bulgaria because its opposition was so small, and had very little experience interacting either with dissidents from other states in the bloc or with the West. Indeed, there was more pressure for change from the Soviet Union, despite its refusal to interfere, than from the Bulgarian population. Only after Zhivkov's fall did the possibility of change appear widely to be felt by the population. This contrasts with other East European states, where the sense that there was hope for change played an important role in catalyzing pressure from below against regimes. In Bulgaria, hope for real change remained relatively low even in 1990—glasnost and perestroika seemed fine models there—and there was little independent political tradition to draw on.[72] Paradoxically, the model of reform that developed in Bulgaria was probably one that Moscow would have preferred throughout the Eastern bloc: change introduced from above, regulated and moderated by the ruling party.

---

71. Bulgaria's reputation had also suffered from its alleged involvement in the assassination attempt on Pope John Paul II, the drug smuggling in Sofia, and its earlier attempts at forced assimilation. See Brown, *Surge to Freedom*, pp. 184–185, 195; see also Lévesque, *The Enigma of 1989*, p. 172.

72. Ramet, *Social Currents in Eastern Europe*, p. 287

Chapter 7

Late Reform: Mixed Signals in the Romanian Upheaval

Romania's regime change in December 1989 was the last in the Soviet bloc. To say that Romania also reformed would be overstating the case; the new government announced many changes, but its policies largely continued the previous Communist-led system. The transition without reform resulted from the complex nature of the change in power in Romania. While a popular uprising was the stimulus that impelled Party leader Nicolae Ceaușescu's overthrow, members of the Romanian Communist Party (RCP) leadership managed to secure power during the revolution, and continued to lead Romania until 1996.

Romania's rejection of reforms resulted from Nicolae Ceaușescu's unwillingness to consider change or to loosen his control over the country. Ceaușescu insisted on preserving the distorted method of socialism that he had created in Romania. Convinced of his own infallibility and legitimacy, he was unable to adjust to events in surrounding countries; instead, he exhorted his erstwhile allies to defend the cause of socialism, with force, if necessary. Ceaușescu's fall was provoked by a spontaneous popular revolt against his rule, triggered by growing restlessness and awareness of the wave of change in the Warsaw Pact. The absence of strong opposition figures allowed some members of the country's elite to draw upon their long-standing plans for a coup, and to seize the opportunity of Ceaușescu's demise to take control of Romania's government. In consequence, the Communist leader was deposed by popular revolt from below, but members of the Communist leadership continued to rule the country.

In this chapter, I use the theories on cognition and on the demonstration effect outlined in Chapter 1 to explain why Ceaușescu was unwilling or unable to recognize the need for change, and why popular passivity changed to widespread protest within a matter of days. The next section examines Ceauşescu's rise, rule, and fall. It then assesses the effect of cognitive factors and the demonstration effect on the population and leadership to evaluate the incomplete transition in Romania.

The Transition in Romania

Nicolae Ceauşescu was appointed General Secretary of the RCP in 1965, after the death of Gheorghi Gheorghiu-Dej, Romania's Communist leader since the end of World War II. As part of his efforts to solidify his leadership position, Ceauşescu maintained the fairly moderate domestic policies that had been instituted in the early 1960s by Gheorghiu-Dej.[1] Ceauşescu also sustained and even expanded the independent stance within Eastern Europe that Gheorghiu-Dej had established prior to his death.[2] In the late 1950s, for example, the Romanian leader rebuffed Soviet leader Nikita Khrushchev's call for specialization within the CMEA, since this would have constrained Romania's potential industrial growth. The Romanian leadership also carved itself some political distance from the Soviet Union to enhance the RCP's legitimacy in the eyes of the population.

Ceauşescu exploited this independence to gain additional stature at home, as well as to secure external support. The high point of this independence came in August 1968, when Ceauşescu denounced the Warsaw Pact's invasion of Czechoslovakia. Because of residual anti-Soviet sentiment in the country and the population's strong national pride, Ceauşescu's public profession of Romanian solidarity over socialist values enhanced his esteem with much of the population, and even gained him genuine popularity. Ceauşescu's patriotism was to be his most en-

---

1. For useful overviews of developments in Romania during the communist period, see Jonathan Eyal, "Romania: Between Appearances and Realities," in Jonathan Eyal, ed., *The Warsaw Pact and the Balkans, Moscow's Southern Flank* (Houndmills, Hampshire: Macmillan, 1989), p. 100; and J.F. Brown, *Surge to Freedom: The End of Communist Rule in Eastern Europe* (Durham, N.C.: Duke University Press, 1991), pp. 199–201.

2. Gheorghiu-Dej was a "home" communist, who spent the war years in Romania, rather than a "Muscovite," who stayed in exile in the Soviet Union. Stalin eventually insisted that the more trusted Muscovite factions of the Communist Parties take power in the rest of his East European satellite states. One reason why this did not occur in Romania was that the Romanian communist party leaders who had spent the war years in Moscow were mostly Jewish, and they fell from grace in the late 1940s due to Stalin's anti-Semitism. See J.F. Brown, *Eastern Europe and Communist Rule* (Durham, N.C.: Duke University Press, 1988), p. 265.

during source of legitimacy, lasting well after all other aspects of his rule were discredited. In addition to augmenting his domestic position, Ceaușescu's defiance of the Soviet Union in 1968 brought international acclaim and backing. He also played an active role in the third world, which served two purposes: it gave him a way to promote Romania's support for the autonomy of small and medium-sized states; and by cultivating a very visible international position, it helped to insulate him from Soviet punishment.[3]

Throughout the 1970s, Ceaușescu continued to use foreign policy independence to gain favor in the West and keep the Soviet Union at a safe distance.[4] At the same time, Ceaușescu tightened his control over domestic politics and the economy in Romania, and gradually dissolved the moderate policies that he had endorsed in the 1960s. For many years Western analysts assumed that Ceaușescu maintained strict domestic policies as a way to ensure that the Soviet Union would not invade Romania; if an Eastern bloc country wanted foreign policy independence it must show its orthodoxy in domestic policy, or vice versa.[5] However, by the 1980s it was obvious that Ceaușescu's domestic policies were more a function of his own rigidity and megalomania than part of a carefully honed plan.[6] Ceaușescu's actions grew increasingly despotic, and his growing lack of trust of his colleagues and subordinates showed signs of paranoia.[7] Ceaușescu's policies distorted Romania's political structure to

---

3. Brown notes this latter benefit of Romania's policy, and suggests that this was a lesson Ceaușescu learned from watching Marshall Tito's efforts to maintain Yugoslavia's independent position in the face of harsh disapproval from Moscow. See Brown, *Eastern Europe and Communist Rule*, pp. 270–271.

4. The regime's recalcitrance about defense spending enhanced Romania's autonomous image in the West at a comparatively low cost. In 1978, for example, Romania very publicly rejected Moscow's proposal that all Warsaw Pact members increase their defense spending by 3 percent.

5. The opposite example given was that of Hungary; Kádár maintained careful support for Moscow's foreign policy line, while allowing experimentation with different types of economic management and even some marketization throughout much of the 1970s. For an elaboration of this hypothesis, see Christopher Jones, *Soviet Influence in Eastern Europe: Political Autonomy and the Warsaw Pact* (New York: Praeger, 1981).

6. It is true that Ceaușescu structured Romania's defense policy so as to avoid a Soviet invasion, but what he apparently wanted to defend was his own position. The army was poorly equipped to do much to defend the borders, and the population was not well prepared for the "defense of the entire people" that the country's defense doctrine proclaimed. See Eyal, "Romania: Between Appearances and Realities," pp. 69, 107.

7. Brown depicts Ceaușescu's mental state succinctly: "A willful refusal to take advice; a toleration for nothing but sycophants; a nepotism ever-growing in dimensions;

the point that it resembled the other communist-led governments only superficially. All power came to be concentrated at the top, in the hands of Ceauşescu and his wife, Elena. His lack of trust for others meant that he gradually filled many of the high-level positions in the government with family members, leading to the derisive observation that Romania was practicing "socialism in one family." Other Politburo members and government officials were subjected to a rotation policy apparently designed to keep any of them from building an independent power base. As a result, the people running the government and economy became increasingly deprofessionalized and ill-equipped to do their jobs since they were unable to build expertise in any area.[8]

Ceauşescu was also unwilling to accept any form of criticism. His hold over the country and reliance on an increasingly pervasive secret police network (the Securitate) cowed both Party members and the population into quiescence. By the 1980s the country had an appalling human rights record due to Ceauşescu's desire to "homogenize" the population by forcibly replacing village life (for Romanians and ethnic Hungarians alike) with a more centralized, socialist model;[9] this was magnified over time by Ceauşescu' reliance on repression, and his increasingly grandiose visions for the country, which led him to uproot large segments of the population in order to create new monuments or more "efficient" forms of economic management.[10] Ceauşescu's paranoia and belief in his own infallibility were accompanied by insistence on ever greater adulation from both his former colleagues and the population. As a result, the country lapsed into a state of national sycophancy, with only occasional

---

an intolerance visibly hardening as absolute power corrupted absolutely; a self-defeating impatience clamoring for instant success; an inconsistency and unpredictability; a conglomerate of convictions and prejudices; a pretentiousness reflecting little but bad taste; a suspiciousness bordering on paranoia; a wife, Elena, who encouraged the bad and stifled the good in her husband; a self-promoting personality cult the sheer ludicrousness of which insulted, humiliated, angered, or amused most Romanians." See *Eastern Europe and Communist Rule*, p. 276.

8.   Istvan Deak points out that Ceauşescu also succeeded, through these policies, in destroying the prewar Romanian elite. "Survivors," *New York Review of Books*, March 5, 1992, p. 48.

9.   Brown, *Surge to Freedom*, pp. 202–206; and Gail Kligman, "The Politics of Reproduction in Ceauşescu's Romania: A Case Study in Political Culture," *East European Politics and Society*, Vol. 6, No. 3 (Fall 1992), p. 368.

10.   The most horrific examples were his remodeling of central Bucharest in order to build what would have been the largest building in the world, and the plan announced in 1988 to "systematize" the countryside by leveling up to 5,000 villages and transferring their inhabitants into agro-industrial complexes.

incidences of resistance to Romanian policy. By the 1980s, Ceauşescu's self-aggrandizement reached such a point that the Communist Party regime in Romania was legitimating its rule more by equating Ceauşescu with all the positive connotations of the Romanian nation, than by relying on Marxist-Leninist concepts.[11]

By the 1980s, then, the political system in Romania was distinct from that in the other Eastern bloc states. Though nominally socialist and unquestionably centralized, Communist Party rule under Ceauşescu had changed from collective rule to a one-man dictatorship, under which the regime demanded more rigid control over all aspects of life than did the regimes in the other states in the Warsaw Pact.

FRAGMENTS OF OPPOSITION

While the pervasive distrust and fear that was inculcated by the Securitate meant that no organized dissent emerged in Romania, there were nonetheless some signs of opposition to Ceauşescu's policies during the 1970s and 1980s. Within the RCP, for example, there were sporadic attempts to constrain Ceauşescu's encroachment on all aspects of rule in the country.[12] Some of those who emerged as leaders in 1990 had formed tiny clandestine opposition groups within the Party, the military, and possibly the Securitate.[13] No concerted effort appears to have been made to oppose Ceauşescu's policies or to remove him from power. The tight control enforced by Ceauşescu kept the Party quiescent, and he established a branch within the Securitate devoted to investigation of Romania's nomenklatura.[14]

---

11. It has been suggested that the closest comparison to Ceauşescu's leadership in the communist world was North Korea's Kim Il Sung. See Brown, *Eastern Europe and Communist Rule*, p. 276; and Joseph Rothschild, *Return to Diversity: A Political History of East Central Europe Since World War II* (New York: Oxford University Press, 1989), p. 165.

12. The two notable examples of opposition within the party to Ceauşescu were the failure of the 11th Party Congress to confirm Ceauşescu as General Secretary for life in 1974, and a public condemnation of his policies by Constantin Pirvulescu, then a member of the Party leadership, at the 12th Party Congress in 1979. The fact that this latter protest took place on live television was remarkable, but it did not appear to engender additional protests in the country. Brown, *Eastern Europe and Communist Rule*, pp. 279–281.

13. Nestor Ratesh, *Romania: The Entangled Revolution*, The Washington Papers, No. 152 (New York: Praeger, 1991), pp. 85–102.

14. James F. Burke, "Romanian and Soviet Intelligence in the December Revolution," *Intelligence and National Security*, Vol. 8, No. 4 (October 1993), p. 28.

There was more popular protest against the regime's actions—and it was more open than in any Eastern bloc state save Poland. Protest took the form of sporadic workers' strikes and riots. The most notable example was a strike by workers in the Jiu Valley in 1977, protesting against low wages. In March 1979, prior to the emergence of Solidarity, a free trade union was established, and it enlisted 2,000 members across the country before it was dispersed.[15] Another round of workers' riots took place in Brasov in 1987. This led to the publication of a letter by Silviu Brucan, one of the few Communist Party members willing to challenge Ceauşescu's policies publicly, criticizing Ceauşescu's repressive policies for the damage they had inflicted on both society and the Party.[16] Yet as with the scattered opposition within the Party itself, public protests against the Romanian government were inchoate, isolated incidents of outrage, not the result of organized dissent. The Securitate appears to have suppressed any efforts at greater organization. It carried out reprisals against the miners who struck in 1977 and 1987; the leaders of these protests disappeared.[17]

Predictably, Ceauşescu did not follow Moscow's example after Gorbachev introduced glasnost and perestroika in the Soviet Union; the regime had not followed the Soviet lead in policy for decades. Rather than ignoring Gorbachev's initiatives, however, Ceauşescu stated his opinion of Gorbachev's domestic reforms shortly after the 27th CPSU Congress in 1986. He praised the Soviet Union's foreign policy line, pointedly reiterating Gorbachev's statements regarding relations between independent states, and noted that Romania had no need to introduce internal reforms.[18]

More visible signs of Romania's rejection of the new Soviet model appeared during Gorbachev's visit to Romania in May 1987. Gorbachev bluntly promoted reform, and insisted that the Romanian model had

---

15. Ratesh, *Romania: The Entangled Revolution*, p. 11.; Doina and Nicolae Harsanyi, "Romania: Democracy and the Intellectuals," *East European Quarterly*, Vol. 27, No. 2, (June 1993), p. 252.

16. Ratesh, *Romania: The Entangled Revolution*, p. 99.

17. Brown, *Surge to Freedom*, pp. 213–214; and Gail Stokes, *The Walls Came Tumbling Down: The Collapse of Communism in Eastern Europe* (New York: Oxford University Press, 1993), p. 160.

18. Bucharest Agerpress, March 7, 1986, in *Foreign Broadcast Information Service: Eastern Europe* [hereafter *FBIS:EEU*], March 10, 1986, as quoted in Karen Dawisha, *Eastern Europe, Gorbachev and Reform: The Great Challenge*, (Cambridge: Cambridge University Press, 1988), p. 170.

grave problems. His host responded by praising the Romanian model of socialism. Ceauşescu stressed Romania's improved growth since its implementation of its "New Economic Mechanism" in 1973, whose goals he claimed would be achieved by the end of the decade. He also emphasized the importance of strengthening the Party's leadership role in order to guarantee the attainment of these goals, rejecting Gorbachev's exhortation to reduce Party bureaucracies.[19]

In addition, Ceauşescu continued to proclaim his independence in foreign policy. He criticized Moscow's refusal to de-link the basing of nuclear weapons in Europe from the issue of missile defenses in 1986 following the Reykjavik summit between Gorbachev and U.S. President Ronald Reagan. Ceauşescu also again raised the issue of defense spending, unilaterally cutting Romania's defense budget in 1987.[20]

In 1988, while most other East European states were giving at least lip service to reform, Ceauşescu introduced a plan to "systematize" agriculture by demolishing up to 7,000 of the 15,000 villages in the countryside and to resettle the inhabitants in large agro-industrial complexes as part of his ongoing effort to "homogenize" the population. This aggravated Romania's relations with Hungary, which claimed that the move was intended to destroy the ethnic identity of the Hungarian minority in Romania; 1,500 of the villages slated for abandonment were largely inhabited by ethnic Hungarians.[21] This move worsened the grim situation in the countryside and hurt Romania's already poor international standing.

As the pace of reform in Eastern Europe and the Soviet Union began to accelerate early in 1989, Romania's opposition to change became more pronounced. The nature of Ceauşescu's control in Romania appeared to be unaffected by developments elsewhere in the bloc, and the adulation of Ceauşescu and his wife, which by the end of the 1980s characterized his rule, continued unabated.

---

19. See speech by Nicolae Ceauşescu, May 25, 1987 from Agerpres, in *Summary of World Broadcasts: Eastern Europe* (hereafter *SWB:EEU*), May 27, 1987.

20. This was probably done primarily for domestic reasons, since Romania was in financial straits. See "Romania," in *Eastern Europe and the USSR: Structure and Analysis* (London: Economist Intelligence Unit, 1988), pp. 161–180.

21. The ethnic Hungarian minority was not the only group affected by Ceauşescu's plan; ethnic Romanians, gypsies, and ethnic Germans would also be uprooted. Moreover, "systematization" hit towns as well as the countryside. Twenty-nine towns had their traditional centers razed and replaced with the concrete buildings Ceauşescu was so fond of. Gale Stokes, *The Walls Came Tumbling Down: The Collapse of Communism in Eastern Europe* (New York: Oxford University Press, 1993), pp. 160–161.

ROMANIA'S REVOLUTION

Romania's political paralysis gave way abruptly in mid-December 1989. The regime's efforts to exile an ethnic Hungarian priest, László Tökés, from his parish in Timosoara catalyzed a protest there on December 16 and 17, which quickly took on an antigovernment tone.[22] Both ethnic Hungarians and Romanians had surrounded Tökés' home to prevent his removal. The growing crowd coalesced into an antigovernment protest and spread to other parts of the city. Army and Securitate forces were called in to quell the demonstrations, and when riot control methods failed to dampen the spreading protests on December 16, the army opened fire on crowds of demonstrators on December 17. It appears that this step was taken because Ceauşescu demanded that the demonstrators be "liquidated," and sent one of his closest subordinates to Timosoara to oversee the situation.[23] Despite the bloodshed, the riots and demonstrations that this incident spawned continued in Timosoara, and spread rapidly to other cities. Within five or six days, a state of emergency was declared in Timis county, and the clashes had spread to Bucharest. On December 21, antigovernment demonstrations of up to 150,000 were reported in Timosoara, and the army had withdrawn from the city. A meeting was held there between the Romanian prime minister and a committee of protesters in order to discuss their demands, though nothing concrete developed from their meeting.[24]

Ceauşescu reacted to the protests by dismissing the head of the Securitate and the ministers of defense and interior, and sending his representative to Timosoara. He then left for an official visit to Iran on December 18. Returning on December 20, Ceauşescu attacked the demonstrators as "hooligans" and blamed the crisis on foreign manipulation, denouncing Hungary in particular. The next day, Ceauşescu's address to an organized progovernment rally in Bucharest was interrupted by protests; within hours the Securitate began firing on demonstrators, and what appeared to be civil war erupted.[25]

---

22. The leadership of the Hungarian Reformed Church had bowed to pressure from the regime to move the priest, and unsuccessfully attempted to transfer him in May 1989. By December, the church had asked for government assistance in removing Tökés. See Ratesh, *Romania: The Entangled Revolution*, pp. 19–21.

23. Ibid., pp. 28–30.

24. Ibid., p. 34. The army apparently withdrew because it was unwilling to inflict massive casualties. Mircea Munteanu, "New Evidence on the 1989 Crisis in Romania," Cold War International History Project Website *CWIHP.si.edu*, e-Dossier No. 5.

25. The protests were apparently started by citizens who had joined the official dem-

Ceauşescu and his wife Elena fled Bucharest the next day as battles raged throughout the city, and army troops began to fraternize with the population. An organization calling itself the National Salvation Front (NSF) declared itself the new government of Romania on national television on December 22. Fighting continued in the capital and elsewhere during the following days. The Ceauşescus were captured by army troops on December 22, and tried by a military tribunal and executed on December 25, 1989.[26] The army pledged support for the new government after the defense minister, Vasile Milea, refused to order troops to open fire on the population and then was officially reported to have committed suicide.[27] Army leaders apparently agreed to support the NSF only after receiving assurances that "serious politicians" would be in charge, rather than "poets."[28]

The NSF was initially portrayed as a loose coalition between many of the disaffected groups in the country, including the few prominent dissidents who remained in Romania, and former members of the RCP. Led by Ion Iliescu, the NSF quickly declared its intention to be an interim government until a multiparty system could be created in Romania; it abolished the leading role of the Communist Party, and proclaimed that free elections would be held in April 1990. Additionally, it reiterated Romania's commitment to the Warsaw Pact, in ironic contrast to Ceauşescu's hostility toward the alliance.

The NSF's integrity came into question almost immediately as former dissidents accused former Communists who were members of the NSF of trying to continue communist rule under a new name. After vacillating during the first few weeks of its existence, and in spite of popular anger against some of its peremptory methods, in January 1990 the leaders of the NSF declared that "naturally" the NSF would field candidates in the spring elections. Suspicions were also raised about the origins of the

---

onstration in the hope of finding support in the crowd. Ratesh, *Romania: The Entangled Revolution*, pp. 38–40.

26. For a chilling account of the trial, see the published transcripts. The bodies of Ceauşescu and his wife were also shown on television, in order to leave no illusions that they might be alive. "Recording of Trial," Vienna Television Service, December 27, 1989, in *FBIS:EEU*, December 28, 1989; and "Trial Reported on Radio," Bucharest Domestic Service, December 26, 1989, in *FBIS:EEU*, December 27, 1989.

27. His "suicide" was hotly disputed. See "Funeral of Former Defense Minister," Agerpres (Romania), December 29, 1989, in *SWB:EEU*, January 3, 1990.

28. Burke, "Romanian and Soviet Intelligence in the December Revolution," p. 33; and Ratesh, *Romania: The Entangled Revolution*, p. 52.

rebellion that had overthrown Ceauşescu, and it was suggested that this had in fact been a coup, rather than a popular uprising. The leaders of the NSF denied that there had been a coup, or that external forces had been involved in its planning, insisting instead that the changes in December were a spontaneous reaction to events.[29] But other figures associated with the NSF claimed that the core of the group had been plotting some action for about six months.[30] Silviu Brucan and General Nicolae Militaru, who left the government early in 1990, claimed that attempts to overthrow Ceauşescu had been discussed among a small group of Party, military, and Securitate leaders for years, if not decades.[31]

Some of the methods adopted by the NSF in its first weeks in power kindled doubts about the origins and intentions of the group and others clearly illustrated the influence of events throughout the bloc; the NSF's behavior showed a contradictory mix of steps taken by opposition and communist party regimes in other countries. The initial goals proclaimed by the NSF, for example, were the introduction of a multiparty system, the dismantling of the RCP's leading role in the country, free elections, and a shift to a market-oriented economy.[32] In this, it followed the pattern of opposition groups such as Solidarity and Civic Forum. At the same time, the NSF announced its willingness to hold negotiations with "opposition groups" in Romania—as if *it* were the previously recognized government. The NSF's hostility toward other opposition groups was seen also in its claims to represent "all patriotic and democratic forces" in the country, implying that groups trying to operate outside its auspices were either redundant or against these aims.[33] Similarly, when concerns about

---

29. The foreign force suspected of involvement was the Soviet Union; its quick support for the fledgling NSF bolstered the impression that Moscow may have been involved in some way. NSF spokesmen vehemently insisted that this was not the case. See "Brucan Visits Moscow; Soviet Support Expressed," Budapest Domestic Service, January 3, 1990, and "Further on Moscow Visit," London ITV Television, January 3, 1990, both in *FBIS:EEU*, January 4, 1990.

30. "Lupoi on Formation of National Salvation Front," *Le Figaro* (Paris), January 3, 1990, in *FBIS:EEU*, January 11, 1990; and Ratesh, *Romania: The Entangled Revolution*, pp. 39–40.

31. Ratesh, *Romania: The Entangled Revolution*, p. 84–102.

32. "Communique Issued by the Council of the National Salvation of Romania," Bucharest Domestic Service, December 22, 1989, in *FBIS:EEU*, December 26, 1989; and "Decree on NSF Constitution," Bucharest Domestic Service, December 28, 1989, in *FBIS:EEU*, December 29, 1989.

33. The NSF statement of December 28 declared that "the NSF has been established and represents the unification of all patriotic and democratic forces of our country for

the NSF's connections with the former Communist Party led to demonstrations against it, the NSF's response was that it would be impossible to keep all former RCP members out of political life. The new government then issued a decree that banned meetings in the main public squares of Bucharest and proscribed the types of meetings which could be held elsewhere.[34]

Nonetheless, faced with growing criticism, a succession of resignations by disgruntled members—including Silviu Brucan, one of its most prominent members—and demonstrations in several major cities during January, the NSF agreed to create a governing body called the Provisional National Unity Council (PNUC), comprised of representatives of both the NSF and some 30 opposition groups, which would lead the country until elections could be held at a new, later date of May 20, 1990. This concession did not happen overnight, however. On January 12, it agreed to accept several of the demands presented at a major demonstration in Bucharest, including the banning of the Communist Party and the holding of a referendum on the death penalty, but the NSF rescinded these measures only days later and insisted that it could not give in to mob pressure.[35] When elections were finally held in May 1990, the NSF won 67 percent of the vote; Ion Iliescu, its candidate for president, won 85 percent.[36]

---

overthrowing Ceauşescu's dictatorial plan; for uniting the aspirations of the largest masses of people and of our country for a free and dignified life, and ensuring the framework for their assertion." See "Decree on NSF Constitution;" and "Romanian Democratic Party Presents Platform," Bucharest Domestic Service, December 26, 1989, in *FBIS:EEU*, December 26, 1989. See also "NSF Offers to Hold Talks with Other Parties," Paris AFP, January 4, 1990, in *FBIS:EEU*, January 5, 1990.

34. Many of those allegedly affiliated with the NSF, such as the student groups that participated in the rebellion, protested against their "puppet" role in the NSF, and objected to the individuals chosen to represent their interests. "Hundreds Demonstrate against Leadership in Sibiu," Paris AFP, January 3, 1990, and "Students Protest Jobs for Ceauşescu Loyalists," Paris AFP, January 4, 1990, both in *FBIS:EEU*, January 4, 1990; and "Cornea Asks NSF to Clarify Democratic Position," Paris AFP, January 9, 1990, in *FBIS:EEU*, January 11, 1990.

35. See "Rally Held on `Discontent' with NSF Communists," *Rompres* (Romania), January 13, 1990, in *FBIS:EEU*, January 16, 1990; "Peasants Party Requests Election Postponement," *Rompres,* January 13, 1990, and "Iliescu Reportedly Agrees to Postpone Elections," Paris AFP, January 13, 1990, both in *FBIS:EEU,* January 16, 1990; and "Daily Calls for Dumitru Mazilu's Resignation," *Romana Libera,* January 13, 1990, in *FBIS:EEU,* January 17, 1990.

36. Ratesh, *Romania: The Entangled Revolution,* p. 142. The elections were generally perceived as fair.

Explaining the Regime's Rejection of Early Reform

The Romanian regime's early rejection of reform can be explained by Nicolae Ceauşescu's attitude toward reform, and his perception of the legitimacy of his rule. This section examines Ceauşescu's views of these issues.

Ceauşescu made it no secret that he rejected the policies Gorbachev was advocating at home and in the Eastern bloc. After the 1987 Plenum of the CPSU Central Committee, which dealt with questions of democratization of the Party, Ceauşescu said bluntly that he thought democratization a "dangerous" direction for the Party to take.[37] Ceauşescu's private meeting with Gorbachev and his wife, Raisa, during Gorbachev's May 1987 visit to Bucharest degenerated into a shouting match over reforms.[38] As late as the Warsaw Pact meeting following Gorbachev's December 1989 meeting with U.S. President George Bush in Malta, Ceauşescu continued to try to convince the Soviet Union to stop the changes underway in the bloc (with force if necessary), or at a minimum, to continue to defend socialism.[39]

Added to his rejection of reform, Ceauşescu's belief in the legitimacy of his rule appeared unshaken.[40] Ceauşescu's control over the Party and the country was absolute. The state structure had been heavily centralized, and the RCP's rule was officially grounded in the canons of Marxist-Leninist ideology. Yet Ceauşescu's rule was more Stalinist in nature than in other East European states, even the other conservative regimes, based on maintaining fear and distrust throughout society. Further, as his control over the Party and country tightened, Ceauşescu increasingly claimed to embody the Romanian character, and to legitimize his rule through this association, rather than with socialist principles alone.

Like Honecker and Zhivkov, Ceauşescu's extended tenure meant that no generational change had taken place. Yet to an unprecedented degree, Ceauşescu had claimed credit for all of Romania's achievements. While his resistance to reform could possibly stem from a recognition that he would have to take the blame for all of his government's failures, this

---

37. M. S. Gorbachev, *Zhizn' i Reformii* [Life and reforms], vol. 2 (Moscow: Novosti, 1995), p. 318.

38. Ibid., pp. 397–398.

39. Ibid., p. 403. See also "Minutes of the Meeting between Nicolae Ceauşescu and Mikhail S. Gorbachev, Moscow, 4 December 1989," *Cold War International History Project Bulletin*, Issue 12/13 (Fall/Winter 2001), pp. 217–225.

40. Ratesh, *Romania: The Entangled Revolution*, p. 74. See also "Recording of Trial."

does not appear to have been the case; Ceauşescu seems to have been completely blind to the failures of the system he had created.

With such a leader, it is unsurprising that the Romanian regime was loath to emulate Gorbachev's policies or introduce liberalizing measures. Yet the reasons for this rejection go beyond the criteria laid out here: whether the regime recognized the need for reform, or felt that it could survive in a more open climate. The means by which Ceauşescu ruled, and his utter lack of contact with reality, would suggest that while he was in power change simply was not an alternative.

Romania's economic situation, and Ceauşescu's management of it, further confirm that he was unable to comprehend the need for change. The country had made impressive economic gains in the 1960s and 1970s. Its independent political stand gained it enthusiastic trade partners abroad, including the United States, and Romania had the fastest industrial growth rate in the Eastern bloc during this period.[41]

These gains made the economy an additional source of legitimacy for the regime in the 1970s, but by the end of the decade the economy was faltering. Once Ceauşescu had solidified his position in the political leadership, he insisted on controlling Romania's economy as well. Ceauşescu became utterly opposed to spontaneity, which meant that no reforms could involve decentralization or the tolerance of greater initiative by managers or workers.[42]

The apparent advantage of Romania's raw materials base also created a problem for the country over the longer term. Beginning in the 1960s, the government built an enormous petrochemical industry to take advantage of the country's oil reserves. But with a waning in domestic production and the oil shocks of the early 1970s, this became an immense economic drain; indeed, the industry proved to be a major contributor to the country's indebtedness by the end of the decade. Diminishing domes-

---

41. The United States gave the regime access to Western machinery at a time when this was denied to other Eastern bloc states, and accorded it the most favored nation (MFN) trade status in 1975. Ceauşescu later renounced MFN in 1988, since it had become clear that the U.S. Senate would not renew it in light of Romania's human rights record. For a comprehensive overview of Ceauşescu's struggles with the United States over MFN in the late 1980s, see Roger Kirk and Mircea Raceanu, *Romania Versus the United States: Diplomacy of the Absurd, 1985–89* (New York: St. Martin's Press, 1994). See also Rothschild, *Return to Diversity*, p. 163.

42. In agriculture, Ceauşescu's grip translated into a particularly harsh form of collectivization, with an almost total rejection of private plots for the peasantry. In industry, the heavily centralized economy was maintained with little change throughout the 1960s and 1970s. Some revisions were made in economic methods during this period, and a "New Economic Mechanism" was introduced in 1973, but these merely tinkered with the existing structure. Brown, *Eastern Europe and Communist Rule*, pp. 283–284.

tic supplies compelled the regime to import large quantities of oil to keep its facilities running, and when prices on the international market rose, it had to rely on Western credits to finance these purchases. This left the country with a $10.2 billion debt in 1981, which the government was unable to service. Ceauşescu responded by enacting a draconian austerity program to pay off the country's debt as rapidly as possible. This entailed increasing the country's exports while reducing imports, regardless of the impact on domestic living standards. The program successfully reduced Romania's debt to $6 billion in 1986, and Ceauşescu announced in the spring of 1989 that the entire debt had been repaid. But the cost to the population was severe. The country suffered food shortages throughout the 1980s, and the amounts of electricity and heat available to the population were sharply curtailed, even during several particularly severe winters.[43]

SUMMARY

In almost any other state, the disastrous condition of the economy would have led the regime to consider making drastic changes in its economic management structure. But Ceauşescu's grip on the country and his megalomania made him unconcerned about and probably unaware of the population's suffering and discontent. Further, the absence of an opposition movement within the country—though undoubtedly due to pervasive fear of the Securitate—gave Ceauşescu little reason to suspect that his long-standing reliance on repression and tyranny from above could not continue. He thus rejected the option of introducing reform.

In Lieu of Late Reform: Revolution

Since Ceauşescu appears to have been unable to understand the depth of change in the political climate around him—thereby ensuring that he would not initiate reform—change in Romania would likely begin with protests from below. The demonstration effect helped impel people to protest. This section examines Ceauşescu's cognitive resistance to change by looking at his continued support for the existing system and his opposition to reform. It also assesses leaders' and the population's awareness

---

43. Citizens were allowed only one 40-watt bulb for each room, and ambulances stopped picking up pensioners as a cost-cutting measure. Stokes, *The Walls Came Tumbling Down,* p. 158; and Deak, "Survivors," p. 44. Brown also notes that Ceauşescu's decision to turn the management of the country's electrical system over to the military in the early 1980s was essentially an admission of the government's failure to provide electricity. Brown, *Eastern Europe and Communist Rule,* pp. 285–287.

of developments in other states. Finally, I examine divisions within the Romanian leadership for their impact on the course of events in 1989.

RESISTANCE TO CHANGE

Indications of resistance to change were pervasive in Romania in 1989. Ceauşescu frequently asserted the importance of socialist principles, and shifted from his earlier insistence on independence to calls for interference to stop the process of change in the Eastern bloc states. This indicates Ceauşescu's unease with the process of reform, and also the degree to which he was out of touch with developments in the Warsaw Pact. While Gorbachev was embracing noninterference and was disavowing the use of force, Ceauşescu was calling for intervention.

Ceauşescu's resistance to change, and his continued faith in the system he created, is evident in many ways, such as the continuity in domestic policies in the late 1980s. Indeed, rather than introduce reforms in response to the change in policies in the Soviet Union in 1988, Ceauşescu announced a new phase of his effort to homogenize the population by "systematizing" agriculture in Romania. His effort to pay off Romania's foreign debt at the population's expense continued. Even after Ceauşescu proclaimed that Romania's debt had been paid off in the spring of 1989, the country's harsh economic policies were not revised.[44]

Added to this, the regime continued to disavow any need for reforms by elaborating on the achievements of socialism in Romania. Throughout 1989, Ceauşescu and other government spokesmen pointed to the benefits of the Romanian system for its population, and insisted that the gains made in Romania were clear evidence of the "correctness" of the Party's policy, and of its adherence to the principles of socialism.[45]

Belying this facade of business as usual, however, was the increasingly vociferous defense of the basic tenets of socialism among the Romanian leadership during 1989. This was somewhat out of character for the RCP, which during the previous decade had generally equated Romania's achievements with Ceauşescu's person—not as a socialist, but as the epitome of all that was good about Romania. In 1989, the central theme of

---

44. Ceauşescu's claims to have paid the debt are dubious, and statistics in Romania were notoriously unreliable. The grain harvest for 1989 was reported to be 60,000 tons in October 1989; after the revolution the figure was reduced to under 17,000 tons. Stokes, *The Walls Came Tumbling Down*, p. 159.

45. "President Nicolae Ceauşescu Address on Receiving the Children and Youth's Representatives," Agerpres, December 29, 1988, in *FBIS:EEU*, January 3, 1989; "President Nicolae Ceauşescu's New Year Message," Bucharest Domestic Service, December 31, 1988, in *FBIS:EEU*, January 3, 1989; and "Ceauşescu Views Road Traveled by Socialism," *Scinteia*, October 25, 1989, in *FBIS:EEU*, October 31, 1989.

the promotion of socialism was the regime's adamant defense of the Party's leading role in running the state. As the Hungarian Party leadership moved toward removing its constitutionally protected leading role, for example, the RCP insisted that it was "all the more important" for the Party to lead the way in policy decisions.[46] During the summer, Ceauşescu and the RCP more stridently insisted that questioning the Party's leading role was "like voiding the basic principles of socialism," since the Party's role could not be shared—much less renounced—without jeopardizing the cause of socialism.[47] Along with this defense of the Party's leading role, Ceauşescu also began to attack any suggestion that a multiparty system was acceptable in a socialist country.[48] By the fall, the regime's tone was increasingly beleaguered; in asserting the correctness of its position, the RCP railed against giving up the "revolutionary principles" embodied in the leading role of the Party;[49] the idea of allowing a multiparty system was condemned as "completely wrong" and "harmful."[50]

This insistence on the Party's leading role can be interpreted as a rigorous defense of the existing system, or as an indication of nervousness about the kind of multiparty system emerging in neighboring states like Hungary. Both of these elements were probably present in Romania. Indeed, Gorbachev argues that Ceauşescu may have recognized that the introduction of reforms would jeopardize his rule.[51] But there is no evi-

46. Ion Mitran, "Increasing the Leading Role of the Party—An Objective Requirement of Building and Improving the New System," *Scinteia*, January 19, 1989, in *FBIS:EEU*, January 26, 1989.

47. "Socialism—an Objective Requirement, the Sole Alternative of People's Free Development, of Mankind's Progress—Excerpted Article in *Scinteia* of 12 July," Agerpres, July 12, 1989, in *FBIS:EEU*, July 13, 1989; "Party Leadership—Lawful Requirement of Successful Socialist Construction," *Scinteia*, September 1, 1989, in *FBIS:EEU*, September 7, 1989; and "Growing Leading Role of Party—a Law of Development of the New Society—Article Run by 23 September *Scinteia*," Agerpres, September 23, 1989, in *FBIS:EEU*, September 27, 1989.

48. "President Nicolae Ceauşescu's Interview with the Algerian Weekly *Revolution Africain*," Agerpres, June 29, 1989, in *FBIS:EEU*, June 30, 1989; and "Creative Force of Socialist Democracy," Agerpres, September 2, 1989, in *FBIS:EEU*, September 8, 1989.

49. "A State of Revolutionary Workers Democracy," Agerpres, October 5, 1989, in *FBIS:EEU*, October 25, 1989.

50. Building of a New Social System with the People and For the People—Article in *Scinteia* of 18 October 1989 (Excerpts)," Agerpres, October 18, 1989, in *FBIS:EEU*, October 27, 1989; and "'Socialist Property, A Foundation for the Assertion of Revolutionary Worker Democracy'—An Article Printed in *Scinteia* of November 1, Excerpts," Agerpres, November 1, 1989, in *FBIS:EEU*, November 7, 1989.

51. Gorbachev, *Zhizn' i Reformii*, p. 400.

dence that Ceaușescu ever considered opening the system to reforms. This implies that he was unable to change his views of the situation enough to contemplate change.

The regime's defense of the concept of socialist ownership was equally vigorous, as different concepts of economic management were broached in other East European states. Party spokesmen at first noted that capitalist forms of ownership were "not in accordance with the principles of socialist improvement."[52] By the end of the summer the regime had rejected privatization outright, and asserted that any diminution of socialist property and ownership would jeopardize socialism.[53] The Party also insisted that claims about the benefits of a market economy must be combated, to maintain the purity of the socialist system.[54]

As changes accelerated in Eastern Europe, Ceaușescu's escalating defense of the basic tenets of socialism in domestic policy extended into the foreign policy arena. The regime attacked imperialism, and denounced the anticommunist activities of some Western powers, notably West Germany and the United States.[55] By the fall, with the escalation of the East German refugee crisis and the change of leadership in Poland, Romania's attacks on the West for interference had become particularly heated. In November, Ceaușescu went so far as to assert that there was no fundamental change in the class character of international politics, which remained an explicit struggle between socialism and capitalism.[56] Ceaușescu's disapproval of Moscow's acceptance of moves away from socialism within Eastern Europe was also obvious in his criticism of Western efforts to "deideologize" international relations; "deideolo-

---

52. "Comrade Nicolae Ceaușescu's Interview for *Kansan Uutiset* Daily of Finland," *Scinteia*, February 10, 1989, in *FBIS:EEU*, February 14, 1989.

53. "People Are Governing Society," Agerpres, August 8, 1989, in *FBIS:EEU*, August 9, 1989; and "The Socialist Property the Lasting Foundation of the Homeland's Socio-Economic Progress," Agerpres, August 30, 1989, in *FBIS:EEU*, September 8, 1989.

54. "Speech by Comrade Nicolae Ceaușescu on Problems of Socialism and of the Ideological, Political, and Educational Activity of Developing the Revolutionary Awareness of and Fashioning the New Man, Conscious Builder of Socialism and Communism in Romania," *Scinteia*, October 25, 1989, in *FBIS:EEU*, October 31, 1989.

55. See, for example, *Scinteia* Commentary on Pact Meeting, Agerpres, July 11, 1989, in *FBIS:EEU*, July 12, 1989.

56. "Policy of `Disideologization' Attacked," Agerpress, November 14, 1989, in *FBIS:EEU*, November 21, 1989; and "Socialism the Path of the Peoples' Free Independent Development—Excerpted Article in *Scinteia* of 11 November," Agerpres, November 11, 1989, in *FBIS:EEU*, November 13, 1989.

gization" was a fundamental concept of Gorbachev's "new thinking" in foreign policy.

Ceauşescu's rejection of developments in neighboring states led him to assert the urgency of conformity that Romania had rejected decades earlier. Since 1968, Ceauşescu had been the East European champion of the concept of noninterference in the affairs of other states.[57] His endorsement of this policy continued in the first half of 1989.[58] Yet there was a gradual shift in the tone of Ceauşescu's statements regarding independence within the bloc during the course of the year. As the communist parties in Poland and Hungary accepted new forms of government, Ceauşescu began to propose that the socialist parties engage in discussions on how to safeguard socialism.[59] This suggested that he thought a common approach should be adopted, and that it should reflect long-standing practices, rather than the sorts of changes that were emerging in parts of the bloc. Concurrent with the accelerating changes in neighboring states, the RCP grew more hostile toward the concept of reform, and the Romanian press underscored the regime's defense of the gains of socialism in increasingly blunt tones. This was coupled with more open criticism of steps being taken elsewhere, which the regime considered to be moves backward. The regime began to publish outright attacks on decisions that in its view endangered the Party's leading role in these states, and Ceauseşcu warned that those who jeopardized the "gains of socialism" ought to be punished.[60] The Romanian regime also

---

57. Indeed, Ceauşescu's endorsement of noninterference even led him to warn against external solutions to the Polish crisis in 1980–1981, though he remained adamantly opposed to Solidarity and all that it stood for. Brown, *Eastern Europe and Communist Rule*, p. 273.

58. For example, he reiterated several times the view that reforms must be decided upon on an individual basis, taking into account the varying interests of the states involved. "Comrade Nicolae Ceauşescu's Interview for FRG Newspaper *Die Welt*," *Scinteia*, December 30, 1988, in *FBIS:EEU*, January 6, 1989; Dr. Aurel Zamfirescu, "International Solidarity—An Innovating and Profoundly Mobilizing Concept," *Lumea*, No. 17, April 27, 1989, in *FBIS:EEU*, May 9, 1989; and "Under the Sign of Strengthening Collaboration in Socialist Construction, in the Struggle for Peace and Disarmament, of the Determination to Firmly Reject any Destabilizing Tendencies of Interference in Home Affairs—Article in *Scinteia* of 11 July," Agerpres, July 11, 1989, in *FBIS:EEU*, July 12, 1989.

59. "Ceauşescu RCP Plenum Address Published," *Scinteia*, June 29, 1989, in *FBIS:EEU*, July 7, 1989.

60. "Comrade Nicolae Ceauşescu Has Paid a Friendly Working Visit to the Czechoslovak Socialist Republic," *Scinteia*, May 18, 1989, in *FBIS:EEU* May 24, 1989; and "Ceauşescu RCP Plenum Address Published, "*Scinteia*, June 29, 1989, in *FBIS:EEU*", July 7, 1989.

insisted that problems in different socialist countries were due to a mis-application of the tenets of socialism, not to any problems with the ideas themselves.[61]

Not surprisingly, the regime's opinion of developments in Hungary was negative from the outset of its discussion of reforms. Romania was openly critical of the Communist Party's activities in Hungary from late 1988 onward, and the RCP accused Hungary of betraying socialism.[62] The Romanian regime also struck a nationalist note, attacking Hungary's policy toward Romania as interference.

In contrast, the Romanian regime was almost totally silent about the changes taking place in Poland in early 1989. Only at the end of July did the Romanian regime actively begin to criticize events in Poland, and its criticism was aimed primarily at Solidarity.[63] Yet as Romania's calls for safeguarding socialism grew more urgent, the PUWP (Polish United Worker's Party) came under tacit pressure as well. Ceauşescu apparently tried to compel changes in the PUWP's policies by sending a delegation to Poland to press the Party to forestall the change in government, with force if necessary. PUWP members claimed that the RCP had expressed its "concern" with the situation in Poland, and proposed joint action by the communist states to "defend socialism and the Polish nation"—an offer the PUWP declined.[64]

---

61. "Socialist Property, A Foundation for the Assertion of Revolutionary Worker De-mocracy—An Article Printed in *Scinteia* of November 1, Excerpts," Agerpres, Novem-ber 1, 1989, in *FBIS:EEU*, November 7, 1989; "*Scinteia* on Hungary's Foreign Debt," in *FBIS:EEU*, December 7, 1989; and "*Scinteia* on Polish, Hungarian Economy," analysis of editorial reports in *Scinteia* of November 15 and November 17, 1989, in *FBIS:EEU*, December 19, 1989.

62. Examples of this perspective were seen from March to September, but were espe-cially bitter after the Hungarian government opened its border to East German refu-gees wishing to travel to the West. For some examples, see "Geneva Envoy Attacks Hungary on Rights Probe," Paris AFP, February 28, 1989, in *FBIS:EEU*, March 1, 1989; "From the Foreign Press—Daily *Nepszabadsag* on the Opinion of the MSZMP Marxist Unity Platform," *Scinteia*, June 11, 1989, in *FBIS:EEU*, June 16, 1989; "Related to Grave Anti-Socialist, Revisionist and Anti-Romanian Manifestations Held in Budapest," Agerpres, June 18, 1989, in *FBIS:EEU*, June 19, 1989; Anti-Romanian Hungarian `Prov-ocations' Rejected, Agerpres, June 21, 1989, in *FBIS:EEU*, June 21, 1989; N. Patrascu, "When the Disparagers of Socialism are Allowed to Show Their True Face," *Lumea*, No. 25, June 22, 1989, in *FBIS:EEU*, July 6, 1989; and "Statement on GDR Citizens' `Ille-gal' Passage," Budapest Domestic Service, September 12, 1989, in *FBIS:EEU*, Septem-ber 13, 1989.

63. Mazowiecki, for example, came under vociferous attack for his anti-socialist atti-tude after his nomination as prime minister. See "*Scinteia* on the Situation in Poland," Agerpres, August 20, 1989, in *FBIS:EEU*, August 22, 1989.

64. See *Radio Free Europe Weekly Record of Events*, September 29, 1989.

But the regime's most vehement reaction to the changes elsewhere came in August, in response to the announcement that the Polish Communist Party had accepted the nomination of a Solidarity advisor as prime minister. The Romanian regime tried to convince the Warsaw Pact to join forces to stop this development, arguing that they "ought to take any steps necessary to defend the gains of socialism."[65] This was essentially an appeal for the reactivation of the Brezhnev Doctrine, which Romania itself had rejected in 1968, and which the Warsaw Pact appeared to have renounced only a month earlier at its July summit.[66]

Ceauşescu's attacks on reforming states' policies indicated his awareness of developments in the Eastern bloc, and suggested that the Romanian leadership felt that its position might be threatened by these developments. It also shows that Ceauşescu was unable to conclude that the changes in other countries required a similar shift in policy on his part; instead, the Romanian regime would prefer to see Soviet involvement in the internal affairs of others.

The collapse of East Germany and Czechoslovakia in the fall drew little public reaction from Romania. There was no mention in the Romanian press of the causes of the problems that arose in countries such as East Germany, nor were the changing events covered.[67] As it had done with Poland, the Romanian regime congratulated the emerging Communist leaders on their new positions, and gave scant attention to the noncommunist figures who now dominated the governments in East Germany and Czechoslovakia. The regime also continued its strident emphasis on the importance of efforts to build socialism, even as socialism collapsed throughout the bloc.[68]

---

65. "*Scinteia* on the Situation in Poland," *Agerpres*, August 20, 1989, in *FBIS:EEU*, August 22, 1989.

66. See "Meeting of the Warsaw Treaty Political Consultative Committee: Communique," TASS, July 8, 1989, in *SWB:EE*, July 10, 1989.

67. The collapse of the Berlin Wall and the mass demonstrations in both East Germany and Czechoslovakia were ignored by the Romanian media. This does not mean that the population knew nothing about these changes; Romania was exposed to Soviet radio broadcasts and newspapers, and parts of the country are within radio range of Hungary or Yugoslavia, where the changes were openly reported.

68. "Ceauşescu Views Road Traveled by Socialism," *Scinteia*, October 25, 1989, in *FBIS:EEU*, October 31, 1989; "Socialism, The Peoples' Liberty and Independence are Not Negotiable," Agerpres, November 8, 1989, in *FBIS:EEU*, November 16, 1989; and "President Nicolae Ceauşescu's Interview with *Prenza Latina*," Agerpres, November 16, 1989, in *FBIS:EEU*, November 27, 1989.

Romania's reportage on developments in the Soviet Union was as minimal as that on the changes elsewhere in Eastern Europe. For example, the June 1989 press coverage of the newly created Congress of People's Deputies noted Gorbachev's election as president and some of the measures he pushed through the Congress, but the Romanian press managed to create the impression that this body operated in much the same way that Romania's elected bodies did, with decrees put forward for unanimous approval.[69]

Thus, in late 1989 Romania was transformed from the strongest advocate of independence in the bloc to its most fervent defender of socialism. By the time of the 14th RCP Congress in late November, Romania appeared to consider itself in a state of siege. The leadership's concern was manifested in its utter rejection of the reform process elsewhere in Eastern Europe, and in its growing efforts to keep change out of Romania. This was shown both by the dearth of reportage on developments elsewhere in the bloc throughout 1989, and by the increasing restrictions on the Romanian borders, which by November were meant to keep foreigners out of the country, as well as Romanians in. This latter policy was intensified just prior to the RCP Congress in November 1989. Restrictions were most noticeable with regard to other East Europeans; Hungarians in particular were excluded. While this was partly a function of the continuing tensions over the minority question and the general friction between the two countries, it also appears to have been meant to keep out the sort of reform ideas that had clearly helped to catalyze the rounds of demonstrations that had occurred earlier in both East Germany and Czechoslovakia.[70] This suggests that the regime was well aware of the danger of contagion from outside, and wanted to avert the emergence of such problems at home.

ASSERTIONS OF LEGITIMACY

In spite of his obvious concern about the changes taking place throughout Eastern Europe, Ceauşescu appears to have believed in the legitimacy

---

69. See, for example, "Paper on USSR Deputies Congress Proceedings," *FBIS:EEU*, June 8, 1989.

70. Of course, the popular protests in East Germany and Czechoslovakia were not caused by outside forces alone. But in both cases, knowledge of developments elsewhere, and contacts—particularly among young people from various Eastern European countries—appear to have been critical to rallying people in support of change. That the tiny opposition in Bulgaria also attempted to expand its contacts with other East European opposition movements is further evidence that these groups recognized the importance of learning from others in the bloc.

of his rule until the bitter end. His regime's continued defense of the existing system and socialist principles showed no indication that he contemplated any changes. Instead, Ceauşescu's reaction to the revolution in Romania illustrated his continued confidence in his right to rule, and his inability to comprehend the depth of popular hostility toward him. He was enraged by the protests in Timosoara and wanted the "hooligans" involved there "liquidated." This reaction gave no hint that he felt in any way responsible for popular discontent; rather, he was affronted by it.[71] Ceauşescu's trip to Iran, begun after he declared that the country was in "a state of war," also indicated his confidence about his right to rule; it does not seem to have occurred to him that this was a risky or impolitic move. Even after Ceauşescu and his wife, Elena, fled the crowds in Bucharest, both seemed unable to understand why the population was angry with them. Ceauşescu insisted during their trial that the population lived better under his rule than at any previous time, indicating how out of touch he was with the country: "never was there in the villages as much wealth as there is now. I have built hospitals, schools, no country in the world has such things."[72] Finally, Ceauşescu insisted throughout, from the begining of the protests in Timosoara through his trial on December 25, that the revolt must be the result of foreign interference. He particularly blamed the West and Hungary and the Soviet Union.[73] Again, this underscores his inability to comprehend that the population considered his rule illegitimate.

Yet Ceauşescu's paranoia meant that he perpetually feared overthrow, and had made elaborate plans against such a contingency. His fury at the initial protests in Timosoara and demand that the troops fire on demonstrators shows both paranoia and arrogance, but no concern for the population.[74] After Ceauşescu's death, it came to light that he had a plan to flee the country in case of emergency, though what kind of emergency he had in mind was unclear. His insistence throughout his trial that he was the victim of foreign manipulation, however, suggests that it remained inconceivable to him that the Romanian population, or his subordinates in the party and army, might rebel against him.

---

71. Ratesh, *Romania: The Entangled Revolution*, pp. 26–28.

72. Ibid., p. 75.

73. Ceauşescu apparently believed that the Warsaw Pact was behind the uprising in Timosoara, and that the Soviet Union was planning to invade. "New Evidence on the 1989 Crisis in Romania," Documents 5 and 7.

74. "Immediate measures must be taken to rapidly liquidate what is happening in Timosoara . . . where there is an attempt of anti-government action, liquidate it radically, without a word," Ratesh, *Romania: The Entangled Revolution*, p. 28, fn 8.

KNOWLEDGE OF CHANGE IN EASTERN EUROPE

Awareness of developments in other East European states played a small but notable role in Romania. What is particularly notable is how the communication of developments within Romania itself spread protest throughout the country.

Popular objection to the regime was evident in the number of people trying to escape from the country in 1989. A steady stream of refugees began to leave the country in 1989; by the end of the year at least 24,000 had gone to Hungary.[75] Though the flight was minuscule in comparison to the number of refugees fleeing East Germany and Bulgaria, the consequences of being caught trying to escape Romania were higher, as were the potential reprisals against family members left behind. A majority of those fleeing in 1989 were ethnic Hungarians; the pressure being placed on the Hungarian minority in Romania to conform as part of Ceauşescu's "systematization" program may have led many to try to escape. Positive changes in Hungary's political climate may also have convinced both ethnic Hungarians and the ethnic Romanians and Germans who left to attempt to escape Romania. Ceauşescu ordered defenses along Romania's border with Hungary reinforced in 1989 to quell this emigration, though he canceled this order under pressure from the Soviet Union.[76]

Censorship in Romania under Ceauşescu was high. Western publications were not available, and the only source of reliable information about external events was foreign radio broadcasts. When Gorbachev initiated perestroika in 1986, all political, cultural, and social exchanges with the Soviet Union were cut to an absolute minimum, despite Soviet protests. Distribution of Soviet newspapers and magazines was also curtailed.[77] The Romanian press also censored speeches by Soviet officials visiting the country, taking out references encouraging reform.[78] Nonetheless, a sizable portion of the Romanian population listened to foreign radio broadcasts and so was aware of changes in the Eastern bloc. Of the adult population, 63 percent listened to Radio Free Europe, 31 percent to Voice of America, 25 percent to the BBC, and 16 percent to Deutsche

---

75. This figure was reported in November. Of this number, the Hungarian government said that 18,000 were ethnic Hungarians, 4,200 Romanians, and 1,100 ethnic Germans. See *Radio Free Europe Weekly Record of Events,* November 8, 1989.

76. Burke, "Romanian and Soviet Intelligence in the December Revolution," p. 31.

77. Jacques Lévesque, *The Enigma of 1989: The USSR and the Liberation of Eastern Europe* (Berkeley, Calif.: University of California Press, 1997), pp. 192–194.

78. Burke, "Romanian and Soviet Intelligence in the December Revolution," p. 39.

Welle.[79] The population in Timosoara, where the revolution began, also had access to Hungarian and Yugoslavian television, because Timisoara is close to the border with these states.

Popular knowledge of developments elsewhere proved particularly crucial to the spread of the revolution across Romania. Initial reports of the rebellion and bloodshed in Timosoara were broadcast by Western radio on December 17, the day shooting began, and Radio Free Europe extended its normal broadcast that evening. Romanians have noted that this magnified the sense that something important was underway in the country. Slogans aimed at the regime, such as "Today in Timosoara, tomorrow in the whole country," figured in these radio broadcasts.[80] Ceauşescu's own attacks on "hooligans" and foreign manipulation of Romania in his televised speech on December 20 further increased the country's awareness that something was afoot, despite the absence of official acknowledgement of the crisis.

But the most important media impact came from Romanian television itself, when it unwittingly broadcast the scattered protests in the crowd during Ceauşescu's speech in Bucharest on December 21, and the dictator's reaction. On the live television broadcast, Ceauşescu was visibly taken aback by these protests, and this was "widely reported to have incited many Romanians to begin taking to the streets on the night of the 21st."[81] Though uncertainties remain about who first began to protest at the December 21 demonstration, others responded spontaneously by joining in the protests against the regime.[82]

The media also played an important role in the establishment of the NSF as Romania's new government. As the Ceauşescus fled on December 22, many different groups began to form mini-governing bodies. The NSF, however, broadcast its formation on Romanian television, and appealed to the population to defend the new government and the television station from hostile forces. For the next several days, the locus of government was the television station, which stayed on the air throughout the fighting around the country.[83]

---

79. Ratesh, *Romania: The Entangled Revolution*, p. 35, fn. 14.

80. Ibid., pp. 35–36.

81. Burke, "Romanian and Soviet Intelligence in the December Revolution," p. 33.

82. Deak points out that it was not clear if the anticommunist protest was provoked by the Securitate or was truly spontaneous, one of the many remaining mysteries of the period. "Survivors," p. 49.

83. The television station and tower remained unscathed, while all the buildings around it were severely damaged by the fighting. Similarly, the buildings surrounding

FISSURES WITHIN THE REGIME

The facade of unity within the RCP hid the fact that some members of the Romanian leadership appear to have responded more favorably to Gorbachev's calls for reform than did Ceauşescu or his wife, Elena. Some within the Party and military leadership already opposed Ceauşescu's rule in the 1970s. From late 1987 to early 1989, fragments of this opposition became public. Silviu Brucan's open letter to Ceauşescu, condemning his handling of riots in 1987, is one example; an interview he gave to Radio Free Europe, broadcast into Romania in late 1988, more explicitly attacked Ceauşescu's methods of rule, and advocated linking economic and political reforms.[84] In March 1989 six prominent Party members sent a letter to Ceauşescu, strongly criticizing his repression of the Romanian people and stating that this action discredited "the very idea" of socialism.[85]

While none of these incidents can be traced directly to changes taking place outside Romania, Brucan's comments reflected Gorbachev's policies. Moreover, the timing of these public critiques suggests that changes in the surrounding states had convinced these intellectuals that there might be an opportunity to rally some support for domestic changes.

However, opposition to Ceauşescu's rule within the Party did not translate into support for the kind of democratizing reforms that were implemented in the rest of Eastern Europe. Rather, Ceauşescu's opponents within the leadership wanted to replace him, but not the system. Ion Iliescu, for example, rejected political pluralism shortly after the revolution in December 1989, as "an obsolete ideology of the nineteenth century,"[86] and stressed his support for "renovated" socialism.[87] Silviu Brucan had recommended an alternative program to Ceausescu's rule in 1988, which drew heavily on the process of reform in the Soviet Union.[88]

---

the Central Committee building in the center of the city, where the NSF originally met, were heavily damaged, but it was not. This fed uncertainties about who was fighting whom during Romania's revolution, an issue that remains unresolved. See Andrei Codrescu, *The Hole in the Flag: A Romanian Exile's Story of Return and Revolution* (New York: William Morrow, 1991), pp. 195–206.

84. Ratesh, *Romania: The Entangled Revolution*, pp. 99–100.

85. See the extracts from the open letter to President Ceauşescu, published in the *Independent*, March 13, 1989.

86. Deak, "Survivors," p. 50.

87. Lévesque, *The Enigma of 1989*, p. 199.

88. Ratesh, *Romania: The Entangled Revolution*, p. 102.

SOVIET INFLUENCE

There has been a great deal of speculation about Soviet involvement in Romania's revolution in 1989. Several books were published proclaiming a Soviet hand behind these events.[89] The evidence, however, does not support this speculation—nor would significant Soviet involvement make sense, given Gorbachev's adherence to noninterference throughout the rest of the Eastern bloc.

Moscow unquestionably knew that opposition to Ceauşescu existed within the top ranks of the Party and army in the 1980s, but it chose not to back this opposition in efforts to overthrow Ceauşescu. The Soviet Union refused to support a coup attempt in Romania in 1984, and efforts by some of those who later ousted Ceauşescu to enlist help from the Soviet embassy were rebuffed in the 1980s.[90]

Romanians opposed to Ceauşescu also solicited aid from Moscow both before and after the popular uprising in Timosoara that brought about Ceauşescu's fall. Silviu Brucan traveled to Moscow in 1988 and late 1989 and spoke with representatives at the Kremlin on both visits, informing the Soviet leadership of the existence of a group opposed to Ceauşescu, if not of plans to remove the dictator. On both occasions, the Soviet leadership listened but refused to get involved in Romania's internal affairs.[91] Ion Iliescu apparently called the Soviet Embassy in Bucharest on December 22 to keep Moscow informed about developments in Romania, and to let the Soviet Union know who was involved in the NSF—before its official creation. He also apparently requested Soviet military assistance, which Moscow declined to give. Iliescu's action may have led to a phone exchange that took place between the Soviet embassy and the Romanian Army Chief of Staff, in which a Soviet diplomat apparently offered military aid, which the Chief of Staff, General Guse, declined. Gorbachev announced to the Congress of People's Deputies that the Soviet Union had received a request for aid from Romania, but that

---

89. See, for example, Michel Castex, *A Lie as Big as the Century: Romania, the History of a Manipulation* (Paris: Editions Albin Michel, 1990); Radu Portocala, *Autopsy of the Romanian Coup d'Etat: In the Country of the Triumphant Lie* (Paris: Editions calmann-Levy, 1990); and Anneli Ute Gabanyi, *The Unfinished Revolution: Romania between Dictatorship and Democracy* (Munchen Zurich: Serie Piper, 1990), as cited in Ratesh, *Romania: The Entangled Revolution*, pp. 80–85.

90. General Vasile Militaru apparently tried to get Soviet support in 1987, but was told that its diplomats were "forbidden to interfere in domestic Romanian affairs." Burke, "Romanian and Soviet Intelligence in the December Revolution," p. 42.

91. Lévesque, *The Enigma of 1989*, p 200; and Ratesh, *Romania: The Entangled Revolution*, pp. 103–104.

the Romanian Army's Chief of Staff had assured them that the situation was under control. The Soviet Union did offer humanitarian assistance and ammunition to the new Romanian government, but it does not appear to have gotten involved in the Romanian uprising.[92] As in other countries, Moscow's most significant impact resulted from its refusal to intervene in internal developments. In Romania's case, this was especially significant because Moscow chose not to inform Ceauşescu of potential plans to oust him.[93]

SUMMARY
In spite of the flood of changes across the Eastern bloc by the end of 1989, Ceauşescu appears to have remained opposed to reform, and confident of his ability to continue in power. He was clearly uncomfortable with the changes in neighboring countries, but this led him to call for intervention to stop the process, rather than to introduce reforms himself. Ceauşescu's overthrow resulted from a popular uprising against his rule, as citizens across the country joined protests that were only inflamed by the government's efforts to quell them with force. Members of the ruling party who had long opposed Ceauşescu managed to gain control of the government during the course of the revolution, and introduce a reform Communist government that sustained its position by championing the revolution.

Conclusion

In Romania, the regime decisively rejected the option of early reform, and indeed, the concept of reform as presented by Gorbachev altogether. Nicolae Ceauşescu, Romania's leader, was convinced of his legitimacy and the correctness of his policies. In spite of the country's disastrous economic circumstances for which he was largely responsible, he denied that there was any need for reform.

Late reform would be expected from above if elements within the regime wanted reform, and were sufficiently strong to engineer a change in the Party's leadership. Clearly, some members of Romania's leadership recognized by 1989 that Romania was increasingly isolated by its policy choices, and that these policies were retarding the country's development rather than promoting it. Silviu Brucan, for example, noted that "if we

---

92. Ratesh, *Romania: The Entangled Revolution*, pp. 109–112.

93. These plans were unlikely to succeed on their own, given the failure of previous efforts to remove Ceauşescu.

continue on the same path, Romania will be the first country in the world to deliberately plan its underdevelopment for the year 2000."[94] Opposition to Ceauşescu within the leadership, however, was far too weak to remove him from power. Ceauşescu relied heavily on repression, fear, and surveillance even of those in leadership positions. This effectively ground the majority within the Party as well as the population into passivity. See Table 7.

What appears to have occurred in Romania in December 1989 is a revolution instigated from below, the second possibility in a late reforming state. That demonstrations and protests began in Timosoara is significant; its citizens had greater access to information from outside Romania due to their exposure to radio and television from Hungary and Yugoslavia. They were thus more likely to be aware of events in other parts of Eastern Europe. The process of rebellion did not immediately mimic the earlier pattern in Eastern Europe of demands for democratization and greater freedoms. This can be explained by the purpose of the initial protest—to prevent the eviction of a priest—and the very directed popular anger against Ceauşescu, leading to calls of "down with the dictator." Notably, even in the face of attacks by the army in Timosoara, the crowds appealed for a peaceful protest. As demonstrations spread, more specific demands emerged and local officials attempted to negotiate with popular representatives, a process similar to that adopted by regional leaders in East Germany.

It seems clear that Ceauşescu's downfall was primarily the result of widespread popular protest against his rule, as the Timosoara demonstrations rapidly enveloped the country and the capital. However, the Romanian case differs from other East European cases in several important ways. First, this was the only case in which significant and protracted violence occurred.[95] The Ceauşescu regime was willing to use force against the population, even after the capitulation of several other East European regimes without violence. This reinforces the proposition that Ceauşescu continued to have complete faith in his right to rule. His fury at the public protests and at his trial, as well as his apparent shock at the protests against him during his speech in Bucharest, point to his inability to comprehend either that his rule was viewed by the population

---

94. Ratesh, *Romania: The Entangled Revolution,* p. 100.

95. Some violence occurred in other countries, notably in the beating of peaceful demonstrators by police in Czechoslovakia. The scale of violence in Romania was far greater. The official death toll was 162 throughout the country, and 1107 wounded. "New Evidence on the 1989 Crisis in Romania."

Table 7. Indicators Measuring the Romanian Regime's Attitudes in 1989.

EARLY REFORM

INDICATORS OF REGIME'S RECOGNITION OF NEED FOR REFORM

INDICATOR	ROMANIA	REGIME'S ATTITUDE
Previous reform efforts	No reforms	Rejection of need for reforms
Nature of state's economic and political structure	Distorted Marxist-Leninist model	
Problems facing the state	Severe economic difficulties	
Response to Gorbachev	Negative	

INDICATORS OF REGIME'S PERCEPTION OF ITS ABILITY TO SURVIVE

INDICATOR	ROMANIA	REGIME'S ATTITUDE
Statements of legitimacy	Yes	Perception of rule as legitimate
Intra-regime conflict	Minimal	
Level of repression	High	

UNDERSTANDING LATE REFORM

COGNITIVE PROCESSES: INDICATORS OF REGIME'S RESISTANCE TO CHANGE

INDICATOR	ROMANIA	REGIME'S ATTITUDE
Resistance to need for reform	Yes	Resistant to change
Statements of faith in system	Yes	
Statements of legitimacy	Yes	

EVIDENCE OF THE DEMONSTRATION EFFECT

INDICATOR	ROMANIA	EFFECT WITHIN THE STATE
Communication of developments elsewhere	Yes	Evidence of the demonstration effect
Mimicry	Yes, by regime	

as illegitimate and based on repression, or that changes in the Eastern bloc had undermined the option of continued rule by such methods.

Romania's revolution differed from others also in the nature of the leaders who harnessed and eventually "led" the revolution. As in Bulgaria and East Germany, where the communist regimes had doggedly repressed and restricted opposition to the regime, Romania had virtually no leaders outside the Party with the popular stature to lead the protest or establish a new form of goverment. Instead, the majority of those associated with the NSF were members or former members of the RCP leadership.[96] Instead of opposition figures directing the course of events, those who had earlier opposed Ceauşescu from within the Party rapidly took charge. They were thus able to ensure their control over Romania's new government. While they initially parroted support for democratization and pluralism, reform was in effect hijacked by elements of the Communist leadership. The result was a hesitantly reform-communist goverment more similar to Bulgaria's than to the noncommunist governments that emerged in the rest of Eastern Europe.

Cognitive factors are illuminated starkly in the Romanian case. Ceauşescu's megalomania left little chance that he would perceive the need to modify his rule. His tight grip on power, and the methods he used to ensure that no obvious replacements to him existed, helped sustain his rule by perpetuating fear, passivity, and suspicion throughout population and elite.

The popular revolt reflects the effect of change in Eastern Europe. Earlier protests, including one in 1987, did not spread because of effective repression by the regime. In contrast, in 1989 isolated demonstrations in Timosoara triggered a reaction across the country. The fact that similar protests had succeeded throughout Eastern Europe must have helped incite the population to respond to news of protests. As it became increasingly evident that the regime's efforts to quell demonstrations within the country had failed—most dramatically on national television in Bucharest—ever larger numbers of people were motivated to join the protest against the regime.

Finally, the NSF's behavior mimicked the process in other East European states, at least superficially. At the outset, the NSF presented itself as a coalition of those in favor of "democracy" in Romania, and included in its ranks the most prominent critics of the previous regime. This mimicked the pattern that had developed in Round Table negotiations else-

---

96. The NSF initially included a wide range of figures, including the handful of prominent dissidents in the country. Yet many dissidents first learned of their "inclusion" in the NSF from television broadcasts.

where, in which long-time dissidents had negotiated new political arrangements with failing regimes. The NSF also proclaimed goals similar to those in other states, including the need for pluralism, banning of the Communist Party, and its own interim role as a caretaker government until new elections. Its failure to follow through with these promises indicated some of the long-term consequences of Ceauşescu's rule. Not only was there no real democratic opposition able to challenge the former Communists, but these ex-communists found it hard to relinquish Ceauşescu's methods of relying on repression and the centralization of control.

Chapter 8

Conclusion

During the Cold War, most observers perceived the states of the Warsaw Pact as relatively homogenous, sharing communist-led regimes, centralized economies, and passive if discontented populations. The lifting of Soviet control quickly revealed the differences between these states. Variations were first obvious in their acceptance or rejection of the prospect of reform put forward by Gorbachev; greater variation emerged as states yielded to internal and external pressures and initiated reforms.

The collapse of communism took diverse trajectories in Eastern Europe as a result of different regimes' domestic standing and the reaction of domestic actors to developments in neighboring states. In early reforming states, various domestic factors convinced the regimes to accept the opportunity to introduce reforms. The Polish government was compelled to do so to address popular discontent; and Hungary's regime believed it could continue to rule the country in a more open political climate, and at the same time address the chronic problems resulting from the state's socialist structure. In both countries, the regime's perception of its legitimacy and its comprehension of the problems confronting the state played a major role in shaping the initiation of political reforms.

In the late reforming states, the degree to which both regime and population comprehended the depth of changes progressing through Eastern Europe influenced the initiation of reform. Regime leaders in several states were unable to accept the need for change. In some states, the combination of this conservatism and the growing restlessness of a population unhappy with communist rule eventually triggered the widespread popular protests that drove regimes from power. In other states, competing groups within the leadership took advantage of the changes spreading outside and inside the state to remove unpopular leaders and take control.

Patterns of Reform in Eastern Europe

EARLY REFORM

Two variables were critical to a regime's decision to introduce or reject political and economic reforms in Eastern Europe in the late 1980s: whether it recognized the need for substantial reforms; and whether it believed it could endure in freer political circumstances.

A regime's appreciation of the need for political and economic revisions was central to its acceptance or rejection of Gorbachev's advocacy of reform in the Eastern bloc. In both states where reforms emerged early in the reform process, Poland and Hungary, the communist regimes were well aware of the need for change. Moreover, each acknowledged the linkages between economics and politics, and were aware that earlier attempts to tinker with the socialist economic structure without political changes that altered the management of the economy had failed. Only in these two states, whose regimes acknowledged the need for reforms, did such changes emerge early, in response to Soviet leader Mikhail Gorbachev's invitation to reform. See Table 2 in Chapter 1 for an evaluation of how the East European states responded to the challenge of reform.

For decades, efforts by the Polish regime to resolve economic difficulties through price increases and limited structural reforms had led to protests from a population unreconciled to communist rule. This cycle of regime tinkering and protest culminated in the standoff between regime and population in the 1980s, after the regime introduced martial law in an attempt to quell the Solidarity movement that emerged in 1980. When Gorbachev came to power, the Polish regime led by General Jaruzelski was among the first to experiment with political reforms and significant economic changes in an effort to improve its standing with the population and to ameliorate the country's severe economic crisis.

In Hungary, reforms in the early 1980s had already begun to include experimentation with market mechanisms and partial openness to the international market, and a wide-ranging debate about political reform had begun well before 1985. The regime also had tinkered with the Marxist-Leninist economic model in the past, notably with the introduction of the New Economic Mechanism in the late 1960s and early 1970s. Though Party leader János Kádár rejected significant political changes in the early 1980s, the country's experience with prior reform attempts had helped convince many in the Party that political reforms must accompany economic reforms. By the end of 1988, the regime had begun to propose significant changes in the state's political structure.

A regime's perception of its ability to survive in a more open political environment influenced the reform process in two ways. A regime's perception of its legitimacy determined, to a large degree, whether it was willing to risk opening the political process to other forces within the state. If it considered its rule legitimate, the regime was more likely to believe it could compete against other political forces. In addition, conflicts within a regime sometimes led factions to turn to groups outside the regime in an effort to find allies to bolster their own political position in the state. A regime's sense that it could survive was sustained to some degree by its faith that it would retain a controlling stake in a liberalized political system; when political liberalizations appeared in Eastern Europe in 1989, the goal remained a limited political pluralism, rather than a fully competitive political process.

The Polish regime's perception of its ability to survive was mixed, at best. The regime had been discredited by its imposition of martial law and the suppression of Solidarity, and in the mid-1980s the regime appeared to have little legitimacy with the population. Yet Jaruzelski and some of his associates believed that the Party had sufficient legitimacy to survive within the partially open political structure they envisaged when they opened negotiations with Solidarity. Their faith in the Party's ability to compete apparently rested on the population's endorsement of earlier government reform proposals, the decline of support for Solidarity in the years prior to the initiation of Round Table negotiations, and the expectation that the Communist Party's domestic role would be protected in the new system they proposed. Popular support for Gorbachev in Poland probably also bolstered the regime's belief that the introduction of reforms along the Soviet model would gain it greater domestic support. In the end, the Party was shocked by its defeat in the controlled elections of June 1989, and the careful political bargain it had constructed with Solidarity crumbled in the face of popular pressure for broader change.

The Hungarian Party leadership was confident that it could compete in a more open political environment. Both comparatively radical reformers and conservatives in the Party leadership believed that the Party would continue to lead even in a multiparty setting. Opinion polls supported this assumption; the Party continued to be the strongest political force in the state throughout the summer of 1989.

In Hungary, conflict within the regime was a major factor in the Party's loss of its relative popularity and corresponding political position. Power struggles among prominent members of the leadership and differences in their views about the appropriate nature of reforms prevented the Party leadership from formulating a strategy for competing in the new political system it helped to create. This enabled opposition groups to strengthen their standing relative to the Party, leading to its defeat in free elections in 1990.

LATE REFORM

The other states in the Warsaw Pact initially rejected the introduction of reforms, partly because they denied the need for political as well as economic reforms. The economies of most of the late reforming states were not in desperate straits, so the regimes could argue that economic reforms were less urgent and political reforms not called for—though none could claim to have a vibrant, healthy economy. (Romania's economy was in disastrous condition, but the regime insistently denied this.) Several argued that there was simply no need to change the economic and political model their states relied on.

The regime's perceptions of their legitimacy varied. Some leaders rejected reforms in the belief that their rule was ideologically justified or not in danger. Others did so in the belief that they could not keep power in a more competitive political environment. The experience of 1968 in Czechoslovakia, and the artificial nature of East Germany, a separate German state established by the Soviet Union, created fundamental legitimacy problems for these two states. This reinforced the concerns of the regimes in these states, and sustained their rejection of reform. The Bulgarian and Romanian regimes were confident of their legitimacy, but rejected the need for substantial reforms.

In the later reforming states, the initiation of change was influenced by a second set of factors: the regime's comprehension or denial of the inescapability of change over the course of 1989, and the demonstration effect that the changes elsewhere in the Soviet Union and Eastern Europe created.

In several late reforming states, regime leaders were unable to adjust to the changed circumstances within the Eastern bloc. They did not revise their policies to attempt to respond to the changed political climate. Instead, they clung to the old system, insisting that socialism should be defended, that significant economic reforms were not necessary, and that the communist party's monopoly on power remained justified. Their discomfort with events in the bloc was evident in their increasing attacks on the West and on opposition groups within the bloc.

In East Germany and Czechoslovakia, the regimes' behavior and statements by leaders in 1989 suggested an inability to appreciate how dramatically the changes outside their states were influencing the political environment within the state. They also suggest regime paralysis, an inability to change behavior despite awareness of changing circumstances. Both their inability to comprehend what was going on and their incapacity to respond coincide with what cognitive theories would lead us to expect from leaders with long tenures in office, confronted with unfamiliar policy proposals. People's cognitive capabilities are limited, making it difficult for them to recognize the significance of events that do not fit within the parameters of their previous experience. People use cognitive tools to simplify the information they receive. This leads them to fit new information into their preexisting views of the world, and to discount or ignore evidence that threatens their view of the world.

The top leaders must be distinguished somewhat from the regimes in these states, particularly in the case of East Germany. Both East German leader Erich Honecker and Czechoslovak leader Milos Jakeš steadfastly rejected reform, and appeared unable to comprehend the depth of the changes in the Eastern bloc. At least some members of the Party leadership in these states were concerned about the continued rejection of reform, but the strong concentration of power at the top meant that change did not emerge in these states until provoked from below. Like Honecker and Jakeš, Bulgarian leader Todor Zhivkov showed his inability to adjust to the changed conditions in the Eastern bloc. The evidence suggests that he responded to Gorbachev as he had to previous Soviet leaders, by adopting policies that appeared similar to those of the Soviet Union on the assumption that the appearance of compliance would satisfy the new Soviet leadership as it had in the past. Zhivkov's long tenure also meant that, like Honecker and Jakeš, he might be held responsible for Bulgaria's problems if the need for change was acknowledged or reforms were introduced.

The diffusion of ideas and information across borders in Eastern Europe played a critical role in catalyzing the bloc-wide process of reform. This diffusion provoked more people to reject the communist system through flight or protest. The visible emergence of broader protests impelled substantial portions of the population in different East European states to emulate the behavior they were learning about, and join the protests against communist rule.

By the fall of 1989, the regimes in both East Germany and Czechoslovakia were confronted with continual protests, as the population overcame its apathy. (The frontispiece gives an indication of the extent of the demonstration effect in the fall of 1989.) In East Germany, public rejection of the regime was sparked by the East German exodus to the West, which indicated the hopelessness of large segments of the population. The exodus had a snowballing effect, goading others to take similar action. The East German population's cognizance of this hemorrhage—through reportage on Western television and the disappearance of colleagues or friends—provoked a rise in demonstrations calling on the regime to respond to the crisis by introducing reforms. A succession of personnel changes in the Party leadership and promises of new reforms and negotiations with opposition groups failed to halt the demonstrations or flight, leading to the decision that unification of East Germany with West Germany, which occurred in October 1990, was the only way to stabilize the situation in East Germany.

Once protests began in Czechoslovakia in November 1989, word of mouth and handbills printed by students and activists affected the population more than Western television, to which fewer had access. Students and activists worked to spread the message of protest. Working class support for the protests was apparently stimulated by the example of the students' willingness to struggle for change despite the widespread apathy of their elders.

Evidence of the demonstration effect in these two states can be seen in several ways. Opposition groups in both states duplicated calls for dialogue with the regime once negotiations began in Poland and Hungary. Groups expressed their support for dissidents in other states, indicating their awareness of developments in neighboring states. Moreover, the calls for change that emerged in protests echoed the earlier demands in Poland and Hungary. The East German exodus itself resulted from the diffusion of information; news that Hungary had removed its border fences with Austria led people to go there on vacation, to try to escape across the frontier.

Regimes were also affected by the diffusion of information. This was most obvious in states where fractures developed within the ruling regime. In these cases, some groups within the leadership were moved by events at home and abroad to force the removal of inflexible leaders and initiate reform. The transition in Bulgaria showed the demonstration effect at work on the regime; it introduced reforms in the absence of significant pressure from below. Conflict within the regime had not been apparent during Zhivkov's tenure, but discomfort with his refusal to change policies led some members of the Bulgarian Politburo to recognize that real changes were needed to resolve the state's economic problems, and these could only be introduced by removing Zhivkov. Honecker's fall from power in East Germany also was induced by fractures within the regime that were intensified by the spread of popular protests.

Developments in Eastern Europe in 1989, which demonstrated Soviet tolerance for substantial change, clearly influenced the Bulgarian leadership. Members of the Bulgarian leadership had tried to obtain Gorbachev's full support for Zhivkov's ouster in July 1989, and received his by then standard refusal to get involved. Since Bulgaria's leaders were not willing to act independently of the Soviet Union, Gorbachev's noncommittal response served at the time to inhibit their effort to remove Zhivkov. However, Moscow's acceptance of developments in Poland and Hungary during the summer of 1989, and its equanimity as protests swelled in East Germany, indicated Soviet acquiescence to even a communist party's removal from power.

Finally, the Romanian case showed both a regime's utter refusal to adjust and popular rejection of the existing system of rule. During the 1980s, Ceauşescu effectively was the regime. Convinced of his own infallibility, he vehemently rejected the need to change his political and economic policies. Effective repression kept popular opposition to the regime minuscule; within the Party leadership, only a handful of people dared to contemplate alternatives to Ceauşescu's rule. The transition in Romania was sparked by popular protests in a regional capital, which then spread across the country. Yet there were no opposition figures in the state capable of leading the country, and elements of the Party leadership secured control of the government. The result was a popular revolt that led to the removal of Ceauşescu, but not the Communists.

Both the popular revolt and the opposition to Ceauşescu within the Party were influenced by developments in Eastern Europe. Popular objection to the regime's policies had long existed, but earlier protests were isolated and quickly squashed. Over half of Romania's population listened to foreign broadcasts and were thus aware of events elsewhere in Eastern Europe. The protests in December 1989 spread across the country, as Romanians learned of them from Western radio broadcasts. The demonstration effect was evident also in the National Salvation Front's early adoption of calls for democratization, a pluralist system, and the abolition of the Communist Party. These calls mimicked the appearance of reform rather than the reality; the NSF later tried to discredit other opposition groups and rejected substantial economic reforms.[1]

---

1. The demonstration effect was also evident in Hungary, an early reforming state. Its regime had adopted a variation on the Polish model of Round Table negotiations in the spring of 1989, making it the first example of the demonstration effect. By September, when negotiations concluded in Hungary, the political climate in the state had been changed by Soviet acceptance of a Solidarity prime minister in Poland. As the Communist Party in Hungary fragmented during the fall, the opposition was emboldened to take a more anticommunist stance, which helped erode the regime's support, as did Moscow's acquiescence to the rejection of communist party control in succes-

Long-Term Implications for Eastern Europe, and Beyond

How did the shape of the transition in different states affect subsequent developments in Eastern Europe? The region of the former Warsaw Pact has evolved into two groups of states: Poland, Hungary, and the Czech Republic; and the others, Bulgaria and Romania, with Slovakia awkwardly in between. East Germany has been integrated with West Germany since 1990. The former group has had greater success in adopting democratic political models and introducing market reforms. Two factors appear to be involved here: the pull of the West, and the continued rule of ex-communists after 1989 in Romania and Bulgaria, and in Slovakia after its separation from the Czech Republic at the end of 1992.

These factors are related; indeed, one reason the transition in Bulgaria and Romania had a less democratic outcome was because opposition figures and the general population in these states had less exposure to westerners or Western ideas during the Cold War. The variation in levels of interest continued in the 1990s in a self-perpetuating process. The West's lack of attention to the transition in Bulgaria and Romania did little to encourage these states to make greater efforts to democratize, while their failure to democratize was cited as the reason for less Western interest in these states. Poland, Hungary, and the Czech Republic, which enjoyed more Western interest, had a reasonable hope of integration into Western institutions. In these states, the prospect of joining the West helped reinforce the importance of sustaining strong democratic institutions, which were seen as a minimum prerequisite for inclusion in the West. The other states have taken longer to consolidate democratic structures. While the West did not induce the changes in Eastern Europe in 1989, the pull of the West strongly shaped the aspirations of citizens in these states. In this respect, the Western democracies remained an important model during the post–Cold War period. Indeed, the fact that Bulgaria, Romania, and Slovakia continue to strive to establish solid democratic institutions underscores the power that this model, and potential inclusion in the Western community of nations, holds for this region.

The continued rule of ex-communists or reform communists was a second critical factor in the development of the East European states during the 1990s. In the states where the communists (or ex-communists) remained in power, the introduction of market-oriented economic reforms and the consolidation of strong democratic institutions (including multiple political parties) has been slower. In effect, the change in these states

---

sive East European states. The bounds of the system within which the HSWP's calculations of legitimacy had been made had, in essence, dissolved.

in 1989 did not signify a complete rejection of the earlier model, as it did in Poland, Hungary, the Czech Republic, and East Germany. The new leaders imitated the declarations of change made in earlier reforming states but did not relinquish the methods of rule learned during the Soviet period, including the one-party system and obstruction of opposing groups. Certainly, these states were not the only Eastern bloc states to have trouble discarding the previous system; throughout Eastern Europe, leaders and populations struggled to accept ideas such as the need for a loyal opposition, and strong political parties developed slowly because the party model had been discredited by communist party monopoly.[2] Yet the continuation in power of former communists, and the smaller size of opposition groups in these states, made the process of developing new political institutions and methods slower in Bulgaria and Romania, and to some degree in Slovakia.

A third notable factor in the aftermath of the East European transitions is that the perception of legitimacy on which the early reforming states based their actions proved to be more accurate in the long run than it seemed at the end of 1989. In both Poland and Hungary, the reformed communist parties (now called socialist or social democratic parties) regained power in free elections in the mid-1990s. Of course, the parties that regained power in these states were the reform wings of the earlier ruling parties; moreover, they worked hard to reshape themselves and their images in these states. Yet the communist parties benefitted from the difficulties of the economic transition, since the more "democratic" parties that won power at the beginning of the decade suffered from their association with the extreme economic hardships of the first few years of the transition. In effect, the communists in these states had the last laugh, because one motivation behind the establishment of more pluralist governments in 1989 had been the desire by the ruling parties to share the blame with opposition groups for the difficulties that they knew were to come in addressing these states' economic problems.

The peaceful collapse of the Soviet Union's outer empire helped to shape the decline of the imperial core itself. Actors within the Soviet republics learned lessons from the East European example for their own

---

2. For an in-depth analysis of the transition to democracy in parts of Eastern Europe, see Karen Dawisha and Bruce Parrot, *The Consolidation of Democracy in East-Central Europe* (Cambridge: Cambridge University Press, 1997). See also Michael Mandelbaum, ed., *Post-Communism: Four Perspectives* (New York: Council on Foreign Relations, 1996); H. Welsh, "Deal with the Communist Past: Central and East European Experience after 1990," *Europe-Asia Studies*, Vol. 48, No. 3 (1996), pp. 413–428; and Aldona Jawlowska and Marian Kempny, eds., *Cultural Dilemmas of Post-Communist Societies* (Warsaw: IFiS Publishers, 1994).

struggles against Moscow. The nonviolent model that emerged from Eastern Europe helped shape similar peaceful independence campaigns within the Soviet Union, notably in the Baltic republics and Russia itself.[3] Unfortunately, in the former Soviet Union the political reforms introduced by Mikhail Gorbachev have encountered considerably greater difficulties. In Russia and most of the other newly independent states, the spillover from successful reform in Eastern Europe has been distressingly limited.

The reasons that explain the uneven pace of reform in Eastern Europe offer at least a partial explanation. The pull of the West in the former Soviet Union has varied widely over time and in the different republics. Western support for democracy in Russia in particular has fluctuated, as Western leaders responded uncertainly to the prospects for a different relationship with the Soviet Union's successor. Western leaders failed to accept Gorbachev's invitation to change the international system completely by embracing Russia and drawing it in to the major Western institutions.[4] Yet Russia's leaders missed the opportunity as well. Former communists continue to rule in many of the former Soviet republics, and the commitment of these leaders to democratic institutions and market-based reforms varies widely.[5]

The success of democratization efforts in Eastern Europe provides hope for Russia, however. The power of ideas expressed through the actions of a myriad of individuals helped break these states free of the Soviet empire. Beliefs can change, and even when leaders are the impediments to change, they can be moved—or removed—by the demonstration of support for new ideas.

Issues For Further Research

This book has provided a theoretically based explanation for the collapse of communist regimes in Eastern Europe. This explanation has implica-

---

3. See Mark Kramer, "The Collapse of East European Communism and the Repercussions within the Soviet Union." Forthcoming *Journal of Cold War Studies* Vol. 5, No. 3 (Summer 2003).

4. Some in the West continue to argue that Russian inclusion in institutions such as NATO should be seriously considered. See Celeste Wallander, "Why Russia Belongs in NATO," *Christian Science Monitor*, December 31, 1996, p. 19.

5. The notable exceptions are the Baltic republics, Estonia, Lithuania, and Latvia, which rejected communist rule and have introduced signficant political and economic reforms.

tions for international theory at several levels of analysis; I examine them in this section.

REALIST AND CONSTRUCTIVIST APPROACHES

The peaceful erosion of the Soviet Union's outer empire presents hard issues for both realist and constructivist theories. Some scholars have criticized realist approaches for failing to predict or explain the end of the Cold War and the collapse of the Soviet Union, and others have defended realism, arguing that realist theories can explain these events.[6] The peaceful erosion of the empire, and later the peaceful collapse of the Soviet Union itself, have been explained away by realists as merely a reflection of the changing power balance in the international system. But why did the Soviet Union tolerate the loss of Eastern Europe, given that few states or empires concede collapse without a fight? Gorbachev rejected the use of force as a way to protect Soviet gains in Eastern Europe, choosing instead to adhere to the principles on which he based his reform effort in the Soviet Union. His adherence to normative principles contradicts a realist understanding of state behavior in the international system. Realist approaches expect states to act on the basis of their position in the international system, with the primary goal the preservation of the state's security.[7]

The collapse of communism in Eastern Europe also provides a challenge for constructivist theories. Scholars adopting a constructivist approach argue that statesmen interpret the international system on the basis of shared understandings of how the system works; if these shared understandings are changed, the system can also change.[8] Changing the

---

6. For some critiques, see John Lewis Gaddis, "International Relations Theory and the End of the Cold War," *International Security*, Vol. 17, No. 3 (Winter 1992/93), pp. 5–58; and Richard Ned Lebow, "The Long Peace, the End of the Cold War, and the Failure of Realism," *International Organization*, Vol. 48, No. 2 (Spring 1994), pp. 269–277. For approaches arguing that realism can explain the end of the Cold War, see William C. Wohlforth, "Realism and the End of the Cold War," *International Security*, Vol. 19, No. 3 (Winter 1994/95), pp. 91–129; and Kenneth N. Waltz, "The Emerging Structure of International Politics," *International Security*, Vol. 18, No. 2 (Fall 1993), pp. 44–79.

7. Moreover, the Soviet Union's military capability in Europe should have enabled it to prevent the collapse of the communist regimes in Eastern Europe if it chose to; it had over 500,000 troops based in Eastern Europe in 1989. See *The Military Balance, 1989–1990* (London: International Institute for Strategic Studies, 1989), pp. 38–40.

8. See, for some examples, Richard K. Ashley, "The Poverty of Neorealism," *International Organization*, Vol. 38, No. 2 (Spring 1984), pp. 225–286; Alexander Wendt, "The

norms on which international behavior is based, then, should lead to alterations in the way the international system is understood—and in how it functions. While some constructivist scholars have claimed that the peaceful collapse of the Soviet Empire, and then the Soviet Union, represents a "fundamental transformation of the international system" based on changes in the norms underpinning the system, this conclusion seems at best premature.[9] Gorbachev attempted to do just this, but failed.

There are two aspects of this failure. First, Gorbachev was trying to change domestic politics and the international arena simultaneously, and to apply the same principles to both. Gorbachev accepted the results of the East European reform process in 1989 because of his belief in the principles he was trying to inculcate in the Soviet Union. Gorbachev refused to defend the right of the Soviet Union to its gains in Eastern Europe because he recognized that the systemic changes he wanted to make—both at home and abroad—could not survive on a foundation of repression. To use force in Eastern Europe, Gorbachev would have had to renounce the principles on which he was trying to reshape politics in the Soviet Union, thereby jettisoning domestic reform.[10]

Second, Gorbachev wanted to create a world more friendly to the Soviet Union by changing both how world leaders (and citizens) viewed the international system, and the Soviet Union's international reputation. Gorbachev expected to make the East European leaders understand and share his goals, and to convince Western leaders of their efficacy.[11] Yet he

---

Agent-Structure Problem in International Relations Theory," *International Organization*, Vol. 41, No. 3 (Summer 1987), pp. 335–370; Alexander Wendt, "Anarchy is What States Make of It: The Social Construction of Power Politics," *International Organization*, Vol. 46, No. 2 (Spring 1992), pp. 391–425; and Martha Finnemore, *National Interests and International Security* (Ithaca, N.Y.: Cornell University Press, 1996).

9. See, for example, Rey Koslowski and Friedrich V. Krathchwil, "Understanding Change in International Politics: The Soviet Empire's Demise and the International System," in Richard Ned Lebow and Thomas Risse-Kappen, eds., *International Relations Theory and the End of the Cold War* (New York: Columbia University Press, 1995), pp. 127–166.

10. See, for example, Eduard Shevardnadze, *The Future Belongs to Freedom*, trans. by Catherine A. Fitzpatrick (New York: Free Press, 1991), pp. 118–120.

11. The history of Soviet–East European relations illustrates how difficult it is to shape the way people construct their view of the world. Throughout the Cold War, the example of the Western model confounded efforts by Soviet and East European leaders to convince their populations of the superiority of the socialist system. When Gorbachev tried to find a middle ground between communism and capitalism, the Western alternative thwarted his efforts in Eastern Europe. Populations there grasped at freedom and Western-style democracy, rather than perestroika. The pull of the West as an alternative model proved too strong.

failed to establish broad-based support for the vision of a Europe without divisions. Instead, NATO expanded to the east in 1999, admitting three new members from the former Warsaw Pact, violating promises made to Gorbachev by the United States in 1990. Some scholars and policymakers continue to argue that NATO must hedge against a potential Russian threat. While the threat of a major interstate conflict in Europe is lower than it has been for centuries, the dominant structural elements of the Cold War remain; the international system is no longer bipolar, but it has not been fundamentally transformed. An important lesson of Gorbachev's failure is that it takes more than one leader or state to create a new paradigm for the international system. Changing this paradigm may be a matter of changing ideas in many countries, a daunting task.

These approaches, and the international relations literature in general, have few theories that help explain change short of war or revolution. One reason may be the focus on systems-level factors. The peaceful collapse of communism in Eastern Europe, and the subsequent disintegration of the Soviet Union cannot be understood without examining state-level policies, and the perceptions of leaders as well as populations in these states. The sources of conflict today seem increasingly to be generated from domestic causes; the roots of peaceful change are likely to be found at the domestic and individual level as well.[12] Both realist and constructivist approaches would benefit from better integration of state- and individual-level approaches.[13]

Determining how change short of war occurs is particularly important in the nuclear age. Yet understanding the ways that the existence of nuclear weapons (particularly in such large numbers) has changed how international politics are conducted cannot be assessed at the systemic level alone. The crucial question is whether and how nuclear weapons

---

12. For example, Samuel Huntington has highlighted the importance of moderate leaders if transitions to democracy are to result in balanced constitutions and government structures, rather than promoting extremist policies with the potential to lead to strife. Huntington, *The Third Wave: Democratization in the Late Twentieth Century* (Norman, Okla.: University of Oklahoma Press, 1991), pp. 109–163; Michael E. Brown has also stressed the importance of leadership and addressing internal problems to avoid conflict. See Brown, "Internal Conflict and International Action," in Michael E. Brown, ed., *The International Dimensions of Internal Conflict* (Cambridge, Mass: MIT Press, 1996), pp. 606–614.

13. Some scholars in each approach are doing this kind of work. See, for example, Jack Snyder, *Myths of Empire: Domestic Politics and International Ambition* (Ithaca, N.Y.: Cornell University Press, 1991); Elizabeth Kier, *Imagining War: French and British Military Doctrine Between the Wars* (Princeton: Princeton University Press, 1997); and Jeffrey Checkel, *Ideas and International Political Change: Soviet/Russian Behavior and the End of the Cold War* (New Haven, Conn.: Yale University Press, 1997).

have changed the way leaders think about their options, not only with regard to war, but also with regard to domestic and international changes.

For this reason, the role that nuclear weapons played in the peaceful erosion of the Soviet empire deserves more scrutiny. The existence of large nuclear arsenals on both sides of the East-West divide for much of the Cold War makes it hard to attribute Cold War stability to bipolarity alone. We need to know how the existence of large nuclear arsenals affected the choices of statesmen and individuals as the Eastern bloc was starting to unravel in 1989. Did awareness of the inherent dangers if violent protests got out of hand contribute to the peaceful nature of the popular protests in Eastern Europe? Clearly, the superpowers recognized the need for restraint during 1989, but were individuals in different countries in Eastern Europe equally aware of the need for caution? Only a few scholars have directly addressed the question of the role nuclear weapons played in shaping the end of the Cold War.[14] If we want to understand better the positive or negative role nuclear weapons may play in future crises, then we need to determine how important nuclear weapons were in perpetuating peace during the collapse of this empire.[15] This is particularly critical given the emergence of two new nuclear powers in 1998, India and Pakistan, and the startling degree to which the threat posed by nuclear weapons has receded from the public consciousness.

DEMOCRATIZATION AND REGIME CHANGE

Why does one state suffer violent conflict over who has the right to rule, while another makes efforts to negotiate new systems of government peacefully? The state's previous exposure to democracy is clearly part of the answer.[16] The external attention it receives and its affinity with the major democratic countries in the international system, the United States and the states of Western Europe, also appear to be crucial. These variables are particularly evident in the changes within Eastern Europe and the former Soviet Union since 1989. States that felt shared bonds with the West, and could hope to be integrated into the Western community of nations, have been more successful at establishing democratic systems of

---

14. One example is Kenneth A. Oye, "Explaining the End of the Cold War: Morphological and Behavioral Adaptations to the Nuclear Peace?" in Richard Ned Lebow and Thomas Risse-Kappen, eds., *International Relations Theory and the End of the Cold War* (New York: Columbia University Press, 1995), pp. 57–84.

15. On the debate over the future and utility of nuclear weapons, see Scott D. Sagan and Kenneth N. Waltz, *The Spread of Nuclear Weapons: A Debate* (New York: W.W. Norton, 1995).

16. Huntington, *The Third Wave*, p. 42.

government by peaceful means. In states that had less affinity with the West, and received less Western attention and aid and so could assume that they were less likely quickly to be integrated into Western institutions, the process was more likely to be violent, and to have a less democratic outcome.[17] Thus, international attention, and expectations about international links, can affect domestic politics. Moreover, the perception that a state will be included, or that outsiders will pay attention, appears especially important.

This has important implications for arguments about the spread of democracy. The conventional wisdom seems to be that democracy is "winning," due to the impressive spread of democratic governments around the globe in the past twenty to thirty years.[18] Yet the establishment of a democratic system requires more than merely the holding of free elections, and young democratic governments are struggling in many places. The goal of promoting the spread of democracy needs to be accompanied by help in the construction of democratic institutions, to ensure that fledgling democratic goverments have a real opportunity to resolve the problems that previous regimes may have left them, and to ensure leaders and populations that they will be welcomed into the democratic community.

PERCEPTIONS AND INTERNATIONAL POLITICS

This book has focused on regimes' responses to pressure for change. The cases examined here underscore the importance of understanding how people react to information and events. Leaders, like all individuals, are wary of sudden change, and often cannot recognize that the circumstances they confront require radically new approaches.

As the rate of international communication accelerates and its scope expands, the conduct of international politics will come under new pressure. At the same time new actors, ranging from international organizations and nongovernmental organizations to civil society groups, appear to be playing an ever greater role in shaping both domestic and international politics. These new pressures will make it increasingly important

---

17. On this point, see Thomas Carothers, "Democracy without Illusions," *Foreign Affairs*, Vol. 76 (January–February 1997); Jane M. O. Sharp, "Spreading the Security Blanket," *Bulletin of the Atomic Scientists*, Vol. 54, No. 1 (January–February 1998); and Renée de Nevers, "Conflict Prevention in Multi-Ethnic Societies," in G. Bonvicini, E. Greco, B. von Plate, and R. Rummel, eds., *Preventing Violent Conflict: Issues from the Baltic and the Caucasus* (Baden-Baden: Nomos Verlagsgesellschaft, 1998).

18. This is what Samuel Huntington has called the "third wave" of democratization. See Huntington, *The Third Wave*.

to understand the mechanisms by which leaders and governments confront changing circumstances.

The collapse of regimes in Eastern Europe showed the difficulty people have in changing their beliefs and responses when confronted by new situations. The increased speed of transactions and change is likely to make it harder for leaders to comprehend the challenges or the choices they face, yet they will probably have less time to respond. In such circumstances, understanding peoples' psychological reactions may be a critically important tool for analyzing leaders' and governments' behavior—and also for avoiding dangerous mistakes in political judgment.

THE DEMONSTRATION EFFECT

The demonstration effect also deserves further study in the international arena, especially with the spread of media penetration around the globe. The flow of information across borders is taken for granted in most countries, from personal communications and news reports to financial information and transactions. The Soviet and East European regimes tried to control the flow of information into and within their states, with limited success.[19] The rapidly increasing pace of communication, and greater connections across borders and among populations around the globe, is likely to make it increasingly difficult for authoritarian regimes to control information flows in the future.

Are some ideas more likely to catch on than others? In particular, should we assume that the example of democracy and the diffusion of democratic ideas has a particularly strong impact, or are other ideas equally strong influences?[20] The nature of technological change is value neutral. The Internet, for example, provides a means to spotlight human rights abuses—but it also allows fascist groups to spread their message with ease. Information flows may lead to more democracy, but why should they not also provoke violence and repression?

In Eastern Europe, the popular protests triggered by the perception of a fleeting window of opportunity to push for democracy remained largely peaceful, and resulted in greater political freedoms. But the more

---

19. At a time when personal computers were becoming household items in the West, Soviet scholars concurred that the efforts of communist rulers to constrict the flow of information constrained these states' ability to compete economically with the West.

20. For example, Stephen Van Evera has argued that the danger of more anti-democratic regimes' spreading is lessened in Europe by the social leveling that occurred during the Soviet era. More democratic ideas, then, are likely to find a more receptive audience. Van Evera, "Primed for Peace: Europe After the Cold War," in Sean Lynn-Jones, ed., *The Cold War and After: Prospects for Peace* (Cambridge, Mass.: MIT Press, 1992), pp. 229–230.

negative consequences that can be provoked by the demonstration effect were seen in Rwanda in 1994. Mass killings in Rwanda were fomented by exhortations on hate radio.[21] Similarly, riots in Indonesia in the summer of 1998 were provoked by popular discontent with plunging living standards and rising unemployment—the consequence of a financial crisis in Asia triggered by currency speculation and the flight of international financial capital from the region, both made possible by the speed and range of international communications and financial networks. But rather than protest only against the government for its mishandling of the crisis and half-hearted efforts to solve the population's problems, people attacked the ethnic Chinese population in Indonesia, a group that was perceived as responsible for many of the country's inequities. The Rwandan case shows that regimes or hate groups can use the demonstration effect to their own destructive ends, while the Indonesian case illustrates how populations may respond when regimes do little to address growing domestic crises.[22]

The power of ideas is strong, but this is not limited to positive ideas. This is too clearly evident in the history of the twentieth century. To avoid the catastrophes of the past, we need a better understanding how ideas spread across borders, and under what circumstances they are likely to lead to changes for the better.

---

21.   On the use of hate radio in Rwanda, see Dan Lindley, "Collective Security Organizations and Internal Conflict," in Michael E. Brown, ed., *The International Dimensions of Internal Conflict* (Cambridge, Mass.: MIT Press, 1996), p. 563.

22.   On the issue of the demonstration effect and development issues, see Andrew C. Janos, *Politics and Paradigms: Changing Theories of Change in Social Science* (Stanford, Calif.: Stanford University Press, 1986), pp. 84–95.

About the Author

Renée de Nevers is an Assistant Professor in Political Science and International and Area Studies at the University of Oklahoma. Previously she was a Program Officer at the John D. and Catherine T. MacArthur Foundation, with responsibility for grantmaking in the area of International Peace and Security.

Dr. de Nevers received her B.A. degree from Stanford University, and her master's degree and doctorate in political science from Columbia University. She has been a fellow at the Belfer Center for Science and International Affairs at Harvard University, Stanford University's Center for International Security and Arms Control, and the Hoover Institution, and has worked at the International Institute for Strategic Studies in London. She has published articles and monographs on Russian foreign policy, European security, democratization and ethnic conflict, and international regimes.

Index

BCSIA Studies in International Security

Published by The MIT Press

Sean M. Lynn-Jones and Steven E. Miller, series editors
Karen Motley, executive editor
Belfer Center for Science and International Affairs (BCSIA)
John F. Kennedy School of Government, Harvard University

Allison, Graham T., Owen R. Coté, Jr., Richard A. Falkenrath, and Steven E. Miller, *Avoiding Nuclear Anarchy: Containing the Threat of Loose Russian Nuclear Weapons and Fissile Material* (1996)

Allison, Graham T., and Kalypso Nicolaïdis, eds., *The Greek Paradox: Promise vs. Performance* (1996)

Arbatov, Alexei, Abram Chayes, Antonia Handler Chayes, and Lara Olson, eds., *Managing Conflict in the Former Soviet Union: Russian and American Perspectives* (1997)

Bennett, Andrew, *Condemned to Repetition? The Rise, Fall, and Reprise of Soviet-Russian Military Interventionism, 1973–1996* (1999)

Blackwill, Robert D., and Michael Stürmer, eds., *Allies Divided: Transatlantic Policies for the Greater Middle East* (1997)

Blackwill, Robert D., and Paul Dibb, eds., *America's Asian Alliances* (2000)

Brom, Shlomo, and Yiftah Shapir, eds., *The Middle East Military Balance 1999–2000* (1999)

Brom, Shlomo, and Yiftah Shapir, eds., *The Middle East Military Balance 2001–2002* (2002)

Brown, Michael E., ed., *The International Dimensions of Internal Conflict* (1996)

Brown, Michael E., and Šumit Ganguly, eds., *Government Policies and Ethnic Relations in Asia and the Pacific* (1997)

Carter, Ashton B., and John P. White, eds., *Keeping the Edge: Managing Defense for the Future* (2001)

de Nevers, Renée, *Comrades No More: The Seeds of Political Change in Eastern Europe* (2003)

Elman, Colin, and Miriam Fendius Elman, eds., *Bridges and Boundaries: Historians, Political Scientists, and the Study of International Relations* (2001)

Elman, Miriam Fendius, ed., *Paths to Peace: Is Democracy the Answer?* (1997)

Falkenrath, Richard A., *Shaping Europe's Military Order: The Origins and Consequences of the CFE Treaty* (1994)

Falkenrath, Richard A., Robert D. Newman, and Bradley A. Thayer, *America's Achilles' Heel: Nuclear, Biological, and Chemical Terrorism and Covert Attack* (1998)

Feaver, Peter D., and Richard H. Kohn, eds., *Soldiers and Civilians: The Civil-Military Gap and American National Security* (2001)

Feldman, Shai, *Nuclear Weapons and Arms Control in the Middle East* (1996)

Feldman, Shai, and Yiftah Shapir, eds., *The Middle East Military Balance 2000–2001* (2001)

Forsberg, Randall, ed., *The Arms Production Dilemma: Contraction and Restraint in the World Combat Aircraft Industry* (1994)

Hagerty, Devin T., *The Consequences of Nuclear Proliferation: Lessons from South Asia* (1998)

Heymann, Philip B., *Terrorism and America: A Commonsense Strategy for a Democratic Society* (1998)

Kokoshin, Andrei A., *Soviet Strategic Thought, 1917–91* (1998)

Lederberg, Joshua, *Biological Weapons: Limiting the Threat* (1999)

Shaffer, Brenda, *Borders and Brethren: Iran and the Challenge of Azerbaijani Identity* (2002)

Shields, John M., and William C. Potter, eds., *Dismantling the Cold War: U.S. and NIS Perspectives on the Nunn-Lugar Cooperative Threat Reduction Program* (1997)

Tucker, Jonathan B., ed., *Toxic Terror: Assessing Terrorist Use of Chemical and Biological Weapons* (2000)

Utgoff, Victor A., ed., *The Coming Crisis: Nuclear Proliferation, U.S. Interests, and World Order* (2000)

Williams, Cindy, ed., *Holding the Line: U.S. Defense Alternatives for the Early 21st Century* (2001)

The Robert and Renée Belfer Center for Science and International Affairs

Graham T. Allison, Director
John F. Kennedy School of Government
Harvard University
79 JFK Street, Cambridge, MA 02138
(617) 495-1400
http://www.ksg.harvard.edu/bcsia   bcsia_ksg@harvard.edu

The Belfer Center for Science and International Affairs (BCSIA) is the hub of research, teaching and training in international security affairs, environmental and resource issues, science and technology policy, human rights and conflict studies at Harvard's John F. Kennedy School of Government. The Center's mission is to provide leadership in advancing policy-relevant knowledge about the most important challenges of international security and other critical issues where science, technology, and international affairs intersect.

BCSIA's leadership begins with the recognition of science and technology as driving forces transforming international affairs. The Center integrates insights of social scientists, natural scientists, technologists, and practitioners with experience in government, diplomacy, the military, and business to address these challenges. The Center pursues its mission in four complementary research programs:

- The **International Security Program** (ISP) addresses the most pressing threats to U.S. national interests and international security.

- The **Environment and Natural Resources Program** (ENRP) is the locus of Harvard's interdisciplinary research on resource and environmental problems and policy responses.

- The **Science, Technology and Public Policy** (STPP) program analyzes ways in which science and technology policy influence international security, resources, environment, and development, and such cross-cutting issues as technological innovation and information infrastructure.

- The **WPF Program on Intrastate Conflict, Conflict Prevention and Conflict Resolution** analyzes the causes of ethnic, religious, and other conflicts, and seeks to identify practical ways to prevent and limit such conflicts.

The heart of the Center is its resident research community of more than 140 scholars: Harvard faculty, analysts, practitioners, and each year a new, interdisciplinary group of research fellows. BCSIA sponsors frequent seminars, workshops and conferences, maintains a substantial specialized library, and publishes books, monographs, and discussion papers.

The Center's International Security Program, directed by Steven E. Miller, publishes the BCSIA Studies in International Security, and sponsors and edits the quarterly journal *International Security*.

The Center is supported by an endowment established with funds from Robert and Renée Belfer, the Ford Foundation and Harvard University, by foundation grants, by individual gifts, and by occasional government contracts.